ETHICS AND MORAL PHILOSOPHY

SCM AS/A2

Ethics and Moral Philosophy

David Mills Daniel
with
Dafydd E. Mills Daniel

scm press

© David Mills Daniel and Dafydd E. Mills Daniel 2009

Published in 2009 by SCM Press
Editorial office
13–17 Long Lane,
London, EC1A 9PN, UK

SCM Press is an imprint of Hymns Ancient and Modern Ltd (a registered
charity)
St Mary's Works, St Mary's Plain,
Norwich, NR3 3BH, UK
www.scm-canterburypress.co.uk

Scripture quotations are from the Revised Standard Version of the Bible,
copyright 1946, 1952 and 1971 by the Division of Christian Education
of the National Council of the Churches of Christ in the USA. Used by
permission. All rights reserved.

British Library Cataloguing in Publication data
A catalogue record for this book is available
from the British Library

978 0 334 04171 9

Typeset by Regent Typesetting, London
Printed and bound by
CPI William Clowes, Beccles NR34 7TL

Contents

CONTENTS

CONTENTS

For Jenny, Edmund,
Dafydd and Megan

Setting the Scene

The SCM AS/A2 Ethics and Moral Philosophy textbook

While this book should be of interest to anybody looking for an introduction to moral philosophy and ethics, its purpose is to support the teaching and learning of the AS/A2 Ethics/Religious Ethics modules in the AS and A2 Religious Studies specifications of all the examination boards in England and Wales, and also the moral philosophy elements of AS/A2 Philosophy. Therefore, the book's content is determined by the content of those specifications, and the kind of questions candidates are expected to answer.

The book's structure

The book is divided into three parts, corresponding to the three main divisions of ethics: **Part 1 Metaethics; Part 2 Normative Ethics; and Part 3 Applied Ethics.**

Part 1

Metaethics sounds a lot more intimidating than it actually is. It is what is known as a 'second order' activity, and concerns not ethical principles themselves, or what we ought to do, but such issues as ethical concepts, ethical language and its meaning, and the nature of moral discourse. For example, an enquiry into whether we ought always to perform actions that maximize happiness is part of normative ethics, but an enquiry into whether 'good' means 'that which maximizes happiness' is a metaethical one. There is a sense in which the distinction between metaethics and normative ethics (see below) is artificial. Many important philosophers, such as Kant (see **pp.**

69–85), Mill (see **pp. 93–8**) and Bentham (see **pp. 27–9, 87–92**) deal with both. Indeed, G. E. Moore, who is critical of both Mill and Bentham (see **pp. 37–8, 95** and **pp. 22–3, 29–31, 89**), maintains that many moral philosophers have often tried to answer ethical questions, without being clear about what the questions are, and, as a result, have made metaethical errors.

Part 1 deals with the questions of why we should be moral and whether there are moral truths or facts; the key metaethical issues of the is/ought gap and the naturalistic fallacy; and discusses the main modern metaethical theories: ethical intuitionism, ethical emotivism, universal prescriptivism and ethical descriptivism.

Part 2

A norm is a rule that governs behaviour, or a criterion by which it is assessed, and **normative ethics** concerns the objects or ends that we should regard as good, and the rules or principles that we ought to adopt to govern and/or assess our conduct.

Part 2 covers the major ethical theories that are covered in the AS/A2 Religious Studies specifications: deontological and Kantian ethics; consequentialist and utilitarian ethics; virtue ethics; natural law ethics and justice; situation ethics; and conscience. There are also chapters dealing with the general relationship between religion and ethics, Christian ethics and the issue of moral responsibility.

Part 3

Applied ethics is about the application of normative ethical principles to ethical issues.

Part 3 covers ethical issues examined in the AS/A2 specifications: abortion; euthanasia; assisted conception and embryo research; human and sexual relationships; equality and human rights; issues of war and peace; and animal and environmental ethics.

Religion

For AS/A2 Religious Studies, candidates are required to be familiar with the main ethical principles of *one* religion.

For reasons of space, this book deals with only one religion: **Christianity**, which is the religion chosen by a large number of schools and colleges for study at A-level.

In Part 2, Christian ethics is discussed in general terms, and in Part 3 the relevant Christian beliefs, teachings and ethical approaches, with particular reference to the Church of England, the Roman Catholic Church and the Methodist Church, are considered in relation to each ethical issue.

The book's approach

Different approaches are possible in a textbook. The one adopted here is to focus on the writings of particular philosophers, ethicists and religious and other thinkers.

In Parts 1 and 2 the major book, or one of the major books, on the subject is taken as the core text for a particular ethical theory, and the theory is discussed in relation to that book. All quotations from the book are referenced, in **non-bold type**, to a cheap and easily available edition of the book, or to an internet source, so that students can gain quick access to the relevant sections of the text, and read more of it for themselves. The discussion of each core text concludes with an '**Assessment**' sub-section, which sums up the strengths and weakness of the particular theory. At the end of each chapter in Parts 1 and 2, there is a **brief bibliography**, with details of the core texts and other useful books and internet sources for further study and research.

Part 3 contains a detailed discussion of each ethical issue, including a historical perspective; relevant UK legislation; UK government reports on the subject; any useful statistical information; the views of philosophers, ethicists and other thinkers; Christian teachings about, and approaches to, the issue; and the views of other organizations that are interested or involved in the issue. At the end of each chapter, there is a list of references and suggestions for further reading and research, including a range of internet resources, to help students to carry out further study and research for themselves, and to follow their own lines of enquiry.

Terms and their use

Numerous technical terms are used in ethics and moral philosophy, particularly to describe the various metaethical theories. This book does not claim to contain all of them, but all those that feature in the book appear in the index. The terms 'moral' and 'ethical', and their various permutations and applications, as in 'moral realism', 'ethical cognitivism', and so on, are used interchangeably in the text, and as reflects common usage. For example, we usually talk of 'moral responsibility' rather than 'ethical responsibility'.

However, while this book refers to, for example, ethical intuitionism, this is exactly the same as moral intuitionism.

Are ethics and moral philosophy different things? Probably not; but we seem to use 'moral philosophy' to refer to philosophical study and reflection on ethics, and 'ethics' to refer to the activity of laying down actual rules of conduct and discussion of whether or not they should be followed. However, there are different views on this!

Page references in bold type

There is a great deal of overlap between all the theories and issues discussed in this book. The **references in bold type** are there to alert readers to other parts of the book that are relevant to the topic they are studying.

AS/A2 questions

The theories and issues discussed in this book are of great intrinsic interest, and will enrich the lives of those who study them. However, knowledge and understanding of them is also going to be tested in examinations. 'In Conclusion' contains a selection of the kind of questions that are set for AS/A2 Religious Studies and Philosophy examinations, with references to the pages in this book where the relevant information can be found. It also has the website addresses of the four examination boards in England and Wales.

The Index

This contains brief biographical information about the authors of the main non-core books referred to in the text.

How to contact the author

The author is happy to answer any enquiries about the contents of this book, and can be contacted via the **SCM Brieflys website**, at **www.scmbrieflys. co.uk**. Click on **'Ask the Author'** to send him a message.

Part I Metaethics

3 reasons you'll love Pact Coffee:

☐ **Quality is key.** Pact sources top-notch beans from the best farmers in the world.

☐ **We take freshness very seriously.** Fresh coffee tastes better, that's why each 250g bag of Pact Coffee is shipped within 7 days of roasting.

☐ **You'll never run out of coffee you love.** Pact offers convenience and flexibility in one handy service.

For you

Worth £6.⁹⁵

Pact for £1

For a friend

Worth £6.⁹⁵

Pact for £1

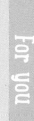

SHAVE CLUB CUSTOMERS
£1 OFFER

Offer for you, offer for a friend!

Up to 15 cups of fresh coffee, roasted within a week, ground to order, posted through your letterbox and yours for only £1. We've even thrown in a £1 first bag for your friend too.

It takes five minutes to sign up and if you order before 1pm Monday – Friday, you'll get your coffee the next day. We like to keep things flexible, so you can set your delivery frequency and amend your order at any time. Easy.

All you need to sign up is one of these or a computer

For you

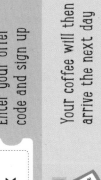

1 pactcoffee.com
Jump on to www.pactcoffee.com

2 SCUK
Enter your offer code and sign up

3 YOUR COFFEE
Your coffee will then arrive the next day

For a friend

1 pactcoffee.com
Jump on to www.pactcoffee.com

2 SCUK2
Enter your offer code and sign up

3 YOUR COFFEE
Your coffee will then arrive the next day

Share the love with a friend...

1 Addressing Some Metaethical Issues

1 The issues: Why be moral? Are there moral truths?

Why be moral?

Well, why should we be? There are many definitions of ethics and morality: distinguishing between right and wrong, or good and bad; the power to do so; the study of right and wrong conduct. Obviously, ethics concerns human conduct, its evaluation, and putting forward views about what we ought and ought not to do. But why should we, as individuals, get involved in it? Why not just go our own way? One obvious reason is that, although you and I are individuals, with our own thoughts, feelings and aspirations, we do not live in sealed compartments. Every day, in all sorts of ways, we interact with other people: our family, friends, neighbours and work colleagues. In addition to those with whom we have actual contact, we are part of wider society, as inhabitants of our town or village, citizens of Britain, taxpayers, shoppers at our local supermarket, and so on. In all these contacts and connections with others, we (not necessarily consciously) apply moral rules to our conduct. For example, we do not feel that we ought to drive a car, when we have been drinking alcohol, even if we think we could get away with it, because of the possibility of harming others, which we consider wrong. On a more trivial level, we do not elbow our way to the front of a queue in a shop, and demand to be served first.

But why do we not do these things? Why do we think they are wrong? Different people will give different reasons, but it will be possible to describe most of the reasons they give as ethical principles, which lay down rules about how people (including ourselves) should, or should not, be treated: for example, that we ought not to behave towards others in ways that cause them pain or unhappiness; that human life is valuable and we should not endanger it; that we should treat others with the respect we owe them as fellow human beings.

Are there moral truths?

Ethical principles vary from individual to individual, and from culture to culture; and even people who have a lot of ethical principles in common may attach different degrees of importance to them. However, are all these principles equally valid? In other words, is there **moral knowledge**? Are there **moral truths** or **moral facts**, such that we can say that some things and actions are always definitely good or right, while others are always definitely bad or wrong?

The view that there are moral truths or facts, which are not subjective or relative to individual preferences or the norms (standards) of particular societies or cultures, but based in some sense on the nature of things, is known as **moral realism** or **ethical objectivism**. This approach includes more than one theory. Plato (see below) argues that there are moral truths, but that they are transcendental: they exist at a different level of reality from the ordinary empirical world, but provide standards of goodness and rightness which should be applied and followed in it. Plato's ethical theory would give us **moral absolutes**: absolute standards for making ethical judgements and determining conduct. So too would a **divine command theory**, which identifies moral truth with God's commands. Kierkegaard, for example, holds that these always take precedence over human ethical standards (see **pp. 176–80**). Other philosophers, such as the utilitarians Bentham and Mill, are **ethical naturalists** (see **pp. 87–98**). They argue that moral truths or facts relate not to transcendental properties, but to such natural properties as pleasure or happiness. In their view these are the ultimate good, and right actions are those that promote pleasure/happiness, and wrong actions those that prevent it. Moral realists are also **ethical cognitivists** (concerned with knowledge): they hold that ethical utterances or statements are not just expressions of opinion, but propositions that can be true or false. For the utilitarian, a moral statement that advocates inflicting pain is simply false. However, there is a complication, which is picked up by G. E. Moore (see **pp. 29–31**). Bentham, for example, in some places seems to argue that its being productive of pleasure is the only legitimate reason for regarding an action as right, whereas, in others, he seems to argue that 'productive of pleasure' is what 'right' means: so that it is not merely wrong, but self-contradictory, to deny that an action which minimizes pleasure is wrong (see **pp. 27–9**).

Opposed to moral realism are **ethical relativism** and **ethical projectionism** or **expressivism**. These take their inspiration from Hume's famous passage about the 'gap' between 'is' and 'ought' (see **pp. 23–7**), which is traditionally interpreted as maintaining that it does not follow from any statement of fact (for example, that there has been a car accident on the road outside) that we ought to take some particular action in relation to it (such as going to see if we can help, or phoning the emergency services). Ethical relativism is the view that there are no moral truths, and that moral principles or standards are relative to particular individuals or societies. However, it also describes the position of some utilitarians and situation ethicists (**see pp. 86–102, 138–53**), who believe that many ethical rules, including such apparently fundamental ones as those that condemn killing or theft, should only be followed if they help achieve what is held to be the ultimate good, such as maximizing happiness or doing the most loving thing. Ethical projectivism or ethical expressivism holds that there are no objective moral standards, and that ethical judgements merely express individual moral attitudes or feelings. However, as these are being projected on to the world, people are often misled (or mislead themselves) into thinking that they correspond to moral truths, which are part of the nature of things. This position, which includes **ethical emotivism** (see **pp. 50–3**), is **non-cognitivist**: it contends that ethical utterances cannot be true or false, because there is no objective criterion by which to determine their truth or falsity.

Discussing the issues

In section 2 'Why be Moral?' Plato, Mill, Nietzsche and G. J. Warnock give us reasons for being moral: that is, for not just reluctantly accepting that we have to be, because we need to rub along with others, but for proactively embracing moral conduct; and also for thinking carefully about it. In section 3 'Are there moral truths?', Plato, J. L. Mackie and G. J. Warnock give their different views about whether or not there are moral truths or facts.

2 Why be moral?

Plato's *Republic* (see recommended edition on **p. 31**)

Plato (c. 429–347 BC)

Plato's contribution to the development of western philosophy is immense. A pupil of Socrates, he became disenchanted with Athenian democracy and all existing forms of government, after Socrates, who had devoted his life to the pursuit of truth, was tried and executed for undermining belief in the gods and corrupting youth. Plato spent the rest of his life teaching and writing, and he founded the Academy, the world's first university, in 386 BC. He concluded (as he argues in *The Republic*) that states must be ruled by philosophers, who, after rigorous intellectual training, would understand the true nature of goodness and justice, and govern well and in their people's interests. His other books include the *Theaetetus*, *Symposium* and *Laws*.

A conventional view of justice and morality

The Republic opens with Plato, through Socrates, exploring reasons for being moral or just. Polemarchus upholds the conventional view that doing right is giving 'every man his due', and justice consists of helping friends ('good, honest men') and injuring enemies ('the reverse') (pp. 8, 12). But Socrates wonders how we are to identify good and honest people. He also argues that, as justice concerns human excellence, and harming bad men will make them worse, justice cannot be giving people their due, if this involves harming enemies: 'it is never right to harm anyone at any time' (p. 14).

Thrasymachus' rejection of conventional morality

Thrasymachus then proposes a cynical approach, which identifies morality or justice with the interests of the powerful. The role of justice is to help the powerful to exploit the weak: what is right or just is what is in the stronger party's interest. In a state, this is the government, so it is right to obey those in power. But Socrates points out that a government may misjudge its own interests, which would make it right for subjects to obey laws that are not in the stronger power's interests. He also argues that those with professional skills, such as doctors, should exercise them not for reasons of self-interest but for the benefit of others. The same should be true of those in government, whose responsibility is to put their subjects' interests, not their own, first.

Thrasymachus rejoins that shepherds look after their flocks for profit. Similarly, justice or morality is someone else's good: that of the ruler, at the subject's expense. Unjust people fare better, and are happier than just ones, especially if like tyrants they do wrong on a grand scale. People condemn wrongdoing through fear of suffering from it, not of doing it. But Socrates reminds Thrasymachus that:

> no profession or art or authority provides for its own benefit, but . . . what benefits the subject of which it is in charge, thus studying the interest of the weaker party and not the stronger. (p. 28)

6

He then argues that the unjust man is bad and ignorant, because unlike the just man, he competes with other unjust men, as well as with just men. The just man, on the other hand, competes only with unjust men; therefore he is the one with knowledge, who is wise and good.

Injustice and immorality are sources of disunity and weakness

Socrates also shows that to succeed unjust people must behave justly. The citizens of an aggressor state, or a band of thieves, would fail in their objectives if they behaved in a purely self-interested way, and wronged each other. Being unjust leads to quarrels, ruling out co-operative effort:

> Injustice . . . whether it occurs in a state or family or army or in anything else . . . renders it incapable of any common action because of factions and quarrels, and sets it at variance with itself. (p. 36)

Further, something with a function has its own particular excellence. As justice is the particular excellence of the mind, the just man with a just mind will lead a good life, while the unjust man will lead a bad one. As the man with the good life is prosperous and happy, 'the just man is happy, and the unjust man miserable' (p. 39).

Justice and morality are merely a matter of convenience

Glaucon (Plato's brother) is not convinced that right actions are always better than wrong ones. He divides good things into three categories: those, like pleasure, wanted for their own sake; those, like wisdom, wanted for their own sake and their consequences; and those, like medical treatment, which though painful are chosen for their benefits. He asks Socrates where justice (or morality) belongs. Socrates puts it in the second and highest category. Glaucon then argues that most people put it in the third, referring to the common opinion that it is good to inflict wrong, but bad to suffer it. As we cannot always inflict wrong, or avoid suffering it, we agree to prevent both. Justice is the middle ground between what is most and least desirable: people would prefer to do wrong, but cannot, and so practise justice unwillingly:

> This is the origin and nature of justice. It lies between what is most desirable, to do wrong and avoid punishment, and what is most undesirable, to suffer wrong without being able to get redress; justice lies between these two and is accepted not as being good in itself, but as having a relative value due to our inability to do wrong. (p. 42)

No one believes justice pays. So-called just men pursue self-interest if they can get away with it. Unjust men often prosper, while just men can lead miserable lives. Gods and men seem to offer a better life to the unjust than the just. Certainly, all will be well with the unjust man, provided he is not caught out. Glaucon wonders what a man who wanted not just to appear to be, but to be just, would do if contrary to the facts he gained a 'reputation for wickedness' (p. 45). Would he continue to be just when there was no advantage in it?

People do the right thing only for what they can get out of it

Adeimantus (another of Plato's brothers) agrees that justice is commended, not because it is valued in itself, but for the good reputation and heavenly rewards it brings. Unjust men are respected as long as they are rich and powerful, and seem respectable. He urges Socrates to demonstrate the ill effects of injustice, and the beneficial effects of justice:

> You have agreed that justice falls into the highest category of goods . . . which are worth choosing not only for their consequences, but . . . for themselves . . . Let us . . . hear you commending justice for the real benefits it brings its possessor, compared with the damage injustice does him . . . Prove to us . . . not only that justice is superior to injustice, but that, irrespective of whether gods or men know it or not, one is good and the other evil because of its inherent effects on its possessor. (pp. 51–2)

So, what is justice?

Socrates stresses the difficulty of determining the nature of justice, and does not answer Adeimantus directly. Instead, he begins by exploring what constitutes justice in society. A civilized society evolves from a primitive one, because its members recognize the disadvantages of trying to be self-sufficient and the benefits of specializing in particular jobs and services; and such specialization becomes increasingly important, as society develops. As well as farmers and tradesmen (wealth-creators), a civilized society also needs a professional army, to defend its territory, and, most important of all, a class of philosophically trained professional administrators, whom Plato calls 'Guardians', to govern it.

Why be moral?

Socrates concludes that justice in the state is this specialization of functions, with each member of society doing the job for which he is best suited. A state is just when each of its three classes of wealth-creators, Auxiliaries (professional soldiers) and Guardians (rulers) concentrate on their own job, and do not meddle with each other's. It is the same with the individual, whose personality consists of three elements: reason, the irrational appetite, and reason's ally, spirit or indignation (which an individual feels when his desires impel him to actions of which reason disapproves). Justice in the individual is the three elements performing their particular function, with reason, supported by spirit, ruling, and thus controlling the irrational appetite, leading to a well-disciplined person:

> Justice is produced by establishing in the mind a . . . natural relation of control and subordination among its constituents, and injustice by establishing an unnatural one. (p. 154)

Thus, justice or morality, in the state or the individual, is an appropriate division of responsibilities among the elements that constitute it, and the integration, self-discipline and effective functioning that this produces; and this is the reason for being just or moral.

John Stuart Mill's *On Liberty* (see recommended edition on p. 31)

John Stuart Mill (1806–73)

For brief biographical details of John Stuart Mill, see **p. 93**.

The principle of liberty

In *On Liberty*, Mill offers a number of reasons for being moral. One is to uphold individual freedom, and to express minority opinions. Even in democratic societies, individuals and minorities, though not subject to political persecution, as they would be in a totalitarian state, are often oppressed by the tyranny of public opinion, which tries to coerce them into acceptance of the majority view. Mill enunciates his 'principle of liberty', to demarcate the boundary between individual freedom and society's legitimate interference with individual conduct:

That the only purpose for which power can be rightfully exercised over any member of a civilized community, against his will, is to prevent harm to others. His own good, either physical or moral, is not a sufficient warrant . . . The only part of the conduct of any one, for which he is amenable to society, is that which concerns others. In the part which merely concerns himself, his independence is, of right, absolute. Over himself . . . the individual is sovereign. (p. 14)

Freedom of expression benefits society

Mill maintains that we should express our opinions, not just because we wish to do so, but because society gains from it. Most human opinions and conduct are 'rational' because they can be corrected through 'discussion and experience' (pp. 24–5). Truth is usually arrived at through the interaction of opposite points of view. A 'suppressed' opinion may be the true one, or contain an important, but 'neglected', part of the truth: and, even if the majority view is true, unless challenged, it will be held as a mere 'dogma' (pp. 52, 59). And, we must not worry about expressing our views moderately: people with strong views often put them forward with a passion that opponents find objectionable, but this is the nature of public debate.

Setting an example and challenging convention

We must also express our individuality in the way we lead our lives; again, society is the gainer. For Mill, mid-nineteenth-century English, European and American society was increasingly dominated by mass public opinion, as reflected in mass-circulation newspapers, which discouraged individuality and originality, and impoverished human life. People were too willing to let society decide how they should live, rather than choosing for themselves. (Democratic) governments pandered to masses that voted for them, creating a society ruled by the 'despotism of Custom' (p. 78):

individuals are lost in the crowd. In politics . . . public opinion now rules the world. The only power deserving the name is that of the masses, and of governments while they make themselves the organ of the tendencies and instincts of masses. (p. 73)

But, progress depends on diversity of opinions and lifestyles, which clash with and challenge each other, giving people a real choice. Mill urges cultivation of individuality. Society needs eccentrics, who will flout mass opinion.

Their value lies less in their being right than in their refusal to conform, which sets an example to others:

> the mere example of nonconformity, the mere refusal to bend the knee to custom, is itself a service. Precisely because the tyranny of opinion is such as to make eccentricity a reproach, it is desirable . . . that people should be eccentric. (p. 74)

Why be moral?

To enrich human society, and to ensure human progress, we need to express our opinions, and contribute to the melting-pot of different ideas that challenge accepted views, and from which truth emerges. By leading, or allowing or encouraging others to lead, distinctively individual ways of life, we help to ensure a range of lifestyles that confront the conventional pattern, and offer people a choice as to how to lead their own.

Friedrich Nietzsche's *Beyond Good and Evil* (see recommended edition on p. 31)

Friedrich Nietzsche (1844–1900)

Nietzsche was educated at the Universities of Bonn and Leipzig, and taught philology at the University of Basle. In 1889, he was committed to a mental asylum, and was then cared for by family members until his death. As well as the controversial and thought-provoking *Beyond Good and Evil* (1886), which deals with such issues as the will to power, the shortcomings of Christianity, and master and slave morality, Nietzsche's books include *Human, All Too Human: A Book for Free Spirits* (1878) and *On the Genealogy of Morals: A Polemic* (1887).

Aristocratic values

As the title suggests, in *Beyond Good and Evil*, Nietzsche puts forward an individualistic and perverse theory of morality and why we should be moral, which seeks to challenge conventional morality, and to provoke traditional moralists.

Aristocratic hierarchical societies (he believes), which attach different values to people and practise slavery, are the ones that have always elevated human beings. For intellectual and cultural progress, there needs to be real distance between social classes, with the ruling class looking down at its 'underlings and tools' (p. 151). Not injuring, abusing, or exploiting others makes for good manners between individuals, but these are only for members of the same class. Trying to make them society's basic principles denies life, the essence of which is exploitation and oppression of the weak. To pursue their will to power, and to dominate their society, members of a healthy aristocracy do to others what they refrain from doing to each other:

> 'Exploitation' is not part of a decadent or imperfect, primitive society: it is part of the *fundamental nature* of living things . . . it is a consequence of the true will to power, which is simply the will to life. (p. 153)

'Master' and 'slave' morality

For Nietzsche, there are two basic types of morality: '*master moralities* and *slave moralities*' (p. 153).

Master morality

The masters define 'good' in terms of proud, exalted states of the soul, regarding the difference between 'good' and 'bad' as that between 'noble' and 'despicable' (p. 154). They despise the cowardly, the self-disparager, the craven, the flatterer and the liar: 'The noble type of person feels *himself* as determining value – he does not need approval, he judges "what is harmful to me is harmful per se" . . . he *creates values*' (p. 154).

The aristocrat may help the unfortunate, but from excess of power, not pity. He relishes his own power, particularly that over himself, and respects all that is severe and harsh. Such people believe and take pride in themselves. They disdain empathetic feelings, and are far removed from a moral code based on 'pity or altruistic behaviour' (p. 155). The aspect of the master morality that is most at odds with current taste is that duties extend only to peers, and that masters are entitled to treat those beneath them as they wish: in a manner that is beyond good and evil. Noble morality is characterized by the ability and duty to be grateful or vengeful, within a circle of equals; a refined concept of friendship; and a need for enemies, as outlets for envy and combativeness.

Slave morality

Slave morality reflects the value judgements of 'the oppressed, the suffering, the shackled, the weary' (p. 155). They gain nothing from the virtues of the powerful, and so stress the moral qualities of pity, kindness and helpfulness, which improve the sufferers' existence, or help them to bear oppression. One who arouses fear, through being powerful and dangerous (in master morality, the good person), is evil, while the good person is harmless and good-natured. Slave morality equates good with stupid, and emphasizes longing for freedom, while reverence and devotion characterize the aristocratic mentality. Nietzsche maintains that the fundamental tendency of contemporary, democratic societies, which reflect the morality of the slave or the herd, is to make ourselves small.

The new philosophers

Nietzsche longs for a new breed of philosophers, who will champion master morality and challenge the false values of democratic society. Courageous, independent and self-reliant, they will not engage with truth simply because they like it, or it exalts them. They will not be sympathetic to Christian teaching, which sides with the oppressed and suffering, or the values of parliamentary democracy. They will (Nietzsche hopes) not be mere thinkers and writers, but:

> commanders and lawgivers. They say, 'This is the way it should be!' Only they decide about mankind's Where to? and What for? (p. 105).

Thus, they will 'create values', based on the will to power (p. 105).

Challenging contemporary values

As men of tomorrow, the new philosophers will be at odds with contemporary society, and will expose its hypocrisy, smugness and falsehood. They will denounce weakness of the will, and advocate strength and the will to power. In a society that honours only the herd animal, and clamours for equal rights, which inhibit the development of the individual, they will proclaim the importance of difference and of being able to live independently. They will affirm the truth that the greatest person is one who is 'beyond good and evil' (p. 106).

Why be moral?

From Nietzsche's point of view, the exponents of master morality must be morally active, to ensure its victory: they must challenge the (corrosive) egalitarian values of democracy. However, those who oppose the master morality in principle, or who feel that they will be losers, rather than winners, if it prevails, also have a reason to be moral: they must prevent it succeeding.

G. J. Warnock's *The Object of Morality* (see recommended edition on **p. 31**)

G. J. Warnock (1923–95)

For brief biographical details of G. J. Warnock, see **p. 59**.

Moral evaluation and the human predicament

In *The Object of Morality*, Geoffrey Warnock considers the purpose of morality. The point of moral evaluation is to make rational beings act better than they otherwise would, and thus to improve the human predicament. Things often go badly, but they could go better if human beings were to act differently:

> the general object of moral evaluation must be to contribute . . . by way of the actions of rational beings, to the amelioration of the human predicament . . . of the conditions in which *these* rational beings, humans, actually find themselves . . . the human predicament is inherently such that things are liable to go badly . . . but also something at least can be done . . . to make them go at least somewhat better. (pp. 16–17)

Our environment naturally satisfies some human needs, wants and interests, but not all. This is partly because the world's resources are limited, and human intelligence and skill do not enable us to increase them to a level at which all existing needs can be satisfied. We are forced to compete with one another for resources, so when one person succeeds in satisfying his needs, it may be at others' expense.

The problem of limited sympathies

This situation is made worse by the fact that we put satisfaction of our own wants first, even if those of others are more pressing. This would not be so serious if we were more intelligent, more rational, less egotistical and more willing to work together. But (Warnock believes) the single most important cause of 'the badness of the human predicament' is 'limited sympathies' (p. 26). The principal object of morality, and the main reason for its importance and for engaging in it, is to help to persuade us to overcome our limited sympathy for our fellow human beings; to make us as concerned about others' welfare as our own:

> the 'general object' of morality . . . is to contribute to betterment . . . of the human predicament . . . to countervail 'limited sympathies' and their potentially most damaging effects . . . to expand our sympathies, or, better, to reduce the liability to damage inherent in their natural tendency to be narrowly restricted. (p. 26)

Why be moral?

We need to be moral, in order to try to improve the human predicament, by overcoming our limited sympathies for other people. We can thus make the world a better place for ourselves and others.

3 Are there moral truths?

The theory of the forms and the Form of the Good in Plato's *Republic* (see recommended edition on **p. 31**)

Plato (c. 429–347 BC)

For brief biographical details of Plato, see **pp. 5–6**.

The need for philosopher-rulers

In *The Republic*, Plato, through Socrates, argues that the problems of existing states (and humanity) will not end until 'philosophers become kings in this world, or till those we now call kings and rulers really and truly become philosophers' (p. 192). Socrates accepts that this is a controversial view, but Plato believes that states must be ruled by those who love their country, are mentally quick and dependable, and (most important of all) who have reached the very highest form of knowledge: the Form of the Good.

Two orders of reality and the theory of the forms

And, this is why Plato insists that only philosophers are fit to rule. He believes there are two orders of reality, and that individual things, in the ordinary, visible world, which are experienced through the senses, acquire their identity by being (in some way) copies of the unchanging forms, or essential natures, of these things in an intelligible, transcendent world, to which only the mind has access. A particular thing is beautiful or just by being a copy of, or participating in, the form, or essential nature, of beauty or justice:

> Socrates. . . . there are many particular things that are beautiful, and many that are good, and so on . . . we . . . speak of beauty-in-itself, and goodness-in-itself, and . . . all the sets of particular things which we have regarded as many; and we proceed to posit by contrast a single form, which is unique, in each case, and call it 'what really is' each thing . . . we say that the particulars are objects of sight but not of intelligence, while the forms are the objects of intelligence. (p. 232)

Things in the ordinary visible world are not perfectly just or beautiful, but only approximate to the beauty or justice of beauty-in-itself or goodness-in-itself. Those who know only particular things, such as beautiful objects or just acts, and not beauty itself and justice itself, do not really 'know' these things. They merely have opinions:

> Socrates. Those then who have eyes for the multiplicity of beautiful things and just acts . . . but are unable . . . to see beauty itself and justice itself, may be said in all cases to have *opinions*, but cannot be said to know any of the things they hold opinions about. (p. 203)

Only those who do not 'confuse particular things' with their form or essential nature have knowledge (p. 199). The philosophers who have reached this stage are fit to govern:

> Socrates. The good, then, is the end of all endeavour, the object on which every heart is set . . . though it finds it difficult to grasp just what it is . . . Can we possibly agree that the best of our citizens, to whom we are going to entrust everything, should be in the dark about so important a subject? . . . At any rate a man will not be a very useful Guardian of what is right and valuable if he does not know in what their goodness consists. (p. 230)

The Form of the Good

Presiding over the forms in the intelligible world, and having the same relation to them as the sun does to visible objects in the visible world, is the Form of the Good, the source of reality, truth and goodness. Only those philosophers who have seen this, which is the essential nature of goodness, possess the highest form of knowledge and know what is good in itself and which things and actions really are good, right and just. As they possess this vital moral knowledge, they must govern the state. This part of *The Republic* contains Plato's famous Simile of the Sun, which compares the Form of the Good to the sun:

> **Socrates.** . . . [the sun] bears the same relation to sight and visible objects in the visible realm that the good bears to intelligence and intelligible objects in the intelligible realm . . . what gives the objects of knowledge their truth and the knower's mind the power of knowing is the form of the good . . . The sun . . . not only makes the things we see visible, but causes the processes of generation, growth and nourishment . . . The good . . . [is] the source . . . of the intelligibility of the objects of knowledge, but also of their being and reality. (pp. 233–4)

Training the philosopher-rulers

Plato describes the advanced studies that will enable trainee Guardians to see the Form of the Good and thus to gain access to moral truths. Concentrated study of mathematics will shift students' focus away from the world of change; while 'dialectic', an intense programme of philosophical enquiry and discussion, will enable the mind to penetrate to the essential nature of things. Those who reach the final stage, and see the Form of the Good, will become the rulers, reluctantly taking turns to govern their state and train their successors, while devoting the rest of their time to their preferred occupation of philosophical study:

> **Socrates.** . . . those who have come through all our practical and intellectual tests with distinction must be brought to their final trial, and made to lift their mind's eye to look at the source of all light, and see the good itself, which they can take as a pattern for ordering their own life as well as . . . society. (p. 273)

Are there moral truths?

Thus, while the masses, ignorant of wisdom and truth, and ruled by their desires, pursue false pleasures, the philosopher-rulers, who have penetrated to the intelligible world of unchanging and eternal truth, know what good itself is, and so will lead lives guided by reason and knowledge. As they possess moral knowledge, they will be fitted to govern the state. Of course, not everyone agrees that there are two orders of reality, or that the ordinary world, experienced through the senses, is less real than an invisible, intelligible one. It runs counter to common sense and sense experience, and Plato does not explain how the intelligible and visible worlds relate to each other. However, even if we reject Plato's theory of forms, and the view that there is an essence of goodness located in a different level of reality, we can take from *The Republic* the message that discovering, or deciding, what is good or right requires intellectual effort and careful enquiry.

Error theory in J. L. Mackie's *Ethics: Inventing Right and Wrong* (see recommended edition on p. 31)

John Mackie (1917–81)

The Australian philosopher John Mackie studied philosophy at Sydney University and at Oriel College, Oxford. After being professor of philosophy at the Universities of Otago (New Zealand), Sydney and York, he became a fellow of University College, Oxford. As well as *Ethics: Inventing Right and Wrong* (1977), his books include *Truth, Probability and Paradox* (1973) and *Hume's Moral Theory* (1982).

Objective moral values and Plato's theory of the forms

Mackie believes that, as a result of Plato's theory of the forms, European moral philosophy has been misled into treating moral values as objective entities, which exist out there in the world, and which are completely independent of human beings. The forms may not be visible, or empirically knowable, but still these 'eternal, extra-mental, realities' are believed to be somehow part of the world's structure; and it is argued that the philosophers, who are acquainted with them and with the Form of the Good, will not only know what is good and right, but will be 'impelled' to pursue and do them (pp. 23–4).

Where are they, and how do we find out about them?

However, Mackie thinks it is hard to imagine just what it would mean for such eternal, objective values to be 'part of the fabric of the world' (p. 24): they would be 'utterly different from anything else in the universe' (p. 38). How would they fit into our picture of the world? They would completely change our view of it, because we would have to accommodate a different level of reality; and, for Mackie, this is a compelling reason for thinking that they do not exist. Again, we could only become aware of them through some special faculty of moral perception or intuition, of the kind argued for by G. E. Moore (see **p. 59**), which would be utterly different from our ordinary ways of knowing things.

Moral scepticism and the error theory

Mackie's own position is **moral scepticism**, at least in relation to any theory which holds that there are independently existing objective values, located in a different level of reality. To challenge such theories, moral scepticism must take 'the form of an **error theory**' (p. 48). This must recognize, not only that there is a general 'belief in objective values', but that this error is now 'built into ordinary moral thought and language' (pp. 48–9). However, in arguing against this error, moral scepticism can draw support from the fact that different people and societies adopt very different ethical principles, suggesting that they do not come from one source. It can also highlight the extent to which ethical principles depend on experience and cultural factors, and the 'metaphysical [concerned with ultimate reality] peculiarity' of the thesis that principles that are supposed to guide human actions come from (empirically unknowable) eternal, transcendent entities (pp. 49).

Are there moral truths?

Mackie thinks not. For him, moral realism is based on a metaphysical error, deriving from Plato, which has gone on misleading people for two and a half thousand years, and which has been incorporated into our thought and language. However, Simon Blackburn claims that Mackie misses the point. He accepts ethical expressionism: that when we make ethical statements, we are expressing our attitudes, not referring to objective moral truths. However, when we talk about our attitudes, we project them on to the world, as if they do express moral truths; and there is nothing wrong with our doing so. His position is known as **quasi-realism:**

we talk as if there were a truth in that talk, that's why the *quasi*. We talk as if there were a reality, a normative reality, the kind . . . Plato believed in . . . Mackie thought that that was an error. I said 'No! The talk is okay, it is the philosopher who is wrong.' The philosophers make the error when they are demanding some fact, some kind of Platonic forms in the world. (Dall'Agnol, pp. 102–3)

Moral facts in G. J. Warnock's *The Object of Morality* (see recommended edition on **p. 31**)

G. J. Warnock (1923–95)

For brief biographical details of G. J. Warnock, see **p. 59**.

Are there moral facts?

In *The Object of Morality*, Warnock asks whether there are moral facts. Like Mackie, he believes that ordinary usage suggests that there are. Thus, if he were to state that Goebbels did some morally abominable things, someone might intelligibly reply, 'That's true'; and we often say that people do things 'knowing' they are wrong (p. 118). Unlike Mackie, Warnock does not think that this is an error in need of correction. It is a legitimate response. However, the moral facts Warnock argues for are not transcendental moral truths, of the kind Plato proposes in *The Republic*. Warnock's contention is that moral facts concern the actions or situations that can correctly and meaningfully be described as 'right' or 'good'; and he offers an example of a moral truth. If a country's ruler engaged in lying, assassination, judicial murder and military aggression, involving the deaths of many innocent people, with no justification other than to cling to power, then the term 'morally wrong' would have to be applied to his actions by anyone who understands the meaning of the term:

> if the phrase 'morally wrong' is not absolutely meaningless . . . there are some things, such as those described, from which that appellation *could* not be withheld by anyone not unaware of the meaning of the expression, or not deliberately misusing it. Accordingly, that *some* things anyway are morally wrong can be shown to be true, every bit as decisively . . . as . . . that . . . snow is white. (p. 124)

Assessment

For Warnock, moral truths are not objective features of the world, in the way that physical qualities are, or as Plato's forms would be. There would be no moral facts without rational beings. But, this does not make moral issues just a matter of opinion, or moral principles just a matter of choice. Particular individuals may be indifferent to the fact that lying, murder and gratuitous violence, for example, are morally wrong, but it is difficult to disagree with Warnock's view that it is a fact that they are. Warnock's position, known as **ethical descriptivism** (see **pp. 59–64**), is close to ethical naturalism. However, Warnock is not maintaining that moral propositions are only true if they relate to one natural property, such as the maximization of pleasure/ happiness, or that this is what 'good' or 'right' means. He is saying that we do have **moral knowledge**; that we know that actions that harm people, or make the world a worse place to live in, are wrong; that morality is grounded in (general) human needs; and that ethical terms such as 'good' or 'right' are used inappropriately if applied to situations or actions that do not meet these needs.

Simon Blackburn suggests the **indefeasibility** (unwillingness to give it up) of a moral view as the test of whether or not we regard it as part of our **moral knowledge**. He gives the examples of his beliefs that there ought to be a minimum wage and that it is wrong to be unkind to children. He can conceive of arguments that would convince him to relinquish the first (overall, it might do more harm than good, by reducing the number of jobs available) but not the second: 'I can't envisage a . . . position . . . which undermines my conviction that you ought to be kind to children' (Dall'Agnol, p. 104).

4 The issues: What is the is/ought gap? What are ethical naturalism, the naturalistic fallacy and the open question argument?

Moving from facts to values: the is/ought gap

As we have seen (pp. 4–5, 15–21), there are differing views about whether there are moral facts, but moral evaluation invariably involves ordinary facts. The people of less developed countries face poverty, lack of food and disease every day of their lives. Ought people in the countries of the prosperous, developed world (and to what extent) to sacrifice some of their material well-being, in order to help them? An old man is terminally ill, and in terrible pain. He wants his doctors to help him to die. Would it be right to allow them to do so, if they are willing? At a party, a female friend asks if her new dress suits her. I do not think so, but it is too late for her to change it now. Ought I to be honest, or should I reassure her with a white lie?

All these situations present us with certain facts. We evaluate them, and then act accordingly. Of course, in the case of the first two, we could evade the issue, unless we are confronted by someone in the street collecting money for a third-world charity, or are related to the old man. But all three situations raise the issue of the relationship between facts and evaluation. How do we move from the facts of a situation to what we ought to do about it?

Should facts dictate moral judgements and actions?

For some moralists, the answer is straightforward. Certain facts dictate particular moral judgements and actions. If people are suffering, we ought to help them, because we ought to maximize general happiness or satisfy human interests and needs (a utilitarian view: see **pp. 86–103**). Indeed, some moral philosophers would argue that, unless it concerns meeting human needs, and improving the human predicament, a response would not even qualify as a moral one (see **pp. 20–21, 59–64**). On the other hand, a follower of Nietzsche might argue that we should not do so, as it perpetuates the existence of weak and inadequate people, whom the world would be better off without (see **pp. 11–14, 281**).

Ethical naturalism

Ethics is almost entirely **anthropocentric** (but see **pp. 318–41**): it concerns how we ought to behave towards other people and ourselves. But, surely, this must simplify ethics. We know a great deal about human beings, so, if ethics is about how we should treat ourselves or others, what is good or right must be about doing what pleases or satisfies us. But is it that simple? As human beings, we have a lot in common, but we are also very different from each other. What satisfies the interests of one may be wholly repugnant to another. Nonetheless, some philosophers have argued that, despite these difficulties, what we regard as right or wrong, good or bad, needs to take account, in general terms, of human nature and what human beings like or want. This is ethical naturalism. For example, with few exceptions, we all want to survive; so, principles of conduct that encourage people to kill others indiscriminately cannot be moral. We all want to be happy. Indeed, this seems to be the ultimate good. So, actions that promote (the greatest amount of) human happiness must be right.

The naturalistic fallacy and the open question argument

Many philosophers have argued that either the nature or situation of human beings (see **pp. 20-1, 59–64**), or widely shared human desires, such as that for happiness (see **pp. 86–98**), should be the basis of morality and moral evaluation. However, some go (or are accused of going) further, arguing that natural properties like happiness are part of the definition of 'good' or 'right'. Below, Jeremy Bentham, appears to do so; and he (and also John Stuart Mill: see **pp. 36–8, 95**) are taken to task by G. E. Moore for this. Moore describes any attempt to define 'good' in terms of a natural property, like happiness, as a **'naturalistic fallacy'**. He also points out that it is always an **'open question'** whether anything described as good actually is: people can deny that it is good without contradicting themselves. Moore makes out a powerful case against the naturalistic fallacy; but it is less clear whether Mill, in particular, actually commits it.

5 What is the is/ought gap?

Hume and the is/ought gap in *A Treatise of Human Nature* (see recommended edition on **p. 31**)

David Hume (1711–76)

David Hume, perhaps the greatest British philosopher, was educated at Edinburgh University, and published his first major philosophical work, *A Treatise of Human Nature*, in 1738–40. His empirical approach to philosophy meant that he became known as a sceptic and even an atheist, making him an object of suspicion to the religious and cultural leaders of eighteenth-century Scotland. Hume published further works of philosophy, including *An Enquiry Concerning Human Understanding* (1748) and *An Enquiry Concerning the Principles of Morals* (1751), but turned increasingly to writing about the history of England, which brought him considerable fame.

Hume's evasiveness

In the following tantalizingly elusive passage from his *Treatise of Human Nature*, David Hume draws attention to the issue of the relationship between facts and evaluation, between **'is'** and **'ought'**, without telling us clearly what it is:

I cannot forbear adding to these reasonings an observation, which may, perhaps, be found of some importance. In every system of morality, which I have hitherto met with, I have always remark'd that the author proceeds for some time in the ordinary way of reasoning, and establishes the being of a God, or makes observations concerning human affairs; when of a sudden I am surpriz'd to find, that instead of the usual copulations and propositions *is* and *is not*, I meet with no proposition that is not connected with an *ought*, or an *ought not*. This change is imperceptible; but is, however, of the last consequence. For as this *ought* or *ought not*, expresses some new relation or affirmation, 'tis necessary that it shou'd be observ'd and explain'd; and at the same time that a reason shou'd be given, for what seems altogether inconceivable, how this new relation can be a deduction from others, which are entirely different from it. But as authors do not commonly use this precaution I shall presume to recommend it to the readers; and am persuaded, that this small attention wou'd subvert all the vulgar systems of morality, and let us see that the distinction of vice and virtue is not founded merely on the relations of objects, nor is perceiv'd by reason. (p. 334)

Hume notes that, in every moral system he has studied, the author first discusses facts (or alleged facts), from the existence of God to observations about human beings and human affairs, all of which are expressed in propositions containing 'is' or 'is not'. He is then, he tells us, surprised to discover that the factual propositions have given way to statements containing only an 'ought' or an 'ought not'. This change happens imperceptibly, but is obviously important. Hume says that he cannot conceive how an 'ought' proposition can be what he calls 'a deduction' from an 'is' one, and, as there is a 'gap' between the two kinds of proposition, the writers should give reasons to justify their move from one type of proposition to the other. However, they generally fail to do so. Hume adds, enigmatically, that observing (and, presumably, challenging) this move would undermine 'all the vulgar systems of morality'.

Assessment and interpretations of Hume from W. D. Hudson (ed.), *The Is/Ought Question* (A. C. MacIntyre and Antony Flew) (see recommended edition on p. 31)

The evasive and ambiguous nature of this passage is confirmed by the radically different ways in which other philosophers, such as Alasdair MacIntyre and Antony Flew, have interpreted it. The traditional view is that

Hume is being ironic: that when he says that he does not understand how the move, from what is the case to what we ought to do, can be made, and wants it to be explained, he is actually saying that it cannot be made, and that such a move, as from 'x is suffering' to 'we ought to help x', is logically flawed, as no evaluation (what we ought to do) follows from any factual statement. According to some philosophers, we cannot move from a minor premise ('x is starving') to a conclusion ('we ought to give x food'), except by way of a major premise, which here would be, 'We ought always to feed those who are starving'. But, although putting in a major premise creates a syllogism, and satisfies the demands of logic, is this what Hume is getting at? The substantial question is: does a particular situation, or people being in a particular situation, as when they are suffering, require that we should act, and act in a particular way? Not all philosophers accept the traditional interpretation of this passage.

Alasdair MacIntyre (born 1929)

For brief biographical details of A. C. Macintyre, see **pp. 114–5**.

Morality is based on a consensus of interests

In 'Hume on "is" and "ought"', Macintyre rejects the traditional interpretation. In his view, Hume believed that abiding by moral rules is justified by the fact that doing so is in everyone's long-term interests: which is to derive an 'ought' from an 'is'. For Hume, the concept of what we ought to do only makes sense in terms of the idea of a consensus of interest. To say that we ought to do something is to state that a commonly accepted rule exists, and the fact that there is such a rule assumes general agreement about what serves our common interests. So, what we ought to do is precisely what our common interests dictate:

> the notion of 'ought' is for Hume only explicable in terms of the notion of a consensus of interest. To say that we ought to do something is to affirm that there is a commonly accepted rule; and the existence of such a rule presupposes a consensus of opinion as to where our common interests lie. (pp. 40–1)

Thus, while for John Stuart Mill (see **pp. 93–8**), it would be morally wrong, but intelligible, to deny that we should do whatever is to the advantage of most people, for Hume it would make no sense. To separate 'ought' from the notion of a consensus of interest would be to deprive it of meaning. This makes Hume an **ethical naturalist** (see **pp. 22, 27–9,**) and a forebear of **ethical descriptivism** (see **pp. 59–64**), the metaethical theory that moral terms like 'ought' or 'right' are being misused if they do not relate to judgements or actions that benefit human beings.

Bridge notions

MacIntyre also proposes the idea of **'bridge notions'**, such as 'wanting, needing, desiring, pleasure, happiness, health', to span the apparent gap between 'is' and 'ought' (p. 46). We can see these functioning as informal major premises. To take our earlier example of '*x* is starving' and 'we ought to give *x* food', our bridge notion might be '*x* is unhappy, but food would make him happy', enabling us to move from minor premise to conclusion. What Hume does in this passage (MacIntyre maintains) is to indicate where we 'pass from "is" to "ought"', and that we should do so (p. 46).

Vulgar systems of morality

But, what does Hume mean by his reference to undermining vulgar systems of morality? According to MacIntyre, he is attacking those popular eighteenth-century moral systems that based what we ought to do on Christian teachings, not human needs, interests, desires, and happiness:

> it is against ordinary morality that Hume is crusading . . . Hume is . . . repudiating a religious foundation for morality and putting in its place a foundation in human needs, interests, desires, and happiness. (p. 46)

So far from trying to establish the autonomy of morals, and a gap between moral judgements and facts, Hume is pointing out the proper factual basis of morality, which is logically grounded in human needs and happiness.

Antony Flew (born 1923)

Antony Garrard Newton Flew read Greats at St John's College, Oxford, taught philosophy at Christ Church, and held professorships at the Universities of Keele and Reading. A strong advocate of individual liberty, and known as a committed atheist, he has written extensively about philosophy of religion. His books include: *New Essays in Philosophical Theology* (1955: co-editor with Alasdair MacIntyre), *Hume's Philosophy of Belief* (1961) and *God, A Critical Enquiry* (1988).

Hume as an ethical subjectivist

Flew argues in 'On the Interpretation of Hume' that Hume is not claiming that moral judgements can be analysed in terms of human needs, happiness or any other statements about objective reality. He is saying that it is impossible to analyse them in a way that treats them as 'entirely independent of human sentiments and human desires' (p. 66). For Flew, Hume is the forebear, not of the **ethical descriptivists**, but of the **ethical subjectivists**, who define rightness and goodness in terms of feelings of approval, and the **ethical emotivists** (see **pp. 50–3**), who hold that the function of morality, and the meaning of moral terms, is to express and arouse feelings.

Human interests

What Hume says about 'is' and 'ought' is a rejection of any attempted reduction of moral judgements to facts about either the 'natural (or supernatural) world' (p. 67). They are related to human interests, not, as MacIntyre contends, by being logically grounded in them, but psychologically, in that these are the things that matter to human beings, and about which they express their feelings and preferences in the form of moral judgements. Flew thinks Hume could, and should, have been more explicit. This passage from Hume's *Treatise* is his equivalent to A. J. Ayer's *Language, Truth and Logic* (see **pp. 50–3**), and he should have proclaimed boldly that:

> when we say *This is wrong* we are not stating anything, not even that we have certain feelings, but rather we are giving vent to our feelings. (p. 67)

6 What are ethical naturalism, the naturalistic fallacy and the open question argument?

Ethical naturalism in Jeremy Bentham's *Introduction to the Principles of Morals and Legislation* (see recommended edition on **p. 31**)

Jeremy Bentham (1748–1832)

For brief biographical details of Jeremy Bentham, see **pp. 87–8**.

The principle of utility and ethical naturalism

In *An Introduction to the Principles of Morals and Legislation*, Bentham defines the **principle of utility** as:

> that principle which approves or disapproves of every action . . . according to the tendency which it appears to have to augment or diminish the happiness of the party whose interest is in question: or, what is the same thing . . . to promote or to oppose that happiness. (p. 2)

'Utility' is the property in any object (or action) whereby it tends to produce pleasure or happiness and/or to prevent pain or unhappiness in the 'party whose interest is considered' (p. 2). This may be the community as a whole, or a particular individual. What Bentham argues, at this point, is that, when we evaluate a potential action, its tendency to promote the natural property of happiness, and/or to diminish the natural property of pain, in the individual or individuals affected, should be the criterion by which we decide whether, and how far, it is right or wrong. This makes Bentham an **ethical naturalist**. For him, moral value is determined by the presence or absence of natural properties: those of pleasure or pain.

A test of what is right, or what 'right' means?

Actions (Bentham continues) that meet, or fail to meet, the criterion set by the principle of utility are those that ought, or ought not, to be done: they are respectively right or wrong actions. But Bentham then goes on to say that moral terms like 'ought', 'right' and 'wrong' only have meaning when they are applied to actions that pass or fail this test; otherwise, they have no meaning:

> Of an action that is conformable to the principle of utility one may always say either that it is one that ought to be done . . . One may say also, that it is right it should be done . . . at least that it is not a wrong action. When thus interpreted, the words *ought*, and *right*, and *wrong* . . . have a meaning: when otherwise, they have none. (p. 4)

He also maintains that the only people who challenge the principle of utility are those who do not appear to know what these moral terms mean. It is simply not true that the word 'right' has any meaning, unless it refers to the principle of utility:

Admitting any other principle than the principle of utility to be a right principle . . . admitting (what is not true) that the word *right* can have a meaning without reference to utility, let him say whether there is any such thing as a *motive* that a man can have to pursue the dictates of it. (p. 7)

Assessment

It seems that Bentham shifts his ground. He starts off by proposing the **principle of utility** as a criterion for deciding whether an action is right or wrong, but ends up by claiming that it is what the word 'right' means. Thus, for Bentham, a moralist who argues that an action is right, even though it does not promote the happiness of the individuals affected, is not applying a different standard of rightness, but showing ignorance of what 'right' means. However, if this is Bentham's view, he is guilty of what G. E. Moore calls the **'naturalistic fallacy'**: he deprives 'right' of its evaluative force. When he states that an action that promotes happiness is right, all he is saying is that an action that promotes happiness is one that promotes happiness.

The naturalistic fallacy and the open question argument in G. E. Moore's *Principia Ethica* (see recommended edition on **p. 31**)

G. E. Moore (1873–1958)

For brief biographical details of G. E. Moore, see **p. 34.**

The naturalistic fallacy

In *Principia Ethica*, Moore accuses other moral philosophers, including Bentham (pp. 69–72), of committing a logical error, in relation to what he regards as the fundamental question of ethics: how 'good' and other moral terms are to be defined. They have been guilty of **ethical naturalism**, of trying to define or analyse 'good' in terms of a natural property, holding that it simply means such a natural property. Moore calls defining 'good' (or any other moral term) as a natural property, the **'naturalistic fallacy'** (p. 62). 'Good' (he insists) cannot be defined, because it is a simple, unanalysable, indefinable, non-natural property or quality of things, which is known by **intuition**; and to say that something is 'good' is to say it has this simple, unanalysable property. Complex things, such as a horse, can be analysed or broken down into their simple or most basic constituent parts; but, these basic constituent parts will all be objects of thought that cannot be defined, because they are ultimate terms of reference:

> 'Good,' then, if we mean by it that quality which we assert to belong to a thing, when we say that the thing is good, is incapable of any definition . . . It is one of those innumerable objects of thought which are themselves incapable of definition, because they are the ultimate terms by reference to which whatever *is* capable of definition must be defined. (p. 61)

Like 'yellow', good is one of these ultimate terms of reference (p. 62).

The open question argument

Philosophers (Moore points out) who define 'good' as a natural object do not agree among themselves: one says it is pleasure, another 'that which is desired', and so on (p. 62). But, if good is just *'defined* as something', there is no possibility of proving any of these definitions to be right or wrong (p. 63). Moore hammers this point home in another way. However 'good' is defined, it can always be asked intelligibly, of the thing so defined, 'whether it is itself good' (p. 67). But, if 'good' just means, for example, 'pleasure', it would not make any sense to ask whether pleasure is good. Whether or not pleasure is good would not be the '**open question**' that it obviously is:

> If we start with the conviction that a definition of good can be found, we start with the conviction that good *can mean* nothing else than some one property of things; and our only business will then be to discover what that property is. But if we recognise that, so far as the meaning of good goes, anything whatever may be good, we start with a much more open mind . . . [and will not insist that] 'This is not an open question'. (p. 72)

Assessment

Even if Moore's definition of 'good' seems rather odd (and agreeing with him about the naturalistic fallacy does not mean having to accept his **ethical non-naturalism**: see **pp. 33–4, 35, 41**), he does make an extremely important point here. Some philosophers do (as Bentham appears to) define 'good' and other ethical terms as a natural property, such as pleasure, and hold that it simply means that natural property. However, this is clearly a fallacy. Unless good and, for example, pleasure are different, saying pleasure is good is pointless, as it is just to state the tautology: 'pleasure is pleasure'. However, when people say pleasure is 'good', they do not think they are uttering a tautology; they believe they are evaluating or commending it. Thus, 'good' cannot just mean pleasure. Again, whatever people claim to be good, it is always an open question (one that can be asked meaningfully) whether it actually is good.

Core texts

Jeremy Bentham, *An Introduction to the Principles of Morals and Legislation*, Mineola, NY: Dover, 2007.

Antony Flew, 'On the Interpretation of Hume', in W. D. Hudson (ed.), *The Is/Ought Question*, London: Macmillan, 1969.

David Hume, *A Treatise of Human Nature*, Mineola, NY: Dover, 2003.

J. L. Mackie, *Ethics: Inventing Right and Wrong*, Harmondsworth: Penguin, 1977.

Alasdair MacIntyre, 'Hume on "is" and "ought"', in W. D. Hudson (ed.), *The Is/Ought Question*, London: Macmillan, 1969.

John Stuart Mill, *On Liberty*, in *On Liberty and Other Essays*, ed. J. Gray, Oxford and New York: Oxford University Press, 1998.

G. E. Moore, *Principia Ethica*, ed. T. Baldwin, rev. edn, Cambridge: Cambridge University Press, 1993.

Friedrich Nietzsche, *Beyond Good and Evil*, trans. M. Faber, Oxford and New York: Oxford University Press, 1998.

Plato, *The Republic*, trans. H. D. P. Lee, 2nd edn (revised and reissued with new Further Reading), London: Penguin, 2003.

G. J. Warnock, *The Object of Morality*, London: Methuen, 1971.

Suggestions for further reading and research

S. Blackburn, *Essays in Quasi-Realism*, Oxford and New York: Oxford University Press, 1993.

D. Dall'Agnol, *Quasi-realism in Moral Philosophy: An Interview with Simon Blackburn*, at http://www.cfh.ufsc.br/ethic@/ethic12.html.

W. D. Hudson, *Modern Moral Philosophy*, London: Macmillan, 1970 (chapters 1–3).

D. Mills Daniel, *Briefly: Mill's On Liberty*, London: SCM Press, 2006.

D. Mills Daniel, *Briefly: Plato's The Republic*, London: SCM Press, 2006.

D. Mills Daniel, *Briefly: G. E. Moore's Principia Ethica*, London: SCM Press, 2007.

D. Mills Daniel, *Briefly: Bentham's An Introduction to the Principles of Morals and Legislation*, London: SCM Press, 2009.

D. Mills Daniel and D. E. Mills Daniel, *Briefly: Nietzsche's Beyond Good and Evil* (Sections 1–3, 5, 6, 9: 257–70), London: SCM Press, 2007.

C. Pidgen, 'Naturalism', in P. Singer (ed.), *A Companion to Ethics*, Cambridge: Cambridge University Press, 1993.

G. Sayre-McCord, 'Metaethics', in E. N. Zalta (ed.), *Stanford Encyclopaedia of Philosophy*, at http//:plato.stanford.edu.

G. Sayre-McCord, 'Moral Realism', in E. N. Zalta (ed.), *Stanford Encyclopaedia of Philosophy*, at http://plato.stanford.edu.

2 Ethical Non-naturalism and Intuitionism

1 An alternative to ethical naturalism

Just knowing what is good or right

Ethical intuitionism, the view that normal human beings have an immediate awareness of moral values, and in some sense 'know' what is good or bad, right or wrong, has a long history, and has been held by such British philosophers as the 3rd Earl of Shaftesbury (Anthony Ashley Cooper, 1671–1713) and Richard Price (1723–91). However, this chapter deals with the ethical intuitionism of two more recent philosophers, G. E. Moore and W. D. Ross, who both reject **ethical naturalism**, which holds that 'good' or 'right' mean, or at least always refer to, such natural properties as pleasure. For utilitarian philosophers, like Jeremy Bentham and John Stuart Mill (see pp. 86–98), pleasure/happiness, or the absence of pain, are the only things that are good in themselves, and right actions are those that produce (most) pleasure/happiness. Moore rejects ethical naturalism, and accuses both Bentham (see pp. 23, 27–31) and Mill (see pp. 23, 36–8, 95) of committing a 'naturalistic fallacy'.

Two kinds of intuitionist

Both Moore and Ross believe that there is **moral knowledge**, but this knowledge is of a special kind: it relates, not to natural properties, such as pleasure, but to non-natural properties of goodness and rightness. For Moore, an **ethical non-naturalist** and intuitionist, goodness is a simple, unanalysable, non-natural property that things simply have, and which can only be known through intuition. However, in *Principia Ethica* (he subsequently came closer to Ross's view), he is also a **consequentialist**: he believes that right actions are those that have the consequence of producing the greatest amount of good. Ross is a **deontological intuitionist**: he believes that we know what is right, as well as what is good, through intuition. However, unlike his Oxford contemporary, H. A. Prichard, Ross did not maintain that we simply 'know' what is right and there is no more that can be said. He believed there are certain *prima facie* **duties** that, on the face of it, human beings are under an obligation to perform. However, we need intuition to tell us which of these it is our duty to perform in a particular situation.

2 Ethical non-naturalism and intuitionism in G. E. Moore's *Principia Ethica* (see recommended edition on p. 47)

G. E. Moore (1873–1958)

George Edward Moore read classics and moral sciences at Trinity College, Cambridge, and was professor of philosophy there from 1925 to 1939. A major influence on Bertrand Russell and Ludwig Wittgenstein, his work, particularly *Principia Ethica*'s emphasis on beauty and friendship, inspired such Bloomsbury Group members as John Maynard Keynes and Virginia Woolf. Moore promoted an analytical approach to philosophy, and his defence of common sense, especially in relation to knowledge of the external world, and his interest in metaethics, to clarify and try to resolve ethical problems, had a lasting effect on the direction of twentieth-century British philosophy. As well as *Principia Ethica* (1903), his books include *Ethics* (1912) and *Some Main Problems of Philosophy* (1953).

How not to answer ethical questions

In *Principia Ethica*, Moore observes that, when we describe a person or thing as 'good' or 'bad', or say a particular course of action is 'right' or 'wrong', we are making a moral or ethical judgement. However, in his view, philosophers have often tried to answer ethical questions without being clear about what the questions are. As a result, a lot of moral philosophers have committed metaethical errors: mistakes about the meaning and use of such moral terms as 'good' and 'right'.

The questions ethics needs to address

For Moore, there are only two basic ethical questions: 'What kind of things ought to exist for their own sakes?', that is, are good in themselves, or have intrinsic value; and 'What kind of actions ought we to perform?', that is, what are the sort of things that are right (pp. 33–4). Moore holds that propositions about what things are good in themselves are intuitions: they are 'self-evident', directly apprehended, and incapable of proof (p. 34). However, questions about what we ought to do (or what is right) are capable of proof, at least in theory. To decide what we ought to do, we need to know, through intuition, what things are good in themselves. We can then examine the consequences of our actions, and perform those that will produce the greatest quantity of intrinsically good things.

Ethical non-naturalism and intuitionism

Thus, as far as goodness is concerned, Moore is an ethical non-naturalist and an intuitionist: he believes that goodness is a non-natural property that a particular thing or state of affairs has, which can only be apprehended by intuition. However, in relation to doing what is right, he is a consequentialist: we need to decide, through observation and experience, which actions will lead to the best possible outcome. He is not a deontological intuitionist: one who holds that what is right can also be known through intuition.

The naturalistic fallacy and the open question argument

See **pp. 27–31** for discussion and assessment of the naturalistic fallacy and the open question argument.

Good in itself and good as a means

Moore explains that ethical terms such as 'good' are used in two ways: to say that something is good in itself, or to say that it is good as a means to something that is good in itself. However, it is hard to establish that a thing or action definitely is good as a means, and will maximize good, because we would need to know (which we rarely do) that a certain kind of action will always have a particular effect: 'to find causal judgements that are universally true is notoriously a matter of extreme difficulty' (p. 73).

Complex wholes and the principle of organic unities

Again, many things that are good in themselves are not single things, but complex wholes, and we must not assume that the value of the whole is '*the same as the sum of the values of its parts*': the value of the whole may be much greater than the sum of the values of the things of which it is made up (p. 79). Moore gives the example of consciousness of a beautiful object, consisting of the object and consciousness of it. This has great intrinsic value, but a beautiful object seems to have little value, if no one is conscious of it, while, if the object is not beautiful, the consciousness is not valuable either. Thus, although a beautiful object and consciousness have great intrinsic value, when combined in a whole, they have little by themselves. Moore gives the name '**organic unity**' to what he describes as this 'peculiar relation' between part and whole (p. 82).

Different kinds of ethical theory that commit the naturalistic fallacy

Having identified the naturalistic fallacy and other errors in ethical reasoning, Moore goes on to show how often they have been committed. He divides ethical theories that commit the naturalistic fallacy into two groups: naturalistic ones, which define 'good' by reference to a natural object, such as pleasure; and metaphysical ones, which define it by reference to 'supersensible reality'. Defining 'good' in terms of what God commands would commit a naturalistic fallacy.

Naturalistic ethical theories that do not maintain that pleasure is the sole good

Moore divides naturalistic ethical theories into those that maintain that pleasure is the sole good, and the rest. Some philosophers argue that there is a natural good, which is fixed by nature. However, it is a fallacy to claim that something is good or bad because it is, or is not, natural. 'Good' does not mean that which is natural, and it is always an open question whether what is natural is good.

Naturalistic ethical theories that maintain that pleasure is the sole good: Mill's utilitarianism

(See also **pp. 93–8** for discussion of Mill's *Utilitarianism*.)

Moore considers that, since the most commonly committed naturalistic fallacy is in relation to pleasure, which many people think is involved in the definition of good, it is not surprising that utilitarianism has become the most widely held ethical theory; and he accuses one of the major nineteenth-century British philosophers, John Stuart Mill, of committing the naturalistic fallacy in his book *Utilitarianism*.

John Stuart Mill and the naturalistic fallacy

Mill maintains that pleasure or happiness is desirable (in Moore's terms, 'good as an end'), and the only thing desirable as an end, while other things are only desirable as a means to it. As proof, Mill offers an analogy with visibility: their being seen is the only proof that things are visible, so the only proof that something is desirable is that people desire it. People desire happiness individually, while general happiness is the happiness of the aggregate of all persons. Moore labels Mill's argument a 'naïve' use of the naturalistic fallacy, because Mill has not given 'desirable' its proper meaning: it does not mean '"able to be desired" as "visible" means "able to be seen." . . . [but] what *ought* to be desired' (p. 118).

Further criticisms of Mill's arguments

Moore points out what he sees as further flaws in Mill's argument. As he has (wrongly) defined 'good' as 'desired', in order to show that pleasure alone is good, he must prove that it is the only thing that people actually desire as an end. However, people clearly desire other things as ends, such as virtue or money. According to Moore, Mill tries to get round this problem by arguing that there is no real conflict here. Although other things are (initially) desired as a means to happiness, they become so closely identified with it that they come to be regarded as part of it, and are then desired 'only as "a part of happiness"' (p. 123).

Are Moore's criticisms of Mill fair?

Although Mill does seem to commit the naturalistic fallacy, it has been argued that he does not claim to be offering a strict proof that happiness is (the only thing) desirable as an end, but merely inviting his readers to note that it is the only thing that people do actually value. Again, Mill concedes that questions of ultimate ends are not capable of direct proof. His own view is that pleasure is the only thing that people desire as an end, but he asks people to look around them, and judge for themselves whether this is the case. Moore acknowledges that Mill is not attempting a strict demonstration of his theory, but he seems to criticize him as if he were offering one, instead of what Mill calls an 'indirect proof'.

Is pleasure the only thing that is good as an end?

Moore accepts that it may be the case that only pleasure is good as an end, but the truth of this can only be known by intuition. However, he thinks there are considerations that incline the mind against it. One of these is Mill's own argument, again in *Utilitarianism*, that pleasures differ in quality, and that intellectual pleasures are to be preferred to purely physical ones. Moore argues that this is inconsistent with strict utilitarianism. If pleasure alone is good as an end, one pleasure is as good as any other; but, if pleasures differ qualitatively, they must be complex, consisting of pleasure and what produces it. Introducing different qualities of pleasure rules out the claim that pleasure alone is good as an end, as there must be something in the higher-quality pleasures, not present in all pleasures, which is also good as an end:

> if you say . . . quality of pleasure is to be taken into account . . . you are no longer holding that pleasure *alone* is good as an end, since you imply that something else, . . . which is *not* present in all pleasures, is *also* good as an end . . . If we do really mean 'Pleasure alone is good as an end,' then we must agree with Bentham that 'Quantity of pleasure being equal, pushpin is as good as poetry.' (p. 132)

Is pleasure valuable in itself?

Moore asks if pleasure is valuable in itself, or only when human beings are conscious of it, as a person could lead a life of intense pleasure, while lacking intelligence, memory or knowledge. In fact, pleasure does not seem valuable without consciousness of it, suggesting that pleasure cannot be the only desirable thing, as consciousness of it is more desirable still:

> pleasure would be comparatively valueless without the consciousness . . . we are bound to say that pleasure is *not* the only end, that some consciousness at least must be included with it as a veritable part of the end. (p. 141)

We must remember the principle of organic unities. The fact that enjoyment of beauty is valuable, while just contemplating it is not, does not mean that all the value lies in the pleasure. It does not follow that, because there is no value in one part of an organic whole, when taken by itself, all the value is in the other part. Both may be equally necessary parts of something intrinsically good, but (comparatively) valueless by themselves.

Does pleasure by itself have any value?

As pleasure seems a 'necessary constituent of most valuable wholes', it is easy to think that, if the other elements lack value by themselves, all the value lies in it (p. 145). However, when judging things as ends, people often prefer less pleasant to more pleasant states, agreeing with Mill that there are higher and more valuable pleasures.

Ethical theories that define 'good' as a supersensible property, and thus commit the naturalistic fallacy

Ethical theories which hold that ethical truths follow from metaphysical ones also commit the naturalistic fallacy, because 'good' cannot be defined in terms of a supersensible property any more than it can in terms of a natural one. Even if the existence of a 'supersensible reality', such as God, could be established, it would still be an open question whether it (or what it decreed) is good (p. 165).

What is right is to produce the greatest possible sum of good

What is right, or what we ought to do, involves ethical judgements about what is good in itself, and empirical knowledge of the kind of effects particular actions produce. When ethics prescribes duties, it means acting in ways that will always produce the greatest possible sum of good; and this is where Moore's intuitionism differs from that of the deontological intuitionists, who maintain that what is right is, like what is good in itself, intuitively certain. However, Moore does not believe that ethics can give a definite list of actions we ought to perform. This would require information about all the future effects of a possible action and their value, but even establishing the probability that a particular action will produce a better total result than another is very difficult. All practical ethics can do is lay down general rules about the few alternative actions that will, 'on the whole, produce the best result', in the short term (p. 201).

The importance of following well-established and generally practised rules of common sense morality

Given the difficulty of calculating the consequences of actions, people should keep to the rules of **common sense morality**, such as those prohibiting murder and theft, which experience has shown to be essential for preserving a civilized society. Indeed, generally practised rules should always be followed, for, even if they are not always appropriate, people are unlikely to be right about when not to follow them, and they will set a bad example to others if they do not follow them. Thus, Moore advocates extreme conservativism towards well-established common sense rules of morality: only when there is no generally practised rule to hand should people consider 'the intrinsic value or vileness of the effects' of possible actions, and act accordingly (p. 215). Virtues (see also **pp. 104–19**), which Moore defines as 'habitual dispositions' to carry out actions that usually 'produce the best possible results', are generally regarded as having intrinsic value, but the same test of whether they are a means to good should be applied to them as to duties (p. 221).

Moore's ideal

What does Moore consider to have the highest value? Moore has no doubt that they are 'the pleasures' of human relationships and 'enjoyment of beautiful objects' (p. 237). Moral philosophy's fundamental truth is that it is only for their sake that there is any purpose in doing any public or private duty, or being virtuous. He considers that these complex wholes are the rational ultimate end of human action.

Great positive evils

He also discusses great positive evils, of which there are three types: 'admiring contemplation', or love, of what is evil, as in cruelty and lust; mixed evils, which involve 'cognition of what is good', together with an 'inappropriate' emotion, as in hating the good; and pain, which would not be an evil without 'consciousness' of it (pp. 257–60). Moore defines mixed goods as positively good wholes that contain intrinsically evil elements, as with such virtues as courage and compassion, which require cognition of something evil and hatred of it.

Assessment

Principia Ethica has been criticized on a number of grounds. Given the range of possibilities, Moore's view that the pleasures of human relationships, and enjoyment of beautiful objects, are the rational ultimate end of human action may seem eccentric. His **ethical non-naturalism** and **intuitionism** seem to make deciding what is good a highly individual and mysterious process, and to turn moral debate into an exchange of different intuitions. His caution about our ability to calculate the consequences of our actions appears excessive, while his insistence that people should always abide by generally practised rules of **common sense morality** would prevent departures from them, even when the circumstances clearly warrant it, and would make challenging accepted moral principles hard, even if they need reform. Moore's harsh criticisms of Mill do not appear to do justice to Mill's arguments in *Utilitarianism*.

However, *Principia Ethica* is a landmark in British philosophy. Its emphasis on **metaethics**, its concern with the nature of moral argument and the meaning and use of moral terms, and, in particular, Moore's identification of the **naturalistic fallacy** and the **open question** argument, made an invaluable contribution to moral philosophy, and played a major a part in determining the direction it would take in the twentieth century.

3 Deontological intuitionism in W. D. Ross's *The Right and the Good* (see recommended edition on **p. 47**)

W. D. Ross (*1877–1971*)

William David Ross read classics at Edinburgh and Greats at Balliol College, Oxford, and was then elected to a fellowship at Oriel College. He was White's Professor of Moral Philosophy (1923–8), Provost of Oriel College (1929–47), Vice-Chancellor of Oxford (1941–4), and was knighted in 1938. An Aristotelian scholar, his publications include a translation of Aristotle's *Nicomachean Ethics* (1908), *Aristotle* (1923), *Aristotle's Metaphysics* (1924) and *Kant's Ethical Theory* (1954). Ross's important works of moral philosophy are *The Right and the Good* (1930) and *Foundations of Ethics* (1939).

'Morally right' and 'morally good' mean different things

Ross is a deontological intuitionist, holding that morally 'right' (what it is our absolute duty to do in a particular situation), and morally 'good', mean different things. For example, 'a right act may be morally bad' (or a wrong act 'morally good'), because the right thing is done from a bad motive (p. 7): a parent may punish a child appropriately, but through anger with the child, not a desire to improve his/her behaviour.

Rejection of consequentialism

In *The Right and the Good*, Ross rejects Moore's (consequentialist) defini-tion of 'right', as that which produces most good, maintaining that the right-ness of certain types of action is a matter of intuition: it is 'self-evident', at least to those with a 'certain degree' of ethical maturity (p. 12); and he uses promises to illustrate his view that an action's rightness does not relate to its consequences. When someone keeps a promise, because he thinks he ought to do so, he does not think about the consequences, much less whether they will be the best possible ones. And, if he thinks he ought to relieve distress, rather than fulfil a promise (for example, if he stops to help a motor accident victim, which prevents him keeping an appointment, as promised), it is not because he thinks that relieving the accident victim's distress will produce more good, but because it seems the right thing to do:

> besides the duty of fulfilling promises I . . . recognize a duty of relieving distress, and . . . when I think it right to do the latter at the cost of not doing the former, it is not because I think I shall produce more good . . . but because I think it the duty which is in the circumstances more of a duty. (p. 18)

Prima facie *duty and duty proper*

So, Ross does not think that an agent should regard either relief of distress or the keeping of promises as an absolute duty, which it would always be right to perform in any circumstances. Rather, they are both *prima facie* or conditional duties, either of which, depending on the circumstances, could be the right thing for an individual to do; and these *prima facie* duties are known through intuition. When two or more such duties conflict, the ethi-cally mature person must study the situation, until he can decide which of them is more incumbent on him than any other: this *'prima facie* duty' is his 'duty *sans phrase*' (duty proper), the right thing for him to do, in that situation (p. 19).

Our prima facie *duties*

What are these *prima facie* duties? Ross gives a list, maintaining that there is nothing arbitrary about it: each *prima facie* duty has undoubted moral significance. They are fidelity (keeping promises), reparation (making amends for wrongful acts), gratitude, justice, beneficence (doing good, by making others' lives better), self-improvement (developing our own virtue and intelligence) and non-maleficence (the duty not to harm others). Ross acknowledges the problem of the lack of any clear criterion for determining our duty proper in situations where these *prima facie* duties conflict:

> It may ... be objected that our theory that there are these various and often conflicting types of *prima facie* duty leaves us with no principle upon which to discern what is our actual duty in particular circumstances. (p. 23)

What is the answer? Ross has already explained that we must rely on the intuition of the ethically mature individual. However, beneficence is one of our *prima facie* duties, and we have a self-evident obligation to bring into existence as many 'intrinsically good' things, such as virtue, knowledge and pleasure, as we can (p. 24). This suggests that, in situations of conflicting conditional duties, we should decide which course of action will produce most good.

Our duty proper and the difficulties of deciding what it is

Ross provides further analysis of the difference between *prima facie* duties and duties proper. That fulfilling a promise, or effecting a just distribution of goods, is our *prima facie* duty is self-evident. Indeed, for Ross the (self evident) 'moral order' expressed in such propositions is as much part of the universe's 'fundamental nature' as its 'spatial or numerical structure' (pp. 29–30). However, the tendency of a course of action to be our duty is only what he calls a parti-resultant attribute of any act we may perform, which it has in virtue of one component in its nature. Our duty proper is a toti-resultant attribute, which belongs to an act in virtue of its whole nature. Thus, judgements about our actual duty, in concrete situations, lack the certainty attaching to *prima facie* duties, because of the difficulty of being sure that we have fully grasped the whole nature of any act we may perform. So, we must reflect carefully on the *prima facie* rightness or wrongness of various possible acts, and, after establishing all the facts of the situation, we should be able to determine that one *prima facie* duty is more pressing, and therefore the right thing to do, in that situation. But, as moral acts invariably have different characteristics, which tend to make them at the same time '*prima facie* right and *prima facie* wrong', we may be mistaken; therefore, there is truth in the view that 'the right act' is 'a fortunate act' (pp. 31, 33). Sometimes, too, the morally wrong act is an unfortunate act, due to the fact that the agent's action is the result of, or is significantly affected by, factors outside his control; but he still incurs blame for it. For example, two people are rushing to catch a bus, and paying no attention to the people around them; both trip, and plunge forward. One collides with a lamppost, harming only himself, and incurs no blame. The other collides with a frail old lady, knocks her down and seriously injures her. He incurs a great deal of blame for his reckless and irresponsible behaviour. The two people behaved in exactly the same way, but the second lacked what Bernard Williams has called '**moral luck**'.

Doing what produces most good

Ross has already accepted that, at times, the right act will be the one that produces most good, and he also believes that many typical acts that are judged right do seem to produce most good. So, if we are not under an obligation, such as that of fidelity, we ought to do what will produce most good, and, even when we are, it is legitimate to regard the tendency of acts to promote good as one criterion of their rightness. However, he feels that the sanctity of a *prima facie* duty, such as fidelity, does not involve, and, in certain situations, may be at odds with, doing good. Often, we will consider it right to fulfil a *prima facie* duty, such as promise-keeping, even though doing so will bring less good into existence than not:

> One of the most evident facts of our moral consciousness is the sense which we have of the sanctity of promises, a sense which does not . . . involve the thought that one will be bringing more good into existence by fulfilling the promise. (p. 37)

The data of ethics: the moral convictions of thoughtful and well-educated people

Ross holds that a lot of what we think about moral questions (both in rela-tion to rightness and goodness) is actually knowledge. The moral convic-tions of 'thoughtful and well-educated people are the data of ethics', and, as ethically mature individuals, we will be well equipped to decide which of all the possible acts we may perform in a particular situation, such as whether or not to keep a promise, has the greatest balance of *prima facie* rightness (pp. 40–1). What we must recognize is that the intrinsic rightness of certain kinds of acts does not depend on their consequences, such as increasing general welfare, but on their own nature.

The meaning of 'good'

Ross also discusses the meaning of 'good' and the nature of goodness. As an ethical non-naturalist, he defines the intrinsically good as that which is 'good apart from any of the results it produces'; and, following Moore, divides intrinsically good things into two classes: those which, though in-trinsically good as wholes, contain elements that are not, and those (whether or not they consist of a number of elements) which are intrinsically good in their entirety, the 'ultimately good' (pp. 67–8).

The nature of goodness

Goodness or value is a non-natural property or quality of things, but how does it relate to their other qualities? For Ross, a thing's goodness, unlike its natural properties, such as yellowness, or being in a state of pleasure, which are *differentiae*, that is 'fundamental or constitutive attributes' of it, is a 'consequential attribute': it is based on all the thing's qualities, that is, its whole nature (p. 121). Nevertheless, goodness is entirely objective and intrinsic to the things that are good.

Things that are good

So what things are good? Virtue, the disposition to give pleasure or save pain to others, and the actions that flow from it, are good in themselves, apart from any consequences they may have. However, as Kant 'had to recognize' (see **pp. 74–84**), 'while virtue alone is morally good', happiness that is deserved because of virtue, is not just a 'source of satisfaction to its possessor, but objectively good' (p. 136). For sentient beings, 'a state of pleasure is always in itself good', while their being 'in a state of pain' is 'always in itself bad', unless the latter is an element in a complex fact that has some other characteristic, relevant to goodness or badness, such as appropriate apportionment of pain to the vicious (p. 137). Indeed, in Ross's view, four things appear to be intrinsically good: 'virtue, pleasure, the allocation of pleasure to the virtuous, and knowledge' (p. 140).

Degrees of goodness

Ross refers to Mill's contention that there are grades of pleasure and that higher pleasures, such as those of the intellect, are more valuable than merely physical ones as evidence that there are qualities other than pleasantness, in virtue of which states of mind are good. His own view is that pleasure is 'definitely inferior' in value to virtue and knowledge (p. 149). Although many people regard 'promotion of the general happiness' as the 'highest possible ideal', they fail to recognize that much of its pleasantness derives from such activities as practice of virtue and knowledge of truth (p. 149). As to the relative value of knowledge and moral goodness as ends, he considers (see also pp. 112–3) the latter to be infinitely superior; and that this superiority is most conspicuous in the case of the highest form of moral goodness, the desire to do one's duty:

> The infinite superiority of moral goodness to anything else is clearest in the case of the highest form of moral goodness, the desire to do one's duty. (pp. 152–3)

As one of our principal duties is to produce as much good as we can, it is essential that we are aware of the comparative goodness of different kinds of good things.

Moral goodness

It is also essential to distinguish between moral goodness and rightness: acts are right, not in virtue of their underlying motives, but from 'the nature of what is done' (p. 156). Ross does not agree with the view, implied by Kant (see p. 71), that an individual's goodness is to be measured by the extent to which he has to fight his inclinations, in order to act rightly, or that doing one's duty, when it conflicts with one's inclinations, has more moral worth than when it accords with them:

Goodness is measured not by the intensity of the conflict but by the strength of the devotion to duty. (p. 159)

When a genuine sense of duty clashes with other motives, the former's precedence must be recognized. One who acts from a sense of duty 'without fuss or conflict' seems better than one who acts from inclination without thought of duty; but one 'who acts from both sense of duty and virtuous inclination is in a still better state' (p. 165).

Assessment

Ross' **deontological intuitionism** is less mysterious than that of his Oxford contemporary Harold (H. A.) Prichard, and even than Moore's version of **consequentialism**, which, in most situations, forces the agent to depend on common sense ethical principles, because of the problems of calculating which action will produce most good. Of course, what is intuitively certain is not the action that will be right in a particular situation, but the types of action that will be. However, these *prima facie* **duties** seem pre-eminently sensible, and could be justified on utilitarian grounds as likely to contribute to the well-being of humanity, or on the Kantian principle of always treating human beings as ends, never merely as means. Further, unlike Kant, Ross recognizes that ethical principles may conflict, and that a choice may have to be made, as to which one to follow. Included among these *prima facie* duties is that of doing good, and Ross suggests that, in circumstances where *prima facie* duties conflict, the right action may well be that which does most good. However, when it comes to making specific moral decisions, mystery still remains: the individual must rely on his moral judgement, which, if he is ethically immature, and the situation is complex, could well be mistaken. Therefore, Ross emphasizes the importance of being a thoughtful, well-educated and ethically mature individual, who is therefore likely to make the right moral judgements. However, Simon Blackburn has criticized this kind of view as 'elitist', and indicating an 'aristocratic and rather aesthetic ethics' (Dall'Agnol, p. 108).

Core texts

G. E. Moore, *Principia Ethica*, ed. T. Baldwin, rev. edn, Cambridge: Cambridge University Press, 1993.

W. D. Ross, *The Right and The Good*, London: Oxford University Press, 1930.

Suggestions for further reading and research

D. Dall'Agnol, *Quasi-realism in Moral Philosophy: An Interview with Simon Blackburn*, at http://www.cfh.ufsc.br/ethic@/ETICA~1.prn.pdf.

J. Dancy, 'Intuitionism', in P. Singer (ed.), *A Companion to Ethics*, Cambridge: Cambridge University Press, 1993.

W. D. Hudson, *Ethical Intuitionism*, London: Macmillan, 1967.

W. D. Hudson, *Modern Moral Philosophy*, London: Macmillan, 1970 (chapter 3).

B. Hutchinson, *G. E. Moore's Ethical Theory: Resistance and Reconciliation*, Cambridge: Cambridge University Press, 2001.

D. Mills Daniel, *Briefly: G. E. Moore's Principia Ethica*, London: SCM Press, 2007.

G. E. Moore, *Ethics*, ed. W. H. Shaw, Oxford: Clarendon Press, 2005.

H. A. Prichard, *Moral Obligation*, Oxford: Oxford University Press, 1949.

W. D. Ross, *Foundations of Ethics*, Oxford: Oxford University Press, 1939.

W. D. Ross, *The Right and the Good*, ed. P. Stratton-Lake, London and New York: Oxford University Press, 2002.

Bernard Williams, *Moral Luck*, Cambridge: Cambridge University Press, 1981.

3 Three Post-intuitionist Metaethical Theories

1 Ethical emotivism, universal prescriptivism and ethical descriptivism

Ethical naturalism and **ethical intuitionism** both hold that moral terms like 'good' and 'right' refer to, and derive their meaning from, a property that things or actions have: either a natural property, such as pleasure, or an unanalysable, indefinable, non-natural moral property, which we know through intuition.

Ethical emotivism, which was developed in detail by C. L Stevenson, in *Ethics and Language*, is eloquently stated by A. J. Ayer in his *Language, Truth and Logic* (discussed below). It rejects any idea that moral terms refer to, or derive their meaning from, a natural or non-natural property, holding that their meaning is to be found in the emotions they express, or the effects they (are intended to) have. For example, Ayer argues that a moral term like 'wrong' adds nothing to the factual content of a statement about stealing money, and cannot be true or false: it simply expresses our feelings about such an act, and/or attempts to arouse disapproval in others.

Universal prescriptivism was propounded by R. M. Hare in *The Language of Morals, Freedom and Reason*, and 'Universal Prescriptivism' (discussed below), and reflects his view that the meaning of moral language is to be found, not in its (intended) effects, but in certain rules of moral reasoning. Moral terms are held to be prescriptive, that is, they express approval and guide choices, in relation to certain actions or states of affairs, and therefore express a type of imperative; they are supervenient, in that they invoke or affirm certain ethical principles, standards or rules for choosing between actions or states of affairs; and they are distinguished from other prescriptive judgements by being universalizable: an action described as 'morally right' must be right for all people in all comparable situations.

Ethical descriptivism: ethical naturalism and Moore's and Ross's **intuitionism** are descriptivist, but Hare uses '**ethical descriptivism**' specifically to identify the critics of ethical prescriptivism, such as G. J. Warnock (see below). Warnock's ideas, as set out in *Contemporary Moral Philosophy* and *The Object of Morality*, are taken as representative of the descriptivist position. It also locates the meaning of moral language in its use. However, it challenges Hare's approach on a number of levels. It questions whether moral judgements are always prescriptive; maintains that the meaning of moral terms is determined by their content, not their form; and argues that morality is logically grounded in human needs.

2 Ethical emotivism in A. J. Ayer's *Language, Truth and Logic* (see recommended edition on **p. 65**)

A. J. Ayer (1910–89)

Alfred Jules Ayer read Greats at Christ Church, Oxford, where he became a lecturer and research student (fellow) in philosophy. He was Grote Professor of the Philosophy of Mind and Logic at University College, London (1946–59), Wykeham Professor of Logic at Oxford and fellow of New College (1959–78), and was knighted in 1970. His approach to philosophy was influenced by Bertrand Russell, G. E. Moore, Ludwig Wittgenstein, the logical positivists and David Hume's empiricism. His books include *Language, Truth and Logic* (1936), *The Foundations of Empirical Knowledge* (1940), *The Problem of Knowledge* (1956) and *Russell and Moore: The Analytical Heritage* (1971).

No such thing as moral knowledge

Language, Truth and Logic is a robust statement of Ayer's version of **logical positivism**: the view that, to be significant, propositions must be either tautologies, which it would be self-contradictory to deny, or (conclusively) verifiable in experience; and of his view that philosophy should confine itself to analysis, avoiding metaphysical and theological speculation. The book had an immediate impact, one of its most controversial aspects being Ayer's treatment of moral (and religious) issues. He rejects the view that there can be two kinds of speculative knowledge: of empirical fact and questions of value (ethics and aesthetics: appreciation of beauty). Ethical judgements simply express emotions, and 'can be neither true nor false' (p. 104).

Ethical judgements are normative

Ayer accepts that for ethical subjectivists, who define goodness and rightness in terms of people's feelings of approval, and utilitarians, who define them in terms of pleasure or happiness (and who both commit Moore's 'naturalistic fallacy': see **pp. 29–31**), statements of ethical value can always be translated into non-ethical ones: about whether the things in question are approved of or pleasant. However, although we sometimes use ethical terms, like 'good' and 'right', descriptively, this is not how they are generally used in ethical discussions. Most ethical statements are normative: they express judgements of value and/or prescribe conduct; and, as it is always an open question (it can be asked intelligibly: see **p. 30**) whether anything that is said to be good actually is, ethical statements cannot be reduced to non-ethical ones. It is certainly not (Ayer argues) 'self-contradictory' to hold that things or actions that are 'generally approved of' are not right or good, or to say that an action that would probably maximize happiness is wrong (pp. 106–7):

> what we are denying is that the suggested reduction of ethical to non-ethical statements is consistent with the conventions of our actual language . . . we reject utilitarianism and subjectivism . . . as analyses of our existing ethical notions . . . in our language, sentences which contain normative ethical symbols are not equivalent to sentences which express psychological propositions, or indeed empirical propositions of any kind. (pp. 107–8)

Ethical statements have an emotive function

For Ayer, ethical statements are not literally meaningful, because they just express emotions. For example, adding an ethical symbol, like 'wrong', to a statement about stealing money, 'adds nothing to its factual content'; it only expresses moral disapproval of the action, and cannot be true or false (p. 110). In fact, Ayer espouses an emotivist theory of ethics, that ethical terms have the purely emotive function of expressing and arousing feelings, stimulating action, and functioning as commands:

> ethical terms do not serve only to express feeling. They are calculated also to arouse feeling, and . . . stimulate action . . . we may define the meaning of the various ethical words in terms both of the different feeling they are ordinarily taken to express, and also the different response which they are calculated to provoke. (p. 111)

Ethical disputes never concern questions of value

But, if ethical statements are just about feelings, how can there be disputes about questions of value? Ayer denies that there are disputes about moral values, as opposed to the motives for, and effects of, actions. In ethical disputes, people hope that, by securing their opponent's agreement about the facts of, or the motives behind, a (proposed) action, they will change their moral feelings:

> When someone disagrees with us about the moral value of a certain action . . . we . . . resort to argument in order to win him over . . . But we do not attempt to show by our arguments that he has the 'wrong' ethical feeling . . . we attempt to show . . . he is mistaken about the facts . . . has misconceived the agent's motive. (pp. 114–15)

Moral philosophy is metaethics

Ayer identifies the major causes of moral behaviour and debate as fear of God's displeasure or of society's disapproval, which is why moral precepts are often regarded as categorical commands; and moral sanctions are invoked to promote or prevent behaviour that increases or diminishes society's well-being. However, there is no objective way to determine the validity of any ethical system or principles; and, instead of attempting to do so, moral philosophy should confine itself to metaethics.

Assessment

Even if we agree with Ayer that **normative ethical statements** (statements that say what we ought to do) are not ordinary empirical propositions, and accept that ethical terms (often) have an **emotive function**, his account does not seem to do justice to (the complexity of) ethics and ethical debate. An ethical dispute may well involve facts, but will not be confined to them. It could be about the facts of a particular situation; given different views of the facts, about which course of action would be most likely to maximize happiness; and about whether happiness is the ultimate good. Again, those who take the view that morality is grounded in the needs of intrinsically valuable human beings would probably regard the statement that murder or torture is wrong as clearly true. **Ethical emotivism**'s strength is its recognition of the dynamic nature and persuasive purpose of moral language: that it is used to influence behaviour. Emotivism's weakness is that it makes moral terms mean different things to different people, depending on the emotions expressed, or the effects produced. It also seems to debase moral argument to the level of propaganda.

3 Universal prescriptivism in R. M. Hare's 'Universal Prescriptivism' (see recommended edition on **p. 65**)

R. M. Hare (1919–2002)

Richard Mervyn Hare read Greats at Balliol College, Oxford, and was White's Professor of Moral Philosophy there (1966–83). He reacted against **ethical emotivism**, and his moral philosophy was influenced by J. L. Austin's focus on the study of ordinary language and Ludwig Wittgenstein's view that meaning is found in use. He is particularly associated with the metaethical theory of universal prescriptivism, set out in *The Language of Morals* (1952), *Freedom and Reason* (1963), *Moral Thinking: Its Levels, Method and Point* (1981) and 'Universal Prescriptivism' (1993). His other books include *Essays on Religion and Education* (1992).

Descriptivist and non-descriptivist metaethical theories

Hare divides modern metaethical theories into descriptivist ones, which hold that the world contains 'moral qualities or facts' that moral statements describe, and non-descriptivist ones, which do not (p. 451). He illustrates the difference by discussing the *'truth-condition* theory' of meaning: that to understand a statement's meaning is to understand the conditions, or facts, which would have to exist for it to be considered true (p. 451). While ethical descriptivists hold that the meaning of sentences that express moral statements or judgements is determined by their truth-conditions, ethical non-descriptivists, including prescriptivists, maintain that, although ethical judgements have descriptive meaning, which is determined by truth conditions, there is:

> a further element in their meaning, the prescriptive, evaluative, or . . . emotive, which . . . expresses prescriptions or evaluations or attitudes which we assent to without being constrained by truth-conditions. (p. 452)

Ethical naturalists and non-naturalists

Ethical descriptivists fall into two types: ethical naturalists, like Bentham, and ethical non-naturalists, like Moore and Ross. The first believe that the truth-conditions of moral statements are provided by such non-moral truths or properties as pleasure or the absence of pain (see **pp. 27–9** and **86–92**); the second by non-natural properties, which are known through moral intuition (see **pp. 33–48**). For Hare, both their theories collapse into 'relativism' (p. 453). With ethical naturalists, this is because the truth conditions, or facts, which, in their view, give moral statements their meaning, are those applying in a particular society, at a particular time. For example, the 'ought' statement 'wives ought to obey their husbands in all things' would, according to ethical naturalism, be true, if certain non-moral statements were true: for example, that wives being obedient would contribute to society's stability (p. 453). However, feminists would reject the moral principle of wifely obedience, even if it made society more stable, arguing that some of a husband's demands should be resisted, even at the price of social destabilization. What happens, Hare explains, when non-moral facts are held to supply the meaning of moral statements, is that the 'substantial moral principle' (in this case, that one ought to do what contributes to social stability), has got:

> promoted into an analytic truth, true in virtue of the meaning of 'ought'. But it is not an analytic truth. If it were . . . the feminists . . . would be contradicting themselves, by saying something which the very meaning of 'ought' establishes as false. If 'ought' has its meaning fixed by truth-conditions . . . then one cannot in logical consistency say what the feminists are saying. (p. 453)

With intuitionism, the truth-conditions that have to exist to make a moral statement true are the non-moral properties of things or actions, which are intuited by the moral agent. However, these invariably turn out to be the 'common moral convictions that all morally educated people have' (see pp. 40, 45); but again, these vary, as they are 'relative to particular societies' (p. 454).

Emotivism

One non-descriptivist theory is emotivism. This is non-rationalist, because the emotivists, in rejecting descriptivism, concluded that it is impossible to 'reason about moral questions', as ethical statements merely express, and seek to arouse, 'non-rational attitudes of approval or disapproval' (p. 455). In Hare's view, they were led to this conclusion because, like A. J. Ayer:

> they added an additional premise which is false, namely that the only questions one can reason about are factual ones. (p. 455)

Hare's universal prescriptivism originated in recognition of the falsity of this premise, and the quest for a form of non-descriptivism that is rational; and this was achieved by showing that rules of reasoning govern non-descriptive, as well as descriptive, speech acts. Emotivists believe that imperatives derive their meaning from their causal properties, that is, the effects they have on those to whom they are addressed. However (Hare maintains), 'verbal shoves and psychological prods' are not part of the meaning of either imperatives or moral statements (p. 455). The rules of reasoning, relating to ethical thinking and discussion, are to be found in a combination of the rules that govern ordinary imperatives, and those that govern 'ought' and other duty words, such as 'must', when they are used in a moral context.

The distinguishing characteristics of ethical statements

So, what, according to universal prescriptivism, are the distinguishing characteristics of ethical statements? Their key characteristic is:

> the 'universalizability' of 'ought'-sentences and other normative or evaluative sentences . . . One cannot with logical consistency, where a and b are two individuals, say that a ought, in a certain situation specified in universal terms . . . to act in a certain way . . . but that b ought not to act in a similarly specified way in a similarly specified situation . . . in any 'ought'-statement there is implicit a principle which says that the statement applies to all precisely similar situations. (p. 456)

There is a contradiction involved in a person specifying that someone ought to do something in one situation, but then saying that a person exactly like the one who ought to do it in the first situation ought not to do it in a precisely similar situation. This is made even clearer if the reasons why it ought to be done in the first situation are given: such as its being a promise, and there are no conflicting duties that prevent the promise being kept. Ethical statements are 'supervenient' on certain non-moral facts, which are given as reasons why something is good or bad, or an action is right or wrong. Thus, when someone says that a particular action would be right, he is invoking a universal ethical principle, to the effect that one should always behave in a certain way, given those facts: keeping promises one has made; always repaying debts; and so on. If one person says that another person ought to do something, and the reason is the universal principle that one ought to keep a promise, then, unless there are overriding reasons for not keeping it, he cannot consistently apply the principle in one situation but refuse to apply it in a precisely similar one.

The point about another duty possibly overriding the promise is an important one. In a particular situation, there may be a good reason for not keeping a promise: for example, a promise to attend a meeting might be broken, in order to help a car accident victim (see **p. 18**). The universal principle is not, 'you ought always to keep a promise, even if the heavens fall', but, 'you ought always to keep a promise, unless there is a good reason for not doing so'. Thus, there needs to be careful attention to all the specifics of the particular situation, to take account of the relevant considerations, including people's desires: different desires make the situation different, and the application of broadly drawn principles may not always accommodate these. A universal ethical principle of, 'you ought always to help old people across the road' sounds unobjectionable, but would not accommodate those old people who prefer to see themselves across the road.

Universality is not generality

Indeed, Hare stresses the importance of not confusing universality with generality. Ought statements can be, and will often need to be:

> highly specific, complex and detailed . . . my moral principles do not have to be as general as '*Never* tell lies': they can be more specific, like 'Never tell lies except when it is necessary in order to save an innocent life, and except when . . . and except when . . . (p. 457)

Again, it is no objection to the universalizability thesis that there can be duties owed to only one person, provided that the person, such as a mother, can be specified in universal terms. Hare mentions Sartre's story about being consulted by a student, as to whether he should join the Free French, or stay at home and care for his widowed mother. Sartre had wrongly concluded that universal ethical principles are useless: not, as he should have done, that very general universal principles do not always fit complex ethical dilemmas. The student should have been able to form a 'highly specific' principle, which would apply to 'situations *just* like his' (p. 457).

The prescriptive nature of ethical judgements

Universal prescriptivists hold that, like ordinary imperatives, ethical judgements are prescriptive (whatever their precise form, they prescribe how people should act), but differ from them in being universalizable. To subscribe to an ethical judgement is to commit oneself to performing the action specified in the judgement, or to be guilty of insincerity. And most people (Hare believes) think that it is conceptually, as well as morally, wrong to say, 'You ought to do so and so, but don't do it.' Of course, this does not mean that an individual will always perform an action that he says he ought to perform, even though he is not physically prevented from doing so. He may be too afraid of the consequences, or morally weak.

Can moral judgements be true or false? In a sense: because of their universalizability. To make an ethical judgement is implicitly to invoke some ethical principle. In a fairly stable society, ethical principles will be stable, too. So, when one person says that another did as he ought, people will know what he means, according to the commonly accepted descriptive meaning (that is, truth-conditions) that the word 'ought' has in that society. So, prescriptivism permits a limited role for truth-conditions in determining the meaning of moral terms, in a particular society; but they will not have the same descriptive meaning in a different one.

A rational process of ethical thinking and argument

As moral judgements have descriptive meaning, in this sense, can an 'ought' be derived from an 'is'? Can we infer moral judgements from non-moral facts (see also **pp. 21–2, 23–7**)? Hare thinks it is easy to see how such a belief arises. In certain societies, particular ethical principles have become so deeply embedded that some 'ought' conclusions appear inevitable. But:

> Prescriptivists have to deny this, because they hold that moral judgements commit the speaker to motivations and actions, but non-moral facts by themselves do not . . . the prescriptive . . . element is not there in the bare description of the facts. (pp. 459–60)

As prescriptivists are not constrained by non-moral facts, or facts of moral intuition, to regard a particular moral principle, or action, as good or bad, right or wrong, they could consistently prescribe principles of male chauvinism or racism, provided they universalized them, and did not exempt particular individuals, including themselves, from their effect, if they were female or members of a particular race. However, Hare suggests a rational process to help prevent people adopting such principles. As moral judgements are prescriptive and universalizable, the logic of moral concepts is that they should be, as Kant argues (see **pp. 72, 74**), capable of functioning as universal laws. Before we formulate or accept moral principles, we must imagine ourselves as other people, putting ourselves fully into their position, to see how they would be affected by our principles. Hare points to well-established examples of ethical principles that embody this approach, such as the Golden Rule (see **p. 192**), and the version of the categorical imperative that requires rational beings to be treated always as ends, never merely as means (see **p. 75**).

Two levels of ethical thinking

Hare also makes the important point that, in relation to the two levels of ethical thinking, 'critical' and 'intuitive', we should not always prefer the former. Judging, and acting, intuitively may prevent some of the undesirable consequences of, for example, utilitarian calculation of the comparative quantities of happiness to be produced by killing, or not killing, an innocent person, and then deciding to do so: better to follow our intuition that an innocent life should always be preserved. People should:

> school themselves to have good dispositions or virtues [see **p. 108**] which will lead them . . . to do what an unbiased and otherwise perfect critical moral thinker would bid them to do – if necessary without too much thought. (p. 461)

Like Ross, Hare acknowledges the reasonable presumption that the moral convictions of thinking people are the right ones; but we must guard against incautious acceptance of the ethical 'wisdom of the ages': white supremacists and Muslim fundamentalists, who 'know' that it is right to stone adulteresses, preach and practise long-held ethical principles (pp. 461–2).

Assessment

Thus, if somebody says that we ought always to give money to a beggar in the street, he is prescribing a universal ethical principle that it is always right to assist the unfortunate with gifts of money. A rational moral argument with an opponent might follow. The opponent might challenge the principle (arguing, for example, that such generosity encourages idleness); might seek to qualify it (only give such assistance if you can afford it without depriving your family; only give to those who are deserving); or, while accepting the principle, question its application in this instance (perhaps on the grounds that this particular 'beggar' is a fraud).

As **universal prescriptivism** maintains that the meaning of moral terms is determined by their use, it is **anti-descriptivist**; but it affirms that such use is governed by a logical structure. Indeed, a particular strength of this theory is that it lays out a rational procedure for moral debate. While the meaning of moral terms cannot be equated with certain facts, facts are relevant to moral judgements, and it shows how acceptance of new facts may change the judgements. In the case above, the advocate of giving may, if convinced that the beggar's poverty is not genuine, conclude that his **universal ethical principle** of charity does not apply in this case. If convinced that giving always causes idleness on the part of the recipient, he may (though not necessarily) modify his principle. On the other hand, he may say that such consequences do not matter, as poverty should always be relieved.

4 Ethical descriptivism in G. J. Warnock's *Contemporary Moral Philosophy* and *The Object of Morality* (see recommended edition on **p. 65**)

G. J. Warnock (1923–95)

Geoffrey James Warnock read PPE at New College, Oxford. He was Principal of Hertford College (1971–88), Vice-Chancellor of the University of Oxford (1981–5), and was knighted in 1986. Strongly influenced by the work of J. L. Austin, Warnock co-edited his *Philosophical Papers* (1961), and prepared his lectures for publication as *Sense and Sensibilia* (1962). In *Contemporary Moral Philosophy* (1967) and *The Object of Morality* (1971), he argues that morality has a definite content and purpose. His other works include *Berkeley* (1953) and *English Philosophy Since 1900* (1969).

Rejection of intuitionism, emotivism and prescriptivism

In *Contemporary Moral Philosophy*, Warnock explains that he finds the three main metaethical doctrines of **ethical intuitionism** (see **pp. 33–48**), **ethical emotivism** and **universal prescriptivism** unsatisfactory. Their accounts of morality are inadequate, because they do not consider what moral utterances actually say or mean, or the grounds on which they are based.

The subject matter of morality

He identifies four factors that have been regarded as the central characteristic of morality. First, there is people's powerful consciousness that it is right or wrong to act in a certain way, and the guilt that follows failure to do so. However, there are no grounds for regarding how people feel about an issue as evidence that it is a moral one. Second, a person's moral principles are held to be those that guide his life, but, as in the case of followers of Nietzsche (see **pp. 11–14** and **281**), some people's guiding principles would not be considered moral. Third (as with Hare), there is the view that moral principles are those that are prescribed universally. However, individuals and groups, as in primitive societies, have prescribed universal principles that we would not regard as moral. The fourth, which Warnock espouses, is that the essential characteristic of morality is its subject-matter. He argues that what makes a view moral is its content, the range or type of considerations on which it is founded, reflecting such objects as promoting human happiness and interests, and satisfying human needs.

Satisfying human needs

Warnock's metaethical theory is 'descriptivist', not in the sense that he believes that moral terms like 'good' or 'right' refer to, or mean, a natural property, such as 'pleasure', but that concern with satisfying human needs, and promoting human well-being, furnishes the criterion for determining whether or not a principle is a moral one. Someone claiming to make a moral judgement must recognize that concern with the welfare of human beings provides the logical boundary of moral debate, and that what he proposes as morally right must be beneficial to them:

> it appears at least enormously plausible to say that one who professes to be making a moral judgment *must* at least profess that what is in issue is the good or harm, well-being or otherwise of human beings – that what he regards as morally wrong is somehow damaging . . . morally right . . .

beneficial ... this would not be a sufficient characterisation of moral judgment ... [but one] any intelligible theory must recognise to be of central importance. (pp. 57–8)

Good and bad, right and wrong

For Warnock, principles or ideals involving what is destructive or damaging to human beings cannot be moral ones. But surely, as human beings are different, what promotes the well-being of some may be harmful to others? Warnock does not think that different tastes or preferences affect the fundamental issue. We all know that the answers to some questions about what is good or bad for people are not debatable:

> I believe that we all have . . . the conviction that at least some questions as to what is good or bad for people . . . are not in any serious sense matters of opinion. That it is a bad thing to be tortured or starved, humiliated or hurt, is not an opinion: it is a fact. That it is better for people to be loved, and attended to, rather than hated or neglected, is again a plain fact, not a matter of opinion. (pp. 60–1)

While it may be a matter of factual judgement whether a person would be helped or harmed, if a certain action were performed, once the facts have been established, and the outcome is known, the morally right course of action, which will be the one that promotes human well-being, will be obvious. Following a course of action that caused harm to others would not be to apply an alternative moral principle, but not to apply a moral principle at all, and those who did so would be morally wrong.

Human welfare as a necessarily relevant criterion of moral evaluation

Warnock rejects the view of anti-naturalist philosophers that description and (moral) evaluation are not just different, but logically independent of each other. Following Hume (see **pp. 21–2, 23–7**), they maintain that, logically, no description ever requires any particular evaluation: we can accept the description, but, without 'logical inconsistency', reject a particular evaluation (p. 64). Warnock insists that, when we discuss things, we do not in fact separate out description and evaluation. We mix them up, because they belong together. So, it may be possible to describe Mussolini's career in such a way that any evaluation of it could be accepted or rejected without logical error. But it would be hard, and we would not expect anybody who claimed to be expressing a moral judgement to commend Mussolini's career.

What 'ethical' means

While it may be the case that, in moral evaluation, no one is ever logically bound to accept any particular thing as good or bad, or right or wrong, this does not mean that just anything can be so regarded. Of course, to say that certain things must necessarily be accepted as criteria of moral value does not imply that everyone necessarily evaluates things by those criteria. But, to engage in moral debate, they must do so. People must accept the relevance to their judgement of a certain range of considerations, centring on human well-being, if their claim to be evaluating morally is to be taken seriously: 'we do not *choose* that this should be so; it *is* so, simply because of what "moral" means' (p. 67).

A course of action would definitely be morally wrong if it could be shown that its consequences would cause indisputable harm to an innocent person or persons, while generating no counterbalancing greater good to anyone else.

Things that are definitely morally wrong

For example, it can be demonstrated conclusively that it would be morally wrong for Warnock to induce heroin addiction in his children; and anyone who:

> denies that the conclusion follows ... that ... it would *not* be morally wrong ... shows either that he has not really followed the argument, or that he does not know what 'morally wrong' means. (p. 70)

These considerations about good or harm to people, which figure analytically in setting moral standards and moral principles, and which constitute the basis of moral argument, are (Warnock holds) matters about which the majority care, not because they choose to, but simply because they do. Further, our common moral vocabulary proves the existence of general agreement about what is desirable and undesirable in human affairs:

> That there is ... a very widespread ... consensus as to what is desirable and undesirable in human affairs is a condition of the existence of a common moral vocabulary. (pp. 71–2)

What matters is the content of ethics

In *The Object of Morality*, Warnock gives further consideration to the purpose and subject-matter of morality (see also **pp. 14–15** and **20–1**). He argues that analysing ethical language will not illuminate the subject of morality. When someone makes a moral judgement, he is not necessarily, as emotivists and prescriptivists contend, engaged in persuading or prescribing. It is only necessary to consider the huge range of contexts in which, and subjects about which, moral judgements are expressed to appreciate the falsity of the view that moral debate has only one purpose. What is distinctive of moral debate, which generally involves the evaluation of actions, is not its language, but its content. Ethical naturalists and non-naturalists had misinterpreted ethical language, maintaining that it refers to natural or non-natural properties. Having rejected this analysis, the emotivists and prescriptivists had looked for another unique use. They are all wrong, as the essential characteristic of moral debate is its subject-matter, the kinds of reasons given for, and considerations regarded as relevant to, the moral judgements made.

The scope of morality

To whom does morality apply? Rationality is a necessary condition of being a moral agent and of moral principles applying to one's actions. Further, if morality's object is to improve rational beings' predicament, a rational being cannot, in general, claim to be an agent to whom moral principles do not apply, when he is deciding what he ought to do, while moral principles must embrace as potential beneficiaries not only all human beings, which is what lies behind the widely held view that morality's essence is 'respect for persons' (p. 150 and see **pp. 21–2, 23–7**), but all sentient creatures: 'the principles of morality apply to (as agents) all rational beings, and (as patients) all creatures capable of suffering' (p. 152 and see **pp. 318–22, 323–5**).

The principle of universalizability is also important. If a person has a reason for not acting in a certain way, because it will cause him suffering, this is a reason for his not following courses of action which will cause other persons to suffer. For:

> what makes my sufferings rationally relevant to practical questions is that they are sufferings, and not that they are mine. (p. 163)

Assessment

Ethical descriptivism locates the meaning of moral language in its use, but rejects Hare's approach. First, it questions whether moral judgements are always prescriptive. According to Warnock, moral terms may be used to do lots of different things: advise, exhort, command, condemn, confess and so on. But, are all these apparently different speech-acts still, in some sense, forms of prescribing? Are those who use moral terms always, whether directly or indirectly (and perhaps without being aware of it), guiding choices? For example, is condemning a cruel act, such as striking a child, or confessing to it, also saying, or implying, 'you ought not to do this kind of thing', or 'I ought not to have done this, and you should not either'?

A more fundamental descriptivist criticism of **universal prescriptivism** is that moral discourse, and the meaning of moral terms, is determined by their content, not their form. Warnock argues that morality is logically grounded in human needs. To qualify as a moral judgement, 'good', 'right', 'ought', or any other evaluative terms, must have a definite content that relates to a concern with human wants or needs, simply because of what the word 'moral' means. For Warnock, anyone who maintains, having heard all the facts, which would include the long-term effects of such a state, that it is not wrong to induce heroin addiction in his children, either (a) has not understood all the facts, or (b) does not understand the meaning of 'morally wrong'.

An appeal to common sense usage seems to support Warnock's argument. In response to such an outrageous assertion as the above, would we be more likely to say, 'I don't agree with your moral judgement', and proceed to debate the matter, or to exclaim, 'You don't know what you're saying!' (that is, are ignorant of the facts), or 'If you think that's not morally wrong, you don't understand what "morally wrong" means!' We should also ponder the cogency of Warnock's explanation (see **pp. 14–15**) of why we need moral discourse at all: that its existence and importance reflect certain undeniable needs and wants of, and facts about, human beings and the world they inhabit, such as their vulnerability, the inadequacy of material resources, and the human tendency to be self-interested and unsympathetic to the hardships of others. While the **emotivist** emphasis on the dynamic quality of moral discourse, and Hare's on its **prescriptive** nature, may seem persuasive, so, too, is the **descriptivist** claim that, to be meaningful, moral discourse (and therefore moral terms) must be **grounded in human needs**.

Core texts

A. J. Ayer, *Language, Truth and Logic* (reprinted with an Introduction by Ben Rogers), London: Penguin, 2001.

R. M. Hare, 'Universal Prescriptivism', in P. Singer (ed.), *A Companion to Ethics*, London: Blackwell, 1991.

G. J. Warnock, *Contemporary Moral Philosophy*, London: Macmillan, 1967.

G. J. Warnock, *The Object of Morality*, London: Methuen, 1971.

Suggestions for further reading and research

R. M. Hare, *The Language of Morals*, Oxford and New York: Oxford University Press, 1952.

R. M. Hare, *Freedom and Reason*, Oxford and New York: Oxford University Press, 1963.

T. Horgan and M. Timmons (eds), *Metaethics After Moore*, Oxford and New York: Oxford University Press, 2006.

W. D. Hudson, *Modern Moral Philosophy*, London: Macmillan, 1970 (chapters 4–6).

D. Mills Daniel, *Briefly: Ayer's Language, Truth and Logic*, London: SCM Press, 2007.

J. Rachels, 'Subjectivism', in P. Singer (ed.), *A Companion to Ethics*, Cambridge: Cambridge University Press, 1993.

G. Sayre-McCord, 'Metaethics', in E. N. Zalta (ed.), *Stanford Encyclopaedia of Philosophy*, at http://plato.stanford.edu.

C. L. Stevenson, *Ethics and Language*, New Haven and London: Yale University Press, 1965.

M. Warnock, *Ethics since 1900*, rev. edn, Oxford and New York: Oxford University Press, 1966.

Part 2 Normative Ethics

4 Deontological Ethics

1 The deontological approach

Right in itself, not because of its consequences

What makes actions right? For some moral philosophers, it is their **consequences** (see **pp. 86–103**): they are right because of the results they produce (or which we hope they will produce), such as happiness. However, other moral philosophers think this approach fails. Even if we could calculate all the consequences of our actions, should (and, indeed, do) we evaluate actions (mainly) on this basis? For example, there are many actions, such as persecuting minority groups in society, which might make a lot of people happy, but which we would condemn as wrong. **Deontologists** say that rightness has little or nothing to do with an action's consequences, and everything to do with the action itself; and that we have a duty to perform certain actions, such as keeping promises, telling the truth, and not harming others, because of their intrinsic rightness. They may also maintain, like W. D. Ross (see **pp. 41–7**), that, in complex situations, we may just have to rely on our intuition to determine what the right action is: although Ross does give a list of what he calls *prima facie* or **conditional duties**, which it is generally our duty to perform.

Kant's ethical system

The most significant deontological system is that of Immanuel Kant, which is discussed below. Kant both explains why consequences cannot (in his view) be the basis of moral decision-making (happiness, for example, is an indeterminate concept, which means different things to different people, and depends on empirical elements, which cannot be guaranteed), and, in the various formulations of his **categorical imperative**, sets out the basis of morality: the absolute worth of rational beings, including human beings, who must always be treated as ends in themselves, never merely as means; and the universal nature of true ethical principles, which must always be such that they can be willed as universal laws, governing the conduct of all rational beings, in all situations. Kant also stresses the importance of the moral agent's intention: to act morally, we must carry out our moral principles (in Kant's terms, obey the moral law) for their own sake, and not for any other motive, such as personal advantage.

Issues that arise

Perhaps, the greatest strength of Kant's moral philosophy is its insistence on the **absolute worth of human beings**: it is hard to think of any other basis for morality. But, is he right to rule out consequences altogether, when making moral decisions? Do not most people's ethical principles embody a mixture of deontological and consequentialist elements: for example, we accept that, in general, we ought to tell the truth, but not if the consequences would cause someone great distress. Again, we may agree that ethical principles should apply universally, but what if they conflict? How do we decide which to apply (see also **pp. 42–5**)? This question seems to bring us back to consequences. Further, ethical principles are not much help if they are inflexible: they may need to be adapted or elaborated, to fit complex ethical dilemmas. Kant seems to argue too that the moral worth of an action relates to the purity of the agent's intention, but is motive relevant to an action's rightness (see **pp. 46–7**)? Kant also stresses the importance of freedom, if there is to be genuine moral responsibility (see also **pp. 215–17**).

2 Kant's moral philosophy

Immanuel Kant (1724–1804)

Immanuel Kant's ideas on metaphysics, moral philosophy and the philosophy of religion have profoundly influenced thinking in all these areas. After studying at the University of Konigsberg, he became a lecturer and then professor of logic and metaphysics there (1770). He devoted his life to study, thought and writing, rising before five o'clock in the morning, and giving fixed periods of time to each activity. As well as *Groundwork of the Metaphysics of Morals* (1785), *Critique of Practical Reason* (1788) and *Religion within the Boundaries of Mere Reason* (1793), his books include: *Critique of Pure Reason* (1781; 1787), *Prolegomena to any Future Metaphysic* (1783), *Critique of Judgement* (1790), and *Metaphysics of Morals* (1797).

The moral law: *Groundwork of the Metaphysics of Morals* (see recommended edition on **p. 84**)

A supreme principle of morality

In the preface to the *Groundwork*, Kant tells us that its purpose is to discover the supreme principle of morality, which, he believes, will not be found in human nature, or ordinary experience, but *a priori* (known before or without experience), in our reason. The book contains a deontological moral system, in which actions are right or wrong in themselves, and moral principles (what Kant calls the moral law(s)) are followed for their own sake, and not because of their consequences, or because they are believed to meet specific human needs.

Only a good will is good without limitation

Kant begins by maintaining that only a good will is 'good without limitation' (p. 7). It is one that seeks to carry out moral duties for their own sake, and not for personal advantage, to satisfy desires or inclinations, or because of what it 'effects or accomplishes' (p. 8). For example, a shopkeeper may not overcharge his customers, but his honest behaviour may be due to a desire to retain his customers, rather than the duty not to cheat them, and so lack moral worth. On the other hand, the actions of a philanthropist who is out of sympathy with humanity, but who continues his charitable acts despite their being contrary to his inclinations, definitely have moral worth.

Acting against our inclinations

Kant is saying that, in order to do the right thing, we sometimes have to act against our inclinations, and that it is sometimes hard to tell whether people are doing the right thing for the right reasons, as opposed to self-interested ones. He also seems to be saying that actions that are contrary to our inclinations have more moral worth than those that are not, even if the latter are right (see also **pp. 46–7**). So, the actions of those who, unlike his philanthropist, find an 'inner satisfaction' in helping others, fit in with their inclinations and so lack true moral worth (p. 11).

The will must be determined by universal law

Kant's most important point is that an action's moral worth lies in the maxim or subjective principle/rule of conduct upon which it is decided, not in its consequences. An action that excludes personal inclination, or consideration of consequences, will be right, because it is determined solely by the *a priori* moral law that comes from the reason. For the will to be absolutely good, it must be determined by what Kant calls 'universal law' as such (p. 14).

Kant gives the example of a man in difficulties, who contemplates making a false promise in order to get himself out of them, and argues that a maxim of not making a false promise because it would mean not being trusted in future would be based on consequences, which is not the same as being truthful from duty. However (Kant argues), the maxim of making false promises when in difficulties could not become a universal law because it would destroy itself: a universal law to lie would end all promises, as it would be pointless to make them: there would then be 'no promises at all' (p. 15). But, although there does seem to be a contradiction between the concept of a promise and a universal law allowing false promises, this example suggests that undesirable consequences would follow if such a maxim became universal: confidence in promises would be undermined.

Possible criticisms

Parts of Kant's argument are easier to accept than others. Doing the right thing often involves acting against inclination, and this factor influences our judgement of an action's moral worth. We are more likely to praise actions that involve sacrificing the agent's inclinations than those that allow him to follow his inclinations, even if we think his chosen course of action is morally right. But can all consideration of consequences be excluded from moral decision-making? Leaving aside the influence on us of utilitarianism and the connection between moral decisions and promoting happiness, human needs, and the consequences of our actions in relation to satisfying those needs, do seem to play a big part in our decisions about what is right and wrong, and which courses of action we should follow.

A test of moral maxims

There are reasons for Kant's rejection of consequences and human nature as the basis of morality, which he develops later in the *Groundwork*, but he has made a point which it is difficult, even for his critics, to reject: that moral principles apply universally (or are universalizable: see also **pp. 49–50, 53–9, 100–02**). People should not perform an action unless they can will that the rules of conduct by which they act should become universal laws: the moral principles they adopt should apply for all people ('rational beings', as Kant calls them) in all situations. Therefore, if supposed moral principles are put forward that apply only to some people or particular circumstances, or which favour some groups or individuals rather than others, they should be challenged.

Moral principles cannot be grounded in human nature

Kant makes it clear that moral principles cannot be grounded in human nature, because the conditions of humanity are 'merely contingent' (p. 23): the way that human beings are depends on a range of empirical factors, which could have been different, and which may change in the future. Kant, however, is looking for moral principles that will be valid for all rational beings, irrespective of any purely empirical factors. Therefore, they must be derived from the reason, not from human experience.

It could be argued that human beings are the only rational beings that concern us, so we should relate our moral principles to (satisfying) human needs. However, Kant's point is important, even for those who base their moral principles on human needs. While there are common human needs, differences among human beings mean that (at least some of) their needs differ. This applies even to the purpose that Kant acknowledges all human beings pursue: happiness. It is an indeterminate concept, because different people include different things in their idea of happiness, and it depends upon empirical elements, which cannot be guaranteed in either the present or the future. Therefore, any attempt to link morality to happiness is bound to fail. Again, if we try to base morality on what (particular groups of) human beings actually consider to be right or wrong, we have to recognize that their inclinations, desires or self-interest may influence their views:

One need only look at attempts at morality in that popular taste. One will find . . . now perfection, now happiness, here moral feeling, there fear of God, a bit of this and also a bit of that . . . without its occurring to them to ask whether principles of morality are to be sought at all in acquaintance with human nature. (p. 22)

The categorical imperative

Kant explores how morality works. Only rational beings possess a will and the ability to act according to moral principles that come from the reason. However, human inclinations and interests may be at variance with the moral law, so it is expressed in commands or imperatives. For imperfect human beings, with wills influenced by their inclinations, morality is presented as things that they ought to do. However, a divine or holy will would not need imperatives, because, free of inclinations, it would already accord with the moral law.

Kant explains the difference between hypothetical and moral imperatives. The former are conditional, indicating an action which is necessary in order to achieve an end that is optional. But moral imperatives are unconditional or categorical: they command actions that are necessary in themselves; and this categorical imperative (which Kant formulates in various ways) is to act only in accordance with a maxim that can, at the same time, be willed as a universal law:

> a *categorical* imperative . . . contains, beyond the law, only the necessity that the maxim be in conformity with this law, while the law contains no condition to which it would be limited, nothing is left with which the maxim of action is to conform but the universality of a law as such . . . There is, therefore, only a single categorical imperative . . . *act only in accordance with that maxim through which you can at the same time will that it become a universal law.* (p. 31)

In *Utilitarianism*, John Stuart Mill argues that this principle could result in adoption of outrageously immoral rules of conduct. But this first formulation of the categorical imperative enables us to test our maxims. If they cannot function as universal moral laws, applicable to all rational beings, they should be rejected.

However, Kant's examples do not work particularly well. He considers a man who is prospering, but who sees that others are not. He follows his inclination, which is to look after himself, and ignore others' difficulties. Kant accepts that humanity would be able to survive adoption of this maxim, but it could not be willed as a universal law, because it would conflict with itself, ruling out the possibility of the help which everyone needs at times. However, it is hard not to feel that the root objection to this maxim is that it would have such undesirable consequences.

The absolute worth of human beings and the kingdom of ends

But why should we be moral at all? Kant observes that the will is determined by an end. However, most of our ends have only relative worth, in relation to achieving particular desires. Therefore, they cannot be the source of universal moral principles and categorical imperatives. An end in itself, which has absolute worth, is needed; and this yields another formulation of the categorical imperative, that the only things that have absolute worth are human and all rational beings:

> So act that you use humanity, whether in your own or in the person of any other, always at the same time as an end, never merely as a means. (p. 38)

Whatever view is taken of Kant's moral philosophy as a whole, this is a convincing basis of morality. Even if we believe that actions are right or wrong, to the extent that they promote happiness, why should we worry about other people's happiness, as opposed to concentrating on our own, unless we attach some value to other human beings? Kant, of course, goes much further. Human beings have absolute worth, and every maxim we adopt should lead only to actions that always treat them as ends in themselves, and never simply as means to achieving our own ends. Again, Kant gives examples, including that of one who makes a false promise. Here the promise-maker uses the promisee as a means, not an end. Kant provides a compelling image of how we should discharge our moral responsibilities with his idea of all rational beings regarding themselves as members of a kingdom of ends, acting as if they are adopting maxims that are to serve as universal laws for all rational beings, and treating themselves, and others, as ends not means:

> Morality consists, then, in the reference of all action to the lawgiving by which alone a kingdom of ends is possible . . . to act only *so that the will could regard itself as at the same time giving universal law through its maxim.* (p. 42)

The autonomy of the will

For Kant, the will's autonomy is the supreme principle of morals, while its heteronomy is the source of all spurious ones. Heteronomy arises when, in making moral decisions, people allow their will to be determined by considerations other than the fitness of their maxims to serve as universal laws for all rational beings. The obvious sources of spurious moral principles are empirical factors, such as human desires and inclinations. The example Kant gives is of someone who adopts the maxim of not lying, not because it is wrong, but to preserve his reputation; but 'I ought not to lie even though it would bring me not the least discredit' (pp. 47–8).

However, heteronomy would also arise if moral principles were taken from an all-perfect divine will. Kant's point is that morality is autonomous: things are not right because they satisfy certain desires, maximize happiness, or reflect God's will. If they were, moral decision-making would involve only deciding whether or not a particular course of action will promote happiness, or please God; and there could be no question as to whether what promotes happiness, or pleases God, is right.

Freedom

(See also **pp. 215–17**.)

To be autonomous is to be free, and Kant maintains that, to have wills that are their own, and to be able to adopt as maxims universal principles to which they hold themselves subject, rational beings (and therefore human beings) must be free. But what proof is there that we are free, when we know that we are subject to the causality of laws of nature? Kant's answer is that we cannot prove that we are free, any more than we can prove the existence of categorical imperatives. However, he distinguishes between the world of sense (that is, things as they appear to us, because of the kind of beings we are), of which our senses give us knowledge, and within which our actions are determined by desires and inclinations, and the world of understanding (that is, things as they are in themselves), to which, because we possess reason, human (and all rational) beings belong. Therefore, we have two standpoints from which to view our relationship with the moral law. As part of the world of sense, we are subject to laws of nature, but as part of the world of understanding, we are subject to moral laws that come from the reason and are independent of nature. However, because, as part of the world of sense, our actions are determined by desires and inclinations, moral laws have to be expressed as imperatives.

The limit of moral enquiry

Kant acknowledges that the freedom claimed seems to contradict the natural necessity of laws of nature, and, while freedom is only an idea of reason, laws of nature are an objective reality. Indeed, Kant admits that there is no possibility of explaining matters that are not determined by laws of nature, so the limit of moral enquiry has been reached. However, as we cannot give up the idea of freedom, which is essential, if there is going to be moral responsibility, we have to accept that, although we cannot explain it, there actually is no contradiction between holding that beings who are subject to the laws of nature are also independent of them, and subject to moral laws given by pure reason:

> how a categorical imperative is possible, can indeed be answered to the extent that one can furnish the sole presupposition on which alone it is possible, namely the idea of freedom. (p. 64)

Assessment

Kant's moral system, as set out in the *Groundwork*, is not straightforward, and getting to grips with it is not helped by Kant's complex, and sometimes opaque, style of writing. However, it does repay the effort. Kant has a lot to offer, and even those who do not accept his moral system, in its entirety, cannot deny his important contribution to moral philosophy.

There are some obviously unsatisfactory elements. Kant does not seem to recognize that applying very general moral principles, such as 'do not lie', 'do not steal', or even 'do not kill', in an inflexible way, to complex ethical dilemmas, will probably not help to resolve them. As Hare points out (**pp. 53–9**), **universality** is not the same as **generality**. Moral principles may have to be very specific, to fit particular situations, so that a general principle, such as 'do not lie', becomes: 'in general, do not lie, except in these and those circumstances, when you may have to'. Ross (see **pp. 42–4**) draws attention to the problem of moral principles being in **conflict** with each other, when a choice may have to be made about which one to follow. Again, what Ross says about the distinction between moral goodness and rightness (see **pp. 46–7**) seems wholly convincing. Further, we may feel that consideration of human needs, and of the consequences of actions, cannot be (wholly) excluded from moral decision-making; indeed, we often apply a general principle, such as always keeping promises, or not telling lies, to a situation in the light of the kind of consequences we expect it to have in that situation.

However, Kant makes us aware of the dangers of basing our moral principles on human desires, including happiness, or on what human beings consider to be right or wrong at a particular point in history. Again, unless human beings are free, they cannot be held morally responsible for their actions. Finally, and perhaps most importantly, it is difficult to see why we should engage in moral activity at all, unless we regard **human beings as ends in themselves,** to whom we have duties and obligations, and not just as means to our own ends.

The postulates of the practical reason: the *Critique of Practical Reason* (see recommended edition on **p. 84**)

The practical reason and the postulates of the practical reason

Kant holds that morality is based on the idea that, as rational beings, human beings are **free,** but also bind themselves by moral laws, which they discover through their reason. Kant accepts that human freedom cannot be proved, but maintains that without it there can be no morality. Thus, freedom is essential to morality, and practical reason (reason when it considers or investigates moral issues) must assume or postulate it, in order to make sense of morality. Although, in his *Critique of Pure Reason*, Kant shows that speculative reason cannot prove God's existence, in the *Critique of Practical Reason*, he argues for two other **postulates of the practical reason: God** and **immortality.**

The highest good

Kant is emphatic that postulating God's existence does not compromise the autonomy of morality, for which he has argued in the *Groundwork*. The moral law is to be obeyed for its own sake, and God is not required to make human beings recognize or perform their duty. However, although morality is independent of religion, human beings have an idea of the highest good, in which performance of duty is rewarded by proportionate happiness. Only an all-powerful God can make this highest good possible, while immortality gives human beings the opportunity to achieve moral perfection.

An ambiguity in the concept of the highest good

In fact (Kant explains), the concept of the highest good is ambiguous: it can mean either the supreme good, or the whole or complete good. There is no doubt that virtue, that is, worthiness of being happy, through obeying the moral law, is the supreme good, and the condition of the possibility of human pursuit of happiness; but it is not the complete good. This requires '*happiness* too' (p. 141). However, unlike virtue, happiness, though always agreeable, is not 'by itself alone good absolutely' (p. 142).

The antinomy of practical reason

Kant points to an antinomy or contradiction, discovered by the practical reason. In human beings' idea of the highest good that they can achieve through their will, 'virtue and happiness are thought as necessarily linked', so that the practical reason cannot think of one without the other (p. 144). This could mean, either that the human desire for happiness is the motive for behaving morally, or that doing so causes happiness. The first is absolutely impossible, for, if human beings were to behave morally, only in order to satisfy their longing for happiness, their motivation would be wrong, as they would not be obeying the moral law for its own sake. However, the second is also impossible, because, in this world, happiness does not necessarily follow 'meticulous observance of moral laws': virtuous people do not always receive the happiness they deserve (p. 145).

Human beings belong to both the world of sense and the world of understanding

Kant resolves this contradiction by again invoking the distinction between the worlds of sense and understanding, and human beings' membership of both. As members of the world of sense, the causality of laws of nature apply to them, as to everything else; but, as members of the world of understanding, they are not subject to natural laws, and are free:

> one and the same acting being *as appearance* . . . has a causality in the world of sense . . . but, with regard to the same event . . . as *noumenon* (as pure intelligence . . .) . . . he can contain a determining basis . . . which is itself free from any natural law. (pp. 145–6)

While it is absolutely false that pursuit of happiness can be a basis for moral behaviour, the idea that virtue necessarily produces happiness is false, only if 'this attitude is regarded as the form of causality in the world of sense (p. 146). They are connected in the world of understanding, so virtuous people will ultimately receive the happiness they deserve.

Immortality

The necessary object of a will that conforms to the moral law is to bring about the highest good in the world. However, the highest good's supreme condition is a will that is completely adequate to the moral law, and that does not require it to be expressed in imperatives in order to obey it. This is moral perfection, or holiness of the will, which human beings cannot achieve during their lives, because human interests often clash with the moral law's precepts. It is only possible for human beings to achieve holiness of the will if there is infinite progress towards it. Therefore, the practical reason must assume an indefinite continuation of human beings' existence and personalities:

> it can be encountered only in a progression proceeding *ad infinitum* toward that complete adequacy; and according to principles of pure practical reason it is necessary to assume such a practical advance ... This infinite progression, however, is possible only on the presupposition of an *existence* and personality – of the same rational being – continuing *ad infinitum* (which is called the immortality of the soul). (p. 155)

In fact, Kant does not foresee a point when human beings will actually achieve holiness of the will, but immortality is their only hope of doing so.

God

The first part of the highest good, virtue, led to the postulate of immortality, in order to enable human beings to achieve moral perfection; the second element, happiness in proportion to virtue, leads the practical reason to postulate a cause capable of bringing it about: God:

> it must lead to the presupposition ... of a cause adequate to this effect ... it must postulate the *existence of God*. (p. 158)

The moral law itself promises neither happiness, nor a necessary connection between moral behaviour and proportionate happiness; and the natural order offers no evidence of a necessary link between the latter and obeying the moral law. Therefore, the practical reason must postulate the existence of a supreme cause of nature as a whole, which contains the basis of this connection:

> there is in the moral law not the slightest basis for a necessary connection between morality and the happiness, proportionate thereto ... Therefore the existence of a cause of nature as a whole ... which contains the basis of this connection ... is also *postulated*. (pp. 158–9)

Of course, God's existence does not need to be postulated as a basis for behaving morally, as this would compromise the autonomy of the moral law.

Christianity

For Kant, Christian teaching brings together the ideas of the supreme good and the complete good. The moral law requires moral perfection, or 'holiness of morals', but does not promise happiness as a result; it leaves human beings with nothing but infinite progress towards becoming ever more virtuous (p. 162). However, in view of this, they are entitled to hope for infinite existence, in order to pursue moral perfection; and ultimately to receive happiness in proportion to their virtue:

> The *holiness* of morals is assigned to rational beings as a standard already in this life; but the well-being proportionate to it, i.e. *bliss*, is conceived as attainable only in an eternity . . . happiness . . . is made solely an object of hope. (p. 163)

Christian morality is not heteronomous: it does not teach that the human will should be determined by what God wills, rather than the moral law's commands. On the contrary, it teaches that the proper incentive for obeying the moral law is duty alone. However, this leads to religion, and to seeing the duties prescribed by the moral law, also as *'divine commands'* (p. 164). The moral law commands human beings to make the highest possible good in the world the ultimate object of all their conduct, but they can only hope to bring this good about if their will is in harmony with that of the world's 'holy and benign originator' (p. 164). Further, although morality concerns not how human beings can make themselves happy, but how they can make themselves *'worthy* of happiness', it is only from religion, and belief in God, that the hope of (ultimately) achieving the happiness they deserve arises (pp. 164–5).

God's ultimate purpose in creating the world

God's *'ultimate purpose'* in creating the world was not to make human beings happy, but so that they could achieve the highest good (p. 165). Therefore, nothing glorifies God more than human beings, who are ends in themselves, and have absolute worth, respecting his command, which is that they obey the moral law for its own sake; and those who are worthy of happiness achieving it:

> nothing glorifies God more than . . . respect for his command, observance of the holy duty that his law imposes on us, when this is supplemented by his splendid provision to crown such a beautiful order with commensurate happiness. (p. 166)

Moralizing Christianity: *Religion within the Boundaries of Mere Reason* (see recommended edition on **p. 84**)

Jesus: a morally perfect human being

In *Religion within the Boundaries of Mere Reason*, Kant interprets Jesus' life and death in a way that fits in with his system of morality. God wants to see humanity in its full moral perfection. As one who, despite temptations, carried out all human duties, and suffered for the world's sake, Jesus represents the idea of a morally perfect human being. He is the moral '*prototype*', and a model for humanity; and it is human beings' duty to emulate his moral disposition (p. 80). For Kant, it does not matter whether Jesus was a real person. The important point is that human beings have an idea of one who is able to obey the moral law:

> There is no need . . . of any example from experience to make the idea of a human being morally pleasing to God a model to us; the idea is present . . . in our reason. (p. 81)

However, it can be expressed in terms of Jesus being God's only-begotten Son, and human beings becoming God's children, by adopting his disposition.

The doctrine of the incarnation

Kant explores the issues that arise from the doctrine of the incarnation: that Jesus has a divine origin (see also **pp. 186–8**). While saying that Jesus came down from heaven makes his moral perfection seem more comprehensible, it has practical disadvantages, as ordinary human beings must seek the prototype they see in him in themselves. Putting Jesus above 'the frailty of human nature' makes it harder for human beings to emulate him (p. 82). But what matters is that, when a teacher is like Jesus, and perfectly exemplifies what he teaches, and it is everyone's duty to do the same, it must be ascribed to his having a morally pure disposition; and this is always valid, for all human beings everywhere.

Assessment

Throughout the *Groundwork*, Kant stresses the autonomy of morality, and that the moral law is to be obeyed for its own sake, not because of inclinations or for the sake of any external factor. Then, in the *Critique of Practical Reason*, he brings God into the picture, and seems to contradict all that he has said previously. But this is not the case. We must be clear what Kant is saying. Postulating God's existence does not compromise the **autonomy of morality**. The moral law is to be obeyed for its own sake: and God is not needed, either to provide the content of morality, or to make human beings recognize or perform their duty. Moral laws do not come from God, nor do they depend upon him in any way.

However, although morality is independent of God and religion, Kant points out that human beings have an idea of the **highest good**, in which they not only do their duty, but receive the happiness they deserve. Indeed (he maintains), there is an ambiguity in the concept of the 'highest good': it can mean the 'supreme good', which is worthiness of being happy, through obeying the moral law for its own sake, or the 'complete good', which requires happiness as well. This does not mean that human beings should be moral because they hope to be rewarded by happiness: this would compromise the autonomy of morality by making (the desire for) happiness a motive for being moral. Rather, it is to recognize that those who are moral deserve to be happy. As David Ross puts it, Kant acknowledges that, although only virtue is morally good, happiness, which is deserved because of virtue, is not just a 'source of satisfaction to its possessor, but objectively good' (see **pp. 45–6**). Clearly, this is not always the case in this world, so, like freedom, God, and also immortality, are necessary postulates of the practical reason. Without freedom, there could not be moral responsibility (see **pp. 215–17**); without God, to apportion happiness to moral desert, the complete good would not be attainable; and, without immortality, human beings would lack the opportunity to achieve moral perfection, or to receive the happiness their moral conduct merits.

In his *Religion*, Kant links morality specifically to Christianity: Jesus (whether or not he actually existed: and, for Kant, whether he did so or not is irrelevant) is the **moral prototype** or exemplar; and the duty of human beings is to emulate his moral disposition, and thereby to attain moral perfection. In striking contrast to Kierkegaard (see **pp. 176–80**), for Kant, religion simply is morality, because there is no other service that God requires from human beings other than moral conduct:

> *Apart from a good life-conduct, anything which the human being supposes that he can do to become well-pleasing to God is mere religious delusion and counterfeit service of God.* (*Religion*, p. 166)

And, in *Religion*, Kant is scathing about those who hold that subscribing to Christian doctrines, or taking part in religious rituals or practices, as opposed to being moral, will please God directly. More orthodox Christians may think that Kant simply does not understand what such sacraments and practices as baptism, communion or private prayer mean. However, even if they do not agree with him, few will deny that there is something grand and inspiring about Kant's conviction that only those who seek to be well-pleasing to God through moral conduct give him the veneration he wants.

Core texts

Immanuel Kant, *Critique of Practical Reason*, trans. W. S. Pluhar, Indianapolis/Cambridge: Hackett, 2002.

Immanuel Kant, *Groundwork of the Metaphysics of Morals*, ed. M. Gregor, Cambridge: Cambridge University Press, 1997.

Immanuel Kant, *Religion within the Boundaries of Mere Reason*, eds A. Wood and G. di Giovanni, Cambridge: Cambridge University Press, 1998.

Suggestions for further reading and research

F. Copleston, *A History of Philosophy*, vol. 6, Part II (Kant), New York: Image Books, 1964 (chapter 14).

R. Johnson, 'Kant's Moral Philosophy' (revised 2008) in *Stanford Encyclopaedia of Philosophy*, at http://plato.stanford.edu.

Immanuel Kant, *Critique of Pure Reason*, ed. M. Gregor, Cambridge: Cambridge University Press, 1997.

M. Kuehn, *Kant: A Biography*, Cambridge: Cambridge University Press, 1998.

D. Mills Daniel, *Briefly: Groundwork of the Metaphysics of Morals*, London: SCM Press, 2006.

D. Mills Daniel, *Briefly: Religion within the Boundaries of Mere Reason*, London: SCM Press, 2007.

D. Mills Daniel, *Briefly: Critique of Practical Reason (The Concept of the Highest Good and the Postulates of the Practical Reason)*, London: SCM Press, 2009.

O. O'Neill, 'Kantian Ethics', in P. Singer (ed.), *A Companion to Ethics*, Cambridge: Cambridge University Press, 1993.

H. J. Paton, *The Categorical Imperative*, Philadelphia: University of Pennsylvania Press, 1971.

P. Rossi, 'Kant's Philosophy of Religion' (rev. 2005), in E. N. Zalta (ed.), *Stanford Encyclopaedia of Philosophy*, at http://plato.stanford.edu.

R. J. Sullivan, *Immanuel Kant's Moral Theory*, Cambridge: Cambridge University Press, 1989.

5 Consequentialist Ethics

1 The consequentialist approach

Evaluating actions by their consequences

While **deontological ethics** locates the basis of morality in the intrinsic value of certain actions and our obligations or duties to others, due to their moral status as rational beings, **consequentialism** locates it in the value of the consequences of actions. But, what sort of consequences? In a consequentialist system of ethics, actions are regarded as the means to producing or promoting some object or end, which is held to be a good, or the principal or ultimate good for human beings; and actions are right to the extent that they further this good, and wrong to the extent that they prevent its realization.

Pleasure and happiness

Is there 'a', or 'the', good for human beings, which they do (or should) regard as the object of their actions, and by the criterion of which they should determine the rightness of their own and others' actions? For those who believe in God, and who believe that God created human beings, and intends to give them a life after physical death, the good for human beings might be to obey God's command, and to conform to his will. However, consequentialist ethicists usually look at the nature of human beings, and at what human beings actually desire or aspire to, in this world, rather than the next. There seem to be very many such things; but consequentialists generally argue that all the objects human beings pursue are in fact means to achieving one ultimate object, **pleasure or happiness,** or to avoiding its opposite, pain. This is utilitarianism: the utility or usefulness of an action is evaluated by the quantity of pleasure or happiness it produces.

Types of utilitarianism and the issues they raise

There are several types of utilitarianism, but this chapter explores the views of three of the leading exponents of utilitarian consequentialism: Jeremy Bentham (**act utilitarianism**), John Stuart Mill (**rule utilitarianism**) and Peter Singer (**preference utilitarianism**). Their discussion of utilitarianism raises a number of issues, some of which have already been examined. Among them are: is maximization of pleasure or happiness simply a standard for evaluating human actions, chosen because it is what most people want, or is 'productive of pleasure' part of the meaning of moral terms like 'good' or 'right' (see **pp. 27–31, 36–8**)? Is it a contradiction to assert that what produces most pleasure is wrong? Do most people actually seek pleasure or happiness above everything else? Are all pleasures of equal value, or are some superior to others? Is pleasure the same as happiness? To what extent do we know the consequences of our actions? Do we have to apply the maximization-of-happiness test to every action we contemplate (act utilitarianism), or should we follow general principles, such as, 'it is wrong to murder' and 'it is wrong to steal', which have been shown, on balance and over time, to maximize happiness, even if they do not do so in a particular situation (rule utilitarianism)? Should consequentialists think in terms of satisfying preferences (preference utilitarianism), rather than maximizing happiness? Why should we bother about maximizing other people's happiness? Should we be concerned about the happiness only of rational beings, or about that of conscious beings (animals) as well (see also **pp. 318–29**)?

2 The utilitarianism of Jeremy Bentham, John Stuart Mill and Peter Singer

Jeremy Bentham's *Introduction to the Principles of Morals and Legislation* (see recommended edition on **p. 102**)

Jeremy Bentham (1748–1832)

After graduating from The Queen's College, Oxford, Jeremy Bentham trained as a barrister, but then concentrated on writing and research. Highly critical of such doctrines as natural rights, natural law and the idea of a social contract, he espoused legal positivism, the view that laws are commands of the sovereign power, and sought to establish the greatest-happiness principle as the all-important standard in ethics, law and government. He was an influential advocate of legal, penal and social reform, and was involved in setting up the University of London. During his lifetime, Bentham's publications included *A Fragment on Government* (1776), *An Introduction to the Principles of Morals* (1789), *Panopticon* (1787), *Punishments and Rewards* (1811) and *Church-of-Englandism* (1818).

A statement of act utilitarianism

Bentham's *Introduction to the Principles of Morals and Legislation* is the classic statement of act utilitarianism: that the rightness or wrongness of individual actions should be determined by the extent to which they maximize pleasure and/or diminish pain, and that the effects of potential actions, particularly those of legislators, governments and judicial authorities, need to be tested against this criterion.

Two fundamental motivations

Bentham argues that nature has placed human beings under the control of two 'sovereign masters': the fundamental motivations of pleasure and pain (p. 1). Our conduct is hedonistic: we naturally always seek those things that give us pleasure, and avoid those things that cause us pain. He also maintains that, as (pursuit of) pleasure and (avoidance of) pain are what, in fact, determine our conduct, we should accept them as our standards of right or wrong. As we regard pleasure as (the ultimate) good, and pain as bad, a right action is one that causes or increases pleasure, and a wrong action one that causes or increases pain:

> Nature has placed mankind under the governance of two sovereign masters, *pain* and *pleasure*. It is for them alone to point out what we ought to do, as well as to determine what we shall do. On the one hand the standard of right and wrong, on the other the chain of causes and effects, are fastened to their throne. (p. 1)

He is thus an **ethical naturalist**, as he holds that ethical standards should be determined by the natural properties of pleasure and pain, and how these affect human beings.

The principle of utility: maximizing pleasure, minimizing pain

Bentham explains that the **principle of utility** recognizes that pleasure and pain determine human conduct, and makes this fact the basis of a moral system, designed to maximize human happiness, by approving or disapproving of actions, on the basis of the extent to which they 'augment or diminish the happiness of the party whose interest is in question' (p. 2). He also explains that 'utility' is that element in an action or its object which produces benefit, pleasure, good or happiness, or prevents pain, evil or unhappiness to the interested party, which may be a 'particular individual' or the wider 'community' (p. 2).

A test of what is right, or what 'right' means?

Bentham's development of his case for utilitarianism also raises the meta-ethical issue of whether he commits the naturalistic fallacy. See **pp. 22–3, 27–31**.

No direct proof of the principle of utility

Bentham accepts that, as it is the fundamental or first principle of morality, the principle of utility 'cannot itself be proved'; rather, it is the criterion against which actions must be tested (p. 4). However (he maintains), the collective experience of humanity does provide proof of a kind: most people, on most occasions, do apply it, while what are presented as arguments against it often turn out to be based on it. Alternative principles that are put forward as the basis for moral judgements and actions are purely subjective, reflecting individual likes or dislikes, without regard to consequences.

Alternatives to the principle of utility

Bentham thinks that there are two main kinds of alternative moral principle to the principle of utility: that of asceticism, which is wholly opposed to it, and that of sympathy and antipathy, which sometimes is. According to the first, subscribed to by some pleasure-hating religious people, but which (he contends) no human being, particularly anyone in government, pursues consistently, an action is judged right or wrong in 'inverse' proportion to the extent that it maximizes or minimizes happiness (p. 9). The second, which Bentham considers more commonly held, particularly among those in government, arises from the laziness of those who prefer to follow their feelings, instead of investigating the reasons for and against possible courses of action, and testing them against the 'external standard' of the principle of utility (p. 17). Bentham also considers what he calls the *'theological principle'*, which relates the standard of right and wrong to what God wills (p. 21). However, he does not regard this as a distinct principle, but merely a (more authoritative) way of expressing one of the other three principles. For Bentham (see also **pp. 170–2**), God wills a thing because it is right; it is not right because God wills it. Thus, whatever is right will be 'conformable to the will of God', but first we need to test it against the principle of utility, to check that it is (p. 22).

Pleasure and pain as sanctions

Bentham believes that, for lawmakers and those in government and the judiciary, ensuring the happiness of the individuals in the communities for which they are responsible should be their sole object, which they can only achieve by legislating and governing in ways that conform to the principle of utility. Further, 'pleasure and pain' are the only means by which they can secure compliance with their laws and decisions (p. 24). Bentham identifies four distinct sources of pleasures and pains: physical (the fundamental one), political, moral and (insofar as it relates to this life, rather than any future existence) religious. Governments can use them all as *'sanctions'*, to give binding force to their laws (p. 24). For example, a law against theft would be enforced by imprisonment, involving physical sanctions, such as relatively harsh living conditions and arduous work, and the political sanction of deprivation of liberty; and these could be reinforced by the moral sanction of society's disapproval of anti-social behaviour and the religious sanction that it breaches a religious teaching, such as the Seventh Commandment (see **pp. 185–6**). However, Bentham points out that governments can be hindered, as well as helped, by moral and religious sanctions, if their laws and decisions run counter (perhaps, by not conforming to the principle of utility) to the interests of the community or religious teachings.

Applying the principle of utility: calculating the consequences of actions

To make the best use of the motivations of pleasure and pain, lawmakers and rulers need to understand how they affect people, and how to test moral judgements and potential actions against the principle of utility, to ensure that they maximize pleasure and minimize pain. For the individual, several factors determine the value of a pleasure or pain: its *'intensity'*, *'duration'*, the *'certainty* or *uncertainty'* of its occurrence, and its *'propinquity* or *remoteness'*; to which, if more than one person is involved, would be added the *'number* of persons' it affects (pp. 29–30). Thus, when deciding whether or not to perform an action, governments and individuals should use these factors to carry out a 'felicific calculus' (calculation of happiness). They should weigh the pleasures it will produce against the pains, and decide whether or not to perform the action, on the basis of its *'good'* (more pleasures than pains) or *'evil tendency'* (vice versa) (p. 31). Bentham is realistic enough to recognize the impossibility of making this calculation before every single moral judgement, legislative act or judicial decision, but thinks that it should always be kept in view, and done whenever possible; and that judgements and actions will be better, the more precisely it is performed. However, even this concession ignores the problems, pointed out by Moore (see **pp. 39–40**), of determining more than a few of the possible effects of any action before it is performed. As Mill argues (see **p. 95**), there is a lot to be said for utilitarians accepting established moral rules and laws, such as those that prohibit theft, which humanity has found to work over time, and to produce a balance of happiness; and to invoke the principle of utility only if these conflict.

Simple and complex pleasures and pains

Bentham divides pleasures and pains into complex and simple ones, with the former being reducible to the latter. The simple pleasures are those of sense, wealth, skill, friendship, good name, power, piety, benevolence, malevolence, memory, imagination, expectation, association and relief; the simple pains, the above, excluding wealth, friendship, good name, power and relief, but including privation, awkwardness, enmity and ill name. Bentham accepts that what may be a source of pleasure to one person, such as the exercise of power, or the indulgence of malevolence, may cause 'pains' to another (p. 41): once again underlining the problem of carrying out an accurate felicific calculation, and determining the consequences of actions, in terms of the balance of pleasure(s) against the pain(s) they produce.

Assessment

Bentham's statement of the **utilitarian principle** raises many issues. He begins by talking about pleasure and pain, which are transitory (and possibly measurable) sensations, and which arise from various sources, but then seems to equate these with happiness or unhappiness. But, human beings are rational beings, and their happiness or unhappiness does not seem to be determined solely, or even mainly, by (transitory) experiences of pleasure or pain: a person in a drug-induced, vegetative state may experience some kind of perpetual pleasure, but we would not equate this with human happiness, which is not a transitory experience, and seems to arise, in part, from coping successfully with life's sometimes painful challenges (see also p. 112).

Again, it is perfectly intelligible to say that the right thing to do is not the one that produces most (immediate) pleasure (see also p. 51). For example, telling a person that he has a terminal illness will not increase his pleasure, but, even if we could avoid telling him, we may think it right to do so, because that would be honest, and/or because, as a rational being, he is entitled to know facts that mainly affect him, and to be in a position to decide how to lead the rest of his life in the light of them.

Further, while equating pleasure(s) with happiness, and, even more vaguely, with 'good', Bentham fails to define it. Are all pleasures, or their sources, equivalent, or are there higher and lower pleasures? For example, are those associated with eating, drinking and gambling equivalent to, and as worthy of being promoted as, intellectual or creative pleasures, like studying philosophy, or learning to play the clarinet? Bentham's concern is only with **quantity of pleasure**, but this was not the view of his fellow utilitarian philosopher John Stuart Mill, who believed that pleasures should be distinguished **qualitatively** as well as quantitatively (see p. 94). And, if quantity of pleasure is the sole criterion, are actions such as organizing cruel activities like gladiatorial contests, which please large numbers of people, right, even when they do so at the expense of a minority?

This raises the issue of whose pleasure(s) we are to consider. Bentham's utilitarianism concerns maximization of pleasure as such: it does not matter who experiences the pleasure. He talks of interested parties, who are the individual(s), or community, to or from the 'sum' of whose pleasures an act may add or subtract; says that an action conforms to the principle of utility, when its tendency to 'augment' the individual's or the community's happiness is greater than its tendency to 'diminish' it; and describes a utilitarian as one who bases his approval or disapproval of an action on this principle (pp. 3–4). But, although community-orientated actions are likely to produce a larger quantity of pleasure overall, why should we, as self-interested individuals, choose to perform actions that benefit others, rather than those which, although producing less pleasure overall, create more for us? Doing so seems to require us to be altruistic, and to give other people's 'interests' at least equal weight with our own; and thus to recognize them as valuable beings, whose pleasure or happiness should matter to us.

John Stuart Mill's *Utilitarianism* (see recommended edition on **p. 102**)

John Stuart Mill (1806–73)

John Stuart Mill, the son of the philosopher James Mill, worked for the East India Company, where he became a senior administrator, for 35 years, and was Liberal MP for Westminster (1865–8). During this time, he also wrote about philosophical and political issues, and developed his own version of utilitarianism. *On Liberty* (1859), *Utilitarianism* (1861), *Considerations on Representative Government* (1861) and *The Subjection of Women* (1869) continue to have a major influence on ethics and political philosophy, as well as on thinking about the rights of individuals and minorities, and the relationship between the individual and the state. His other works include *System of Logic* (1843), *Principles of Political Economy* (1848) and *Three Essays on Religion* (published posthumously).

The utilitarian principle

In *Utilitarianism*, Mill argues for a consequentialist theory of ethics, holding, like Bentham, that the fundamental principle of morality is the utilitarian one: that actions are right to the extent that they promote pleasure and happiness, and wrong to the extent that they cause pain. Pleasure and absence of pain are the only things which are desirable as ends:

> The creed which accepts as the foundation of morals 'utility' or the 'greatest happiness principle' holds that actions are right in proportion as they tend to promote happiness; wrong as they tend to produce the reverse of happiness. By happiness is intended pleasure and the absence of pain; by unhappiness, pain and the privation of pleasure . . . the theory of life on which this theory of morality is grounded . . . [is] that pleasure and freedom from pain are the only things desirable as ends; and that all desirable things . . . are desirable either for pleasure inherent in themselves or as means to the promotion and the prevention of pain. (p. 7)

He accepts that what he calls the 'ultimate ends' of the utilitarian system cannot be proved, although he maintains that they can be reasoned about, and rationally debated and argued for (p. 4).

Quantity of pleasure versus quality of pleasure

However, his version of utilitarianism differs from Bentham's, as he is not solely concerned with quantity of pleasure and determining the rightness or wrongness of actions through attempts to calculate the amounts of pleasure or pain that different possible courses of action may produce. He believes that there are grades or levels of pleasure, and that those associated with the mind, such as literary and artistic pursuits, are more valuable than purely physical ones, such as eating and drinking:

> It is better to be a human being dissatisfied than a pig satisfied; better to be Socrates dissatisfied than a fool satisfied. (p. 10)

That intellectual pleasures are more valuable than physical ones is shown (he contends) by the fact that those who have experienced both think that they are, while such people are also qualified to decide which of any two pleasures is the more worthwhile. Those who enjoy intellectual pleasures may be more aware of life's imperfections, but would not change places with those who do not.

Thus, Mill's version of utilitarianism is not open to the accusation of being crudely hedonistic. Intellectual pleasures are rated above non-intellectual ones, while he emphasizes its unselfishness: utilitarians should be as concerned about the pleasures and happiness of others (the 'greatest amount of happiness altogether', or the general happiness) as they are about their own (p. 11). Mill mentions the ideal of Jesus' golden rule: whatever you wish that people would do for you, do the same for them.

Objections to utilitarianism

Mill deals with various objections to utilitarianism. He does not believe that happiness is unattainable, because it is not a permanent state of exalted pleasure that is being aimed at. He explains what he means by happiness: a well-balanced life, offering a range of (worthwhile) pleasures, little pain, enjoyment of family relationships and friendships, and involvement in the wider affairs of society. And, with the social reforms and general improvement in living standards that were taking place in the nineteenth century, such a way of life was being achieved by growing numbers. He does not feel that it is unreasonable to ask people to be concerned about the happiness of others, because they are not expected to devote all their time to doing so. To the criticism that utilitarianism is godless, Mill's response is that it is consistent with God's purpose, if that purpose is (as Mill considers it should be) ensuring his creatures' happiness.

Use of secondary principles

Mill also points out that his version of utilitarianism does not require people to try to calculate the effects of all possible courses of action on the general happiness before doing anything. Established moral principles, such as those forbidding murder or theft, can be used, because experience has shown that, in general, they promote happiness. The fundamental principle of utility need only be invoked in situations where secondary principles conflict with each other:

> defenders of utility often find themselves called upon to reply to such objections as . . . there is not time, previous to action, for calculating and weighing the effects of any line of conduct on the general happiness . . . But . . . to pass over the intermediate generalization entirely and . . . to test each individual action directly by the first principle . . . It is a strange notion that the acknowledgement of a first principle is inconsistent with the admission of secondary ones. (pp. 23–4)

A 'proof' of utilitarianism

Mill wishes to prove the utilitarian view that happiness is both desirable and the only thing desirable as an end, and, therefore, that the principle of utility is the sole criterion of morality. The proof he offers is an analogy with visibility. Their being seen is the 'only proof' that things are visible, so the only proof that something is 'desirable is that people do actually desire it'; people desire happiness individually, while general happiness is the happiness of the 'aggregate of all persons' (pp. 35–6). Therefore, happiness is an end of human conduct, and the principle of utility (that actions are right to the extent that they promote pleasure and happiness, and wrong to the extent that they promote the reverse) a criterion of morality.

G. E. Moore criticized this so-called proof in *Principia Ethica* (see **pp. 29–31** and **36–8**), as involving the naturalistic fallacy: '"desirable" does not mean "able to be desired" as "visible" means "able to be seen" . . . [but] "what it is good to desire"; but when this is understood, it is no longer plausible to say that our only test of that, is what is actually desired'. But Mill does not seem to be attempting a strict proof that happiness is desirable as an end: indeed, he acknowledges that it is impossible to do so. Rather, he is inviting his readers to observe what their fellow human beings actually value. Happiness is obviously one of these things.

Happiness as the sole criterion of morality?

But is happiness the only thing people desire as an end, and, therefore, the sole criterion of morality? Mill argues that there is no real conflict with, for example, virtue, which people seem to desire as an end. Although happiness is the ultimate end, some things, like virtue, are good as a means to that end: virtuous utilitarians will seek to promote happiness. So, although utilitarians originally valued virtue because it helped to promote happiness, loving virtue (and thus promoting happiness) has now become so closely associated with happiness that it has become part of the end: part of what makes some people happy. Mill concludes that if human beings desire only things that are a part of, or a means to, happiness, it is the sole end of human action, while promoting happiness is the sole standard of morality:

> if human nature is so constituted as to desire nothing which is not either a part of happiness or a means of happiness – we can have no other proof, and we require no other, that these are the only things desirable. If so, happiness is the sole end of human action, and the promotion of it the test by which to judge of all human conduct; from whence it necessarily follows that it must be the criterion of morality, since a part is included in the whole. (p. 39)

He asks people to observe themselves and others, to see whether or not he is right.

However, although this is the way that utilitarians see virtue, it does not alter the fact that others connect virtue with doing things that are right in themselves, irrespective of whether or not they promote happiness. Further, there are those who will simply deny that happiness is the only, or even the most important thing that they desire as an end: unless 'happiness' is just being used to embrace every possible end of human action (see also **pp. 101–2**).

Utilitarianism and justice

Mill considers whether justice is, as some claim, a major obstacle to accepting utility as the criterion of right and wrong, and argues that it does not appear to be an absolute standard, as people's ideas of it vary, and change over time. He analyses justice as consisting of: a rule(s) of conduct, which must be common to all human beings, and which is intended for their good; a desire to punish those who break the rule(s); and somebody whose rights under the rule(s) have been violated, and who can validly require society to uphold those rights. Mill acknowledges that justice is the most important part of morality, because it concerns moral rules, such as those forbidding people to hurt one another, which are 'the essentials of human well-being', and which it is essential for society to enforce (p. 59). But he maintains that utility is the reason why people should protect others' rights; only thus will all members of society have that security without which nothing can be enjoyed.

However, this does not seem to be an adequate account of justice. While it is true that ideas of what is just vary and change, at the root of the idea of justice, and attempting to be just, there seems to be recognition that human beings are entitled to fair and equal treatment, because they matter and are worthwhile in themselves (see also **pp. 131–6**).

Assessment

At one level, Mill's argument for a **hierarchy of pleasures** is convincing. It seems only sensible to recognize **qualitative** as well as **quantitative** distinctions among pleasures. And it also seems to be the case that those who have experienced both intellectual and non-intellectual pleasures value the former more highly than the latter, and wish them to be accessible to, and enjoyed by, other people (which does not mean, as Mill seems to imply, that they will despise all non-intellectual ones). But, Moore's observations, in *Principia Ethica* (see **p. 38**) are fair: grading pleasures, and assessing their value by criteria other than the quantity of pleasure they produce, is a departure from pure, Benthamite utilitarianism. And, indeed, Mill's account of happiness seems to have far less in common with the maximization of pleasure than with Aristotle's *eudaimonia* (see **pp. 111–4**). Further, is a focus on pleasure and grades of pleasure, or even happiness, always relevant to moral decisions? Does it not accord more with our actual experience to relate much of morality and moral decision-making to meeting (the wide range of) human needs? And sometimes satisfying basic, non-intellectual needs takes priority over meeting intellectual ones, as when there are starving people who need to be fed.

Mill's handling of the relationship between utilitarianism and God's purpose is superficial:

> if men believe, as most profess to do in the goodness of God, those who think that conduciveness to the general happiness is the essence or even only the criterion of good must necessarily believe that it is also that which God approves. (p. 28)

However, this fails to recognize that, according to Christian teaching (Christianity is the religion Mill has in mind), God's purpose in creating the world was not just to make his creatures happy (see **pp. 182, 184–5**).

There are problems, too, with using **secondary moral principles**. Doing so may be sensible, but may mean performing actions that will not create most pleasure or happiness in that particular situation. Again, there can be no doubt that happiness is one of the things that people desire, and that, when deciding on a course of action, it is difficult to ignore its (anticipated) effect on one's own or others' happiness. However, it simply does not seem to be the case that it is the only thing that people desire as an end. What Mill has to say about virtue and justice, for example, are unconvincing, and this undermines the argument that the principle of utility should be the sole criterion of morality.

Mill also fails to explain why people ought to be as concerned for others' happiness as their own. He refers to concern for the happiness of others harmonizing with the obligations people naturally feel towards other members of society. But this is no more than an expression of hope or an empirical assertion, which may or may not be true. In *Utilitarianism*, Mill explicitly rejects one version of Kant's **categorical imperative**, arguing that acting only in accordance with a maxim through which you can at the same time will that it become a universal law would allow 'outrageously immoral rules of conduct' to be adopted. However, another formulation of the categorical imperative is so to act as to use humanity, whether in one's own person or another's, always as an end, never merely as a means (see **p. 75**). While consequences, and what promotes or diminishes happiness, in particular, are important elements in moral decisions (and Kant can be criticized for ruling out consideration of consequences), is it not because we value human beings and consider them to be intrinsically valuable ends in themselves, not merely means to our own happiness, that we consider it important to try to satisfy their needs, and, indeed, to promote their happiness?

Peter Singer's *Practical Ethics* (see recommended edition on p. 102)

Peter Singer (born 1946)

Peter Singer studied philosophy at the Universities of Melbourne and Oxford, and was Professor of Philosophy and Director of the Centre for Human Bioethics at Monash University, Melbourne. He is now Ira W. DeCamp Professor of Bioethics at Princeton. He is best known for developing utilitarian theory, to focus on the satisfaction of interests and preferences, rather than the maximization of pleasure/happiness, and applying it to a wide range of bioethical issues, including human treatment of animals, abortion, euthanasia and infanticide. His books include *Animal Liberation* (1975), *Practical Ethics* (1979), *Applied Ethics* (1986), *A Companion to Ethics* (ed.) (1993) and *A Companion to Bioethics* (co-ed.) (1998).

What are ethical standards?

Singer asks what it means to say that people live according to ethical standards, and how we would decide whether or not they are living by ethical standards. One way would be to observe their behaviour: we could then say that those who do not 'lie, cheat, steal, and so on' live by ethical standards, while the liars, fraudsters and thieves do not (*Practical Ethics*, p. 9). However, this approach would ignore two distinctions: that between living according to what are judged to be the right ethical standards, and living according to mistaken ones; and that between living by some ethical standards, and living by none. It may not be the case that the liars, fraudsters and thieves lack ethical standards, but that they have adopted mistaken or unorthodox ones:

> those who hold unconventional ethical beliefs are still living according to ethical standards, *if they believe, for any reason, that it is right to do as they are doing.* (p. 10)

Justifying our decisions and actions

For Singer, living by ethical standards is linked to living in ways, or by principles, that one is prepared to defend or justify. It is their ability to do this that brings people's standards 'within the domain of the ethical' (p. 10). If they are unable to defend or justify their actions, they are not living by ethical standards, even though their behaviour may conform to generally accepted ethical standards. However, being able to justify our standards is a necessary, but not a sufficient, condition of their being ethical. We cannot justify how we behave simply in terms of our own self-interest: 'the notion of ethics carries with it the idea of something bigger than the individual. If I am to defend my conduct on ethical grounds, I cannot point only to the benefits it brings me' (p. 10).

Self-interest and the universal aspect of ethics

Ethical conduct requires a point of view that goes beyond our own personal interests, and which is **universal**; and this universal perspective is common to great moral teachers and ethicists of the past. Jesus taught his followers to love their neighbours as themselves, and to do unto others as they would be done by (see **pp. 189–91, 192**); Kant's categorical imperative requires that the maxims we adopt can be willed as universal laws (see **pp. 72, 74**); and a fundamental utilitarian principle is that each should count for one and none for more than one:

> Ethics requires us to go beyond 'I' and 'you' to the universal law, the universalisable judgment, the standpoint of the impartial spectator or ideal observer, or whatever we choose to call it. (p. 12)

The theory of the **ideal observer** has a long history, going back to David Hume and Adam Smith, and holds that the correct moral judgement about a particular situation is most likely to be made by someone who is impartial: one who does not stand to gain, or be affected, by the outcome. The 'ideal observer', who, in addition to impartiality, can be thought of as possessing such characteristics as omniscience and benevolence, can be invoked as a test of moral decisions: is x the decision that an ideal observer would approve?

Considering the interests of others

Singer concedes that such bare universality can accommodate many different ethical theories, but maintains that ethics' universal aspect supplies a 'persuasive, although not conclusive, reason for taking a broadly utilitarian position' (p. 12). If, when we think ethically, we accept that our own interests cannot count for more than those of others, simply because they are ours, the logic of the universal aspect of ethics is that we must extend our very natural concern with taking care of our own interests to the interests of others. Acknowledgement that our own interests cannot count for more than those of others means that we have to consider how our actions will affect the interests of others: we will have to weigh up all their interests, and 'adopt the course of action most likely to maximise the interests of those affected' (p. 13).

Calculating consequences

Singer warns that there are good consequentialist reasons for not trying to calculate the consequences, and their impact on the interests of others, of every ethical decision. It may be difficult to make an accurate calculation, and the outcome may be consequences that are less beneficial to the interests of others than applying a general principle, or making an intuitive decision. However, we should perform such calculations when we are making decisions in unusual situations, and certainly when we are 'reflecting on our choice of general principles to guide us in future' (p. 13).

He gives an example of the difficulties of calculating the consequences of what appears to be a very straightforward ethical decision: whether or not to share fruit that has been gathered. It seems obvious that the consequences of sharing it out equally are better than those of not doing so. However, it may reduce the total amount gathered in future, as some people will stop gathering if they think that they can get all they need from others.

Utilitarianism: the ethical default position

Singer points out how his version of utilitarianism differs from classical utilitarianism:

> 'best consequences' is understood as meaning what, on balance, furthers the interests of those affected, rather than merely what increases pleasure and reduces pain. (p. 14)

He accepts that no version of utilitarianism, including his own, can be simply deduced from the universal aspect of ethics. Other ethical theories, such as, for example, those based on recognition of individual rights, sanctity of life or justice, are also 'universal in the required sense' (p. 14). But, he does believe that, once the universal aspect of ethics is recognized, and applied to ethical decisions, it quickly leads to a utilitarian position, placing the burden of proof on those who want to go beyond it. It is an ethical default position: the 'first base that we reach by universalising self-interested decision making' (p. 14).

Assessment

It is hard to disagree with Singer's view that ethical conduct requires us to go beyond our own interests, and to consider the interests of others. And Singer explains that the difference between his **'interest'** or **'preference' utilitarianism** and that of Bentham and Mill is that his version evaluates actions by the criterion of the extent to which they further the interests of the individuals or groups affected, rather than by how much they maximize pleasure or minimize pain. However, he also notes that Bentham and Mill use 'pleasure' and 'pain' broadly, so as 'to include achieving what one desired as a "pleasure" and the reverse as a "pain"' (p. 14); which, he maintains, means that the difference between the two versions disappears. Or, does this mean that both are equally vague?

Bentham talked about the two 'sovereign masters' of pleasure and pain, and his **felicific calculus** (see **pp. 88, 90–1**) is designed to measure, in a more or less scientific way, the quantity of pleasure or pain that different courses of action produce. But, both he and, to an even greater extent, Mill, also talk about happiness, and this raises the question of whether pleasure and happiness are at all the same thing, and whether the latter is even theoretically measurable (see **p. 92**).

So what would we count as 'interests' or 'preferences'? If we evaluate actions by the extent to which they satisfy the 'interests' or 'preferences' of rational (and perhaps conscious) beings (see **pp. 319–22**), which interests or preferences do we use? Are we concerned with the basic interests or preferences of humans and other living creatures, such as survival, security and physical well-being, and, in the case of human beings, freedom and self-determination? Or, do we take into account what individuals consider to be their interests, or those that particular societies or communities judge to be those of their members? And how do we decide between competing interests? Contrary to Bentham's intention, utilitarianism becomes highly subjective. Further, there is still the question of why we should consider the interests of others, instead of concentrating exclusively on satisfying our own.

Core texts

Jeremy Bentham, *An Introduction to the Principles of Morals and Legislation*, Mineola, NY: Dover, 2007.

John Stuart Mill, *Utilitarianism*, ed. G. Sher, 2nd edn, Indianapolis/Cambridge: Hackett, 2001.

Peter Singer, *Practical Ethics*, 2nd edn, Cambridge: Cambridge University Press, 1993.

Suggestions for further reading and research

Jeremy Bentham, *Selected Writings on Utilitarianism*, ed. R. Harrison, Ware: Wordsworth, 2000.

D. Brink, 'Mill's Moral and Political Philosophy' (rev. 2007), in E. N. Zalta (ed.), *Stanford Encyclopaedia of Philosophy*, at http://plato.stanford. edu.

R. E. Goodin, 'Utility and the Good', in P. Singer (ed.), *A Companion to Ethics*, Cambridge: Cambridge University Press, 1993.

R. Harrison, *Bentham*, London: Routledge and Kegan Paul, 1983.

T. Jollimore, 'Impartiality' (rev. 2006), in E. N. Zalta (ed.), *Stanford Encyclopaedia of Philosophy*, at http://plato.stanford.edu.

John Stuart Mill, *Autobiography*, ed. J. M. Robson, London: Penguin, 1989.

John Stuart Mill, *On Liberty and Other Essays*, ed. J. Gray, Oxford and New York: Oxford University Press, 1998.

D. Mills Daniel, *Briefly: Mill's Utilitarianism*, London: SCM Press, 2006.

D. Mills Daniel, *Briefly: Bentham's An Introduction to the Principles of Morals and Legislation*, London: SCM Press, 2009.

W. Sinnott-Armstrong, 'Consequentialism' (rev. 2006), in E. N. Zalta (ed.), *Stanford Encyclopaedia of Philosophy*, at http://plato.stanford.edu.

W. Thomas, *John Stuart Mill*, Oxford and New York: Oxford University Press, 1985.

M. Warnock, *Utilitarianism*, London: Fontana, 1970 (which includes Mill's Essay on Bentham).

H. R. West, *An Introduction to Mill's Utilitarian Ethics*, Cambridge: Cambridge University Press, 2004.

6 Virtue Ethics

1 The virtue ethics approach

A focus on the agent not the action

The **deontological** and **consequentialist** approaches to ethics focus on what we do, rather than on who does it: on the actions, rather than the agent. But, is this the right approach? Do not right actions flow almost automatically from people of high moral calibre? Instead of trying to decide what is good, or 'the' good, for human beings and the kind of actions that will achieve it, or what our duties are and to whom we have obligations, perhaps we should concentrate on developing in ourselves those qualities or **virtues** which will lead us to conduct ourselves well instinctively, so that we will always act appropriately towards others, and also towards ourselves.

Moral excellences

This is the virtue ethics approach, which emphasizes the development of virtues: admirable character traits, or **moral excellences**, such as justice, prudence and courage, which will lead people to behave well. This approach is particularly associated with Aristotle's *Nicomachean Ethics*, in which he describes virtues as dispositions to act in certain ways, which will benefit the individual and the wider community. Of course, what are considered virtues will vary from society to society and culture to culture. A warrior society will attach the highest value to such virtues as courage, fortitude and tribal or national loyalty. Religious communities will take a different view. Traditionally, Christianity has valued the virtues of faith, hope and love or lovingness (see 1 Corinthians 13.13), and, in the Sermon on the Mount, Jesus praises such virtues as meekness, (thirst for) righteousness and purity of heart (see Matthew 5.3–10 and **pp. 191–2**).

Aristotle's virtue ethics

For Aristotle, the virtues are those **excellences of character** the presence and practice of which will produce a well-integrated and well-balanced individual, who will fulfil himself, and thus achieve personal happiness, and who will also be a useful member of society in a Greek city-state, such as Athens. They are not qualities, such as self-abasement and extreme self-denial, that are imposed on human beings, or which they impose upon themselves and which go against the grain of human nature. They are qualities that relate, and lead, to human beings achieving what their nature has determined is their highest good: that is, happiness. They are not primarily to do with morality, but with the self-fulfilment that results in happiness; by cultivating these virtues in ourselves, we can become fulfilled and happy.

Intellectual and moral virtues

So, what are they? First and foremost, human beings are rational beings, so what matters most is that we cultivate the **intellectual virtues**. We must develop our intellects, for, according to Aristotle, human happiness derives mainly from leading a 'contemplative life', that is, one concerned with intellectual pursuits (see **pp. 110–12**). We must also live responsibly and, as social beings, coexist with others: so, we must cultivate the **moral virtues**, such as courage, temperance and liberality. Those who develop both the intellectual and moral virtues will be well-integrated, well-balanced individuals, who will achieve *eudaimonia*, happiness or well-being, in their lives.

This chapter focuses on Aristotle's discussion of the virtues in his *Nicomachean Ethics*, and Alasdair MacIntyre's revisiting of virtue ethics in *After Virtue: A Study in Moral Theory*. For Aristotle's discussion of justice, see **pp. 133–6**, and for his discussion of voluntary and involuntary actions, see **pp. 202–4**.

2 Aristotle's *Nicomachean Ethics* (Books I–III, VI and X) (see recommended edition on **p. 119**)

Aristotle (384–22 BC)

Aristotle studied and taught at Plato's Academy in Athens, and was tutor to the future Alexander the Great. Later, he set up his own school, the Lyceum, just outside Athens, where he built up a large library of manuscripts and a museum of natural objects, reflecting his interest in science and natural history. He was critical of Plato's philosophical ideas, including his theory of the forms (see also **pp. 15–18**). His own approach to philosophy emphasized careful analysis of concepts and the role of experience and observation. *The Nicomachean Ethics* is so called, because it was probably edited by his son, Nicomachus. Aristotle's other books cover logic, metaphysics, politics, science and poetry and rhetoric.

A teleological view of the world

Aristotle had a teleological view of the world: everything has a *telos* (end or purpose), determined by its nature or function. The (supreme or highest) good for all things, including human beings, is to fulfil this *telos*, so it is both what they ought to aim at, and also what they actually do aim at. The task of ethics is to identify human beings' supreme or highest good. This has an important bearing on how people lead their lives, as they are more likely to achieve their aim with a definite target to aim at.

The supreme end or purpose for human beings: happiness

So what is this supreme good? Both ordinary and educated people agree that 'it is happiness' (the Greek word *eudaimonia* means happiness or well-being: p. 7): it is a final end, 'pursued for its own sake', not as a means to something else; it is completely satisfying; and it makes life desirable (p. 14). But views differ as to what constitutes human happiness, with the masses believing it is pleasure or money. Aristotle identifies three main types of happy life: the pleasure-seeking life; one devoted to pursuit of political honours; and the contemplative or intellectual life, devoted to pursuit of philosophical truth and scientific knowledge. The first kind he considers bovine; wealth is a means to something else, not an end in itself; while, in political life, honours depend, not on the individual himself, but on those from whom he receives them. This leaves the contemplative life.

What constitutes happiness for human beings: moral and intellectual virtues

To discover what constitutes happiness for human beings, we have to look at their nature and function, to determine the sort of beings they are. And the distinctive feature of human beings is that they are rational. Thus, Aristotle concludes that human happiness is an activity of the soul, in accordance with a 'rational principle' and the 'best and most perfect kind' of virtue (p. 16). However, for Aristotle, virtue does not have the primarily moral associations it now has; it is any kind of excellence. He explains that the human soul or personality is partly rational and partly irrational, and that the appetitive or desiring part of the latter, which may be classed as rational, along with the rational part proper, is, in self-controlled people, capable of obeying the rational part, as a child does a parent. These two parts of the soul have their corresponding classes of virtues or excellences: the moral (those of character) and the intellectual:

> Some virtues are called intellectual and others moral; wisdom and understanding and prudence are intellectual, liberality and temperance are moral virtues. When we are speaking of a man's *character* we do not describe him as wise or understanding, but as patient or temperate. We do, however, praise a man on the ground of his state of mind; and those states that are praiseworthy we call virtues. (p. 30)

Human happiness consists in pursuing and practising these virtues – although this does not tell us which kind of virtue is better.

Learning from experience and from studying human beings

Aristotle holds that we discover the supreme good for human beings, and what they ought to aim at, by studying them and observing life: not, as Plato believed, in a different order of reality. Thus, he rejects Plato's theory of the forms, and the Form of the Good as the source of reality, truth and goodness (see **pp. 15–18**). He links ethics to politics, which seeks to determine what we should and should not do in society, reflecting the fact that human beings do not lead their lives, and develop their moral outlook, in isolation, but as members of communities. In Aristotle's time this was the *polis*, the Greek city-state, such as Athens, from which its citizens derived their cultural and moral, as well as political, identity.

Developing the virtues that will enable people to lead good lives

Aristotle's interest is not in the ethical qualities of individual acts, but in developing the virtues (the right moral disposition) that will enable people to lead good lives. A good man's function is to lead his life well, and he will then be happy throughout it, as he will spend it in 'virtuous conduct and contemplation' (p. 23). However, only when his life is complete will it be clear that this is how he has spent his life, and that he can rightly be called happy. Aristotle also notes that people need material goods to practise the moral virtues, as fine deeds cannot be performed without resources.

The moral virtues

For Aristotle, the moral virtues are like crafts; they are acquired by habit. People become good builders by building well, and just by performing just acts; so, the habits we develop from the earliest age, through the actions we perform, play a vital part in determining our moral dispositions. We need to recognize that the actions that promote or destroy the moral virtues are of the same kind as those that flow from them. For example, we become temperate by refraining from, not indulging in, pleasures, and are best able to refrain from them when we are temperate. Aristotle stresses the impossibility of giving more than an outline account of right conduct, as we have to consider the circumstances of each situation, but there are some important points to bear in mind. Right conduct is incompatible with excess or deficiency in feelings or actions, which destroy our moral qualities, as eating or drinking too much or too little destroys health. Our attitude towards pleasures and pains is an important indicator of our degree of moral goodness:

> it is with pleasures and pains that moral goodness is concerned. Pleasure induces us to behave badly, and pain to shrink from fine actions. Hence the importance . . . of having been trained . . . to feel joy and grief at the right things. (p. 35)

We must also appreciate that a virtuous act is not virtuous, just because it has a certain external quality, but only if the agent knows what he is doing; chooses to perform the action for its own sake; and does so from a permanent disposition towards it.

Virtues are dispositions

Aristotle describes virtues as dispositions, which are not feelings (like anger or fear), or faculties (being capable of having such feelings), but a condition of being well- or ill-disposed towards something, and being inclined to act towards it in a particular way. Thus, our disposition towards anger is good, if our tendency towards it is moderate: we become angry only for good cause. As to the kind of disposition, a moral virtue is a human excellence which, like any excellence, makes that of which it is an excellence good, and enables it to perform its function well; so, moral virtues are dispositions that make someone a good human being and enable him to perform his function as a human being well.

The doctrine of the mean

The moral virtues involve Aristotle's famous doctrine of the mean. A length of wood, for example, can be divided into two equal parts, which would be the mean (the half-way point) between the two extremes of excess and deficiency. This is an objective mean, as everybody would accept that it is the half-way point. However, there is also a relative mean. 'Six pounds' is the objective mean in relation to ten pounds of food, but a trainer would not necessarily give this amount to a particular athlete, as it might be too much or too little (p. 40). Here, the mean is the appropriate amount for the particular athlete. It is this second, relative mean that the moral virtues, which concern feelings and actions, aim to hit. We can, and do, feel fear, anger, pleasure, and so on, too much or too little. The right way is to avoid excess or deficiency, and have, or do, them to an intermediate degree:

> virtue is a purposive disposition, lying in a mean that is relative to us and determined by a rational principle . . . It is a mean between two kinds of vices, one of excess and the other of deficiency. (p. 42)

This seems clear enough. Aristotle has already said that right conduct is incompatible with excess or deficiency in feelings or actions, and the doctrine of the mean seems to reinforce this point. However, it will not always be easy to determine what the mean is. The mean in relation to anger may not always be a moderate degree of anger. It will vary according to the situation, and sometimes extreme anger will be appropriate. The doctrine of the mean does not provide a clear-cut rule that can be followed easily in every situation. It is a general guiding principle that is difficult to hit.

Its application to particular virtues

Aristotle shows how the doctrine applies to particular virtues. For example, with fear and confidence, courage is the mean, rashness the excess and cowardice the deficiency. With anger, the mean is patience, and the extremes irascibility and lack of spirit. However, the mean is not always equidistant between the extremes of excess and deficiency. For example, the deficiency of cowardice is further from the mean of courage than the excess of rashness. We also tend to view the (wrong) things, towards which we are more inclined, as being more opposed to the mean. Aristotle accepts that being morally virtuous, and achieving the mean point in feelings and actions, is difficult. It is easy to get angry, but hard to feel or act towards the right person, to the right extent, at the right time, for the right reason and in the right way. But there are rules that can help us to hit the mean. We must try to avoid the extreme that is more contrary to the mean; to recognize our individual weaknesses, and force ourselves in the opposite direction; and to be vigilant about pleasures, as we do not judge them impartially.

Courage and temperance

While the rash man and the coward show excess or deficiency, the courageous man, having the right disposition, observes the mean, facing danger as a fine thing to do. He fears what human beings naturally fear (for example, there is nothing cowardly in a man dreading brutality towards his wife and children), but faces it in the right way, and for the sake of what is right and honourable. Temperance is a virtue thought to belong to the irrational part of the soul, and is a mean state in relation to physical pleasures. With these, people err in enjoying the wrong objects, or enjoying things with abnormal intensity (people rarely desire pleasures less than they ought), while the licentious display every form of excess. The temperate person does not enjoy wrong pleasures, but holds a mean position, moderately pursuing pleasures that are conducive to health, and which are not dishonourable, or beyond his means. Reason must control the appetitive element, which needs to be in harmony with the former, so that both have as their object attaining what is admirable.

In other chapters of *The Nicomachean Ethics*, Aristotle discusses other moral virtues, such as liberality, magnanimity and amiability, the nature of pleasure, and friendship.

Intellectual virtues

Aristotle has already explained that human happiness is an activity of the soul, in accordance with a rational principle and the best and most perfect kind of virtue, and involves pursuing and practising moral and intellectual virtues. Having discussed the moral virtues, he turns to the intellectual ones. Of course, the intellect (its calculative, as opposed to its contemplative part) has a role in relation to the moral virtues: good moral choices and conduct involve true reasoning, as well as good character and right desire. There is also the question of whether intellectual or moral virtue or excellence is better.

Practical wisdom or prudence

Aristotle begins by examining the (five) states of mind, or modes of thought, by which truth is reached. While he acknowledges that (theoretical) wisdom, which concerns the most valuable kind of knowledge, is superior to practical wisdom or prudence, the latter, which involves the ability to deliberate, and knowledge of particular circumstances, plays a vital role in deciding how to achieve practical human goods. Indeed, those who lack theoretical knowledge are often more effective in attaining these:

> prudence is concerned with human goods . . . the function of a prudent man [is] to deliberate well . . . the man who is good at deliberation generally . . . can aim, by the help of his calculation, at the best of the goods attainable by man. (p. 154)

Again, political science is a form of practical wisdom, so those who possess it will be equipped to look after the welfare of the wider community, as well as to secure their own good. Resourcefulness (correctness in estimating advantage with respect to the right object, the right means and the right time or opportunity) is also a kind of deliberation, while understanding (the ability to judge soundly in matters requiring deliberation) belongs to the same sphere as practical wisdom.

Both (theoretical) wisdom and practical wisdom are inherently desirable intellectual virtues, and, although the former does not deal with things that make human beings happy as such, given the valuable knowledge with which it is concerned, it does produce happiness. As for the latter, the full performance of a human being's function depends on practical wisdom and moral virtue together:

> choice cannot be correct in default either of prudence or of goodness, since the one identifies the end and the other makes us perform the acts that are means towards it. (p. 166)

Eudaimonia: *the life of happiness*

But what constitutes a life of happiness for human beings? Some think pleasure is wholly bad, but Aristotle regards such views as exaggerated. Undeniably, pleasure plays an important part in forming the character to like (or dislike) the right things, as people choose the pleasant and avoid pain, which leads some to regard it as the good.

Is pleasure the supreme good?

Some had argued that, as all creatures are attracted to pleasure, it must be the supreme good; and also that, as pleasure is desirable in itself, and is never chosen as a means to something else, it is the most desirable thing. However, Aristotle sees a weakness in the further argument that adding pleasure to something good makes it more desirable. Plato had disproved the view that pleasure is the supreme good, by pointing out that intelligence makes the life of pleasure yet more desirable: nothing can be 'the' good, if the addition of something else makes it more desirable. Again, there are many things, such as memory and knowledge, which we wish to have, even if they bring no pleasure. Pleasure seems not to be the supreme good, as not every pleasure is desirable, while some pleasures are superior to others.

Different kinds and qualities of pleasure

Pleasure (Aristotle concludes) is essential to life: all creatures are drawn to it, directing their activities towards the objects they like best. However, as pleasures vary in quality, pleasure cannot be regarded as 'the' good for human beings:

> the pleasure proper to a serious activity is virtuous, and that which is proper to a bad one is vicious ... intellectual pleasures are superior to sensuous ones, and both kinds differ among themselves. (pp. 265–6)

Perfect human happiness: contemplative or intellectual activity

Aristotle maintains that perfect human happiness is to be found in the activity that is proper to human beings, which accords with the highest virtue, and which is pleasantest for them. This is contemplative or intellectual activity, for the intellect is the highest thing in human beings, and apprehends the highest things they can know, such as philosophical and scientific truths. Further, while morally good people need others towards whom they can be just or benevolent, the wise man can practise contemplation alone, so it is a self-sufficient activity, which is appreciated for its own sake:

> contemplation is both the highest form of activity (since the intellect is the highest thing in us ...) ... and also it is the most continuous ... those who possess knowledge pass their time more pleasantly ... Again, the quality that we call self-sufficiency will belong in the highest degree to the contemplative activity. (p. 270)

Moral activity: a source of happiness at a lower level

So, the happiest human beings are those who lead the contemplative life, but Aristotle accepts that moral activity also brings happiness: at a lower level. Although moral goodness is intimately connected with human feelings – so living in conformity with them, and its associated happiness, fits in with our physical nature, and also with the fact that we lead our lives as members of society – the life of moral goodness, unlike the intellectual one, requires resources. Another argument for happiness being contemplative activity is that, of all human activities, it is the one most akin to that of the gods, and, of all living creatures, only human beings have this activity in common with them. Further, neither intellectual activity, nor moral conduct, requires extensive material possessions. Indeed, happy people tend to have a moderate quantity of external goods, to live temperate lives, and to do the finest deeds.

Putting ethical theory into practice: moral education

Aristotle discusses how his ethical theory can be put into practice. Given the intellectual and moral limitations of the majority, developing a (modest) degree of goodness in people may be all that is achievable. He feels that the state should educate its citizens in goodness; and, as people respond better to 'compulsion and punishment than to argument', it should punish the disobedient, as well as appealing to the finer feelings of those who have already developed good habits (p. 279). However, as most states neglect these responsibilities, parents may need to instruct their children in goodness. They should study laws and constitutions closely, as this will enable them to discover why some states are better governed than others; to determine the best 'kind of constitution' and 'system of laws'; and to make their philosophy of human conduct as complete as possible (p. 284).

Assessment

The Nicomachean Ethics has had an enormous influence on thinking about ethics for almost two and a half thousand years. It is hard to fault Aristotle's approach: the best way to discover the supreme good for human beings, and what constitutes their happiness, does seem to be by looking at their nature and function, in order to determine what sort of beings they are; and, as human beings are rational beings, and also social beings, who are part of a community, and interact with others in it, the **intellectual and moral virtues** clearly do have a vital part to play in ensuring human well-being

113

and happiness. His concept of the moral virtues as being like crafts, which people can acquire by early development of the habit of right conduct, so that they will be able to lead morally good lives, is attractive and persuasive. Unfortunately, both the state and parents tend to neglect their responsibilities for children's moral education.

However, Aristotle's view that the happiest human beings are those who lead the contemplative life, while a life devoted to practising the moral virtues produces a lower level of happiness, seems to reflect the priorities of a life spent in pursuit of philosophical truth and scientific research. It is debatable, as it can be argued that the greatest happiness is found in practising moral goodness: in helping others, especially those who suffer. Thus, many people would consider the **moral virtues** to be more important than the **intellectual** ones, because they determine the way we relate to, and treat, others, while some would maintain that ethics' sole concern is with our conduct towards other people.

Indeed, the precedence Aristotle gives to individual intellectual activity may appear selfish. He is concerned with the happiness the individual can attain, through engaging in intellectual activity by himself, and thinks that the wise man, practising the intellectual virtues, has an advantage over morally good people, practising the moral virtues: his activity is self-sufficient, while theirs is not. What is lacking here is altruistic concern with the happiness of others: there is no mention of the utilitarian idea of actively promoting general happiness. On the other hand, cultivation of the intellectual virtues enables people to exercise the moral virtues and practise moral goodness more effectively: while correct moral choices cannot be made without moral goodness, which identifies the end, it is practical wisdom, an intellectual virtue, which enables us to perform the actions that are the means of achieving it.

3 Alasdair MacIntyre's *After Virtue: A Study in Moral Theory* (see recommended edition on **p. 119**)

Alasdair MacIntyre (born 1929)

Alasdair Chalmers MacIntyre studied at the Universities of London and Manchester, and taught at British universities, before moving to the United States, where he was professor of philosophy at (among others) Boston, Notre Dame and Duke Universities. He is particularly associated with revival of interest in Virtue Ethics, as argued in *After Virtue: A Study in*

Moral Theory (1981). His other books include: *Marxism: An Interpretation* (1953), *New Essays in Philosophical Theology* (1955, with Antony Flew) and *Difficulties in Christian Belief* (1959).

Moral facts

Against G. E. Moore's contention (see **pp. 29–31** and **36–8**) that reducing 'good' to a statement of fact involves a **'naturalistic fallacy'**, MacIntyre, following Aristotle, argues that 'statements about what is good . . . just are a kind of factual statement' (p. 148). Like other species, human beings have a specific nature, and so a peculiarly human good must be defined in terms of that nature. Moral statements are factual, because they refer to an understanding of the nature of human beings, and the **end** or **purpose** (*telos*) of human life that is consistent with our nature (see also **pp. 120–9**). Talk about what is good for human beings should focus on what best enables us to achieve our particular *telos*.

The human telos

For MacIntyre, Aristotle's conception of the virtues recognizes and reflects the actual nature of human beings. They express an understanding of human life as a unity, in which being moral enables human beings to be true to their essential nature and to realize their *telos*. But, because they embody human good, they are not just the means by which we come to understand the purpose of human life, but the means by which we can unify our nature and our *telos*, and move from 'man-as-he-happens-to-be' to 'man-as-he-could-be-if-he-realized-his-essential-nature' (p. 52):

> the exercise of the virtues is not . . . *a* means to the end of the good for man . . . what constitutes the good for man is a complete human life lived at its best, and the exercise of the virtues is a necessary and central part of such a life, not a mere preparatory exercise to secure such a life. (p. 149)

The context of the polis

Aristotle (MacIntyre believes) is right to see the *polis* (the political community of the city-state) as the context in which the virtues make sense as values that embody a shared understanding of the human good. Human actions need a context to be intelligible, and as a community, the *polis* presupposes 'a wide range of agreement . . . on goods and virtues' (p. 155).

Through moral education, human beings can learn how to apply the virtues to achieving what the community has identified as the *telos* for human beings. The *polis* gives individual lives and actions a unity, by allowing them to be understood in terms of a connected whole. Within a society of shared values, individual human actions no longer seem arbitrary, but are part of a definite scheme. An individual in such a community learns the virtues from it, and gains a sense of the meaning of his existence, in the context of having ends at which all are aiming.

The importance of having a sense of life as a unified whole

When someone complains that life is meaningless, it is because 'the narrative' of his life has become unintelligible to him; he has no sense of its moving towards a climax or *telos*, and there seems to be no point in doing one thing, rather than another. However, such uncertainty and anxiety is not possible within the *polis*, where there are moral facts. Here, the individual has a sense of his life as a whole, because he is moving towards a common goal or *telos*, as part of: 'a community united in a shared vision of the good for man . . . and a *consequent* shared practice of the virtues' (p. 236).

Further, in such a community, human beings are connected to the past, and are aware of the rightness and fitness of thinking of themselves in a particular way, and as having a particular purpose, which they have inherited from the past:

> I inherit from the past . . . a variety of debts . . . rightful expectations and obligations. These constitute the given of my life, my moral starting point . . . what gives my life its own moral particularity. (p. 220)

Individual fulfilment through the life of the community

Thus, for MacIntyre, we have 'a particular social identity' (p. 221). This inevitably places limits on what we can expect to do, or to be, because we enter human society with roles into which we have been born. However, within these limits, we find what is expected of us clearly defined. We are able to understand the ways we must act, in order to satisfy a correct understanding of ourselves, which we gain through having a perspective on human life as a unified whole. We are in no doubt about what the virtues are, what they mean, and why and how we should exercise them, because we can see how they relate to the meaning and purpose of our own lives, through the way they have contributed to our community's past life, and the way they still do so and will continue to do so in the future. We are protected from becoming lost in dilemmas and anxieties about who we are, or what we must do, because we appreciate our place within our community's ongoing tradition, we are aware of the ways others within it lead their lives, and we have a shared purpose.

The effects of ethical emotivism

However, this idea of the political community as a 'common project' is alien to the 'modern liberal individualist world' (p. 156). Ethical emotivism (see **pp. 49, 50–3**), has helped to create the view that moral judgements merely express the individual's own arbitrary preference for a particular good. However (MacIntyre argues), moral judgements are not simply arbitrary or emotional. Yes, acting virtuously does involve acting from inclinations that have been formed by the cultivation of the virtues, but this requires rational judgement, because:

> An Aristotelian theory of the virtues . . . presuppose[s] a crucial distinction between what any particular individual at any particular time takes to be good for him and what is really good for him as a man . . . Such choices demand judgement and the exercise of the virtues requires . . . a capacity to judge and to do the right thing in the right place at the right time in the right way. (p. 150)

The task of ethics is to educate the passions so that they conform with what theoretical reasoning identifies as the *telos*, and practical reasoning identifies as the right action to do in each particular situation.

The emphasis on the individual and individual ethical preferences

The mistaken emphasis on the individual, as the standard of ethical truth, means that 'the substance of morality is increasingly elusive' (p. 243). Saying that morality is only what the individual decides it is rules out speaking of moral facts in the context of the shared life of a community, and as directed towards an end reflecting common values. The absence of this unifying conception of human life underlies modern denials of the factual character of moral judgement. In the *polis*, on the other hand, what is or is not moral can be identified, because morality is not about individual preference, but the *telos* of human beings and human society as a whole.

Its consequences: competition, fragmentation and aimlessness

Unlike the *polis*, with its communal values and common *telos*, modern society is fragmented, and it is difficult to 'envisage each human life as a whole, as a unity, whose character provides the virtues with an adequate *telos*' (p. 204). When the focus is on the individual, there is competition and a diversity of views about what the supreme good actually is, and this threatens the unity of human life. Isolated from each other, human beings try to justify the meaning of their own existence, independently rather than socially. Actions become aimless, as each is free to decide what is moral for himself. As with Sartre's existentialism, the individual is unique, and must decide for himself what he is and will do. For MacIntyre, without the inheritance of the past, and a shared *telos*, we suffer anxiety and despair: we have no true sense of our meaning or purpose. Even individual life becomes fragmented: we divide ourselves, or are divided, into such categories as 'young', 'old', 'at work or out of work', and so on; modern society excludes the idea that we move through life as unified wholes, and as part of a community, with a shared past, present and future.

Assessment

MacIntyre's virtue ethics emphasizes the individual's involvement with an ongoing tradition and the lives of others in a community, as necessary elements in being moral. We can only understand and embody the virtues, and find meaning and purpose in our own lives, if we view human life as a whole, and in the context of a **community** *telos*. He contrasts the view of society as a common project, in which individuals find their place in relation to the community's common goals, with the modern emphasis on the individual. **Virtue ethics** is sometimes criticized for limiting the individual to a particular social tradition, which could lead to moral relativism, with the individual conforming to the particular values of his or her community, which differ from those of other communities. However, **ethical relativism** seems more prevalent in modern society, with its stress on the individual, and MacIntyre holds that appreciating one's place in a community tradition is just the starting point of the ethical life. Indeed, he insists that we are connected to our community's past life, and it is only if we appreciate this that we can understand who we are and what we ought to do.

Core texts

Aristotle, *The Nicomachean Ethics*, trans. J. A. K. Thomson (notes and appendices by H. Tredennick, Introduction and Further Reading by J. Barnes), further revised edition, London: Penguin, 1976.

Alasdair MacIntyre, *After Virtue: A Study in Moral Theory*, 2nd edn, London: Duckworth, 1985.

Suggestions for further reading and research

J. L. Ackrill, *Aristotle the Philosopher*, Oxford and New York: Oxford University Press, 1981.

J. Barnes, *Aristotle*, 2nd edn, Oxford and New York: Oxford University Press, 2000.

S. Broadie and C. J. Rowe, *Aristotle: Nicomachean Ethics*, Oxford: Oxford University Press, 2002.

R. Hursthouse, 'Virtue Ethics' (rev. 2007), in E. N. Zalta (ed.), *Stanford Encyclopaedia of Philosophy*, at http://plato.stanford.edu.

K. Knight (ed.), *The MacIntyre Reader*, Oxford: Polity Press, 1998.

R. Kraut, 'Aristotle's Ethics' (rev. 2007), in E. N. Zalta (ed.), *Stanford Encyclopaedia of Philosophy*, at http://plato.stanford.edu.

Alasdair MacIntyre, *Whose Justice? Which Rationality?*, London: Duckworth, 1998.

P. McMylor, *Alasdair MacIntyre: Critic of Modernity*, London: Routledge, 1994.

D. Mills Daniel, *Briefly: Aristotle's Nicomachean Ethics*, London: SCM Press, 2007.

G. Pence, 'Virtue Theory', in Peter Singer (ed.), *A Companion to Ethics*, Cambridge: Cambridge University Press, 1993.

J. O. Urmson, *Aristotle's Ethics*, Oxford and New York: Oxford University Press, 1987.

7 Natural Law Ethics and Justice

1 The natural law approach

In ethics, the term 'natural law' does not concern descriptive scientific laws, but the view that human beings can determine what is good and right, through applying their reason to the (God-given) natural order. Advocates of **natural law ethics** hold that human beings can infer (some) ethical principles from the natural order, and/or test the moral principles they adopt against it: if they observe the **natural order**, including **human nature**, they will see that certain ethical principles and courses of action are good or right, because they are consistent with the nature of human beings and the way the world operates, but that others are not. Although it is possible to be an adherent of natural law ethics without believing in God, it is particularly associated with religious belief. For many **Christians**, particularly Roman Catholics, natural law is the way human beings, as rational beings, participate in the **eternal law,** by which God governs the universe, and they must base their ethical principles and decisions on it, in order to achieve their proper end as human beings: that is, to conduct themselves in a way that is appropriate to their nature as rational beings, **made in God's image**. Natural law ethicists are likely to argue that ethical principles are wrong, or not ethical principles at all, unless they conform to standards of morality or justice that derive from the natural order.

Natural law also features in debate about the validity of legislation. For natural law theorists, a law cannot be a law, unless its content conforms to natural law principles. On the other hand, **legal positivists,** such as Jeremy Bentham, are dismissive of natural law claims, and maintain that a law is a command of the sovereign (whether an individual ruler or the state) and is a law if it is duly enacted and enforced, irrespective of its content. We can see the influence of natural law theory in the content of declarations of human rights, such as the Universal Declaration of Human Rights and the European Convention on Human Rights (see **pp. 280–1, 285–94**). This chapter focuses on Aquinas's discussion of, and the Roman Catholic Church's teaching about, natural law, and the view of the philosopher of law H. L. A. Hart, that the laws of a state should reflect a '**minimum content' of natural law**. It concludes with a brief discussion of justice. See also **p. 154** for reference to Aquinas's theory of conscience.

2 Natural law in Aquinas's *Summa Theologica* and in *The Catechism of the Catholic Church* (see recommended editions on **p. 136**)

Thomas Aquinas (1224/5–74)

Thomas Aquinas, the son of Landulf, Count of Aquino, attended the University of Naples, where he decided to enter the order of Dominican Friars, and the University of Paris. His reputation as philosopher and theologian led to his becoming adviser to a succession of popes, while continuing to teach and write prolifically. He was canonized in 1323, and in 1879 Pope Leo XIII declared that his setting forth of Roman Catholic teaching was definitive. His books include *De Ente et Essentia* (1254–56), the *Summa Contra Gentiles* (1258–64), the *De Veritate* (1256–59) and the *Summa Theologica* (*Summa Theologiae*, 1265–72).

Aquinas and Aristotle

Aquinas was a disciple of Aristotle, whom he refers to as 'The Philosopher', and also a Christian theologian and teacher. With natural law, as with other aspects of Aristotle's philosophy, he takes Aristotle's ideas and reconciles them with Christian teaching.

God's eternal law

For Aquinas, God is the creator and sustainer of the universe, and also its ruler. One of the functions of a state's ruler is to make laws that will establish and enforce his conception of what the state or community he governs should be like: 'a law is nothing else but a dictate of practical reason [reason applied to ethical questions and conduct] emanating from the ruler who governs a perfect community' (*Summa Theologica*, Ia IIae q. 91 a. 1). The laws a ruler makes should reflect the 'first principle in practical matters', happiness, which is the 'last end of human life': so, laws must promote happiness, and, as they relate to the whole community, not just that of individuals, but 'universal happiness' (Ia IIae q. 90 a. 2). The relationship between ruler and ruled in an earthly society is parallel to that between God and the universe, which includes rational human beings, whom God has made in his own image. As God rules the universe, its 'whole community' is governed by 'Divine Reason', and God's 'Idea of the government of things' has the 'nature of law' (Ia IIae q. 91 a. 1). And, as God's conception of things, unlike that of human beings, is not subject to time, it is eternal: therefore, God's conception of the government of the world is an eternal law. Obeying God's eternal law will ultimately lead to happiness.

Natural law

But what is the relationship between God's eternal law and natural law? Aquinas explains that there are two ways in which a law can be in a person: it can be in the person that rules, but also in the person(s) ruled by it, who 'partakes' of it (Ia IIae q. 91 a. 2). As all the things in the universe are subject to God's eternal law, 'from its being imprinted on them, they derive their respective inclinations to their proper acts and ends' (Ia IIae q. 91 a. 2). God, as creator, has ordained the proper end of all his creatures, and their inclination towards their proper end, which comes from him (not just, as Aristotle held, from their nature as human beings) is the natural law. By following it, they will be guided towards their proper end, which for human beings is that of rational creatures; they will be able to do the right thing; and they will achieve happiness. Only human beings, who are rational, participate in the natural law in 'an intellectual' way, so it is only in relation to them that we can talk of a law that is something 'pertaining to reason' (Ia IIae q. 91 a. 2). Thus, natural law is the way human beings participate in God's eternal law, and:

> the light of natural reason, whereby we discern what is good and what is evil, which is the function of the natural law, is nothing else than an imprint on us of the Divine light. It is therefore evident that the natural law is nothing else than the rational creature's participation of the eternal law. (Ia IIae q. 91 a. 2)

How do we decide what we ought to do?

However, the fact that human beings participate in the eternal law does not mean that it is always easy for them to decide what they ought to do. As with speculative reason, which is concerned with intellectual matters, the practical reason operates by moving from 'principles to conclusions' (Ia IIae q. 91 a. 3). In the sciences, human beings start from basic principles, and, by making the effort to reason from them, acquire 'knowledge . . . which is not imparted to us by nature' (Ia IIae q. 91 a. 3). Similarly, the practical reason must proceed from the basic precepts or principles of the natural law to moral rules, or 'human laws', which cover specific ethical issues and situations. Aquinas explains that the right thing to do, in a specific situation, may not be self-evident to us, because we participate 'imperfectly' in the 'Divine Reason': we know the 'general principles', but not 'the particular determinations of individual cases, which are . . . contained in the eternal law' (Ia IIae q. 91 a. 3). We will make mistakes in ethical matters, and human laws (whether ethical rules or the laws of a state) are unlikely to be free of error.

Good and bad human laws

The laws of an earthly society or state are the dictates of its ruler's reason. They are intended to be obeyed by his subjects, and their proper effect is to lead them to 'their proper virtue' and to make them good, either 'simply' (in an absolute sense) or 'in some particular respect'; and the former will be the case, if the lawmaker's aim is realization of the true or common good, in accordance with 'Divine justice' (Ia IIae q. 92 a. 1). However, if he aims, not at the true good, but at what is 'useful or pleasurable to himself', which may be contrary to divine justice, his laws will not make his subjects good in an absolute sense, but only (if they obey him) in relation to his particular aims. Where this happens, it is good that subjects obey their ruler, but the overall effect is not. It is a case where good is present, even in things that are bad in themselves, as when someone is 'called a good robber, because he works in a way that is adapted to his end' (Ia IIae q. 92 a. 1).

The basic principle of natural law

Is there one natural law or many? Aquinas explains that there is a certain order in the things that are generally understood by the speculative reason. The notion that is understood first is 'being', because it applies to everything. With the practical reason, it is the notion of 'good' as 'that which all things seek after' as their end; so, the first precept of natural law is that 'good is to be done and pursued', and evil avoided; and all other natural law precepts are based on this one (Ia IIae q. 94 a. 2). Thus, as far as human beings are concerned, what is good, and what they ought to pursue, is that which they are anyway inclined to pursue, because of the kind of (rational, but also physical) beings they are (see also **p. 106**). There is no question of a gap between 'is' and 'ought' (see **pp. 21–2, 23–7**): the good for human beings, and the right actions for them to perform, cannot be separated from their nature:

> all those things to which man has a natural inclination, are naturally apprehended by reason as being good, and consequently as objects of pursuit, and their contraries as evil, and objects of avoidance. (Ia IIae q. 94 a. 2)

The ends to which human beings have a natural inclination

So, what things does human reason identify as good, which human beings are naturally inclined to pursue as ends? There is a hierarchy, reflecting the fact that we are living things, conscious beings, and rational beings. Like all living things, we seek 'preservation' of our being, so whatever tends to preserve human life 'belongs to the natural law' (Ia IIae q. 94 a. 2). We are naturally inclined towards those ends 'which nature has taught to all animals', so natural law includes 'sexual intercourse, education of offspring and so forth' (Ia IIae q. 94 a. 2). Finally, we have an inclination to good, according to our nature as rational beings. Thus:

> man has a natural inclination to know the truth about God, and to live in society: and in this respect, whatever pertains to this inclination belongs to natural law; for instance to shun ignorance, to avoid offending those among whom one has to live, and other such things regarding the above inclination. (Ia IIae q. 94 a. 2)

If we pursue the ends to which we are naturally inclined, according to the natural law, we will be happy. However, if we pursue inappropriate objects, and are not true to our God-given nature, we will not. As to the question of whether the natural law is one or many: all its precepts 'have the character of one natural law, inasmuch as they flow from one first precept' (Ia IIae q. 94 a. 2).

Whether all acts of virtue are prescribed by natural law

Aquinas explains that virtuous acts can be looked at from two perspectives. As part of the totality of virtuous acts, they all belong to natural law, as acts which human beings are inclined to perform according to their nature. But they can also be considered individually, and not all the acts that we regard as virtuous are immediately prescribed to us as such by natural law. For example, temperance relates to our appetite in relation to food, drink and sexual matters. Nature may not incline us to it at first, but we discover, through our reason, that it is 'conducive to well-living' (Ia IIae q. 94 a. 3). He also points out that 'human nature' may refer to what is proper to human beings as rational beings, and in this sense, all sins, as contrary to reason, are also contrary to nature. But, it may also refer to what is common to human beings and animals, and, in this sense, certain special sins are said to be against nature. One example is homosexual inclination and practice, or 'unisexual lust' (see also **pp. 270–7**); this is 'contrary to sexual intercourse, which is natural to all animals', and so is 'an unnatural crime' (Ia IIae q. 94 a. 3). There are also relevant differences between individuals, so acts that are virtuous in some are vicious in others.

Making ethical decisions in specific situations

Again, Aquinas contrasts the positions of the speculative reason and the practical reason. Whereas the former deals with matters of logic and science, in which (for Aquinas, as a medieval thinker) there is a high degree of certainty, both as regards general principles and the conclusions that are drawn from them, in practical matters, although the general principles of the natural law are certain, their application to specific situations is not. Because of the differences between individuals and situations, it may be difficult to decide on the right action in a particular situation; and the more differences there are, the harder it will be to make the right decision. Even in situations where only one course of action would be right, it may not be 'equally known by all' (Ia IIae q. 94 a. 4). Aquinas takes the case of goods held in trust by one person for another. Generally, it would be right for the person to 'act according to reason', and return the goods (Ia IIae q. 94 a. 4). But, there are situations where the general principle would not apply: for example, if they are weapons, which may be used in a war against one's own country. Thus:

the natural law, as to general principles, is the same for all . . . But as to certain matters of detail, which are conclusions . . . of those general principles, it is the same for all in the majority of cases . . . and yet in some few it may fail. (Ia IIae q. 94 a. 4)

Changing the natural law

There are two ways in which the natural law may be changed. First, it may be added to; and there is nothing to prevent it being changed in this way, as many things which benefit human life have been 'added over and above the natural law, both by the Divine law and by human laws' (Ia IIae q. 94 a. 5). Second, it may be changed by something which was in accordance with the natural law ceasing to be so. Although its 'first principles' (Ia IIae q. 94 a. 5) do not change, its secondary principles may be modified, in particular cases. Further, what God specifically commands, even if it is murder (as in the case of Abraham: see **pp. 176–8**), theft or adultery, is not wrong, even though it appears to violate natural law:

> by the command of God, death can be inflicted on any man, guilty or innocent, without any injustice whatever . . . also in natural things, what-ever is done by God, is, in some way, natural. (Ia IIae q. 94 a. 5)

Whether natural law can be abolished from the heart of man

The general principles of the natural law cannot be 'blotted out from men's hearts': human beings are always aware of them, although they may have difficulty applying them, in particular situations, due to greed or other pas-sions (Ia IIae q. 94 a. 6). As to the secondary precepts of the natural law, they can be blotted out, 'either by evil persuasions . . . or by vicious customs, and corrupt habits, as among some men, theft, and even unnatural vices . . . were not esteemed sinful' (Ia IIae q. 94 a. 6).

The Catechism of the Catholic Church

According to Roman Catholic teaching, the natural law expresses 'the orig-inal moral sense which enables man to discern by reason the good' (*Catechism of the Catholic Church*, para. 1954). It is written in every human being's soul, because it is human reason commanding each person to do good and avoid sin. However, it would lack 'the force of law', were it not 'the voice and interpreter of a higher reason', to which we must submit (para. 1954). As our participation in the eternal law, natural law, which is 'natural', not in the sense of the 'nature of irrational beings', but because reason 'properly belongs to human nature', shows us how to attain our proper end as human beings (para. 1955). It gives us the 'first and essential precepts which govern the moral life', which are expressed in the Ten Commandments (para. 1955). The presence and effective operation of natural law hinge upon our desire for God, the 'source and judge of all that is good', as well as our recognition of the equal value and moral status of other human beings. Natural law

> is written [in] every just law . . . The natural law is nothing other than the light of understanding placed in us by God; through it we know what we must do and what we must avoid. God has given this light or law at the creation. (para 1955)

As present in every human heart, and 'established by reason', the natural law is 'universal in its precepts' and immutable; and its authority extends to all (para. 1956). It expresses the 'dignity' of all human beings; provides the basis of their 'fundamental rights and duties'; and is 'immutable and eternal' (paras. 1956 and 1958). While its application must take account of the different circumstances of each situation where a moral judgement has to be made, it is a 'rule that binds men', and imposes 'common principles' on them, despite cultural differences (para. 1957). Natural law precepts may not be clearly or immediately perceived by everyone, as sinful human beings need 'grace and revelation', in order to know 'moral and religious truths' (para. 1960). However, even if natural law is totally rejected (by individuals, or at a point in history), it cannot be 'destroyed or removed from the heart of man'; its principles always reassert themselves (para. 1958):

> The natural law . . . provides the solid foundation on which man can build the structure of moral rules to guide his choices . . . the indispensable moral foundation for building the human community . . . [and] the necessary basis for the civil law . . . whether by a reflection that draws conclusions from its principles, or by additions. (para. 1959)

Assessment

For Aristotle (see **p. 106**), everything in the world, including human beings, has an **end** or **purpose**, determined by its nature or function, and the highest good for all things is to fulfil this purpose. Aquinas puts Aristotle's ideas into a framework of Christian belief: human beings have a purpose that is determined by their God-given human nature. Within the universe God has created, **natural law** is the way that human beings, through the use of their reason, can participate in the **eternal law,** by which God governs the universe. By basing their ethical principles and decisions on it, which they are naturally inclined to do anyway, they can fulfil their proper purpose as rational beings, made in God's image, and thus achieve happiness.

For **Christians**, and those who believe in an all-powerful creator God, this is a persuasive approach to morality. Ethical principles, derived from **natural law**, are ultimately grounded in God, through his eternal law. However, although Aquinas, in a passage reminiscent of Kierkegaard (see **pp. 176–80**), contends that God's commands can never be wrong, even if they involve murder, because whatever God (the author of nature) does is, in some sense, natural, natural law principles are not divine impositions, running against the grain of human nature. On the contrary, they fit the nature of human beings, not just as rational beings, but also as living beings, who seek to preserve their lives, and as sentient beings, who share many inclinations and instincts, such as the desire to reproduce, with other animals. This is why the natural law approach is also attractive to **secular** (non-religious) **ethicists**, as it relates ethical principles to the actual nature of human beings and their needs and wants (see **pp. 59–64**).

However, there are problems with the natural law approach. It is one thing to say that the **natural order** and **human nature** should guide the development and adoption of ethical principles; another to say that they should determine it. To define what is good or right as what is 'natural' would be to commit the naturalistic fallacy. As Moore points out (see **p. 36**), 'good' does not mean what is natural, and it is always an **open question** whether what is natural is good.

Aquinas acknowledges that, even with the basic principles of natural law to guide us, it will not always be easy to decide how to apply them in specific, and possibly complex, situations (see **pp. 125–6**). But particularly for those who are not religious, it may not be straightforward to achieve consensus, even about basic principles or their moral significance. There may not even be agreement about what is natural. For example, Aquinas says that **natural law** includes such ends as sexual intercourse and having children, which are to be encouraged, whereas homosexual inclination and practice, what he calls 'unisexual lust' (see **pp. 270–7**), which is contrary to sexual intercourse, is unnatural, and to be condemned. However, advocates of gay rights would argue that same-sex inclination is a natural inclination, and is certainly not to be condemned, as it is the way of life freely chosen by a substantial minority of people. Supporters of birth and population control would argue that, although the desire to reproduce is a natural one, there are situations in which it needs to be restrained, in the interests of individuals and/or society (see **pp. 263–7**). A great danger with the natural law approach is that it can confine moral decision-making within a straitjacket of what the majority considers to be 'natural' and therefore necessarily good or right.

3 H. L. A. Hart and the minimum content of natural law (see recommended edition on **p. 136**)

H. L. A. Hart (1907–92)

The lawyer and philosopher of law Herbert Lionel Adolphus Hart read Greats at New College, Oxford. After practising as a barrister, he became a fellow and tutor of New College, and was professor of jurisprudence (1952–69) and Principal of Brasenose College (1973–8). As well as the influential *The Concept of Law* (1961), his books include *Punishment and Responsibility* (1968), *Essays on Bentham: Jurisprudence and Political Theory* (1982) and *Essays on Jurisprudence and Philosophy* (1983).

Legal positivism

The Catechism of the Catholic Church refers to natural law as the 'necessary basis for the civil law' (para. 1959 and see **p. 123**). In *The Concept of Law*, Hart describes the **legal positivism** of Jeremy Bentham and John Austin (the first professor of jurisprudence (philosophy of law) in the University of London) as involving at least one of three contentions:

> (1) that laws are commands of human beings; (2) that there is no necessary connexion between law and morals, or law as it is and law as it ought to be; (3) that the analysis or study of meanings of legal concepts is . . . to be distinguished from . . . historical inquiries, sociological enquiries, and the critical appraisal of law in terms of morals, social aims, functions, etc. (*The Concept of Law*, p. 253)

Laws and the minimum purpose of human survival

However, Hart argues that, given the nature of human beings, and the fact that 'their aim, generally speaking is to live', there are certain basic rules of human conduct that must be reflected in the laws of any 'social organization', if it is to be viable (p. 188):

> Such rules do in fact constitute a common element in the law and conventional morality of all societies . . . Such universally recognized principles

of conduct which have a basis in elementary truths concerning human beings, their natural environment, and aims, may be considered the *minimum content* of Natural Law. (pp. 188–9)

Hart is saying about law what G. J. Warnock says about ethical principles (see **pp. 20–21** and **59–64**): that to be valid, laws and ethical principles must relate to the essential facts of human nature and the human situation. Unless they relate to these facts (Hart maintains), laws and ethical principles could not promote the 'minimum purpose of survival', which is the reason why human beings associate with each other; and they would have no reason to obey them (p. 189).

The minimum content of natural law

So what sort of facts about human nature, and the human situation, does Hart have in mind? The first is human vulnerability. Human beings are physically vulnerable: they can be killed or injured by other human beings. If we were not thus vulnerable, there would be no need for the 'most characteristic provision of law and morals: *Thou shalt not kill*' (p. 190). So, law and morality need to require and enforce rules of forbearance, which deter human beings from harming each other. Indeed (Hart asks), what purpose would there be in having any other kind of moral principle or law, unless we have rules covering this issue?

The second fact that laws need to reflect is what Hart calls 'approximate equality' (p. 190). However physically strong and intellectually gifted some people are, no individual or group is so much more powerful or cunning than others that he can 'dominate or subdue them for more than a short period' (p. 190). Again, therefore, laws need to provide a 'system of mutual forbearance and compromise', which not only prevent the strong preying on the weak, but the weak, in combination with each other, from preying on the strong (p. 191). Laws must also reflect, and provide mechanisms for countering, human beings' 'limited altruism' and aggressive tendencies (pp. 191–2).

Another inescapable fact is the world's limited resources, which bear heavily on the human predicament: human beings might have been (but are not), 'like plants, capable of extracting food from air' (p. 192). Laws must impose respect for property, and create enforceable obligations as the basis for the trade, exchange or sale of products. Not all human beings understand that having, and obeying laws, is in everybody's interest, while there are some who choose to disobey laws, when they think it to their advantage. Therefore, laws need to provide sanctions to detect and coerce those who do not practise 'mutual forbearance', and to prevent the interests of those who do obey the law from being sacrificed to the interests of those who do not (p. 193).

Assessment

Hart is not signing up to the whole natural law package, as set out by Aquinas and the Roman Catholic Church; nor does his approach involve regarding **natural law** as an expression of God's **eternal law,** or even belief in God. His contention, that there is a **minimum content of natural law,** against which actual laws can be measured, seems a reasonable one. He is saying that, unless laws embody, and enforce, at least certain basic rules of human conduct, such as not harming others and respect for property, which enable the society in which they operate to be viable, and not one in which people kill and rob each other with impunity, they are not laws at all. To qualify as such, laws must relate to the essential facts of human nature and the human situation.

4 Justice

One standard or many

What exactly do we mean by '**justice**' or '**just**'? One dictionary definition is 'fairness' or being 'fair', and when we refer to actions as 'just' or 'exhibiting justice', or to people as 'just', 'fairness' or 'fair' can usually be substituted. However, we also talk of economic justice, social justice, and what is just in the context of law and punishment; and here, again, the idea of fairness seems relevant. In fact, justice relates to how individuals or groups are treated in relation to other members of a larger group or community, whether it is a family, those convicted of crimes, or society as a whole. It also raises the further question of what exactly is fair in this or that situation. What is the criterion for deciding whether an individual act, the sentence of a court, or a new tax, which seems to benefit some, but penalize others, is fair?

One problem with justice is that we feel that it does (or should) provide an absolute standard by which to judge people and actions. However, as Mill points out (see **pp. 96–7**), people's and society's ideas of justice vary, and change over time. A strict parent, who punishes a child for leaving his room in an untidy state by making him spend a whole weekend cleaning and dusting the house, would consider he was acting fairly in relation to how he treats his other children; but a more liberal-minded parent would not, in relation to the way he and like-minded people treat theirs. We would not expect a free-market economist and a Marxist critic of free enterprise to take the same view of what is just in relation to incomes and the distribution of wealth in society. A penologist (student of punishment) who believes that in order to protect society criminals should serve long prison sentences and be subjected to tough conditions while there as a deterrent to future crime, would take a different view of a just sentence from a penologist whose priority is the reform and rehabilitation of criminals. Law and punishment also illustrate how society's ideas of justice change over time. Fifty years ago, most people in Britain thought that justice required a murderer's execution; now, far fewer do (it is debatable whether a majority is still in favour: see pp. 294–5).

There is also an important distinction between standards of justice and their application. The liberal-minded parent would reject the strict parent's standards of justice, but would acknowledge that he applies them fairly, if he treats all his children equally. However, he would regard the strict parent as guilty of a double injustice, if he applies his (in the liberal parent's mind) unjustly strict standards selectively. The liberal-minded parent would argue that the strict parent's standards are unjust by the standard of what he considers appropriate ways of punishing any child, in relation to how he considers any young human person should be treated; he would consider their application unjust by the standard of what the strict parent claims to be the appropriate way to treat all the children for whom he is responsible, not just some of them.

Creating a just society

As far as society is concerned, it might be easier to create a just one if we could make a fresh start. One long-held idea of the origin of society, which has been put forward by such philosophers as Hobbes (see also **p. 288**) and Locke (see **pp. 285–6**), is that it was created by a **social contract**, which defined citizens' rights, their obligations to each other, and the powers and responsibilities of the government. As no such agreement was ever actually made, the 'social contract' is a hypothetical event, but its 'terms' provide criteria for measuring justice, and/or identifying its absence, in a particular society. John Rawls has suggested that the best way of creating a just society would be for its principles to be selected by rational beings who understand human nature, needs and history, but who are not allowed to know what their own place in the society they are forming is going to be. For example, they would not know whether they were going to be rich or poor; employers or employees; those who depend on health and welfare benefits, or who are heavily taxed to pay for them. The impartiality imposed by this '**veil of ignorance**' is likely to lead to a society based on just principles that all its members can accept, whatever their role in it.

Aristotle on justice

In his *Nicomachean Ethics*, Aristotle discusses the issue of justice and its various applications. First, he considers it in general terms:

> the word ['unjust'] is considered to describe both one who breaks the law and one who takes advantage of another, i.e. acts unfairly . . . both the law-abiding man and the fair man will be just. So just means lawful and fair; and unjust means both unlawful and unfair . . . Since the lawless man is . . . unjust, and the law-abiding man just, it is clear that all lawful things are in some sense just; because what is prescribed by legislation is lawful. (pp. 113–14)

We can take issue with this definition straightaway, because it suggests that there is no such thing as an unjust law. However, the important point Aristotle seems to be making is that the just man, by his law-abidingness, is just or fair to others: unlike the unjust man, he does not act in ways that harm them or their interests. Aristotle goes on to describe general or 'universal' justice, that is, the disposition to be just, as (the) 'complete virtue' (p. 115) (see also **p. 108**). This is because it is exercised in relation to others, not oneself: it is 'the only virtue that is regarded as someone else's good, because it secures advantage for another person' (p. 115). Indeed, he distinguishes between **justice** and (a) **virtue**: they are the same, 'except that their essence is not the same; that which, considered in relation to somebody else, is justice, when considered simply as a certain kind of moral state is virtue' (p. 115). Aristotle is saying that, in the individual, justice or being just is being fair to (considering) others; and, in society, this will involve obeying the laws that exist to ensure justice or fairness for all members of the political community:

> the law directs us to live in accordance with every virtue and refrain from every kind of wickedness. Also the things that promote virtue in general are the regulations laid down by law. (p. 117)

Specific applications of justice

Aristotle considers different forms of justice, **distributive**, **rectificatory** and **reciprocal**, which takes his discussion into the areas of law and economics.

Distributive justice

This arises when there are honours or money to be distributed among individuals or within a community. What is a just apportionment? How should it be determined? Aristotle's answer is not particularly helpful, except as a clear illustration of the relative aspect of justice. He says that what is equal is a mean, and that what is just will be a sort of mean (see **p. 109**); so a just distribution will involve:

> at least four terms: two persons for whom it is in fact just, and two shares in which its justice is exhibited. And there will be the same equality between the shares as between the persons, because the shares will be in the same ratio to one another as the persons. (p. 119)

What this means is that a just distribution is not necessarily an equal one. For Aristotle, distributive justice is achieved, not by sharing things out equally, but by giving to each recipient according to his 'merit' (p. 119). This could simply be according to their deserts. After a war, those who have contributed most to victory get the bulk of the honours; those who have worked hardest receive the greatest financial rewards; and so on. However, what constitutes 'merit' will also depend on the values of a particular society: 'the democratic view is that the criterion is free birth; the oligarchic . . . wealth or good family; the aristocratic . . . excellence' (p. 119).

Rectificatory justice

This arises when one person inflicts an injury or wrong on another, as in a criminal act. How is the wronged party, or society on his behalf, to rectify the wrong, and deliver justice? Aristotle's view is that the law must consider the difference that the injury or wrong has caused, and re-balance the situation between criminal and victim:

> when one party has received and the other given a blow, or one has been killed, the active and passive aspects of the affair exhibit an unequal division . . . the judge tries to equalize them with the help of the penalty, by reducing the gain. (p. 121)

As the criminal has gained by his act, and the victim has lost by it, the law must 'restore equality' (p. 122). This could be by ordering compensation to the victim, but also, as today, by imposing a penalty on the criminal: by spending time in prison, he 'pays back' society for the wrong he has done one of its members.

Reciprocal justice

This approach would involve ensuring that the punishment fits the crime: simply and crudely, 'having done to one what one has done to another' (p. 123). But, some form of what Aristotle calls 'proportional requital' is important in the administration of justice, because people expect to return, not only 'evil for evil', but 'good for good' (p. 124). This is a vital factor in the exchange of goods and services: that people give or receive fair or just value for what they buy or sell. Aristotle uses the illustration of a builder and a shoemaker: if the latter wants a house, a fair ratio of shoes to houses (or a house) has to be established; and, for convenience, society has established 'one standard by which all commodities are measured': money (p. 125).

Equity

Aristotle also explains the relationship of **equity** to legal justice: the former is a 'rectification' of the latter (p. 140). The problem with the law is that it is 'universal': it is formulated to deal with the 'majority of cases' (p. 140). However, cases arise where applying the law would lead to injustice, so there need to be mechanisms for invoking principles of justice, and modifying or disapplying it in these situations: 'to correct the omission by a ruling such as the legislator himself would have given if he had been present . . . [or] if he had been aware of the circumstances' (p. 140).

Assessment

Aristotle's discussion of **justice** highlights the point that, in their relations with others, both as individuals and as members of society, people recognize the importance of fairness; but it also highlights the fact that it is not easy to decide what is fair or just. When we talk about people being 'just', we are talking about those who practise the virtue of justice; who are, or who at least always try to be, fair. Standards of justice vary from society to society, and between individuals within the same society, but people with different standards of justice, such as the strict and liberal parent, can still practise the virtue of justice: they can apply their (differing) standards of justice equally and consistently. And, the same is true of society and states. Two states may have different standards of justice: one may regard the death penalty as the just punishment for murder, while the other does not. However, they can both be just in their application of these standards: in the state with the death penalty, there would be injustice if only members of particular racial or economic groups were executed.

What about standards of justice? Are they relative, or is there a definite standard? They certainly vary, and change over time. However, the view that there is an absolute, or at least a definite standard, persists, and this may indicate the belief that, as with ethical principles and law (see **pp. 59– 64, 129–31**), standards of justice should relate to the nature of human beings and human needs, although the perception of what these are may differ or change; and the principle that all human beings are intrinsically valuable, and therefore, in some sense, equal and equally entitled to consideration. Thus, in any society, there is a need to protect all its members from violence and theft, so it is just that the minority who commit such acts be punished; but different societies and eras will have different views about what constitutes a just punishment. In an economically developed society, it is just that those who are better off should pay taxes, to ensure that the less well off enjoy a reasonable standard of living; but views will differ, within a society, and between societies, about what constitutes a just redistribution of wealth through taxation. Within a family, it is just to ensure that all members make a positive contribution to family life, and abide by agreed rules, but what constitutes a just penalty for those who break them will be debated.

Core texts

Aquinas, *Summa Theologica* Ia IIae q. 90 a. 1–4; q. 91 a. 1–3; q. 92 a. 1–2; q 94 a. 1–6, at http://www.op.org/summa.

Aristotle, *The Nicomachean Ethics*, trans. J. A. K. Thomson (notes and appendices by H. Tredennick, Introduction and Further Reading by J. Barnes), further revised edition, London: Penguin, 1976.

Catechism of the Catholic Church, 2nd edn, at http://www.scborromeo. org/ccc.htm.

H. L. A. Hart, *The Concept of Law*, Oxford and New York: Oxford University Press, 1961.

Other references and suggestions for further reading and research

John Austin, 'The Province of Jurisprudence Determined', in M. Warnock (ed.), *Utilitarianism*, London: Fontana, 1970.

Jeremy Bentham, *An Introduction to the Principles of Morals and Legislation*, Mineola, NY: Dover, 2007.

S. Buckle, 'Natural Law', in P. Singer (ed.), *A Companion to Ethics*, Cambridge: Cambridge University Press, 1991.

A. P. d'Entrèves, *Natural Law*, 2nd edn, London: Hutchinson, 1970.

T. Jollimore, 'Impartiality' (rev. 2006), in E. N. Zalta (ed.), *Stanford Encyclopaedia of Philosophy*, at http://plato.stanford.edu.

M. Murphy, 'Natural Law Tradition' (rev. 2008), in E. N. Zalta (ed.), *Stanford Encyclopaedia of Philosophy*, at http://plato.stanford.edu

J. Rawls, *A Theory of Justice*, Cambridge, MA: Harvard University Press, 1971.

8 Situation Ethics

I The situation ethics approach

In Mark's Gospel (12.28–31), Jesus declares that the greatest commandment is that we should love God with all our heart, soul and mind; and
the second that we should love our neighbour as ourselves (see **p. 192**). But
what does this mean in practice? How should we apply this **love ethic** in
actual situations? Jesus gives some answers in the Sermon on the Mount,
in Matthew's Gospel (see **pp. 191–2**); but, on a day-to-day basis, being loving towards our neighbour(s), or trying to maximize the amount of love in
the world, is both inspiring and vague as an ethical code. The American
theologian Joseph Fletcher takes the love ethic as the point of departure for
his *Situation Ethics*, which he subtitles, rather grandly, '**the new morality**'.
The book, and the approach to ethics it advocates, was indeed fashionable,
and also controversial, when it was published in the 1960s; and it is still
interesting and challenging today. However, the book, and **situation ethics**
itself, suffer from the same vagueness as the love ethic itself, when it comes
to giving an account of how to put it into practice. But, this could be to make
Fletcher's point: which is that no situation that demands an ethical response
is ever exactly like another, so there is never an absolutely right course of
action, which fits all (or every type of) situation(s). Fletcher writes from a
Christian standpoint, but does not maintain that situation ethics can only
be practised by Christians.

2 Joseph Fletcher's *Situation Ethics* (see recommended edition on **p. 153**)

Joseph Fletcher (1905–91)

After teaching at the Episcopal Divinity School, Cambridge (Massachusetts) and Harvard Divinity School, Joseph Fletcher was Professor of Medical Ethics at the University of Virginia. A President of the Euthanasia Society of America, he was particularly interested in bioethics. As well as *Situation Ethics: The New Morality* (1966) and *Moral Responsibility: Situation Ethics at Work* (1967), his books include *Morals and Medicine* (1954) and *The Ethics of Genetic Control: Ending Reproductive Roulette* (1974). In his later years, he became an agnostic.

Three approaches to ethical decisions

In *Situation Ethics*, Fletcher maintains that there are only three broad ways of making ethical decisions: the legalistic, the antinomian, and the situational.

Legalism

This is to approach every ethical decision encumbered with a 'whole apparatus of prefabricated rules and regulations', such as every letter of traditional Christian teaching on an issue (p. 18). In Christianity, Roman Catholic legalism has been related to nature or natural law, with moralists working out ethical rules by applying reason to the facts of nature, and producing what they claim as universal and valid '"natural" moral laws' (p. 21 and see also **pp. 120–9**). Protestant legalism has taken Scripture and based equally inflexible ethical rules on 'the words and sayings of the Law and the Prophets, the evangelists and apostles' (p. 21). Ethical legalism may simplify ethical decisions, but risks falling foul of the implied criticism in Bertrand Russell's comment that: 'Christians think an adulterer more wicked than a politician who takes bribes, although the latter probably does a thousand times as much harm' (p. 20).

Antinomianism

This is the opposite approach: decisions are made 'with no principles or maxims whatsoever' (p. 22). Within Christianity, one form of antinomianism has been 'libertinism', the belief that, through grace and a 'new life in Christ and salvation by faith', rules no longer apply to Christians (p. 22). The 'Gnostic' (knowledge) heresy involved the belief that some people have special knowledge, and will just know what is right. This approach recognizes no basis for general moral principles, but claims a 'sort of built-in radarlike "faculty"' (p. 23). The outcome is that moral decisions are spontaneous and erratic.

Situationism

In contrast (Fletcher explains), the situationist enters every moral decision 'fully armed with the ethical maxims of his community', which he treats with respect for the light they shed on his problems (p. 26). However:

> . . . he is prepared in any situation to compromise them or set them aside *in the situation* if love seems better served by doing so. (p. 26)

The situationist goes some way with the natural law approach, as he accepts reason as the instrument of moral judgement (see **pp. 120–9**), and some way with the scriptural approach, by accepting revelation as the source of the ethical norm: the 'command – to love God in the neighbor' (p. 26). But, because he recognizes love as the only ethical standard, any other general principles he adopts will be hypothetical, deriving from the one universal law, which for Christians is *agape* (self-sacrificing love: see **pp. 186–90**). His ethical decisions and actions will reflect his awareness that 'circumstances alter cases', and that he must apply the law of love in a way that acknowledges that no two situations are exactly the same (p. 29).

Principles, but not rules

However, if no situations are ever identical, how useful are the general ethical principles of his community to the situationist, and how (if at all) does he use them, in combination with the law of love, to reach a decision in each unique situation. They are (Fletcher explains) to be used according to the situationist policy of 'principled relativism': they give insights and guidance, but are not treated as inflexible ethical rules, because '*only* love and reason really count' (p. 31). And, as no two cases are ever sufficiently alike to 'validate a law', Christian ethicists have had to adapt the law of love to new and challenging concrete situations (p. 32). Thus, Dietrich Bonhoeffer (see **pp. 152, 192, 195–7**) was 'executed for trying to kill, even *murder*, Adolf Hitler

– so far did he go as a situationist' (p. 33). However, following the pattern of universal prescriptivism (see **pp. 53–9**), this could be formulated as a universal ethical principle, along the lines that, 'no moral agent should ever kill another person, except where it is obvious that killing him will save many other lives'. To describe the act of killing a particular person as the most loving thing to do in a particular situation obscures the reason that justifies killing in that situation, but not in another.

Situationism in practice

Fletcher recounts a situation in a mental hospital, in the United States, where one patient raped another, an unmarried girl ill with a radical schizophrenic psychosis. Her father asked for an immediate abortion, to end the unwanted pregnancy. This was refused, because that state's law prohibited abortion, except on 'therapeutic' grounds (see **pp. 221–8**), where the mother's life was at risk. What would the situationist do?

> situationists, if their norm is the Christian commandment to love the neighbor, would . . . *in this case*, favour abortion . . . for the sake of the patient's physical and mental health, not only if it were needed to save her life . . . They would . . . reason that it is *not* killing because there is no person or human life in an embryo at an early stage of pregnancy. (pp. 38–9)

While many people would agree with Fletcher and the father that abortion would be justified in this situation, Fletcher does not explore the reasons for agreeing with this view. Those who think that abortion would be the most loving act would maintain that the interests of the suffering girl should take precedence over those (if any) of the unborn embryo/foetus. Fletcher would agree with Peter Singer's distinction between a 'human being', in the sense of 'a member of the species Homo sapiens', which an 'embryo conceived from human sperm and eggs' is, 'from the first moment of its existence', and a 'human person': the key characteristics of a 'human person' being 'ration ality and self-consciousness' (Singer, *Practical Ethics*, pp. 85-7). Singer's point is that not all human beings are persons, because some lack the essential characteristics of personhood, and this is the case with human embryos. On the other hand, rational and self-conscious members of an alien species from outer space certainly would be persons. However, the main reason why many ethicists would oppose abortion, in the case Fletcher cites, is that they reject the Fletcher-Singer view that an embryo, at an early stage of pregnancy, is not a person. Views on the rights and wrongs of abortion hinge on this all-important issue of whether, or when, a human embryo/foetus is, or becomes, a person and its moral status (see **pp. 224–6**), but Fletcher does not discuss it.

Four working principles

Fletcher proposes four working principles, to assist the situationist in his ethical decisions.

Pragmatism

Pragmatism is concerned with what works, and with a successful outcome to problems. Applied to ethical decisions, it does not of itself yield ethical principles or standards; we have to choose these for ourselves. However, approaching ethical problems in a practical, common sense way will enable the situationist to take account of all the aspects and complexities of a situation, and to apply the principle of love effectively to it.

Relativism

As no two situations are ever identical, 'the situationist avoids words like "never" and "perfect" and "complete" as he avoids the plague, as he avoids "absolutely"' (pp. 43–4). The Christian situationist has his absolute norm, or ultimate criterion, that of 'agapeic love' (p. 45). This principle must always be applied, but it must be made relative to the actual situation: the situationist must avoid turning a subordinate principle, which may be helpful in one situation, into an absolute rule which he applies invariably. Fletcher reminds Christians that relativism has a long history: in Christianity, it began 'when Jesus attacked the Pharisees' principle of statutory morality, and by Paul's rebellious appeal to grace and freedom' (p. 46).

Positivism

Fletcher points out that fundamental ethical principles cannot be proved. Like the religious believer's 'leap of faith', they are decisions, not conclusions. Thus, the Christian ethicist cannot prove that love is the fundamental moral principle, any more than utilitarians (as Bentham and Mill concede: see **pp. 88, 95**) can prove that pleasure is the highest good. And this indicates the limits of reason, which can 'note facts and infer relations', but not 'find values (goodness)' (p. 48). Fletcher agrees with Hume that there is no logical bridge from facts to values, 'from isness to oughtness' (see **pp. 21–2, 23–7**); moral choices cannot be verified or validated, only vindicated by their success in use (p. 48). Thus, the Christian ethicist makes *agape* love his key principle by his decision to affirm 'the faith assertion that "God is love" and thence by the logic's inference to the value assertion that love is the highest good'; and he does not understand God in terms of love, but 'love in terms of God as seen in Christ' (p. 49).

Personalism

In situation ethics, people, not things, are the centre of concern, and there are no inherent values unrelated to people's needs: 'value is what *happens* to something when it happens to be useful to love working for the sake of persons' (p. 50). Immorality occurs when Kant's categorical imperative, that people should always be treated as ends, never merely as means (see **p. 75**), is ignored, and people are used and things are loved. In Christian ethics, the central importance of persons is reinforced by belief that God is personal, and has created men in his own image. Situation ethics 'does not ask *what* is good but *how* to do good for *whom*; not what *is* love but how to *do* the most loving thing possible in the situation' (p. 52).

Conscience

Situation ethics treats conscience as a function, not a faculty. Talk of conscience is just a way of describing our efforts to make ethical decisions 'creatively, constructively, fittingly' (p. 53). Again, the situationist's concern is with what Fletcher calls 'antecedent' as opposed to 'consequent conscience', that is with making the right decisions, by appropriate application of agapeistic love, in the situation that confronts him, not with passing judgement on decisions already made (p. 54). The situationist agrees with Paul, who characterized conscience as a '*director* of human decisions rather than simply a reviewer' (p. 54).

Only love is always good

Fletcher insists that, to be successful Christian situation ethicists, we must free ourselves of the view that there are any values that are independent of being loving to persons. No action, thing or state of affairs is worth anything in itself; it acquires value, 'only because it happens to help persons (thus being good) or to hurt persons (thus being bad)' (p. 59). Even accepted and apparently self-evident ethical principles, such as helping those in distress, may fail by the test of what is the most loving action in one, particular situation:

> Persons – God, self, neighbor – are both the subjects and the objects of value; *they* determine it to be value for some person's sake ... What is right in one case, e.g., lending cash to a father who needs it for his hungry family, may be wrong in another case, e.g., lending cash to a father with hungry children when he is known to be a compulsive gambler or alcoholic. (p. 59)

An act's rightness is determined by how it is 'related to circumstances' (p. 59).

Love is a predicate, not a property

For Fletcher, there are no moral properties, either natural or non-natural, that a thing or action must possess in order to be good or right (see **pp. 21–31, 33, 35, 50–3**). Love is not something 'substantive', which 'we *have* or *are*', but 'something we *do*', and which is a predicate of our actions (pp. 60–1). Our task is so to conduct ourselves that 'more good (i.e., loving-kindness) will occur than any possible alternatives'; and we can do this by following the example of Jesus, and loving our neighbours (p. 61): 'Kant's second maxim, to treat people as ends and never as means, is strictly parallel to the New Testament's "law of love"' (p. 64).

Nothing is absolute

Accepting that long-adopted ethical rules are relative, not absolute, is difficult. Fletcher rejects the widely held moral rule that lying is always wrong. It depends on the situation: lying may, or may not be, the most loving thing to do. Someone may only be able to keep a secret by lying. And, he would be right to do so, 'depending upon how much love is served in the situation' (p. 65). Situationism rejects 'legalism and dogmatism' and the view that any principle of value, whether 'life or truth or chastity or property or marriage or anything but love', is good as such (pp. 67–8).

Love is the only norm

Christian situation ethics 'reduces law from a statutory system of rules to the love canon alone', in the same way that Jesus did not hesitate to ignore the obligations of Sabbath observance, and Paul replaced the rules of the Jewish religious law (the Torah) with the 'living principle of *agape*' (p. 69). This does not mean blanket rejection of religious laws, as they are found in, for example, Christianity or Judaism, but accepting that they should be followed only '*if* they serve love'; and recognizing that, as love and law will often conflict, they 'cannot be partners; at best, love only employs law when it seems worthwhile' (p. 71).

The Ten Commandments, the Sermon on the Mount and Christian ethics

Acceptance of some of the Ten Commandments, such as those that prohibit killing, stealing and false witness, seem fundamental to the existence of a civilized society (see **pp. 185–6**), but, for the situationist, they are relative: depending on the situation, love may call on him 'to break . . . *any or all of them*' (p. 74). Apart from the principle of love, there are no universal ethical laws; only empty platitudes, such as 'do the good and avoid the evil' (p. 76). Christians, in particular, must avoid turning 'a collection of scattered sayings, such as the Sermon on the Mount' into a 'rules book', resulting in error and frustration (p. 77). They need to recognize that 'Christian ethics is a situation ethic' and that 'non-reciprocal, neighbor-regarding' agapeic love, embracing everybody, including enemies, is the only moral principle (pp. 77–9). But again, Fletcher seems to minimize the importance of fundamental moral principles, such as those that prohibit murder or theft, without explaining the circumstances in which application of the law of love would justify modifying or suspending them.

Objections to situation ethics

Fletcher confronts the objection that situation ethics is too demanding, that it calls for more critical intelligence, factual information and more commitment to righteousness than most people are capable of. But, this is just a fact of life: ethical decisions often are difficult. Christians are expected to be ethically mature, and prepared to take responsibility and to act responsibly. *Agape* love rules out their being selfish or indifferent, and just minding their own business. Nor can they take refuge in a set of ethical rules, in order to escape the challenges and complexities of responsible decision-making.

Thus, classical pacifism (see **pp. 311–16**), which holds that violence is always wrong, in any situation, is a form of legalism, making the pacifist 'safe ethically', through the inflexible application of his principle, in a way that the situationist can never be (p. 84).

Love and justice

For Fletcher, Christian love must be applied prudently, and this careful calculation is what gives love its necessary 'care-fulness', so that, in applying it to a particular situation, 'it *becomes* justice' (p. 88). However, he redefines justice in a way that fits in with Christian situation ethics. If justice is giving our neighbours their due, what is due to them is love: so, 'Love is justice, justice is love' (p. 89). And, to be just and loving, we need a 'shotgun, not a rifle': we must calculate carefully how, in each situation, we can distribute love as widely, and to as many recipients, as possible (p. 89). To be just, Christians must also think creatively, in relation to biblical teaching, and think in terms of neighbours, not just a neighbour, which risks reducing *agape* to a 'merely one-to-one relationship' (p. 91).

Christian theologians have been too ready (Fletcher thinks) to separate, or to see an antithesis between, love and justice. For example, Reinhold Niebuhr (see **pp. 196–7**) made them alternatives, with love transcendent and impossible, and justice relative and possible. But, instead of saying that love is ideal and justice is actual, we should say that love is maximum justice and justice is optimum love. Talk of rights, as what is due to the neighbour, can also be misleading. What the neighbour has a right to is what is loving; and all alleged 'rights', such as religious freedom, free speech, the vote, even life itself, are relative, not absolute: '*all* are validated only by love' (p. 95). But will this do? Does it make sense to justify or defend basic human rights or freedoms (see **pp. 279–81, 285–93**), which relate to the intrinsic worth and dignity of each individual, on the grounds of 'love'? Whose love? Is my right to life or free speech justified only by God's love, or that of other people? It suggests that a government would be justified in removing these rights and freedoms, if it thought that doing so was the most loving thing to do: a convenient argument for totalitarian states.

Following the example of utilitarianism

Situation ethicists (Fletcher argues) can take over the principle of 'the greatest good of the greatest number' from Bentham and Mill, substituting *agape* for the pleasure principle, and replacing 'the hedonistic calculus' with 'the agapeic calculus', to promote 'the greatest amount of neighbor welfare for the largest number of neighbors possible' (p. 95). While situationism is more readily classified as consequentialist or teleological ethics, as it is directed to maximizing the good of love, it can also be understood within a deontological framework: the situationist's 'duty' is to 'seek the goal of the most love possible in every situation' (p. 96). However, as act utilitarians (see **pp. 87–92**) have found, calculating the consequences of actions is difficult, if not impossible. Certainly, taking one of Fletcher's examples, the situationist's love calculus can throw out some unexpected results, such as President Truman's decision to drop nuclear bombs on Hiroshima and Nagasaki, which was made on a 'vast scale of "agapeic calculus"' (p. 98).

Loving is not liking but benevolence

Agapeic love is not ordinary love (see **pp. 188–9**), which involves emotion or affection. It is primarily an 'active determination of the will', and so, unlike feelings, it can be commanded (p. 105). Its opposite is not hatred, but indifference, not caring about the well-being of others. It can be defined as benevolence or active good will, which reaches out to neighbours, 'not for our own sakes nor for theirs, really, but for God's' (p. 105).

Our neighbour is anybody

Christian love embraces, not just the 'friend-neighbor', the 'stranger-neighbor and the acquaintance-neighbor but even the enemy-neighbor' (p. 107). This is because, unlike ordinary love between two people, which is based on feelings, it is not reciprocal, and (although it may hope for it) does not 'presuppose any return of concern' (p. 108). When the compiler of the Sermon on the Mount (see **pp. 191–2**) portrayed Jesus urging his listeners to 'be perfect as your heavenly Father', he did not mean 'perfect', in the sense of their love having the completeness of God's, but that it should be as 'all-inclusive' as God's *agape* (p. 108).

Self-love and neighbour love

Agape is essentially other-regarding: it reaches out to the neighbour. However, it may be self-regarding, if this is what maximizes love:

> The logic of love is that self-concern is obligated to cancel neighbor-love whenever *more* neighbor-good will be served through serving the self.

The self is to be served rather than any neighbor if *many* neighbors are served through serving the self. (p. 113)

Thus, the only doctor at a train accident should not risk his own life to rescue a victim trapped in a carriage, when his medical expertise may save the lives of ten other victims: it is wrong to love ourselves for our own sake, but right to love ourselves for our neighbour's and ultimately for God's.

It is not cruel to calculate

Successful moral choices, involving effective application of the principle of love to concrete situations, require intelligent assessment, as well as a loving attitude. Only those who 'sentimentalize and subjectivize love' regard calculation of a situation as 'cold or cruel' (p. 116). Again, despite what some Christian ethicists say, it is not true that the end does not justify the means: that is like saying that 'a thing is not worth what it costs, that *nothing* is, that use or usefulness is irrelevant to price' (p. 120).

Means and ends

Indeed (Fletcher maintains), unless we have some purpose or end in view, towards which our actions are directed, they are meaningless. Our prime concern is with the end we seek, which is maximization of love in a particular situation: the means are of secondary importance, but they must be 'appropriate and faithful to that end' (p. 121).

They are not 'merely neutral tools', which are 'ethically indifferent', and must be selected carefully (p. 121–2). As with principles or actions which can be right or wrong, according to the circumstances, a means that is

sometimes good may at other times be evil, and what is sometimes wrong may sometimes be right when it serves a good enough end – *depending on the situation.* (p. 123)

But, if the situation is sovereign, and the end justifies the means, can any means be ruled out as inappropriate, provided it works? It appears not, as Fletcher's reference to the use of nuclear bombs against Japan, in 1945, suggests.

Nothing is intrinsically wrong

The nature of situation ethics is that 'anything and everything is right or wrong, according to the situation' (p. 124). The situation ethicist can escape the trap into which exponents of the intrinsic theory of value fall, as they have to condemn certain acts as intrinsically wrong, irrespective of circumstances which may make them appropriate means to the maximization of love. Fletcher gives the example of telling a lie, to prevent someone committing suicide, or stealing someone's gun, to prevent him shooting another person. The moral absolutists, who issue a blanket ban on lying or stealing, may, by stigmatizing it, prevent people committing a lesser evil, which could lead to a much greater good. An evil means does not invariably 'nullify a good end': it is a matter of the proportions of good and evil, and the situation itself (p. 126). However, the proportions are all-important, requiring the exercise of very careful judgement. The situationist confronts the same problem as the act utilitarian. Is he really going to be able to calculate all the consequences of his action? Can he be certain (as Moore warned: see **p. 40**) that he will be justified in setting aside established, common sense moral rules?

Four factors the situationist must take into account

To assist situationists' ethical decisions, Fletcher stipulates four questions they should always ask, and then balance on 'love's scales': What is the end? By what means is it to be achieved? What is the motive? What are the foreseeable consequences? (pp. 127–8). He points to what he considers a defect of traditional ethics: that to be wrong an action needs to fail only one of these tests, but to be right must pass all four. For the situationist, however, all ends and means are interrelated in a 'contributory hierarchy', and nothing is intrinsically good but the highest good: love (p. 129). An action my fail one or more of the tests, but still be the most loving in the circumstances, and therefore the right one.

Fletcher dismisses an argument that traditional moralists (and also Moore: see **p. 40**) raise against this cavalier approach to established moral rules: even if, by flouting the rule, in this situation, you did the right thing, what about your example, which may discredit established moral rules? Others may copy you, and get it spectacularly wrong. This 'generalization argument' (Fletcher believes) is just an 'antisituational gambit', designed to undermine 'personal responsibility and leave law in control' (p. 131). Love's job is to calculate an action's 'gains and losses', and then decide what is right (p. 132). For example, in a particular situation, one family's well-being may be best served by divorce (see **pp. 267–70**), whereas another's may not be.

Love and freedom

Fletcher recognizes that many people do not welcome the freedom and responsibility of situation ethics, and feel more comfortable with a set of rules, to which they can turn to decide what to do in every situation. The situationist, by contrast, rejoices in being free from the 'dead hand' of law, preferring to 'live as a free man, with all the ambiguities that go along with freedom' (p. 135). Of course, as society, and the ethical issues it throws up, become more complex, the attractions of established rules seem stronger; but, whatever the moral legalist thinks, it is an error to believe that moral decisions are simplified, or that a list of moral rules can offer relief from the burden of responsible moral decision-making.

Jesus' situation ethic

Although this was much truer of the 1950s and 1960s, when he was developing his ethical theory, Fletcher deplores the hypocrisy, masquerading as moral consensus, which pays lip-service to so-called 'moral laws', which are continually broken in practice, because they are 'too petty or too rigid to fit the facts of life' (pp. 137–8). Contemporary Christians need to appreciate that the only view of Jesus' ethics consistent with his actual teaching is the situational one. For example, he has nothing to say about sexual ethics, apart from condemning adultery and divorce (see **pp. 257–9, 268–9**), so whether any particular form of sexual relationship, such as homosexuality, is right or wrong must be judged on the basis of his teaching that the only thing that matters is 'whether love is fully served' (p. 139). Thus, extra-marital relations are not wrong, unless people 'hurt themselves, their partners, or others' (p. 140).

But, would an individual, who wanted to commit adultery, really ask himself if it was the most 'loving' thing to do (the term seems almost self-contradictory in this context), or simply use situationism as a cover for indulging his desires? And, does Fletcher do justice to the Christian tradition, which rules out certain kinds of sexual activity as never being genuine manifestations of Christian love (see **pp. 255–78**)?

Taking account of an action's total context

For Fletcher, an action's rightness (lovingness) cannot be judged in isolation: it must be evaluated in the 'whole complex of all the factors in the situation' (p. 141). He draws a parallel with ecology, which studies the relationship between an organism and its environment. Situation ethics is an ecological ethics: it takes account of the total environment of every moral decision. The situationist may be unable to answer such hypothetical questions as: should a husband lie to his wife, desert his family, or not report an item in his tax return? Indeed, he will probably counter with one of his own: does the questioner have a concrete situation in mind? But, it is hard to see why his answer could not be, 'In general, you should do so and so, because experience has shown it to be the most loving conduct, but you must assess each situation, in case there are morally relevant differences.' This would be more consistent with what he says about the situationist respecting his community's general ethical principles.

Neocasuistry

The pragmatism and relativism of situation ethics offers a new approach to casuistry (the process of working out detailed ethical rules to cover specific situations): but one which is 'case-focused . . . to bring Christian imperatives into practical operation': Agapeic love, seeking to act lovingly towards the neighbour, examines the facts of a situation, and decides what ought to be done (p. 148). In Philippians 1.9, St Paul declares: 'it is my prayer that your love may abound more and more, with knowledge and all discernment'. For Fletcher, this sums up the Christian approach to ethics:

(1) . . . prayerful reliance upon God's grace; (2) the law of love as the norm; (3) knowledge of the facts, of the empirical situation in all its . . . particularity; and (4) judgement . . . which is a matter of responsibility in humility. (p. 152)

Can anyone be a situation ethicist?

Fletcher has discussed Christian situation ethics, but acknowledges that lovingness is often the motivating force behind non-Christian and even atheist ethical decisions. Christians do not have a monopoly of love and its power: through the Holy Spirit, it can operate in those who do not know God. But, Christian love is special, as it is the 'love of gratitude . . . to God for what he has done for us . . . especially in . . . Jesus Christ' (p. 155). God does not stand in need of our service, but our only way of serving him, and of expressing our gratitude to him, is by serving our neighbours.

Assessment

For the **situation ethicist** (Fletcher maintains) love is the only ethical standard, and the only right action, in any situation, is the most loving one. Love is the **first principle of situation ethics**, and, like any first principle, it cannot be proved, but can only be vindicated by success in practice. But, how can the situationist be sure that he will always do the most loving thing? He must recognize that every situation is unique, and that circumstances alter cases. He must be calculating, in the positive sense. He must tease out every aspect of every situation, before he acts, so as to ensure that his action really is the most loving.

Fletcher does not dismiss established ethical principles out of hand. He believes that a situationist should approach every moral decision with his community's ethical principles in mind. And he should treat them with respect for the light they shed on ethical decisions. However, he must not regard them as inviolable, and he must be prepared to modify them, or set them aside completely, if that is what love demands. As love is the only principle, subordinate principles, including even those in the Ten Commandments, however important, and whatever the extent to which experience has shown that following them produces the best outcome, cannot be treated as absolute. For, in this particular situation, applying a firmly established principle may not maximize love. Yes, in general, lying will not be the most loving thing to do; but it could be here and now. The same is true even of killing; and not only, as in Bonhoeffer's case, to rid the world of a mad and murderous megalomaniac, but even when it involves the mass slaughter caused by exploding a nuclear bomb.

However, while Fletcher emphasizes the importance of carefully calculating each moral situation, he does not, in the examples he gives, clearly explain or justify why a particular choice is the most loving. For example, it is possible to explain and justify President Truman's decision to drop atomic bombs on Hiroshima and Nagasaki (see **pp. 308–9**), but Fletcher does not do so. In places, he also seems to suggest that there may be many situations in which it would be right not to apply such fundamental moral principles as not killing or lying, when, particularly with the first, they are likely to be extremely rare. Further, despite what he says to the contrary, he gives the impression that it is relatively easy to determine all the morally relevant aspects of a situation, and, by means of the 'agapeic calculus', to determine the consequences of an action. In fact, as Mill and Moore agree (see **pp. 95**

and **39–40**), it may be extremely difficult to do so: which is why it is generally better to apply a well-tested principle, rather than try to calculate the
consequences of modifying or suspending it.

We come back to the problem that applying the **love ethic**, in actual situations, is far from straightforward; and not only because of the difficulty of
calculating consequences. For what is the most loving action in this or that
situation? There is no objective criterion by which to decide that matter. It
is likely to prove highly subjective, with each situationist judging the most
loving action to be what fits in with his own moral preferences or prejudices,
or even what suits his own self-interest. In practice, the most truly loving actions are likely to be those that apply well-established moral principles, and
that at the very least, embody the principle of non-maleficence (see **p. 43**).

Core text

Joseph Fletcher, *Situation Ethics*, London: SCM Press, 1966.

Other references and suggestions for further reading and research

H. Cox (ed.), *The Situation Ethics Debate*, Philadelphia: The Westminster
   Press, 1968.
Joseph Fletcher, *Morals and Medicine*, Princeton: Princeton University
   Press, 1954.
Joseph Fletcher, *Moral Responsibility: Situation Ethics at Work*,
   Philadelphia: Westminster Press, 1967.
Joseph Fletcher, *The Ethics of Genetic Control: Ending Reproductive
   Roulette*, Garden City, NY: Anchor Press/Doubleday, 1974.
W. D. Hudson, *Modern Moral Philosophy*, London: Macmillan, 1970
   (chapter 5).
D. Mills Daniel, *Briefly: Fletcher's Situation Ethics*, London: SCM Press,
   2009.
J. A. T. Robinson, *Honest to God*, London: SCM Press, 1963 (chapter 6).
Peter Singer, *Practical Ethics*, 2nd edn, Cambridge: Cambridge University
   Press, 1993.
P. Vardy and P. Grosch, *The Puzzle of Ethics*, rev. edn, London:
   HarperCollins, 1999 (chapter 10).

9 Conscience

I The conscience

What is it?

The theory of a **moral conscience** is the belief that all human beings have a God-given conscience, which prescribes moral rules and impels us to follow them. For Calvin, human beings are invested with a moral conscience, through which they may see the difference between good and evil, and follow the natural law (see **pp. 120–8**). This is not to say that the moral conscience is something different from the natural law. Rather, it is that by which we distinguish between right and wrong, which are established by the **natural law**; and this is what is engraved on our hearts as the moral conscience. Although ideas relating to conscience are mainly associated with Christianity, particularly Protestantism, they have a long history outside it, as well.

Development of the theory of conscience

Socrates seems to have a similar conception, and St Paul's statement, 'When Gentiles who have not the law do by nature what the law requires, they are a law to themselves' (Romans 2.14–16), was important for future conceptions of conscience. Medieval scholars, most notably Thomas Aquinas, also developed theories of conscience. They distinguished between conscience and *synderesis*: the latter is an understanding of the general principles of (moral) conduct, while conscience is the means by which human beings apply those principles to guide action in particular instances. Protestantism, by making conscience an independent, authoritative faculty, seems to have more or less collapsed *synderesis* into conscience. For Schopenhauer and

Nietzsche, conscience is largely that which makes us feel guilty after committing what we feel to be, or have been conditioned to consider, immoral acts. John Stuart Mill also thought of conscience as that which impels us to duty through bad feeling. This way of thinking bears some relation to one of the ways that Luther, and to an extent Newman, discuss conscience: as that which is terrified by God and sin.

Recent interpretations

Recent discussions of conscience, in philosophy and theology, do not treat it as an independent faculty. Indeed, the very existence of conscience, as something distinct from the exercise of moral reasoning, rational moral training, or the influence of moral conditioning, is questioned. For Freud, conscience is an aspect of the superego that judges us, with consequent feelings of anxiety, when we (both consciously and unconsciously) fail to conform to the principles of our superego, which is an internalized mixture of parental influences and various social and racial expectations, which (potentially) are modified during an individual's lifetime.

2 The conscience in Joseph Butler's 'A Dissertation upon the Nature of Virtue' and *Fifteen Sermons* (see recommended edition on **p. 165**)

Bishop Joseph Butler (1692–1752)

After graduating from Oriel College, Oxford, in 1718, Joseph Butler became preacher at the Rolls Chapel and Clerk of the Closet to Queen Caroline (wife of George II), and was later bishop of Bristol, dean of St Paul's and bishop of Durham. He published his *Fifteen Sermons Preached at the Rolls Chapel* in 1726 and *The Analogy of Religion* (to which the 'Dissertation on the Nature of Virtue' was annexed), an orthodox Christian response to the Deists, who denied the importance of divine revelation, in 1736. His work made a major contribution to the development of eighteenth-century thought. His ethical theory anticipates Kant's moral philosophy, and his analysis of conscience influenced the moral thinking of David Hume, Adam Smith and others.

'A Dissertation upon the Nature of Virtue'

Human virtue

For Butler, human beings are 'capable of moral government' because we have a 'moral nature' and 'moral faculties of perception and of action' (p. 169). Through an inherent moral faculty, usually termed conscience, we 'naturally and unavoidably approve some actions, under the peculiar view of their being virtuous and of good desert; and disapprove others, as vicious and of ill desert'. We are thus superior to other animals, because, despite being similarly driven to actions only by emotional impulse, 'we have a capacity of reflecting upon actions . . . and making them an object to our thought', and so can control our behaviour (p. 69). Butler thinks it unimportant to decide whether conscience is an aspect of our reason or our emotion. Indeed, for Butler, it is both 'a sentiment of the understanding' and 'a perception of the heart'. But, however one thinks of, or labels, conscience: a 'great part of common language, and of common behaviour over the world, is formed upon supposition of such a moral faculty'; and it is not:

> at all doubtful in the general, what course of action this faculty, or practical discerning power within us, approves and what it disapproves. (p. 69)

As conscience is inherent in human nature, all human beings have the same moral faculty, and not only approve and perform moral actions as individuals, but share a 'universally acknowledged standard' that applies to all human beings (p. 70).

Action and intention

For Butler, the object of conscience is actions, not consequences. We do not judge an action to have been good or bad on the basis of its consequences, divorced from the agent's intention (see also **pp. 46, 71, 77**). If someone intends to cause harm, but their action accidentally produces good consequences, we would still judge the person and the action to be immoral. And, just as we are interested in a person's intention, when we judge them morally, we also consider their power over their situation, and their capacity to understand their actions. We think a criminal deserves punishment for a crime s/he has committed, because s/he decided to perform that act, and intended, for example, to rob another. The criminal has 'ill desert' because s/he is culpable for the act s/he decided to perform (pp. 70–1). But, we would not say that someone deserved to be punished for having bubonic plague, even if s/he had to be left to die, in order to prevent the infection spreading. Here, the individual is unfortunate, not guilty, and so we do not demand punishment, because s/he is innocent of any intention to cause harm. Similarly, before deciding whether an action is good or bad, we consider the agent's capacity to understand their actions. We do not deem a child, or a mentally ill person, to be as morally culpable as an adult of sound mind. A child and a mentally ill person are capable of intending and performing immoral acts, but we do not expect them to have the capacity to understand their actions completely.

Benevolence and utility

Because conscience considers actions and intentions, rather than consequences, benevolence is not 'the whole of virtue' (p. 74). If it were, we would not object to someone stealing something from us, in order to give it to someone else, who would get more enjoyment from it. We regard stealing, or any falsehood or injustice, as wrong in itself, without considering the amount of happiness that it may produce. Thus, the utilitarian conception of virtuous actions, as those that produce most happiness, is not consistent with the actions our conscience actually approves. However, even though we do not approve of actions simply because they have brought someone happiness, Butler holds that, in fact, obeying our conscience will produce the greatest overall happiness for the human race. The conscience limits human beings to approving only of those actions that God 'has directed': that is, 'all ways not contrary to veracity and justice' (p. 74).

Occasionally, human beings may feel that an unjust action, such as stealing, will produce short-term happiness, but if, in the long term, we came to think of stealing as a good thing, the human race would be unhappy, due to high levels of crime and unrest. Our conscience, by preventing us from ever thinking that stealing is morally justified, prevents a situation in which we act to make others happy, but mistakenly increase unhappiness. Thus, the world's happiness is 'the concern of him who is the Lord and Proprietor of it'; we cannot really know which actions will produce happiness, because we cannot see the future (pp. 74–5). We can only follow the direction of conscience, knowing that God gave it to us, because 'he foresaw this constitution of our nature would produce more happiness' (p. 74).

Fifteen Sermons

The human constitution

Human beings (Butler holds), like every work of nature or art, have a system or constitution. Once it is understood, we can determine our purpose, just as we can understand what a watch is for, by looking at its parts and workings. The human constitution consists of 'Appetites, passions, affections, and the principle of reflection' (conscience) (p. 14). However, to gain a clear idea of the human constitution, we need to know not only human nature's various elements, but how they relate to each other. For any machine to work, its parts must be governed by a mechanism that creates the correct constitution, by bringing every individual element into its proper relationship with everything else. In human beings, the conscience is the superior faculty, which, by controlling our appetites, passions and affections, brings them into their proper order, thus forming our constitution. And, because the conscience is a moral faculty, which rules over all our other elements, the human constitution is clearly 'adapted to virtue', just as a watch, according to its constitution, 'is adapted to measure time' (p. 15). If a watch does not measure time, it is not truly a watch, but something that has failed to do what it was made to do. The same is true of those human beings who do not behave morally.

Indeed, for Butler, the nature of the human constitution, as designed for virtuous behaviour under the direction of conscience, gives human beings a prior obligation to morality, which precedes even Christian revelation:

> our being God's creatures, and virtue being the natural law we are born under, and the whole constitution of man being plainly adapted to it, are prior obligations to piety and virtue than the consideration that God sent his son into the world to save it, and the motives which arise from the peculiar relations of Christians, as members one of another under Christ. (p. 25)

Made to be moral

It is as impossible to deny that human beings are made to be moral, as that 'eyes were given . . . to see with' (p. 34). This is why, for Butler, self-love and virtue coincide perfectly. True self-love, far from undermining morality, helps people to realize that only moral behaviour, which gives them social approval, satisfaction of their conscience and benevolent emotions, and a future reward in heaven (see, in particular, *Sermons II, VIII* and *XII*), is in their true self-interest. We need only appeal to a 'person's heart and natural conscience' to uncover a shared human sensitivity to being moral (p. 34). Further: 'everyone may find within himself the rule of right, and obligations to follow it' (p. 36). This is because we all have a God-given conscience, and will agree about what is moral, according to our shared human constitution.

Reflection

Our obligation to be moral, because we were made to be so, and must be so, in order to be true to our nature, is strengthened by the fact that our constitution was put into our own hands. Unlike machines, we can act in ways contrary to our constitution; so, it is up to us to choose to affirm the law of our conscience, and act according to its direction. This is why every human being 'is a law to himself' (p. 37): first, because our conscience supplies us with moral laws, which we must obey if we are to be true to our nature; and second, because, by reflecting on our activities, we can guide our actions independently, according to our conscience's direction. Animals act only in accordance with their strongest passion, whether hunger or lust. Our power of reflection or conscience make us superior to animals; and only by reflecting on our actions can we become autonomous agents. What makes us better than animals is acting according to our reason and judgement, not our passions.

And because, when we reflect on our actions, we bring them before our moral faculty of conscience, we will necessarily be drawn to moral behaviour, because that is what our conscience approves. We are only truly human when we are moral, and thus true to our God-given constitution; and this is to behave rationally.

The authority of conscience

Conscience is human nature's superior faculty, but not always the strongest. A particular passion may override it, impelling us to actions that it condemns. But Butler distinguishes between '*mere power* and *authority*' (p. 39). Our passions may, at times, predominate, but our conscience has absolute authority. Because God gave it to us, so that we may realize our true nature as moral agents, it alone is entitled to govern our conduct. Whenever we fail to be guided by it, and yield to other appetites and passions, our constitution is controlled and corrupted by motivations that are contrary to our obligations as rational, moral creatures. Submitting to our passion is like ignoring the authority of civil government:

> . . . as in civil government the constitution is broken in upon and violated by power and strength prevailing over authority, so the constitution of man is broken in upon and violated by the power faculties or principles within prevailing over that which is in its nature supreme over them all. (p. 41)

Society and human beings can only achieve their goals when unified under proper direction. By resisting conscience or civil government, we cause disharmony, which contradicts the very basis and nature of the individual or society, and we prevent them from functioning properly. A society is only truly a society when everyone obeys the law, and we can only be true to our human constitution, and realize our true human potential, if we accept conscience's absolute authority. For Butler, when we recognize its authority, and affirm our real nature as rational, moral beings, we surmount the lower elements of our nature, which we share with 'the brutes', and attain the highest level of humanity (p. 42). Life's meaning and purpose, our 'whole economy', is contained in our being ruled by conscience (p. 42). God, 'the Author of our nature', gave it to us as 'our natural guide'; and we must recognize our 'duty' to it (p. 43). By conforming to it, we fulfil our obligations to God and to our true nature as moral beings, capable of achieving happiness and the fullest expression of human life, which values love, righteousness and virtue for their own sake:

> Thus morality and religion, virtue and piety, will at last necessarily coincide . . . and love will be in all senses 'the end of the commandment'. (p. 67)

Assessment

Butler's **theory of conscience** is an optimistic response to the views of those, such as Thomas Hobbes (see **p. 288**), who argue that even apparently moral or altruistic human actions arise from selfishness or self-interest. Butler argues that, although we achieve what is best for ourselves by being moral, self-interest is not the motivation. We are moral by nature, and perform moral acts as ends in themselves, so the good we derive from being moral results from doing what nature intended. Similarly, Butler does not think that **utilitarianism** explains human moral behaviour. Our conscience is interested in particular actions as moral. It does not contemplate happiness, or the means of achieving it, only actions that seem right in themselves, but which, under God's guidance, may result in long-term, general happiness.

Butler is not entirely consistent about whether conscience is a rational or an emotional faculty. In the 'Dissertation on Virtue', he argues that the question is not important, and that conscience seems to be an aspect of both reason and emotion. However, in the *Sermons*, he sometimes suggests that its concern is with rational principles of morality; at other times, that it also involves an emotional response. He insists that conscience, as it comes from God, discloses a universal law of shared moral values, consistent with a common human nature. This view ascribes moral potential to all humans, and suggests that we pursue the same moral goals. However, as, in practice, we do not always do so, his theory has been criticized as unrealistic, and as enabling people to claim the right to behave as they wish. If, as Butler maintains, we are a law unto ourselves, according to conscience's direction, then we must be allowed to follow whatever we take to be its law. While some claim that this approach results in the break-up of society, with people obeying their own individual moral standards, it can be argued that it means accepting the core value of a liberal society: that we should be allowed to follow our consciences, as long as we do not harm others.

3 The conscience in John Henry Newman's A *Grammar of Assent* (see recommended edition on **p. 165**)

John Henry Newman (1801–90)

After graduating from Trinity College, Oxford, John Henry Newman became a fellow of Oriel, and was a leading member of the Oxford Movement, which held that the Church of England should be free of the state. In 1845, he became a Roman Catholic, as he thought it was the only true Church. An impressive preacher and a conscientious educator, he set up the first Oratory (members living as a community, but not taking monastic vows) in England (1848), and founded a Roman Catholic university in Dublin (1854). He wrote on education (*The Idea of a University* (1852)), early church controversies (*The Arians of the Fourth Century* (1833)) and his own religious life (*Apologia pro Vita Sua* (1864)), and died two years after being made a Cardinal.

Conscience and the image of God

For Newman, we have a **conscience by nature**. Through it, we 'gain an image of God'; can give 'real assent to the proposition that He exists'; and receive a 'sense of moral obligation', as we feel anxiety, guilt and fear when we behave badly, but experience 'self-approval and hope' when we behave morally (pp. 97–8). From these:

> intimations of conscience with the reverberations or echoes . . . of an external admonition, we proceed on to the notion of a Supreme Ruler and Judge, and then again we image Him and His attributes in those recurring intimations, out of which . . . our recognition of His existence was originally gained. (p. 97)

Conscience gives us 'the materials for the real apprehension of a Divine Sovereign and Judge', because its moral promptings are indications of God's own nature, which he gives us indirectly; and, through them, we feel a greater connection to our idea of him, as both real and present (pp. 97–8).

Conscience and the moral sense

Newman distinguishes between the intellectual and the emotional aspects of conscience:

> The feeling of conscience . . . is twofold: – it is a moral sense, and a sense of duty; a judgment of the reason and a magisterial dictate. (p. 98)

The moral sense is conscience viewed from its rational or intellectual aspect, but Newman's interest is in conscience in its emotional aspect, as the 'sanction of right conduct', as opposed to the moral sense, which delineates the 'rule of right conduct' (p. 99). The emotional aspect of conscience, as 'the dictate of an authoritative monitor bearing upon the details of conduct', is its 'primary and most authoritative aspect', as well as being 'the ordinary sense of the word' (p. 99). We have a natural 'sense of duty and obligation', as we have of 'the beautiful and graceful in nature and art' (p. 99). But, conscience is not a detached taste or sense, admiring moral rules from afar, as we might a beautiful object, without any deep, personal connection to it. Conscience is eminently personal; concerned with 'self alone and one's own actions, and with others only indirectly and as if in association with self'; and it teaches us that God 'is our Judge' (pp. 99 and 304). On the other hand, the moral sense, conscience's intellectual aspect, may have no special relation to persons, and may regard morality as something abstract: as rules of right and wrong that can be rationally formulated and discussed. However, in its truest, emotional sense, conscience does not simply identify rules, but forces them 'on us by threats and by promises that we must follow the right and avoid the wrong' (p. 99).

Something outside ourselves

Conscience, unlike the moral sense or the sense of beauty, does not contemplate objects in themselves, nor does it 'repose on itself' (p. 99). It appeals to something outside itself, to explain the immediacy of its feelings about right and wrong, and 'dimly discerns a sanction higher than self for its decisions' (p. 99). Indeed, of all our tastes and sensations, only conscience is 'a voice, or the echo of a voice, imperative and constraining' (p. 99). This is why we have a bad conscience, feelings of fear and 'a lively sense of responsibility and guilt' when we behave badly, even if no one sees us, and we break no social laws; and perhaps benefit from our immorality (p. 100). Conscience 'is always emotional', because it always involves recognition of a living object, towards which it is directed (p. 100):

> If, as is the case we feel responsibility, are ashamed, are frightened, at transgressing the voice of conscience, this implies there is One to whom we are responsible, before whom we are ashamed, whose claims upon us we fear. (p. 101)

Because God personally appears to us through our consciences, we experience 'the excitement of affection and passion' (p. 100). In its voice, we sense, and so can envisage, God, and we respond emotionally, feeling that we must always act for his and our conscience's approval. If we did not experience God as 'Supreme Governor, a Judge, holy, just, powerful, all seeing, retributive', through our conscience, we would not suffer the inexplicable pangs of guilt that follow bad conduct, or the equally unaccountable feelings of satisfaction and relief when we behave well (p. 101). It makes us aware of God's nature, and we respond emotionally, personally and positively.

The cultivation of conscience

For Newman:

> Conscience . . . teaches us, not only that God is, but what He is; it provides for the mind a real image of Him, as a medium of worship; it gives

us a rule of right and wrong, as being his rule, and a code of moral duties. (p. 304)

Nature has given us a conscience, but we must cultivate it, for it is 'so constituted that, if obeyed, it becomes clearer in its injunctions . . . wider in . . . range, and corrects and completes the accidental feebleness of its initial teachings' (p. 304). The more we heed it, the more distinct our image of God, and thus our knowledge of good and evil, become. Instinctively, children know the difference between right and wrong, and recognize God as their 'Moral Governor', who is intimately connected to them, and will care for, and guide, them in times of crisis (p. 103). As we grow up, our initial sense of God should become clearer and more powerful. We develop an intellectual concept of him, as all-loving and present in the beauty and design of the world. But, if we fail in our duty, by succumbing to the 'the temptations of life', 'bad companions' or 'the urgency of secular occupations', our soul's 'light . . . will fade away and die out'; God's voice will become more indistinct; and our conscience will be weakened (p. 105). It will also be damaged by our giving more weight to intellectual ideas of God than to our emotional attachment to him, through conscience: a process observable in 'the religion of so-called civilization', which focuses on 'the moral sense' and rationality, but fails to appreciate our emotional side (p. 308). As individuals and a society, we seem to be increasingly conditioned out of the conscience's instinctive connection to God, which we had as children. We must always be aware of how the human mind, through conscience's emotional aspect, 'arrives, not only at a notional, but an imaginative or real assent to the doctrine that there is One God'; and this is the only way to understand our relationship to God, as well as being the real meaning and nature of the human moral life (p. 108).

Assessment

Newman's **theory of conscience** is clearly linked to his aim, in *A Grammar of Assent*, to show how personal faith in God is both reasonable and certain, but does not depend on intellectual arguments or formulas, which are only part of faith. Their role is not to supply the image of God, as our emotional conscience does, but to keep it before us, when, for example, we formulate theological principles, to which we can attach our emotional assent to God. Newman is wholly against secularization of human life, and the increasing absence of God and religion from our understanding of the nature and purpose of ethics, education and society. He rejects a liberal interpretation of church membership, which holds that specific religious principles, or emotional commitment, are unnecessary for religious belief. This is why, before his conversion to Roman Catholicism, Newman was such a prominent opponent of the traditional, moderate and inclusive English approach to religion, and a leading exponent of the distinctiveness and depth of faith, which many thought had been lost in the liberal progressiveness of the time.

His analysis of conscience suggests that it gives human beings a sense of something beyond themselves and the visible universe. Newman may be psychologically accurate, but this does not necessarily mean that God exists. Our guilt about immoral acts may come, not from God, but from our social upbringing or our psycho-physical nature. We may feel that Newman's emphasis on fear, as the spur to moral behaviour and recognition of God as judge, does not do full justice to moral actions, which we perform because we consider them good in themselves. Indeed, he emphasizes God's judgement so much that it seems difficult to believe in the possibility of forgiveness. Also, does Newman account for the diversity of religions and moral codes that human beings accept through conscience? His suggestion that it needs to be cultivated implies that differences in culture and education, as well as human ignorance, error and neglect, account for this diversity. So, if only one God speaks to us through conscience, does this mean that we misinterpret it, and that our religious beliefs and moral codes do not reflect God's guidance accurately? If so, what is the criterion for distinguishing erroneous feelings of conscience from those that are authentically the voice of God?

Core texts

Joseph Butler, *Five Sermons* (with 'A Dissertation Upon the Nature of Virtue'), ed. S. L. Darwall, Indianapolis, IN: Hackett, 1983 (selected from *Fifteen Sermons Preached at the Rolls Chapel*).
John Henry Newman, *An Essay in Aid of A Grammar of Assent*, ed. N. Lash, Notre Dame, IN/London: University of Notre Dame Press, 1979.

Suggestions for further reading and research

F. Copleston, *A History of Philosophy*, vol. 5, part 1, New York: Image Books, 1964 (chapter 10).
C. S. Dessain, *John Henry Newman*, London: Adam and Charles Black, 1966.

E. C. Mossner, *Bishop Butler and the Age of Reason*, New York: Macmillan, 1936.

Works and Life of John Henry Newman at www.newmanreader. org.

John Henry Newman, *Newman's University Sermons*, ed. D. M. MacKinnon and J. D. Holmes, London: SPCK, 1970.

10 Religion and Ethics

1 The relationship of religion and ethics

For many **religious people**, especially believers in an all-powerful and all-knowing creator God, the relationship between religion and ethics seems obvious. The second depends on the first: the basis of what is good or right lies in the will of God, and, if we always obey God, we will be morally good, and know the right thing to do. For, what God commands is good or right by definition. But is it that simple? If it were, to know what is good or right would only involve finding out what God wants us to do. The question of whether what God commands is good or right would not arise: indeed, it would be meaningless. However, the question as to whether what God (even if he is all-powerful and all-knowing) commands is good or right, is an intelligible one; it is asked even by religious believers, who sometimes question what they take to be God's commands. Therefore, logically, it is an **open question** whether what God commands is good or right, while to define 'good' or 'right' in terms of God's will or commands would be to commit the **naturalistic fallacy** (see **pp. 29–31**).

In this chapter, Geoffrey Warnock considers the implications of belief in God on attitudes to ethics and ethical issues, and Elizabeth Anscombe argues that Christian belief has shaped the way we think about, and discuss, them. Plato asks whether things are good because God wills them, and makes out a convincing case for holding that they are not. Richard Braithwaite contends that religion can be reduced to morality, while Kierkegaard, using the example of Abraham, maintains that God's commands should always take precedence over morality.

2 Why God and religion make a difference to ethics

G. J. Warnock on religion and ethics (see recommended edition on p. 181)

G. J. Warnock (1923–95)

For brief biographical details of G. J. Warnock, see **p. 59**.

Belief in God has a major impact on ethical questions

In *The Object of Morality*, Warnock makes the point that, whatever the precise relationship between God and ethics, belief in God, and particularly in a monotheistic (one-God) religion, like Christianity, which holds that God is neither all-too-human (infinitely powerful, all-knowing and creator from nothing of all that exists), nor utterly non-human (all-loving and concerned about human beings), is bound to have a major impact on the believer's attitude to ethical questions. There is no parallel, in any secular morality, to a transcendent being who inspires both love and fear in his followers, and demands their obedience:

> a being to which, in quite a unique sense, veneration is owed, which is uniquely an object of both love and fear, and above all to whose behests is owed, uniquely, *obedience*. (p. 141)

Rules of conduct are divine commands

And this is the key point. Even if morality is held to be independent of God (see **pp. 170–2**), and to establish standards by which even God's actions can be evaluated, any rules of conduct God lays down for his followers become divine commands, involving, if disobeyed, not just breaches of ethical principles, which society may condemn, but possibly (eternally) punishable sins against God:

> For where it is supposed that God has spoken on some matter of conduct, then deliberately to act wrongly . . . [has] the . . . character of disobedience, of wilful disrespect, shown towards overwhelming authority, and . . . power. (p. 141)

Warnock does not agree with Kant that there can be a reverential attitude to an autonomous moral law, comparable to the one the religious believer has towards ethical principles that he regards as divine commands. Without God, there is a sense in which anything is permitted; but, once God comes into the picture, there really are imperatives. And, of course, as Jonathan Edwards argues (see **pp. 207–9**), if God exists, his infinite powers have serious implications for human beings' freedom and moral responsibility.

G. E. M. Anscombe on religion and ethics (see recommended edition on p. 181)

G. E. M. Anscombe (1919–2001)

Gertrude Elizabeth Anscombe read Greats at St Hugh's College, Oxford, and, after fellowships at Newnham, Cambridge, and Somerville, Oxford, was professor of philosophy at Cambridge (1970–86). A disciple of Ludwig Wittgenstein, and later one of his literary executors, her publications include a translation of Wittgenstein's *Philosophical Investigations* (1953), *Intention* (1957), *An Introduction to Wittgenstein's Tractatus* (1959) and *Collected Papers* (1981).

No emphasis in Aristotle on moral culpability

In her 'Modern Moral Philosophy', Anscombe notes the fundamental part played by Aristotle's *Nicomachean Ethics* (see **pp. 105–14**) in shaping the course and content of moral philosophy and ethics for over two and a half thousand years. However, his approach differs from that of modern moral philosophers: in particular, in his relative lack of emphasis on the issue of moral culpability. Modern moral philosophy gives terms like 'should', 'needs', 'ought' and 'must', when used in a moral context, a sense which suggests being obliged by law, equating failure to do as one morally ought with breaking a law. If this did not come from Aristotle, how did it arise?

A *law* conception of ethics

Anscombe's answer is: from Christianity, 'with its *law* conception of ethics' (p. 179). As Christianity's ethical rules (such as the Ten Commandments: see **pp. 185–6**) are divinely ordained, breaking them means disobeying the commands of God, the divine law-giver. Anscombe argues that, as a result of Christianity's long dominance of western society, the concept of being bound by law has become so deeply embedded in moral language that it has outlived the belief in divine law in which it originates:

if such a conception is dominant . . . and then is given up, it is a natural result that the concepts of 'obligation', of being bound or required as by a law, should remain though they had lost their root. (p. 180)

Her (debatable) view is that this belief was abandoned after the Reformation; but it is certainly true that only a minority of committed religious believers hold it in today's secular society. Anscombe believes that Hume, in the *Treatise of Human Nature* (see **pp. 23–7**), and modern moral philosophers, have shown that, without belief in God and a divine law conception of ethics (and being punished for disobedience), the idea of 'morally ought' lacks substance and force, and should be dropped:

Hume and our present-day ethicists had done a considerable service by showing that no content could be found in the notion 'morally ought' . . . the latter . . . try to find an alternative (very fishy) content and to retain the psychological force of the term. It would be most reasonable to drop it. It has no reasonable sense outside a law conception of ethics. (p. 183)

3 Are things good just because God wills them?: Plato's *Euthyphro* (see recommended edition on **p. 181**)

Plato (c. 429–347 BC)

For brief biographical details of Plato, see **pp. 5–6**.

An 'unholy' act

In the *Euthyphro*, Plato explores the issue of whether something is good or right (his term is 'holy'), because God (or the gods) loves or wills it, or does God (the gods) love or will it because it is good or right? The scene is set in 399 BC, just before Socrates' trial for undermining belief in the gods and corrupting youth. At the Porch of the King Archon (the chief magistrate for religious matters), in the market-place in Athens, Socrates encounters Euthyphro, a self-professed expert on religion who, Socrates is astounded to discover, proposes to prosecute his father for unintentionally bringing about the death of a day-labourer. The man had murdered a servant, and had died while Euthyphro's father was detaining him. Socrates observes that Euthyphro must have very exact knowledge of what is holy and unholy, to be certain that, in prosecuting his own father, instead of showing him the respect that, in ancient Greek society, sons owed to fathers, he is not committing an unholy act himself.

Which way around is it?

This leads to discussion of what is holy (good or right), during the course of which Euthyphro defines it as 'whatever all the gods love' (p. 13). However, Socrates forces Euthyphro to acknowledge what it means to say that a thing is in a state of 'being loved' or 'being seen'. Its being loved or seen is the consequence of someone loving or seeing it, not the reason why s/he loves or sees it:

> **Socrates.** Then what is loved-by-the-gods is not the holy . . . nor is the holy what is loved-by-the-gods . . . they differ from each other.
> **Euthyphro.** How so . . . ?
> **Socrates.** Because . . . the holy is loved because it is holy, not holy because it is loved?
> **Euthyphro.** Yes.
> **Socrates.** Whereas what is loved-by-the-gods is so because the gods love it. It is loved-by-the-gods by virtue of their loving it; it is not because it is in that state that they love it.
> **Euthyphro.** That's true. (p. 15)

The gods (and the argument can be applied to God) do not love the things that are holy, good or right because these things are in a state of being loved by them, but because, by being things that are holy, good or right, they are things that are lovable, or worthy of being loved by them:

> **Socrates.** But if what is loved-by-the-gods and the holy were the same thing . . . then if the holy were loved because it is holy, what is loved-by-the-gods would be loved because it is loved-by-the-gods; and again, if what is loved-by-the-gods were loved-by-the-gods because they love it . . . the holy would be holy because they love it . . . however, you can see that the two of them are related in just the opposite way, as two entirely different things: one of them is lovable because they love it . . . the other they love for the reason that it is lovable. (pp. 15–16)

Assessment

Therefore, holiness, goodness or rightness cannot be equated with, or defined in terms of, being loved, or willed, by the gods or God; and ethical standards are distinct from, and independent of, God's will. And, indeed, any attempt to define them in terms of what God loves or wills would be to commit a form of the **naturalistic fallacy** (see **pp. 27–31**), and mean that to ask if God loves, or wills, what is good, would only be to ask if God loves, or wills, what he loves or wills. Again, it would not then be an open question (see **p. 36**) whether what God loves, or wills, is good or right; but clearly this question can be asked intelligibly.

4 Trying to reduce religion to ethics: R. B. Braithwaite (see recommended edition on p. 181)

R. B. Braithwaite (1900–90)

Richard Bevan Braithwaite read mathematics and moral sciences at King's College, Cambridge, of which he was a fellow from 1924 until his death. A specialist in the philosophy of science, he was Knightbridge Professor of Moral Philosophy from 1953 to 1967. He became an Anglican in middle age, and was particularly interested in the nature of religious belief and religious propositions, which he explores in *An Empiricist's View of the Nature of Religious Belief* (1955). His other works include *Moral Principles and Inductive Policies* (1950) and *Theory of Games as a Tool for the Moral Philosopher* (1955).

Religious statements are not empirically verifiable

As an empiricist philosopher, inclined to regard only empirically verifiable statements as meaningful, Braithwaite is very aware of the difference between religious statements and ordinary empirical ones. There is an obvious difference between a statement like 'John loves Julia', which is, in principle, verifiable through observation of what John says and does, and 'God loves the world'. How can we verify the second statement empirically? In *An Empiricist's View of the Nature of Religious Belief*, Braithwaite maintains that there are three groups of statements with generally clear methods of verification: those about particular matters of empirical fact; scientific hypotheses and other general empirical statements; and the logically necessary statements of logic and mathematics. Religious statements do not belong to any of these groups; but, this is not true only of religious statements. Moral statements, like 'the utilitarian principle', that actions are right to the extent that they promote happiness, are not logically necessary or empirically verifiable statements either; but, as they guide conduct, they clearly have some sort of meaning (p. 235).

Religious statements are a type of moral statement

Braithwaite thinks that, although moral statements cannot be empirically verified, they are meaningful: they get their meaning from their use, which is to guide conduct. He argues that the same is true of religious statements, which are a type of moral statement. They are used to express a person's attitude: that he will act in the way specified. Thus, the Christian's intention to follow a Christian way of life 'is not only the criterion for the sincerity of his belief in the assertions of Christianity; it is the criterion for the meaningfulness of his assertions' (p. 239).

Religious statements may not refer explicitly to a moral principle

But a lot of religious statements look more like empirical statements than moral ones. Saying that we should act in ways that will maximize pleasure and minimize pain is obviously intended to guide conduct; but what about statements like 'God is Love' or 'God loves the world'? These seem to be about God's nature and his relationship to the world, as well as love. How are they conduct-guiding? Braithwaite's answer is that, unlike moral statements, religious ones may not refer explicitly to a moral principle. Rather, they are representative of a particular religion's statements. The person who makes them indicates his adherence to that religion's way of life. So, to take Braithwaite's example, unless a Christian's assertion that God is love (*agape*) indicates his intention to follow 'an agapeistic way of life' (see **pp. 186–9**), there is no connection between his belief and his practice (p. 240).

Use of concrete examples

Focusing on a statement like 'God is love' strengthens Braithwaite's argument, but, if we look at the Apostles' Creed, it contains statements about transcendent reality (that God is the 'Maker of heaven and earth' and that Jesus Christ was his 'only Son'); historical statements that Jesus lived on earth, and was 'crucified, dead, and buried'; and so on. These do not

173

have even an implicit reference to moral principles and guiding conduct. However, Braithwaite argues that we cannot take a religious statement in isolation, and expect it to specify a rule of conduct. At one level, uttering it commits the individual (in the case of Christianity) to an agapeistic way of life; at another, the moral teaching and the conduct required are embodied in 'concrete examples' of agapeistic behaviour, like the Parable of the Good Samaritan (p. 242). Again, in the 'higher religions', such as Christianity, there is a concern with underlying attitudes, as well as behaviour: with, for example (in the Sermon on the Mount), anger that can lead to violence, as well as violence itself (p. 242).

Distinguishing the religious assertions of one religion from another

So, religious assertions are moral assertions of a special kind. But are there any differences between the 'religio-moral' assertions of one religion and another, if they advocate similar behavioural policies, as do, in Braithwaite's view, the religions he focuses on (Christianity, Judaism and Buddhism)? Braithwaite thinks there are. The actual behaviour policies that religious believers affirm their intention to follow may be common to all three religions, but they are linked to 'different *stories*', which form the different religious traditions (p. 244).

Religious stories

Braithwaite explains what he means by a religious story, and its role in encouraging good conduct. A story is a proposition, or set of propositions, stating certain facts, and this element is lacking in purely moral statements. The religious believer thinks of these stories, and the facts they relate, in connection with his resolution to follow the way of life prescribed by his religion, and they will inspire him to do so. When someone professes his belief in all the stories of, for example, Christianity, he is not truly a Christian, unless he proposes to live according to Christian moral principles and associates his intention of so doing with Christian stories:

> To assert the whole set of assertions of the Christian religion is both to tell the doctrinal story and to confess allegiance to the Christian way of life. (p. 245)

Assessment

Is Braithwaite's characterization of religion correct? Are the stories actually true? Does it matter if they are? Do the followers of particular religions believe that their religion's stories are true? Are they expected to? Does it matter whether they do so or not? Clearly, Braithwaite is not describing most religious people's view of religion. The majority of Christians, when they recite the creed, are saying things they believe to be objectively true, such as that God created the world. They may also believe that this shows that God loves the world, and that they should do likewise, but they do not repeat the statement, Sunday by Sunday, just as an exhortation to love each other. In fact, Braithwaite's use of the word 'story' confuses the issue. Jesus told stories, such as the Parable of the Good Samaritan, to encourage loving conduct, and these are not regarded as records of actual events. But, Christians believe that the story of Jesus' life, however imperfectly recorded in the Gospels, describes actual events. They also believe that teachings about God's existence, nature and loving attitude towards the beings he has created record truths about ultimate reality.

But none of this matters to Braithwaite. Religious stories may refer to human beings (such as Jesus, Moses and the Buddha), who are supposed to have lived in the past, and these people would have been empirically observable, if they had existed; but it is not important whether or not they did, or that religious people should believe that they did (see also **p. 82**). What matters is that the story or stories should be entertained in thought, in order to reinforce good conduct. Indeed, it is almost preferable if the stories are not (regarded as) true, as this removes limits on their interpretation and use. What matters in religious conviction is not the stories, but resolving to follow a morally commendable way of life:

> In religious conviction the resolution to follow a way of life is primary; it is not derived from believing . . . any empirical story. The story may psychologically support the resolution, but does not logically justify it. (p. 249)

A **moral belief** is an intention to behave in a certain way; a **religious belief** is a moral belief, together with the entertainment of certain stories, which are associated with this intention in the believer's mind.

5 Putting God first: Kierkegaard's *Fear and Trembling* (see recommended edition on **p. 181**)

Søren Kierkegaard (1813–55)

Søren Abaye Kierkegaard studied theology at the University of Copenhagen, and then devoted himself to study and writing. His focus on the implications of religious belief, individual choice and despair, and the individual's relationship with God, make him the first existentialist thinker and writer. As well as *Fear and Trembling* (1843), his books include *Either/Or* (1843), *Philosophical Fragments* (1844), *Practice in Christianity* (1850) and *For Self-Examination: Judge for Yourself* (1851). He was a major influence on both theistic and non-theistic philosophers and theologians, such as Paul Tillich, Martin Buber and Jean-Paul Sartre.

Abraham: exemplar of faith

In *Fear and Trembling*, Kierkegaard explores the nature of faith in God; what it means to have such faith; and its implications for how we should lead our lives and make our ethical decisions, by focusing on Abraham, regarded as an **exemplar of faith**. At God's command, Abraham left the comfort of his own country, to become a foreigner in the Promised Land. God has told him that he will be the forefather of many generations, and he goes on believing it, despite the fact that, realistically, he and his wife, Sarah, are too old to have children. And then, when the long-hoped-for son finally arrives, God tests him again, and orders him to sacrifice Isaac. But Abraham's faith is equal to the test:

> he did not doubt . . . He knew it was God the Almighty who tested him, he knew it was the hardest sacrifice that could be demanded of him, but he also knew that no sacrifice was too hard when God demanded it. (p. 18)

So, what does it mean to have faith like Abraham's? It is not a vague hope about what may happen in the next life, but relates to this life, and to the conviction that, for and through God, anything, however absurd, is possible. This is why Abraham can respond cheerfully and trustingly to God's extraordinary command, which shatters all accepted ethical principles, and overturns the responsibilities of father to son, without, as would be the case with one who lacked faith, losing all hope for the future.

Faith and ethics

But (Kierkegaard asks) is Abraham's willingness to sacrifice his son, in obedience to God's command, admirable or outrageous? People say they admire Abraham's faith, and what he did because of it, but what if somebody today showed the same degree of faith, and tried to copy him? Ethically, Abraham intended to murder his son. Would not the same clergy, who commend Abraham as an example, condemn a modern Abraham, and want to put him in an asylum for the insane, or execute him? Society would also discourage such a man in case foolish people tried to copy him. The nature of modern society means that faith and its consequences (particularly its implications for accepted ethical standards) are acceptable only if locked safely away in the past:

> if faith is taken away . . . all that remains is the brutal fact that Abraham intended to murder Isaac, which is easy enough for anyone to imitate who does not have faith . . . Can one then speak candidly about Abraham without running the risk that an individual in mental confusion might go and do likewise? (pp. 24–5)

Kant, Hegel and the universality of ethical precepts

So, do God's commands take precedence over morality? Kierkegaard considers whether, if there is a conflict between God's command and an accepted moral principle (a 'universal' ethical precept), the individual who has faith should obey God's command, or abide by the universal ethical precept. He poses this dilemma in the context of the moral philosophies of Kant (see **pp. 69–85**) and Hegel. Kant had argued that moral laws, which must be obeyed for their own sake, and not for any other motive, or because of their consequences, and which human beings discover *a priori*, in their reason, apply universally and directly to all human beings as rational beings; and that a rational being ought never to act, except in such a way that he could also will that the maxim of his action should become a universal law. However, Hegel had argued that moral laws are expressed in national life, laws and customs. Instead of discovering moral laws in his own reason, the individual complies with his nation's universally accepted ethical precepts, which determine his whole ethical life. The individual abolishes his own individuality, to become the universal, while the ethical has no end beyond itself, but is the end of everything outside itself.

A *teleological suspension of the ethical*

However, this eliminates individual moral decision-making, which is regarded as a form of moral evil:

> The ethical . . . is the universal . . . it applies to everyone . . . It . . . has nothing outside itself that is its telos [end], but is itself the telos for everything outside . . . As soon as the single individual wants to assert himself . . . over against the universal, he sins and only by acknowledging this can be reconciled again with the universal. (p. 46)

But, where does this leave a man of faith, like Abraham, who is prepared to breach a fundamental principle of accepted morality, in order to obey God's command? Either he is wrong, and should be condemned, or he is right, and what Kierkegaard calls the 'paradox of faith' must be accepted: that the single individual is capable of an absolute relation with God, and is higher than universal ethical precepts, which can be set aside, or 'teleologically' suspended, to serve the higher purpose of obeying God:

> Faith is precisely this paradox, that the single individual . . . is higher than the universal . . . that the single individual as the particular stands in an absolute relation to the absolute . . . faith is this paradox . . . or else Abraham is lost. (p. 48)

But what if the man of faith is wrong? Then he is simply a murderer. This underlines the terrifying responsibility the man of faith assumes, when he obeys God, and defies society and its ethical precepts. One who subordinates his individuality to the state or society runs no risks, but the man of faith must bear the full burden of responsibility for his teleological suspension of the ethical. Like Mary, the mother of Jesus, whose response to God's call was unknown to anyone else, he must be prepared to face society's condemnation:

> The story of Abraham contains then a teleological suspension of the ethical. As the single individual he became higher than the universal. This is the paradox that cannot be mediated . . . If that is not the case . . . he is not even a tragic hero but a murderer. (p. 58)

An absolute duty to God

Kierkegaard explores a way around the problem of a clash between duty to God and universal ethical duties: to do as Braithwaite suggests (see pp. 172–5), and subsume the first in the second, so that duty to God becomes just performing ethical duties. For Kierkegaard, this would make Hegel right, and mean that individual moral choice must be given up, in favour of obeying universally accepted ethical precepts. But then God would just vanish into morality, and any other way of serving him would become unacceptable, preventing Abraham being held up as an exemplar of faith:

> The ethical is the universal and as such in turn the divine. It is therefore right to say that every duty, after all, is duty to God, but if no more can be said, then one is saying as well that I really have no duty to God . . . God becomes an invisible vanishing point, an impotent thought, his power being only in the ethical. (p. 59)

However, as there is an individual relationship with, and an absolute duty to, God, the individual is higher than morality, while his relation to God determines his relation to morality, not the other way round. And, if duty to God, and obeying his commands, is absolute, it is ethical precepts that become relative. The paradox of the Abraham story is that, ethically, 'the father must love the son. This ethical relation is reduced to the relative in contradistinction to the absolute relation to God' (p. 62).

The loneliness of those who regard their duty to God as absolute

However, this duty to God cannot be accommodated within society's universally accepted ethical code, according to which Abraham is a murderer. Kierkegaard notes the pressure that society places on the individual to follow its ethical precepts. It wants its members to renounce individual decision-making, fearing the consequences. It would also be much easier for God-obedient individuals, like Abraham, if they could be like everybody else, and abide by society's ethical code. For, as what he is doing is between himself and God, he stands outside society's accepted ethical code, and cannot explain his actions to those whose lives are wholly governed by it.

Ethics and sin

Kierkegaard raises the point of how those who believe that our whole duty to God consists in obeying society's ethical code manage to accommodate sin. If they believe in the God of Christianity, they cannot ignore sin. Yet, if they acknowledge sin, they go beyond society's ethical code, because sin involves the issue of individual disobedience of God and its consequences:

> An ethics that ignores sin is an altogether futile discipline, but if it asserts sin, then it is for that very reason beyond itself. (p. 86)

Assessment

Fear and Trembling makes it clear why Kierkegaard is regarded as the first (Christian) **existentialist** (philosophical approach emphasizing the importance of individual choice) writer. Through the story of Abraham, he sets out the **ethical dilemma** that may confront the religious believer: does he put his relationship with God first, and accept an **absolute duty** to obey God's commands, or does he conform to society's **universal ethical precepts**? The costs of choosing the former may be immense, involving sacrifice, isolation, and social condemnation. Again, society is bound to be suspicious of the single individual who holds that its ethical code can be teleologically suspended. Praising a person of faith from the distant past, like Abraham, is one thing, but coming to terms with having one in its midst is another. Even if it accepts his genuineness, society is bound to be concerned about the impact his example may have on the impressionable and impetuous. However, the person of faith knows that, for God, anything, however absurd, is possible, and that one who loves God needs nothing else.

But does the relationship between faith and the ethical have to be as Kierkegaard describes it? Is it a stark choice: for God or not; for obedience to God, whatever he demands, or for conformity with generally accepted ethical principles? When first told about Kierkegaard's interpretation of the Abraham story, C. S. Lewis was unimpressed, "'Tell me no more," he brusquely interjected; "the man was pathological"' (Keefe, p. 90). However, for some, the choice is a stark one; and many of those who have made the choice against God have found Kierkegaard as inspiring as those who have embraced faith. For others, it is not so dramatic. They prefer to base their decision on careful evaluation of the arguments, and, even if they conclude that God exists and should be obeyed, they also believe that, if God is the all-loving God of, for example, Christianity, he would never issue commands that would breach fundamental ethical principles, or involve harming others.

Core texts

G. E. M. Anscombe, 'Modern Moral Philosophy', in W. D. Hudson (ed.) *The Is/Ought Question*, London: Macmillan, 1969.

R. B. Braithwaite, *An Empiricist's View of the Nature of Religious Belief*, in J. H. Hick (ed.), *The Existence of God*, New York: Macmillan, 1972.

Søren Kierkegaard, *Fear and Trembling*, eds C. S. Evans and S. Walsh, Cambridge: Cambridge University Press, 2006.

Plato, *Defence of Socrates, Euthyphro, Crito*, trans. and ed. D. Gallop, Oxford and New York: Oxford University Press, 1997.

G. J. Warnock, *The Object of Morality*, London: Methuen, 1971.

Suggestions for further reading and research

R. E. Allen, *Plato's Euthyphro and the Earlier Theory of Forms*, London: Routledge and Kegan Paul, 1970.

S. B. Babbage, 'To the Royal Air Force', in C. Keefe (ed.), *C. S. Lewis, Speaker and Teacher*, London: Hodder and Stoughton, 1971.

W. W. Bartley III, *Morality and Religion*, London: Macmillan, 1971 (chapter 2).

A. Hannay, *The Cambridge Companion to Kierkegaard*, Cambridge: Cambridge University Press, 1997.

J. H. Hick, *Philosophy of Religion*, Englewood Cliffs, NJ: Prentice-Hall, 1963 (chapter 6).

W. McDonald, 'Søren Kierkegaard' (rev. 2006), in E. N. Zalta (ed.), *Stanford Encyclopaedia of Philosophy*, at http://plato.stanford.edu.

D. Mills Daniel, *Briefly: Kierkegaard's Fear and Trembling*, London: SCM Press, 2007.

J. Watkin, *Kierkegaard*, London: Geoffrey Chapman, 1997.

11 Understanding and Interpreting Christian Ethics

1 God and ethics

The Christian God

Geoffrey Warnock points out that a God who is neither 'all-too-human' nor 'utterly non-human' will have a major impact on the believer's attitude to ethical questions (see **pp. 168–9**). The Christian God certainly matches Warnock's criteria. An invisible, eternal, transcendent, all-powerful, all-knowing being, who created the universe and all that it contains from nothing, but who has himself always existed, or never not-existed, he is far from being 'all-too-human'. But neither is he 'utterly non-human'. Christians believe that he is a **personal God,** who is all-loving, and cares about each individual human being. Through **Jesus** (called God's son), who was human, but who embodied, and revealed in his life on earth, God's infinite love for human beings, God brought about human beings' salvation. As well as loving human beings, he has an ultimate purpose for them: after physical death, they will have eternal life with him, the proof of which is Jesus' resurrection and ascent to heaven. And, as C. S. Lewis points out, the very idea of eternal life transforms the ethical perspective: 'there are a good many things which would not be worth bothering about if I were gong to live only seventy years, but which I had better bother about very seriously if I am going to live for ever' (Lewis, *Mere Christianity*, p. 68).

The Christian ethical perspective

Christians' world picture, and therefore ethical perspective, is different from that of agnostics or atheists; and Kierkegaard's *Fear and Trembling* makes clear just how different it can be. If the Christian God exists, human beings' ethical universe has to include a transcendent, all-powerful creator; and Kierkegaard's insistence that the believer's relationship to such a God is absolute, and takes precedence over other obligations including generally accepted ethical principles, is understandable (see **pp. 178–9**). Even if God's commands shatter conventional ethical principles, there must be a good reason, which only he knows; and if he is all-loving, what he commands must be right, even if it seems not to be.

God-centred ethics

We sometimes talk of 'Christian ethics', as if it were just one more ethical approach, like consequentialist, deontological or virtue ethics, which can be critically assessed, and then adopted in whole or in part. Often, people focus on the **Sermon on the Mount**, in which Jesus stresses loving attitudes to fellow human beings and the importance of controlling the motives underlying wrong actions, and they think these principles can be used to enrich secular morality. But that is not how Jesus intended them. He was teaching his followers how to lead the lives of members of God's kingdom. Christians are to love other human beings, not just because they are intrinsically valuable human persons, to whose preferences or interests they should give equal weight with their own, but because God created and loves them, and loving them is part of a Christian's duty to God.

Being loving

The Sermon on the Mount has a lot to say about being loving, but how is this to be put into practice, day by day? No ethical system can answer every ethical dilemma, but, from a purely secular point of view, answers are more likely to be found in Kant, Bentham or Mill than in the Sermon on the Mount.

2 Creation (Genesis 1.1 and 26–7)

God and creation

The book of Genesis, which brings together two distinct accounts of creation (the Priestly Account, Genesis 1.1–2.4a; and the J-E Account, 2.4b–25), begins: 'In the beginning God created the heavens and the earth' (Genesis 1.1). It does not provide an accurate scientific or historical account of the universe's origin; its significance is its teaching about the relationship between God and creation. The universe and all it contains owe their existence to God. Nothing would exist, or go on existing, unless God wills it. Therefore, the distinction between creator and all created things is absolute. Whereas God is infinite and has his 'own necessity', the universe and its contents are finite, contingent and dependent: they are things that are possible 'to be and not to be' (Aquinas, *Summa Theologica* Ia q. 2 a. 3). Human beings are as finite and wholly dependent upon God as any other created thing:

> then the Lord God formed man of dust from the ground, and breathed into his nostrils the breath of life; and man became a living being. (Gen. 2.7)

Made in God's image

Yet, human beings are different from the rest of the created order:

> Then God said, 'Let us make man in our image, after our likeness . . . So God created man in his own image . . . male and female he created them. (Gen. 1.26a, 27)

As rational beings, human beings were created in God's 'image', to have a special relationship with him; and their special status in the created order has important ethical implications. Human life is precious to God and uniquely valuable. This is the Christian doctrine of the sanctity of human life, which holds that it must always be respected and preserved: 'Whoever sheds the blood of man, by man shall his blood be shed; for God made man in his own image' (Gen. 9.6).

Human dominion over the rest of creation

Human beings also have a special position in relation to the rest of the created order. God has put them in charge of it:

and let them have dominion over the fish of the sea, and over the birds of the air, and over the cattle, and over all the earth. (Gen. 1.26b)

Their 'dominion' has been variously interpreted. For some, it gives human beings a free hand to use creation as they wish: a view that has had serious consequences for animals and the environment; for others, that God has entrusted them with the care of his creation, of which they must be responsible stewards (see **pp. 322–5** and **332–4**).

Assessment

Christian teaching about the **sanctity of human life** is extremely influential, and is shared by many who are neither Christian nor religious. But it is not altogether straightforward. Is human life to be regarded as uniquely precious and inviolable from the moment of conception; or only from a certain stage of development? This issue arises in relation to abortion and embryo research (see **pp. 224–6** and **249–50**). Human beings' special moral status has contributed to an **anthropocentric** (human being-centred) ethical outlook. But, what about other creatures? Do they have moral status, or does Christianity endorse '**speciesism**' and human exploitation of them (see **pp. 318–25, 328–9**)?

3 The Ten Commandments (Exodus 20.12–17, 20)

Responsibilities to others

During the people of Israel's long journey to the Promised Land, after liberation from slavery in Egypt, Moses receives the Ten Commandments. These contain ethical principles, which are essential to a civilized secular, as well as a religious, society: respect for life ('You shall not kill': Exod. 20.13); respect for property ('You shall not steal': 20.15); and recognition of the importance of honesty and integrity in relation to others ('You shall not bear false witness against your neighbour': 20.16). They also cover sexual relationships ('You shall not commit adultery': 20.14); the importance of curbing the lust and avarice that lead to sexual immorality and crime ('You shall not covet your neighbour's house . . . wife . . . or anything that is your neighbour's': 20.17); and acknowledgement of children's obligations to parents ('Honour you father and your mother': 20.12).

Obligations to God

Human beings and human society have benefited from following these principles. But, in Exodus 20, the commandments relating to God take precedence. He brought the people of Israel 'out of the land of Egypt', so, on pain of punishment, they must not have, or worship, 'other gods' (20.2–5); they must not take his name 'in vain' (20.7); and they must keep every seventh day as 'a sabbath' for God (20.8). Further, the basis of the obligation to adopt and keep the Ten Commandments is not their benefit to human beings or human society, but the obligation to God. The commandments are part of God's covenant with the people of Israel. They will have a special relationship with him ('you shall be my own possession among all peoples'), provided they 'obey my voice and keep my covenant' (19.5), that is, keep his laws.

Assessment

But, what if God orders actions that do not benefit human beings, such as violent and destructive behaviour? Should he still be obeyed? Many Christians would say no (see **pp. 170–2**), but some would say yes: because God is the omnipotent and omniscient creator, and must know best (see **pp. 176–80**). There is the further question of the 'autonomy' of ethics. If God's will is taken to be the (sole) basis, or meaning, of what is good or bad, right or wrong, this seems to commit a special form of the **naturalistic fallacy**, in relation to God (see **p. 36**): the **'supernaturalistic' fallacy**.

4 Jesus, salvation and the gospel of love (John 3.16–21)

God's love for human beings

Christianity teaches that God is infinite and omnipotent; but its key distinguishing doctrine is that God is all-loving, and manifested his love for human beings, by being incarnated ('made flesh') in the historical figure of Jesus Christ, whose teaching, death and resurrection made salvation available to all:

For God so loved the world that he gave his only Son, that whoever believes in him should not perish but have eternal life. For God sent the Son into the world, not to condemn the world, but that the world might be saved through him. (John 3.16–17)

For the theologian and former Archbishop of Canterbury William Temple, this is 'the central declaration' of Christianity. Not only is God 'Love'; he gave his Son for human beings' redemption:

> No object is sufficient for the love of God short of *the world* itself. Christianity is not one more religion of individual salvation ... It is the one and only religion of world-redemption. (Temple, *Readings in St John's Gospel*, p. 48)

However, John's Gospel makes it clear that redemption and eternal life require faith and loving behaviour by human beings. Those who believe in Jesus, and whose own lives reflect God's love for them, will be saved. Those who do not are 'condemned already', because they have 'not believed in the name of the only Son of God' (John 3.18):

> For every one who does evil hates the light, and does not come to the light, lest his deeds should be exposed. But he who does what is true comes to the light, that it may be clearly seen that his deeds have been wrought in God. (John 3.20–1)

Those who are confronted by Jesus, and the love God shows through Jesus, must choose:

> since the Son of God, Himself love, life, light, and truth, has come into the world, and there is no love, light, life, or truth which does not take its origin from Him, acceptance of his witness ... are essential; and rejection of Him or disbelief in Him is therefore acceptance of ... hatred, death, darkness, and falsehood. (Lightfoot, *St John's Gospel*, p. 118)

The incarnation

How can Jesus be the incarnation, in history, of God and his love? Unhelpfully, the traditional Christian creeds speak of him in terms of 'substance', as:

> the only-begotten Son of God ... of one substance with the Father ... Who for us men and for our salvation came down from heaven, and was incarnate by the Holy Spirit of the Virgin Mary, and was made man. (The Nicene Creed)

But can someone be a human being and also 'of one substance' with God? For Kant (see **p. 82**), Jesus' nature, and whether or not he was a real person, do not matter. His significance is to represent the ideal of a morally perfect human being, whom human beings must try to emulate. But, for most Christians, it is important that the incarnation actually happened, 'at a particular time and place' (Temple, *Readings in St John's Gospel*, p. 48).

John Hick explains the nature of the incarnation, by focusing on the distinction between God's metaphysical attributes, such as his eternity, omnipotence and omniscience, and his moral attributes, such as his goodness and love. The Christian doctrine of the incarnation maintains that the latter, but not the former, have been 'embodied . . . in a finite human life, namely, that of the Christ' (Hick, *Philosophy of Religion*, p. 84). This enables Christians:

> to point to the person of Christ as showing what is meant by assertions such as 'God is good' and 'God loves his human creatures'. The moral attitudes of God toward mankind are held to have been incarnated in Jesus and expressed concretely in his dealings with men and women. (p. 84)

In the compassion Jesus showed for the 'sick and the spiritually blind', and his 'forgiving of sins', Christians can see 'God's compassion' and 'God's forgiveness'; and practise them in their own lives (p. 84).

The Christian principle of agape *love*

The First Letter of John declares: 'if God so loved us, we also ought to love one another . . . if we love one another, God abides in us and his love is perfected in us' (1 John 4.11–12). But what is God's love? It is not like ordinary human love, but is *agape* love, of the kind Jesus showed, even to those who persecuted him:

> It knows no boundaries . . . Its sphere is the whole realm of our relationships with other people, both direct and indirect. (Hick, *Christianity at the Centre*, p. 29)

Agape love does not depend on 'the desirableness of its object', nor does it relate to particular relationships or obligations, such as those between sexual partners, family members, or those of the same community, race or culture (p. 29). Christian love is:

> unconditional in its nature and universal in its range . . . a giving love, going out to people not because they have any special characteristics . . . but simply because they are *there*, because they are persons, neighbours under God. (p. 30)

Christians are asked to develop in themselves, and to show to others, this unconditional *agape* love.

Assessment

It sounds magnificent, and the world would no doubt be better for more care and compassion. But, is it possible to 'love' (as opposed to care about) those we do not know, as 'neighbours under God'? We understand what it means for a husband or wife to love each other, or a parent to love a child, but does it make sense to talk of undifferentiated love for (for example) all the poor people in the world? Again, *agape* love is regarded as superior to ordinary human love, because the latter exists between people with a specific relationship to each other. But can we 'love' anyone, apart from those we know, and to whom we stand in a particular relationship; and for whom we are prepared to make any degree of sacrifice?

And, how is *agape* love to be put into practice in specific situations? As situation ethics shows (see **pp. 138–53**), 'being loving' could lead the moral agent in more than one direction. Is it more loving to tell someone he has a few days to live, so he can put his affairs in order; or to withhold the information and spare him fear and pain? Is it more loving for a parent with little money to give £100 to a beggar whose basic needs are not being met, but for whom he has no special responsibility, or to spend it on a new computer, which, though not essential, will help his children, to whom he does have specific obligations, to do their homework more easily?

5 The two greatest commandments (Mark 12.28–31)

In Mark's Gospel, this passage comes at the end of a series of questions, intended to 'entrap' Jesus (12.13). Then a scribe enquires:

> 'Which commandment is the first of all?' Jesus answered, 'The first is, "Hear, O Israel: The Lord our God . . . is one; and you shall love . . . God with all your heart, and with all your soul, and with all your mind, and with all your strength." The second is this, "You shall love your neighbour as yourself." There is no other commandment greater than these.' (12.28–31)

Jesus is saying that loving God, which is a response to his love, and loving human beings, are closely related. Our love of God is reflected in our love of others:

true love of the neighbour springs from . . . love of God . . . there can be no true love of God which does not express itself in love of the neighbour. (Nineham, *The Gospel of St Mark*, p. 326)

Assessment

This underlines the different starting points of **Christian** and **secular ethics**. Whereas the Christian ethic is grounded in God's love of human beings and their love of God, the secular ethic is grounded in human beings' responsibilities to other human beings, whether to maximize their happiness (utilitarian); treat them as ends not means (Kantian); or to develop the virtues that will contribute to the well-being of the individual and society (virtue ethics).

6 The parable of the Good Samaritan: love in action (Luke 10.29–37)

But who are our neighbours? A lawyer tests Jesus, by asking how he can 'inherit eternal life' (Luke 10:25). After Jesus has given the answer, recorded in Mark 12, the lawyer asks Jesus to define 'neighbour'; and Jesus replies with this well-known parable. Despite the mutual hostility between Jews and Samaritans (who were regarded as outcasts and sinners), it is a Samaritan who helps the wounded robbery victim, and treats him as a neighbour. Jesus urges the lawyer to '"Go and do likewise"' (10.37).

The point of the story is clear. Jesus:

tells the story . . . not to answer the question, 'Who is my neighbour?' but to show that it is the wrong question. The proper question is, 'To whom can I be a neighbour?' and the answer is, 'To anyone whose need constitutes a claim on my love.' (Caird, *The Gospel of St Luke*, p. 148)

Assessment

Do we need to understand, or explain, the Samaritan's conduct in terms of 'love'? Did he need to love the injured man as his neighbour? Or was the Samaritan just applying a universal ethical principle (see **pp. 53–9** and **72–3**) of, 'always help people in distress, if you can do so'; and the fact that the former was of a different and hostile race did not constitute a relevant reason for not doing so?

7 The Sermon on the Mount

Selections from Matthew, chapters 5–7

As Joachim Jeremias explains, the Sermon on the Mount is a collection of Jesus' ethical teachings, delivered on different occasions, which spell out the implications of Christian belief for human conduct.

The Old Law and the New (Matthew 5.21–6, 38–42, 43–8)

Here, Jesus contrasts the Old Law, given by Moses, with his New Law, which sets more exacting ethical standards.

Conquering anger

The sixth commandment forbids (unlawful) killing, but Jesus addresses and condemns the motive of anger which impels people to violence and murder: 'every one who is angry with his brother shall be liable to judgment' (5.22). Christians must not insult others ('whoever says, "You fool!" shall be liable to the hell of fire', 5.22), while achieving reconciliation with opponents, including those they have wronged, takes precedence even over religious duties:

> if you are offering your gift at the altar, and there remember that your brother has something against you, leave your gift there before the altar and go; first be reconciled to your brother . . . (5.23–4)

Non-resistance

The Old Law permitted someone who had suffered a wrong to exact appropriate retribution from the perpetrator ('eye for eye, tooth for tooth', Exodus 21.24), but Jesus will not allow Christians to take revenge, resist aggression ('Do not resist one who is evil', Matthew 5.39), or even to insist on their rights.

> if any one strikes you on the right cheek, turn to him the other also; and if any one would sue you and take your coat, let him have your cloak as well; and if any one forces you to go one mile, go with him two miles. (5.39–41)

Jesus' examples make his point powerfully. A blow on the right cheek (with the back of the hand) was regarded as especially insulting. A creditor or court could demand a coat or undergarment in payment, but not the cloak or outer garment. The Roman occupying forces in Palestine requisitioned goods and services from the civilian population: such demands are to be met willingly, not reluctantly, and in excess of what is required. This teaching has had a tremendous influence on attitudes to war (see **pp. 314–16**). Those who take it literally practise pacifism, even in the face of aggression. But was Jesus' behaviour consistent with his own teaching? In Matthew 21.12–13, he is shown overturning the moneychangers' tables, and driving them out of the Temple. And, the evils of Hitler's Germany were so great that Dietrich Bonhoeffer joined in resistance to them (see **pp. 140–1 and 195–7**).

Loving your neighbour

Jesus teaches Christians not to limit their love. The Old Law's command is: 'You shall love your neighbour [Leviticus 19.18] and hate your enemy' (Matthew 5.43). But, for Christians, 'neighbours' include enemies and persecutors: 'Love your enemies and pray for those who persecute you' (5.44). They will thus reflect, in their own lives, the unconditional and indiscriminate love of God, who 'makes his sun rise on the evil and on the good, and sends rain on the just and on the unjust' (5:45).

Forgiveness

Christians must forgive others for the wrongs they have inflicted, because they expect God to forgive the wrongs they have committed:

> For if you forgive men their trespasses, your heavenly Father also will forgive you; but if you do not forgive men their trespasses, neither will your Father forgive your trespasses. (6.14–15)

The Golden Rule

In the 'Golden Rule', Jesus teaches that actions must be based on universal principles (see also **pp. 55–7, 72–30 and 100**). Christians must treat others as they would wish to be treated themselves. Before acting, they must put themselves in the position of those their actions will affect. If they would not like to experience the effects themselves, they should not perform the actions: 'So whatever you wish that men would do to you, do so to them; for this is the law and the prophets' (7.12).

Assessment: Joachim Jeremias, Dietrich Bonhoeffer and Reinhold Niebuhr

Jesus' ethical demands are difficult, if not impossible, to put into practice. Are they to be taken literally? Or, is Jesus setting up an ideal, against which we can measure our conduct, and see its shortcomings? Christian theologians and religious leaders have long debated the interpretation of the **Sermon on the Mount** and its application to the lives of Christians. Below, the views of the biblical scholar Joachim Jeremias, and of two of the twentieth century's greatest Christian theologians and teachers, Dietrich Bonhoeffer and Reinhold Niebuhr, are discussed. Bonhoeffer holds that Jesus meant his teachings as commands, which Christians should carry out, while Niebuhr views them as an ultimate ideal, highlighting the limitations of sinful humanity. Jeremias reminds us that the Sermon's ethical demands must be understood in the context of the early Church's message of salvation (being saved from death) through Jesus.

Joachim Jeremias's *The Sermon on the Mount* (see recommended edition on **p. 199**)

Joachim Jeremias (1900–79)

After studying at the Universities of Tübingen and Leipzig, Joachim Jeremias was Professor of New Testament Studies at the University of Göttingen. A specialist in the history of Judaism and Palestine in Jesus' time, his publications include *The Sermon on the Mount* (1959), *Jesus' Promise to the Nations* (1952), *The Central Message of the New Testament* (1965) and *New Testament Theology* (1971).

A collection of individual teachings

In *The Sermon on the Mount*, Jeremias explains how New Testament scholarship has shown that the Sermon on the Mount is not a sermon Jesus delivered on one occasion, but a later collection of individual teachings. Why was it made?

Kerygma *and* didache

During its earliest period, Christianity had two forms of preaching: proclamation (*kerygma*) and teaching (*didache*). St Paul records the oldest statement of the first in 1 Corinthians:

For I delivered to you . . . what I also received, that Christ died for our sins in accordance with the scriptures, that he was buried, that he was raised on the third day in accordance with the scriptures, and that he appeared to Cephas [Peter], then to the twelve. (15.3–5)

The *kerygma* proclaimed Christ's saving work: that, by his death and resurrection, he had redeemed mankind. The *didache* was ethical teaching, instructing Christians as to how they should lead their lives. So, the Sermon on the Mount was not presented to Christians as a pattern of life they had to follow unaided; it was preceded by the message of salvation: '*the proclamation of the gospel; and . . . by conversion, by a being overpowered by the Good News*' (p. 23).

Your sins are forgiven

Before every saying in the Sermon on the Mount, a protasis or introductory clause must be inserted, to the effect:

'Your sins are forgiven' . . . Therefore, because 'Your sins are forgiven,' there now follows: 'While you are still in the way with your opponent, be reconciled to him quickly'. (p. 30)

Only by beginning with the greatness of God's gifts can 'the heavy nature of the demands which Jesus makes' be understood (p. 32). Further, the Sermon on the Mount is not a complete ethical programme, covering every ethical issue that arises; nor is it a series of rigid regulations that Christians must follow to the letter; rather, its teachings and examples indicate how Christians, conscious of salvation and of God's forgiveness, should lead their lives:

what is here taught is symptoms, signs, examples of what it means when the kingdom of God breaks into the world which is still under sin, death, and the devil . . . the Sermon on the Mount is not law, but gospel. (pp. 33–4)

Dietrich Bonhoeffer's *The Cost of Discipleship* (see recommended edition on **p. 199**)

Dietrich Bonhoeffer (1906–45)

After studying theology at the Universities of Tübingen and Berlin, Dietrich Bonhoeffer became a pastor in the German Lutheran Church. A strong opponent of Hitler, he joined the German resistance during the Second World War, and was arrested in 1943. After two years in prison and concentration camps, he was executed in April 1945. In *The Cost of Discipleship* (1937), Bonhoeffer insists that Christianity offers 'costly' grace. Christians must obey Jesus, and be prepared to face sacrifice and suffering of the kind Jesus endured. His other works include *Act and Being* (1931), *Ethics* (1949) and *Letters and Papers from Prison* (1951).

Cheap grace and costly grace

Bonhoeffer spells out the full implications of what it means to be a Christian. It is tempting to make light of Christianity's demands. Through Jesus' death, God has given human beings grace: unmerited help, to enable them to be saved. But, some Christians think that, because of Jesus' redemptive work, they need make little effort themselves; they believe in cheap grace, not the costly grace of Christianity:

> It is costly because it costs a man his life . . . it is grace because it gives a man the only true life. It is costly because it condemns sin, and grace because it justifies the sinner . . . it is *costly* because it cost God the life of his Son. (p. 37)

And following Jesus may involve suffering, and even death, as it did for Bonhoeffer.

Faith and obedience

Faith (Bonhoeffer insists) means obedience, so, while it is true that only he who believes is obedient, only he who is obedient believes: 'obedience is called the consequence of faith, it must also be called the presupposition of faith' (pp. 54–5). It is the sinner, not the true Christian, who absolves himself from obedience, on the grounds that only those who believe can obey, thus perverting the costly grace of Jesus' call into the cheap grace of self-justification: 'Our sinner has drugged himself with cheap and easy grace' (p. 60). In reality, it is part of every Christian's calling to take up the cross of obedience and suffering.

Following in Jesus' footsteps

The ethical obligations of the truly Christian life are set out in the Sermon on the Mount. It does not contain a list of ideals for Christians to aim at, but clear commands to be carried out. The place for true Christians is, 'on the cross at Golgotha' (p. 103), and they can expect to incur the world's hatred and violence. But this does not excuse them from obedience. They must not feel righteous indignation at offences or wrongs, because Jesus rejects the distinction between it and 'unjustifiable anger', which always attacks 'the brother's life' (p. 116). The true Christian must not be angry, or try to defend himself:

> By his willingly renouncing self-defence, the Christian affirms his absolute adherence to Jesus, and his freedom from the tyranny of his own ego. (p. 128)

Again, if we judge others, we treat them from the outside, in a spirit of detachment; but love has no place for such an approach.

The way of the cross

The distinctive qualities of the lives of Jesus' true followers are self-renunciation, and infinite love, including for enemies and the enemies of Christianity:

> It is unreserved love for our enemies, for the unloving and the unloved, love for our religious, political and personal adversaries . . . it is the love which was fulfilled in the cross of Christ. (p. 137).

Christians can have only 'one all-embracing devotion': to Jesus (p. 157). Many interpretations of the Sermon on the Mount are possible, but there is only one thing Jesus wants from his followers: that they get on with putting it into practice:

> Humanly speaking, we could understand and interpret the Sermon on the Mount in a thousand different ways. Jesus knows only one possibility:

simple surrender and obedience, not interpreting it or applying it, but doing and obeying it . . . he really means us to get on with it. (p. 175)

Reinhold Niebuhr's *An Interpretation of Christian Ethics* (see recommended edition on **p. 199**)

Reinhold Niebuhr (1892–1971)

Reinhold Niebuhr attended Yale Divinity School, and was a pastor in Detroit, before becoming Professor of Christian Ethics at Union Theological Seminary, New York. An active campaigner for social justice, the many terrible events of the first part of the twentieth century impressed on him the extent of human wickedness, and the limits of what human beings and human society can achieve: a position known as Christian Realism. In *An Interpretation of Christian Ethics* (1934), he argues that sinfulness prevents human beings fulfilling the Sermon on the Mount's love ethic. His other works include *Moral Man and Immoral Society* (1932), *The Nature and Destiny of Man* (1941–3) and *Faith and History* (1949).

The nature of a religious ethic

Whereas a secular ethical system concerns regulation of human conduct and making human beings behave better, religious morality probes the original causes of human wickedness and the ultimate purpose of human existence: 'It is concerned . . . with the problem of good and evil, not only with immediate objectives, but with ultimate hopes' (p. 16). Unlike the cultural and ethical values of modern, sceptical and scientifically minded society, it recognizes ultimate sources of good and evil, and the presence in the world of demonic forces, which can impel human beings to extremes of barbarism (as they were in Germany, when Niebuhr wrote his book), and endanger civilization:

> There has been little suggestion in modern culture of the demonic force in human life, of the peril in which all achievements of life and civilization constantly stand because the evil impulses in men may be compounded in collective actions until they reach diabolical proportions. (p. 26)

An uncompromising love ethic

In the Sermon on the Mount (Niebuhr argues), Jesus does not offer a secular ethic, but an absolutist and perfectionist, religious love ethic, which opposes not only selfish human impulses but even the prudent instincts of self-defence. Its only connection is vertical, between God's loving will and that of human beings:

> The absolutism and perfectionism of Jesus' love ethic sets itself uncompromisingly not only against the natural self-regarding impulses, but against the necessary prudent defences of the self . . . It has only a vertical dimension between the loving will of God and the will of man. (p. 49)

An ethic that cannot be fulfilled in the world as it is

Jesus' command to forgive our enemies, and pray for our persecutors, shows his 'intransigence against forms of self-assertion which have social and moral approval in any natural morality', and clearly shows that the Sermon on the Mount does not give 'specific guidance in the detailed problems of social morality where the relative claims of family, community, class, and nation must be constantly weighed' (pp. 55, 61). The basis of Jesus' ethic is eschatological: to do with God's ultimate purpose for the world. His ethic cannot be carried out in the world as it is; it can only be put into practice after God has intervened in the world to change it:

> The ethical demands made by Jesus are incapable of fulfilment in the present existence of man. They proceed from a transcendent and divine unity of essential reality, and their final fulfilment is possible only when God transmutes the present chaos of the world into its final unity. (p. 67)

The role of the ultimate ideal

Faced with the realities of our situation, which springs from evil and sin, human beings have to create an orderly society; and the impossible ideal of Jesus' love ethic will not provide a social ethic, by which to conduct our lives. So, what is its role? It is an ultimate ideal, against which we can measure the shortcomings of a 'prudential social ethic', and which enables us to appreciate the limitations of what we can achieve; to repent; and become recipients of God's grace (p. 61):

It is possible for individuals to be saved from this sinful pretension, not by achieving an absolute perspective upon life, but by their recognition of their inability to do so. Individuals may be saved by repentance . . . the gateway to grace. (p. 99)

Hope, despair and faith

Historically, progress from the basic rights and obligations of early communities to the more extensive ones of advanced societies is an ascent of the ladder of moral possibilities, which gets closer to the law of love. However, human beings must not be over-confident. Christ's example and teaching are our despair, as well as our hope. The key dividing-line is between those who have too much confidence in the potential of human virtue, and those who are so thoroughly aware of its limitations as to despair. Out of this:

arises a new hope centred in the revelation of God in Christ . . . The real crux of the issue between essential Christianity and modern culture lies . . . between those who have a confidence in human virtue which human nature cannot support and those who have looked too deeply into life and their own souls to place their trust in so broken a reed. It is out of such despair . . . that faith arises. (pp. 131–2)

Core texts

Dietrich Bonhoeffer, *The Cost of Discipleship*, rev. edn, London: SCM Press, 1969.

Joachim Jeremias, *The Sermon on the Mount*, Philadelphia, PA: Fortress Press, 1973.

Reinhold Niebuhr, *An Interpretation of Christian Ethics*, London: SCM Press, 1936.

Revised Standard Version of the Bible, New York and Glasgow: Collins, 1971, from which all biblical quotations are taken.

Other references and suggestions for further reading and research

Aquinas, *Summa Theologica*, at http://www.op.org/summa.

G. B. Caird, *The Gospel of Saint Luke*, Harmondsworth: Penguin, 1963.

E. L. Ehrlich, *A Concise History of Israel*, London: Darton, Longman and Todd, 1962.

J. C. Fenton, *The Gospel of Saint Matthew*, Harmondsworth: Penguin, 1963.

R. Gill (ed.), *The Cambridge Companion to Christian Ethics*, Cambridge: Cambridge University Press, 2001.

J. H. Hick, *Philosophy of Religion*, Englewood Cliffs, NJ: Prentice-Hall, 1963 (chapter 6).

J. H. Hick, *Christianity at the Centre*, London: SCM Press, 1968 (chapter 1).

R. H. Lightfoot, *St John's Gospel: A Commentary*, ed. C. F. Evans, Oxford and New York: Oxford University Press, 1956.

C. S. Lewis, *Mere Christianity*, London: Fontana, 1952.

J. Marsh, *The Gospel of Saint John*, London: Penguin, 1963.

C. F. D. Moule, *The Birth of the New Testament*, 2nd edn, London: Adam and Charles Black, 1966.

D. E. Nineham, *The Gospel of Saint Mark*, Harmondsworth: Penguin, 1963.

R. Preston, 'Christian Ethics', in P. Singer (ed.), *A Companion to Ethics*, Cambridge: Cambridge University Press, 1993.

W. Temple, *Readings in St John's Gospel* (chapters 1–12), London: Macmillan, 1939.

J. P. Wogaman, *Christian Ethics: An Historical Introduction*, Louisville, KY: Westminster John Knox Press, 1993.

12 Moral Responsibility: Determinism and Free Will

1 Are we responsible for what we do?

Determinism is the doctrine that every event has a cause. Applied to what are held to be voluntary or freely willed human actions, it suggests they are not actually free. There are three main philosophical responses to the issue. The first is **hard determinism**, which holds that the causal connection between human motives and actions rules out genuine freedom. Below, John Hospers represents this position, while Jonathan Edwards argues for **hard theological determinism**: the view that God's infinite powers (his omniscience and omnipotence) rule out human freedom. The second response is **soft determinism**, represented below by John Locke and David Hume, which maintains that determinism and human freedom are compatible, and that human beings are free (and responsible and punishable for their actions), unless subject to external constraint. The third response is **libertarianism**, represented by Immanuel Kant, which insists that the human will is free, and must be so if human beings are to be held responsible (and punished) for their actions. Aristotle explains the difference between **voluntary** and **involuntary actions**.

2 Voluntary and involuntary actions: Aristotle's *Nicomachean Ethics* (see recommended edition on p. 217)

Aristotle (384–322 BC)

For brief biographical details of Aristotle, see pp. 105–6.

Moral responsibility

Moral responsibility raises the issue of voluntary actions (done of one's own free will) and involuntary (not done of one's own free will): we are held accountable, and praised or blamed, for the former, but not the latter, and, as moral agents, we need to understand the difference between them. Aristotle addresses this question in *The Nicomachean Ethics*.

Voluntary and involuntary actions

Involuntary actions (he explains) arise when a person is subjected to external compulsion or is ignorant of what he is doing, but the dividing-line between voluntary and involuntary actions is not always clear-cut. Mixed actions occur when the agent has the power to perform, or not to perform, the action, but is forced (as by threats to his family) into a wrong action, which he would not normally choose. But, Aristotle does not think that such situations excuse any action, however bad, that the agent performs: there are some things people should 'sooner die than do', and agents are 'praised or blamed' according to how far they have resisted, or yielded to, coercion (p. 51). Further, the agent cannot blame external factors if he succumbs to them easily, or take credit for fine acts but then try to avoid responsibility for disgraceful ones, by attributing them to the compulsive effects of pleasure.

It is ignorance of a particular circumstance that makes an act involuntary

Aristotle further maintains that it is only ignorance of particular circumstances, as when the agent is mistaken about what he is doing, not ignorance of a moral principle, that makes an act involuntary. Someone performing a wrong act, due to the first kind of ignorance, should feel pain, and show repentance, when he realizes what he has done. For example, a person might kill someone accidentally, and the action would be involuntary and excusable, but it would not be, if the agent did it as a result of ignorance that murder is morally wrong. He should know, and would be culpable for not knowing, that it is. Again, there is no distinction, 'in point of voluntariness', between deliberate wrong acts and those due to temper, as both 'considered judgements' and 'irrational fears' are part of human nature, and we must avoid wrong actions, however they arise (p. 54).

Choice

Aristotle notes that moral goodness is closely related to choice, and explores its nature. It follows deliberation, which does not concern ends (what we wish for), but the (best) practical means of realizing our ends: we say we wish to be happy, but not that we choose to be. Having decided the means, we direct our aim; and, as the exercise of the moral virtues relates to means we have chosen, through deliberation, both virtue and vice are in our power. We can do what is right, and not do what is wrong, so we decide what sort of people we are going to be:

> if it is in our power to do a thing when it is right, it will also be in our power not to do it when it is wrong ... if, as we saw, doing right or wrong is the essence of being good or bad, it follows that it is in our power to be decent or worthless. (p. 61)

Rewards and punishments

Aristotle believes that the view that our actions are in our power is borne out by rewards and punishments, which are used to encourage or deter right or wrong actions. People are responsible for their moral state, which reflects how they live; the good or bad qualities they develop correspond to their activities. However, while people who act unjustly or licentiously do so voluntarily, this does not mean they can stop, if they want to. It was in the power of such people not to become so, in the first place, but they may be unable to break free of the bad habits they have developed:

> it was at first open to the unjust and licentious persons not to become such ... they are voluntarily what they are; but now that they have become what they are, it is no longer open to them not to be such. (p. 63)

Assessment

Are we justified in holding people responsible for their moral defects, and therefore their wrong actions, in this way? Has not their character, from which their wrong actions flow, been created by factors, such as heredity and upbringing, over which they had no power? Aristotle tackles the **hard determinist view**: that when people wrongly think that something is good, and aim at it, this is the result of their character, which is outside their control, so they cannot be held responsible or blamed for it; while those who choose what is truly good have an inborn ability to do so, so there is nothing meritorious in their good conduct. He rejects such attempts to diminish human responsibility. Virtue and vice are both voluntary, as good and bad people are equally free in their actions, and perform all the means towards their ends voluntarily, even if they are not free (due to their character) in their choice of ends: 'vice will be no less voluntary; because the bad man has just as much independence in his *actions*, even if not in his choice of the end' (p. 65).

3 Hard determinism

John Hospers's 'What Means This Freedom?' (see recommended edition on p. 217)

John Hospers (born 1918)

Educated at the Universities of Iowa and Columbia, John Hospers taught philosophy at Brooklyn College, California State University and the University of Southern California. A former presidential candidate for the United States Libertarian Party (1972), his publications include *Meaning and Truth in the Arts* (1946), *Introduction to Philosophical Analysis* (1956), *Human Conduct: An Introduction to the Problems of Ethics* (1961) and *Libertarianism: A Political Philosophy for Tomorrow* (1971).

Unconscious motivation

In 'What Means This Freedom?', Hospers focuses on unconscious motivation and its bearing on moral responsibility, arguing that although acts originate in people's character, and they could have acted differently had they wanted to, they should not be held morally responsible for what they do. Their actions result from factors in their personality that they cannot control:

> The deed may be planned . . . it may spring from the agent's character . . . and it may be perfectly true that he could have done differently, *if* he had wanted to; nonetheless his behavior was brought about by unconscious conflicts developed in infancy, over which he had no control. (p. 126)

We are ignorant of these factors, and hold people responsible for their actions even though their behaviour cannot be changed by reasoning, exhortation or threats.

What is the criterion of moral responsibility?

So, what is the criterion of moral responsibility? It cannot be premeditation, because acts can be premeditated, but not responsible. A battered wife may consciously choose to remain with her violent husband, due to an 'unconscious, masochistic "will to punishment"' (p. 128). What about the agent's ability to find reasons for his action? This is not satisfactory either: the 'reasons' may be rationalizations that disguise the unconscious motives, like those Hamlet gave for not doing his duty. This exposes the inadequacy of the soft determinist view, that agents are responsible for their actions unless they are externally coerced. One who is compelled to wash his hands continually by unconscious mental conflicts is not subject to external coercion, but is as little able to control his actions as if his hands were forced under the tap. Such people fail another test of responsibility: giving them reasons for changing their behaviour has no effect. Psychiatric and psychoanalytical research indicates that such behaviour is typical of all people some of the time, of some people most of the time, and, 'once the infantile events have taken place, is inevitable' (p. 130).

Character is shaped by heredity and early environmental factors

How (Hospers asks) can people be held responsible, if their actions derive from their character, which is determined by their heredity and early environmental factors that they did not choose. A criminal will be unaware of the inner forces that cause his violent crimes: he harms others by his acts of aggression, but they are 'the wriggling of a worm on a fisherman's hook', and he is unable to control them (p. 132). When we become aware of the real position, we imprison him, for our and his protection, but tend not to hold him morally responsible. If we discover that his parents brought him up badly, and encouraged his greed and selfishness, we blame his environment for the way he has turned out, and see that it is unreasonable to expect him to have developed acceptable moral attitudes:

we could hardly expect him to have developed moral feelings . . . We no longer want to say that he is personally responsible; we . . . blame nature or his parents for having given him an unfortunate constitution or temperament. (p. 134)

Can these factors be overcome?

Hospers's argument seems to be refuted by evidence of those who have overcome the disadvantages of their early background, and become responsible and law-abiding citizens. He does not deny that this happens, but contends that their ability to do so is itself a product of heredity or 'early environment' (p. 138). We do not 'give ourselves this ability', and so 'cannot be blamed for not having it' (p. 138). Sometimes, moral exhortation may elicit a hitherto untapped capacity for improvement, but it will be pointless if 'the ability is not there' (p. 138). A desire can only be overcome by a stronger contrary desire, and many people lack the means of creating that stronger contrary desire. Those who possess it are simply fortunate.

Two levels of moral discourse

Thus, for Hospers, our 'characters' and desires are the result of 'the influences that made us what we are', over which we had 'no control' and of which we were not conscious at the time they were shaping us (p. 139). We are what we are; we did not choose to be so; and any ability we have to change ourselves is itself the result of heredity and/or environment. So:

> the only meaningful context of 'can' and 'could have' is that of *action*. 'Could have acted differently' makes sense; 'could have desired differently' . . . does not. (pp. 140–1)

Moral discourse operates on two levels: an upper level of actions, and a lower one of the springs of action. 'Can' and 'could' are only meaningful at the upper level, which, as our springs of action, that is, our desires, determine what we do, rules out moral responsibility.

Assessment

Hospers focuses on the behaviour, and the reasons for it, of the psychologically disturbed, and those with criminal tendencies who have been subjected to a bad early environment, but implies that what is true of this minority is true of everyone: that we are all governed by **unconscious motives**, and cannot be held responsible for our actions. But, is this the case? The very fact that we designate certain people as psychologically disturbed or mentally incapable, and not responsible for their actions, indicates that we regard the majority as rational and responsible. Indeed, the minority's abnormal and irresponsible behaviour is defined and identified in relation to the majority's normal and responsible behaviour. Yes, there are people whose behaviour is compulsive, and who do not respond to the reasons they are given for changing it; but they are diagnosed as mentally ill, and receive psychiatric treatment. Most people do not behave in this way. Indeed, Hospers seems to undermine his own argument when he says that compulsive behaviour is typical of all people some of the time and of some people most of the time: therefore, it is not typical of most people most of the time.

Jonathan Edwards' *Freedom of the Will* (see recommended edition on p. 217)

Jonathan Edwards (1703–58)

Jonathan Edwards was educated at Yale and, as a minister in the Congregationalist Church, played a major part in the religious revivals (the 'Great Awakening') in Connecticut, during the 1730s and 1740s. In 1750, he moved to the Indian mission at Stockbridge, and became President of the College of New Jersey (now Princeton University) in 1757. A vigorous and forthright exponent of Calvinist doctrine and its implications for Christian belief and practice, Edwards is particularly associated with the theological determinism of his *Freedom of the Will* (1754). His other writings include *Original Sin* (1758) and *End of Creation* and *True Virtue*, published posthumously (1765).

Theological determinism: God's omniscience imposes necessity on events

Edwards' *Freedom of the Will* contains a robust statement of theological determinism, with Edwards spelling out the implications for human freedom of the existence of the Christian God, whose powers are believed to be infinite. If, as Christians maintain, God is omniscient, and has 'a certain and infallible prescience of the act of the Will of moral agents', which means that he knows, infallibly, every event that will take place, including the voluntary actions of human beings, this makes our choices and actions *'necessary*, with a Necessity of connexion or consequence' (p. 73).

Can human beings be free moral agents?

What is known with absolute certainty, in advance of its occurrence (Edwards argues), is necessary, not contingent: and human choices and actions are indissolubly connected with divine foreknowledge, such that they cannot not take place. Those who think that they are not necessary events, or that it is possible that they should not occur, do not understand the meaning of God's omniscience:

> To suppose the future volitions of moral agents not to be necessary events; or, which is the same thing, events which it is not impossible but that they may not come to pass; and yet to suppose that God certainly foreknows them, and knows all things; is to suppose God's knowledge to be inconsistent with itself. For to say, that God certainly . . . knows that a thing will infallibly be, which at the same time he knows to be so *contingent*, that it may possibly not be, is to suppose his knowledge inconsistent with itself; or that one thing that he knows, is utterly inconsistent with another thing he knows. (p. 75)

Indeed, God's foreknowledge, as well as the exercise of his omnipotence, whereby he decrees what will happen in the world, is equally incompatible with human liberty: they both impose necessity on events. The connection between an event and divine foreknowledge of it (God's omniscience) is as infallible and indissoluble as that between an event and a divine decree that it should take place (God's omnipotence): 'it is no more impossible, that the event and decree should not agree together, than that the event and absolute knowledge should disagree' (p. 76).

God's being eternal makes no difference

Edwards refers to one attempt to get around this problem, by arguing that, as God is eternal, and therefore outside time, and sees things in a perfect, unchangeable overview, not as a succession of events in time, his foreknowledge does not impose necessity on events which occur in time. Edwards dismisses this argument: God's seeing things 'perfectly and unchangeably' does not alter the fact that he has certain foreknowledge of human beings' moral actions, so 'it is now impossible that these moral actions should not come to pass' (p. 79).

Assessment

If God foreknows human choices and actions, infallibly, that does mean that it is impossible for them not to occur. To that extent, we can agree with Edwards. However, is Edwards right to hold that God's **omniscience** and **infallible foreknowledge** are as incompatible with **human freedom** as the exercise of his omnipotence? If a human being were able to foretell the future, including our choices and actions, with total accuracy, we would not regard that as imposing a necessity on them, in the sense of actually determining the choices we make, even though that person could predict exactly what our choices and actions would be. The fact that God's powers are infinite complicates the situation, but we do need to challenge Edwards' view that the effects of God's omniscience, and the exercise of his omnipotence, are the same. If God is omniscient, he knows, infallibly, what we will choose, and what we will do; but that does not mean that he predetermines the moral choices we make. We can still regard ourselves as free beings, because God allows us to be; because he created us as free and morally responsible beings; and so he does not interfere in our choices. However, among the things that God infallibly foreknows are the freely made moral choices and actions of free human beings. As we confront a moral decision, we can believe that God already knows (infallibly) what we will decide and do, but that the choices we make are nonetheless entirely our own.

4 Soft determinism

John Locke's *An Essay Concerning Human Understanding* (see recommended edition on **p. 217**)

John Locke (1632–1704)

John Locke attended Christ Church, Oxford, and then became physician and political adviser to Anthony Ashley Cooper (Earl of Shaftesbury), who, as leader of the anti-Roman Catholic Whig party, tried to exclude Charles's brother James from the throne. During this time, Locke wrote *Two Treatises of Government*, providing the theoretical basis for the 'Glorious Revolution' of 1689, which ousted James II in favour of his Protestant daughter, Mary, and her husband, William III. Locke's most important work, *An Essay Concerning Human Understanding* (1689), is a statement of the empiricist case that knowledge comes from experience. His other works include *Letter on Toleration* (1689) and *The Reasonableness of Christianity* (1695).

Freedom is our power as agents to perform, or not to perform, particular actions

In *An Essay Concerning Human Understanding*, Locke points out that every human being discovers in himself a power to initiate, refrain from, continue or terminate actions, and that it is from the degree of power our minds have over our actions that the ideas of liberty and necessity arise. In fact, the only actions we have any idea of are thinking and moving. So, when we can think or move, as we choose, we consider ourselves free: and not free, when we cannot. Thus, our idea of liberty is that of our power as agents to perform, or not to perform, a particular action, according to our volition. If we lack this liberty, we regard ourselves as under necessity:

> the idea of liberty is the idea of a power in any agent to do or forbear any particular action, according to the determination or thought of the mind . . . where either of them is not in the power of the agent, to be produced by him according to his volition, there he is not at liberty; that agent is under necessity. (p. 167)

For example, a man who falls into a river, when a bridge collapses under him, is not a free agent. He wishes not to fall into the water, but his volition has no effect on what happens to him, so he is not free. With our thoughts, we are free if we can entertain them, or not, as we choose.

The question is not whether the will is free, but whether the human being is free

As liberty is the power to perform actions, or not, according as we will, the proper question is not whether the will is free, but whether the human being is free. Insofar as we can, by the exercise of choice, cause something to exist, or not to exist, we are free. We cannot be freer than to have the power to do what we will:

> so far as anyone can, by the direction or choice of his mind preferring the existence of any action to the non-existence of that action, and *vice versa*, make it exist or not exist, so far he is free . . . For how can we think anyone freer than to have the power to do what he will? (p. 172)

But human beings (Locke observes), with their inquisitive minds, are not content with this concept of freedom. They want more, and insist that a human being 'is not free . . . if he be not as free to will as he is to act what he wills' (p. 172). So, are we free to will? Locke thinks not. Freedom relates to actions, and the power to act or not to act, as we will. We are not at liberty to will or not to will, because we cannot prevent ourselves from willing.

An absurd question

But, if we cannot, a further question arises: are we, given a choice between two or more courses of action, free to will whichever we please? Locke considers this to be an absurd question. To ask whether we are free to will whether we sit or move, speak or remain silent, 'is to ask whether a man can will what he wills, or be pleased with what he is pleased with' (p. 174). Freedom consists in our being able to act, or not to act, according as we will or choose, and the will is just the power of the mind to direct our bodies to motion, rest, or whatever. Thus, the answer to the question of what determines our will is that it is our mind:

> The will being nothing but a power in the mind to direct the operative faculties of a man to motion or rest . . . to the question, 'What is it determines the will?' the true . . . answer is, The mind. (p. 175)

Assessment

Locke says much the same thing as John Hospers: that the only meaningful context of 'can' is that of action, not that of desire or will. However, he draws a different conclusion from this analysis. Instead of holding, like Hospers, that this undermines **freedom**, he says that this is what we mean by freedom: to be free is just to be able to do as we will or desire. As to the question of whether we can not only do as we please, but also will as we please, he dismisses it as an absurd question. Thus, in terms of responsibility, provided a person is not subject to external coercion (which today would include psychiatric disorders), he can be held responsible for his actions.

David Hume's *An Enquiry Concerning Human Understanding* (see recommended edition on p. 217)

David Hume (1711–76)

For brief biographical details of David Hume, see p. 23.

Causation and voluntary human actions

In his *Enquiry*, Hume addresses the issue of causation or determinism, in relation to voluntary human actions, which he believes has been bogged down in confusion and ambiguity. Everybody accepts that, in nature, everything has a cause, which could produce only one possible effect:

> It is universally allowed, that matter . . . is actuated by a necessary force, and that every natural effect is so precisely determined by the energy of its cause, that no other effect, in such particular circumstances, could possibly have resulted from it . . . if all the scenes of nature were continually shifted in such a manner, that no two events bore any resemblance to each other, but every object was entirely new . . . we should never, in that case, have attained the least idea of necessity, or of a connexion among these objects . . . The relation of cause and effect must be utterly unknown to mankind. (p. 149)

People accept that causal necessity applies to the 'voluntary actions of men', agreeing that human nature remains the same down the ages; that human motives operate uniformly; and that motives like ambition and avarice, but also generosity and public spirit, 'always produce the same actions': 'these passions . . . distributed through society, have been . . . and still are, the source of all the actions and enterprizes, which have ever been observed among mankind' (p. 150).

We can draw inferences between human actions and motives, and are able to do so only because we recognize the causal connection between the two: these general observations, based on experience, give us our understanding of human nature, and 'teach us to unravel all its intricacies' (p. 151). However, people are reluctant to acknowledge this causal connection openly, fearing it will undermine belief in free will, and damage religion and morality.

The nature of free will

Hume argues that reconciling freedom and necessity, in relation to human actions, is a 'merely verbal' question: actions are undeniably connected with motives (p. 158). Human freedom, or free will, simply means individuals being free to act, or not to act, according to the determination of their will, in contrast to being subject to external coercion, as they would if a gun were pointed at them. Thus, there is no such thing as human freedom, when it is opposed to causal necessity, not external constraint:

For what is meant by *liberty*, when applied to voluntary actions? We cannot surely mean, that actions have so little connexion with motives, inclinations, and circumstances, that one does not follow with a certain degree of uniformity from the other ... For these are plain and acknowledged matters of fact. By *liberty*, then, we can only mean *a power of acting or not acting, according to the determination of the will*; that is, if we choose to remain at rest, we may; if we choose to move, we also may. (pp. 158–9)

Religious and moral concerns

As for religious and moral concerns, Hume dismisses them. So far from being harmful to morality, the causal connection between motives and actions is essential to it. Unless human actions result from causes within the human character, people cannot be praised, blamed, or held responsible for them. Laws are based on the effects of rewards and punishments, which encourage good, and deter evil, actions:

All laws being founded on rewards and punishments, it is supposed as a fundamental principle, that these motives have a regular and uniform influence on the mind ... According to the principle, therefore, which denies necessity, and consequently causes, a man is pure and untainted, after having committed the most horrid crime. (pp. 160–1)

At the same time, we accept that people cannot be held responsible for things they do under coercion.

Idle philosophical speculation

Hume dismisses the argument that applying causal necessity to voluntary human actions involves a chain of necessary causes that traces human volitions back to God's will and makes him responsible for them. If God is the cause of all human actions, it is hard to deny that he is the author of sin, but Hume regards this as an example of idle philosophical speculation. Hume also considers the serious issue of how to reconcile God's omniscience with human freedom (if God knows everything that is going to happen, everything that happens, including human choices, seems predetermined and inevitable), and concedes that it is beyond philosophy's power to do so:

These are mysteries, which mere natural and unassisted reason is very unfit to handle ... To reconcile the indifference and contingency of human actions with prescience; or to defend absolute decrees, and yet free the Deity from being the author of sin, has been found . . . to exceed all the power of philosophy. (p. 164)

Assessment

Hume's 'soft' determinism, like Locke's, means that human freedom or free will is compatible with determinism: human actions are caused by human motives, but they are free, unless externally coerced. However, contrary to Hospers, Hume argues that, so far from undermining human freedom, this causal connection between motive and action is an essential part of freedom and responsibility. Unless human actions flowed from causes within the human character, they would be random, and people could not be held accountable for them. Hume also maintains that, whatever we may say about the subject, our actual behaviour presupposes a causal connection between actions and motives, because we are constantly drawing inferences from one to the other. Our expectations of others' behaviour and our interpretation of historical events depend on the stable and predictable operation of human nature, and individuals behaving in accordance with their character, as it has developed over the years.

Hume's argument is subtle and persuasive, but not altogether convincing. His points about human nature and individual character are well taken, but freedom and holding people fully responsible for their actions seems to involve the possibility (leaving out those with psychiatric or other mental problems or limitations) that, when they are confronted with a choice between, say, two courses of action, they should, through the exercise of their reason, or the conjunction of reason and sympathy, be able genuinely to choose and to perform either action, not just that they should act in accordance with their desires. For example, a person who sees a wallet full of money lying on the pavement, should be genuinely capable of choosing whether to keep it, or (perhaps after overcoming his inclination to keep it) hand it in to the police. Freedom does not mean that he should keep it if his heredity is bad and/or he has been brought up badly, or hand it in if his heredity is good and/or he has been taught to be law-abiding and honest.

5 Libertarianism: Immanuel Kant's *Groundwork of the Metaphysics of Morals* (see recommended edition on p. 217)

Immanuel Kant (1724–1804)

For brief biographical details of Immanuel Kant, see **pp. 70–1**.

To be able to obey the moral law, human beings must be free

In the *Groundwork*, Kant maintains that, to function as moral beings, that is, to have wills that are their own, and to be able to adopt as their rules of conduct the universal categorical imperatives of the moral law (see **pp. 74, 76**), to which they subject themselves, rational, and thus human beings must be free:

> how a categorical imperative is possible, can indeed be answered to the extent that one can furnish the sole presupposition on which it alone is possible, namely the idea of freedom. (p. 64)

The world of sense and the world of understanding

Kant accepts that, as we are subject to the causality of laws of nature, we cannot prove our freedom, which 'can never be seen by any human reason' (p. 64). However, he accounts for it by invoking his distinction between the world of sense (things as they appear to us, because of the kind of beings we are), of which our senses give us knowledge, and within which our actions are determined by desires and inclinations, and the world of understanding or the intelligible world (things as they are in themselves), to which, because we possess reason, human beings belong. Therefore, there are two standpoints from which to view our relationship with the moral law. As part of the world of sense, we are subject to laws of nature, but as part of the world of understanding, we are subject to moral laws, which come from the reason and are independent of nature:

> the human being claims for himself a will which lets nothing be put to his account that belongs merely to his desires and inclinations, and . . . thinks as possible by means of it . . . actions that can be done only by disregarding all desires and sensible incitements. The causality of such actions lies

in him as intelligence and in . . . actions in accordance with principles of an intelligible world, of which he knows nothing more than that in it reason alone . . . gives the law, and . . . those laws apply to him immediately and categorically, so that what inclinations . . . (hence the whole nature of the world of sense) incite him to cannot infringe upon the laws of his volition as intelligence. (pp. 61–2)

However, because, as part of the world of sense, our actions are determined by desires and inclinations, moral laws have to be expressed as imperatives.

The problem of reconciling freedom with natural necessity

Kant acknowledges the difficulties of his analysis, because the claim that we are free seems to contradict the natural necessity of laws of nature, and, while freedom is a 'mere idea' of reason, laws of nature are an 'objective reality' (p. 63). And, he admits that there is no possibility of explaining matters that are not determined by laws of nature, so the 'limit of all moral inquiry' has been reached (p. 65). However, we cannot give up the idea of freedom, which is essential if there is going to be moral responsibility. We just have to accept that, although we cannot explain it, there actually is no contradiction between holding that beings who are subject to the laws of nature are also independent of them, and capable of freely obeying moral laws given by pure reason:

the idea of a pure world of understanding as a whole of all intelligences, to which we ourselves belong as rational beings (though . . . members of the world of sense), remains always a useful and permitted idea . . . for producing in us a lively interest in the moral law by means of the noble ideal of a universal kingdom of *ends in themselves* (rational beings) to which we can belong . . . when we carefully conduct ourselves in accordance with maxims of freedom as if they were laws of nature. (p. 66)

Assessment

For Kant, the arguments of the **soft determinists** are equivocations. Kant's **libertarianism** might be called 'hard freedom': it is not enough that we should be free of external coercion, and able to act in accordance with our inclinations; we must also be able to overcome these inclinations, so that we have a genuine choice as to whether we perform or do not perform an action. Only if we have this kind of freedom can we be held responsible for our actions. Kant does not play down the difficulties. We know that human beings are subject to the causality of the laws of nature. This is a reality, while freedom is only an idea. Kant surmounts the problem by his distinction between the world of sense and the world of understanding. As physical beings, there can be no doubt that we are part of the world of sense, the physical world, and how we function, as purely physical beings, is wholly determined by laws of nature that are outside our control. But, unlike any other being in the world of sense, we are also rational beings and, because we have the faculty of reason, we are able to understand and obey moral laws that prescribe conduct that is contrary to our inclinations.

Kant's claim is unprovable, but it does seem to accord with reality. We know that we are subject to inclinations that sometimes impel us to behave in ways that are wrong and that harm others; but we are also aware of our ability to reason, which provides us with reasons or moral laws for not giving in to them. The extent to which individuals obey the moral laws of reason, or succumb to their inclinations, could be regarded as the measure of the extent to which they are fully rational members of the world of understanding.

Core texts

Aristotle, *The Nicomachean Ethics*, trans. J. A. K. Thomson (notes and appendices by H. Tredennick, Introduction and Further Reading by J. Barnes), further revised edition, London: Penguin, 1976.

Jonathan Edwards, *A Careful And Strict Inquiry Into The Modern Prevailing Notions Of That Freedom Of The Will*, New York: Leavitt and Allen, 1852; reprinted Whitefish, MT: Kessinger, 2007.

J. Hospers, 'What Means This Freedom?', in S. Hook (ed.), *Determinism and Freedom*, London and New York: Collier-Macmillan, 1970.

David Hume, *An Enquiry Concerning Human Understanding*, ed. T. L. Beauchamp, Oxford and New York: Oxford University Press, 1999.

Immanuel Kant, *Groundwork of the Metaphysics of Morals*, ed. M. Gregor, Cambridge: Cambridge University Press, 1997.

John Locke, *An Essay Concerning Human Understanding*, New York: Prometheus Books, 1995.

Suggestions for further reading and research

R. Clarke, 'Incompatibilist (Nondeterministic) Theories of Free Will' (rev. 2004), in E. N. Zalta (ed.), *Stanford Encyclopaedia of Philosophy*, at http://plato.stanford.edu.

The Determinism and Freedom Philosophy Website, edited by Ted Honderich, at http://www.ucl.ac.uk/~uctytho/dfwIntroIndex.htm.

P. Edwards, 'Hard and Soft Determinism', in S. Hook (ed.), *Determinism and Freedom*, London and New York: Collier-Macmillan, 1970.

Thomas Hobbes, *Leviathan*, ed. J. A. C. Gaskin, Oxford and New York: Oxford University Press, 1996.

J. L. Mackie, *Ethics: Inventing Right and Wrong*, Harmondsworth: Penguin, 1977 (chapter 9).

D. Mills Daniel, *Briefly: Kant's Groundwork of the Metaphysics of Morals*, London: SCM Press, 2007.

D. Mills Daniel, *Briefly: Hume's Enquiry Concerning Human Understanding*, London: SCM Press, 2007.

D. Mills Daniel, *Briefly: Aristotle's Nicomachean Ethics*, London: SCM Press, 2007.

R. Young, 'The Implications of Determinism', in P. Singer (ed.), *A Companion to Ethics*, Cambridge: Cambridge University Press, 1993.

Part 3 Applied Ethics

13 Abortion and Euthanasia, Suicide and Assisted Suicide

1 Abortion

Abortion law in Britain

In Britain, abortion is governed by the Abortion Act, 1967 (as amended by the Human Fertilisation and Embryology Act, 1990), and is permitted, with the agreement of two doctors (or one, if the situation is urgent), on certain specific grounds: (i) continuation of the pregnancy would put the pregnant woman's life at risk; (ii) ending it would prevent serious permanent injury to the pregnant woman's physical or mental health; (iii) continuation would involve greater risk of injury to the pregnant woman's physical or mental health than ending it; (iv) continuation would involve greater risk to the physical or mental health of the woman's existing children than ending it; or (v) there is a substantial risk that the foetus has mental or physical abnormalities. Abortions on grounds (iii) and (iv) can only take place up to 24 weeks of pregnancy (28 weeks before the 1990 Act), as the foetus is deemed to be viable (capable of surviving outside the womb) after that point. There is no time limit to abortions on grounds (i), (ii) and (v).

Not abortion on request

Thus, abortion law does not offer women abortion on request, or even legalize it in general. It permits abortions under specific conditions; and no medical practitioner or nurse is obliged to take part, if they have moral reservations. The law does not give women an absolute right over their own bodies, and does not match John Stuart Mill's principle of liberty: that the 'only purpose for which power can be rightfully exercised over any member of a civilized community, against his will, is to prevent harm to others': in conduct affecting only him or herself, the individual's 'independence is, of right, absolute' (Mill, 'On Liberty', p. 14). Society restricts the freedom of women to have abortions, and thus their right to determine what is in their best interests, in the interests of the unborn embryo/foetus. As society regards the women seeking abortions as autonomous beings, whose choices in matters that affect only themselves should be respected, the debate about abortion hinges on different views of the embryo/foetus's moral status.

Changing attitudes towards abortion

Until 1967, abortion was generally illegal in Britain. The Offences against the Person Act, 1861 defined abortion as a serious criminal offence, even if intended to save the pregnant woman's life. The Infant Life Preservation Act, 1929, as well as establishing 28 weeks as the age when a foetus was viable, and beyond which an abortion could not be performed, authorized a medical practitioner to carry out an abortion if s/he was satisfied that continuation of the pregnancy would put the pregnant woman's life at risk. During the 1930s, the Abortion Law Reform Association campaigned for reform, and in 1938, Mr Aleck Bourne, FRCS, was prosecuted, but not convicted, for performing an abortion on a young woman who had been gang raped, for the sake of her mental well-being. However, every year many women in Britain still died as a result of illegal abortions. The 1967 Abortion Act was introduced as a private member's bill by the Liberal MP David (now Lord) Steel, but received encouragement from the then Labour government.

The embryo and the foetus

In 2006, a total of 193,700 abortions were performed in Britain, of which 87 per cent were paid for by the NHS. However, only 11 per cent of these were performed after the first 13 weeks of pregnancy. This is important, because of the time limit on when abortions can be performed, which reflects the view that the embryo/foetus acquires legal rights as it develops. Many people who do not object to abortion in principle share this view: that an early abortion is more morally acceptable than a late one, because the foetus is less viable, or like a human being. In the wider debate on abortion, while opponents of abortion emphasize the intrinsic value of the human embryo from the moment of conception, and its potential to become a fully developed, rational adult human being, the supporters of abortion stress the differences between the human embryo and the human adult. But who is right?

> Abortion . . . pose[s] difficult ethical issues because the development of the human being is a gradual process. If we take the fertilized egg immediately after conception, it is hard to get upset about its death. The fertilized egg is a single cell. After several days, it is still only a tiny cluster of cells without a single anatomical feature of the being it will later become. The cells that will eventually become the embryo proper are at this stage indistinguishable from the cells that will become the placenta and amniotic sac. Up to about 14 days after fertilisation, we cannot even tell if the embryo is going to be one or two individuals . . . At 14 days, the first anatomical feature, the . . . primitive streak, appears in the position in which the backbone will . . . develop. At this point the embryo could not possibly be conscious or feel pain. At the other extreme is the adult human being. To kill a human adult is murder . . . Yet there is no obvious sharp line that divides the fertilised egg from the adult. (Singer, *Practical Ethics*, pp. 136–7)

Deontological and utilitarian approaches to abortion

The key issue is whether or not the pre-natal embryo/foetus is a person, and therefore a moral subject, and, if so, when it becomes one. If the embryo/foetus has, or at some stage in pregnancy acquires, moral status, then moral principles will apply to it, and it would be difficult for a **deontologist** to support abortion. S/he would have to accept that all the obligations of one human person to another apply to it. For the **Kantian**, in particular, it would be wrong, by aborting it, to treat the embryo/foetus, not as an end, but merely as a means to the happiness (or reduced pain) of the pregnant woman seeking an abortion. For the **consequentialist/utilitarian**, though, the interests or preferences of the unborn embryo/foetus would not be absolute, even if it is regarded as a person. To the extent that they could be ascertained, they would have to be balanced against those of the pregnant woman and anybody else involved. For the **classical utilitarian**, the extent to which the embryo/foetus is capable of experiencing pain would be significant.

223

Religious belief and abortion

Abortion is a matter of great concern to religious believers. For most **Christians**, the embryo/foetus is a person, made in the image of God (see **pp. 164–5**, but also see Peter Singer's definition of a person on **p. 225**). For the **Roman Catholic Church**, abortion involves ending the life of a human person, and is always wrong. According to its teaching, which used to be that 'ensoulment' (receiving a soul) took place at 'quickening' (about 16 weeks into pregnancy), when the foetus begins to move, it is now held to be present from the point that the egg is fertilized: 'The doctrine of the faith affirms that the spiritual and immortal soul is created immediately by God' (*Catechism of the Catholic Church*, para. 382). The **Church of England** shares the Roman Catholic Church's general opposition to abortion:

> In the light of our conviction that the foetus has the right to live and develop as a member of the human family, we see abortion, the termination of that life by the act of man, as a great moral evil. (CofE (a))

However, like many other Protestant denominations, it accepts that circumstances exist where abortion is justified, as when the pregnant woman's life is in danger, but wants such abortions to be carried out as early as possible. The **Methodist Church** recognizes that principled opposition to abortion can accommodate acceptance that there are circumstances when it is the lesser evil:

> abortion is always an evil, to be avoided . . . there will be circumstances where the termination of the pregnancy may be the lesser of evils. These include situations where the embryo is grievously handicapped, the pregnancy is the result of rape or the health, mental or physical, of the mother is at risk. (Methodists (a))

Potential and actual human beings

Opponents of abortion, whether religious or not, insist that the embryo/foetus is the human person, with all his/her individual characteristics, in waiting. All the elements of the future human person are present, so the embryo/foetus is entitled to all the protection given to a human person. Another argument is that, with modern medical techniques, foetuses are viable at ever earlier stages in a pregnancy, so the time limit for abortions should be set earlier. However, there does seem to be a difference between a potential and an actual human person. Biologically, the foetus may be a human being, but is the foetus also a human person, with full moral status? Singer rejects this claim. It is not:

> rational or self-conscious . . . on any fair comparison of morally relevant characteristics, like rationality, self-consciousness, awareness, autonomy, pleasure and pain . . . the calf, the pig and the much derided chicken come out well ahead of the fetus at any stage of pregnancy – while if we make the comparison with a fetus of less than three months, a fish would show more signs of consciousness. (Singer, *Practical Ethics*, pp. 150–1)

He concludes that no foetus can be a person, so no foetus has 'the same claim to life as a person'; therefore, 'an abortion terminates an existence that is of no "intrinsic" value at all' (p. 151).

Developmental moral status

John Mackie contends that it is 'more reasonable to think of the right or claim to life as growing gradually in strength', and as 'very slight immediately after conception' (Mackie, *Ethics*, p. 198). At the outset of a pregnancy, the embryo has no interests or rights, but could be held to acquire them as it develops. Thinking of the foetus as gradually acquiring moral status, and thus entitlement to protection, would make abortions ethically acceptable during the early stages of a pregnancy but less so at more advanced stages.

The foetus and the infant

Of course, Singer's argument seems as applicable to newly born infants as to unborn foetuses, and he acknowledges that 'the grounds for not killing persons do not apply to newborn infants'; they 'cannot see themselves as beings who might or might not have a future, and so cannot have a desire to continue living' (*Practical Ethics*, p. 171). However, it does not seem unreasonable to stand on the distinction between an embryo/foetus (unborn) and an infant (born), and to regard the latter as having, but the former as not having, moral status, or having it only to a limited degree after it becomes viable. Mackie maintains that birth is the 'salient point, a popularly acceptable ground of distinction', so that infanticide is, but abortion is not, regarded as 'the killing of what is now a separately existing human being'. (*Ethics*, p. 199). The law recognizes a clear distinction between the two, allowing the first to be aborted, under certain circumstances, but making the killing or harming of the second a criminal offence. Why should not ethics do the same? It is a distinction that seems acceptable to large numbers of people, despite the efforts of anti-abortion campaigners, during the more than 40 years since the passing of the Abortion Act.

Diminishing respect for human life or for those with mental or physical disabilities

One **consequentialist** argument against abortion is that it may reduce respect for human life. However, there is no evidence that this is the case, nor is there any reason why it should, if the distinction between embryo/(non-viable)foetus and infant is accepted. Another argument is that the absence of any time limit on when a foetus with a physical or mental impairment can be aborted (and, indeed, provision for abortion on this ground) shows society's lack of value for those with disabilities. This is held to promote and perpetuate disability bias, and to be at odds with, for example, the Disability Discrimination Act, 1995 (see **p. 292**), which reinforces equal opportunities for those with disabilities, and prohibits discrimination against them.

However, it does not seem inconsistent to ensure equal rights and opportunities for those with mental or physical disabilities, in order to enable them to enjoy the highest possible quality of life, while holding that their birth should be prevented, if possible, given that, whatever we do, they are likely to experience a lower quality of life than other people, and perhaps to suffer. As to whether allowing abortion on the grounds of disability diminishes respect for those with disabilities, there has been significant growth of legal protection and equal opportunities for those with disabilities, since the passing of the 1967 Abortion Act, suggesting that it does not.

Trying to restrict the grounds for abortion

Abortion legislation in Britain does not give women an absolute right to choose whether or not to continue with a pregnancy, but allows the interests and well-being of a pregnant woman to be balanced against the 'interests' of the embryo/foetus: the assumption that, if it were a conscious or self-conscious being, it would prefer its existence to continue, rather than be terminated. Some anti-abortion campaigners argue that, unless there is a serious risk to the pregnant woman's life or health, she should go through with the pregnancy, because she does not have to keep the child, as there are plenty of people eager to adopt. The **utilitarian** counter-argument to this would be that more weight should always be given to the definite unhappiness/pain of a woman, forced to see an unwanted pregnancy through to its conclusion, than to the possible happiness of the prospective adoptive parents. A **deontologist** might argue that, if the law were to force a pregnant woman to give birth, against her will, for the benefit of potential adoptive parents, it would treat her as means (a kind of brood mare), not an end.

The interests of society

Another consideration is the interests of society. As a result of the Abortion Act, in 2006, more than 193,000 unwanted children, who would otherwise have been born, were not. The abortion rate was highest among 19-year-olds. It could be argued that society benefits from preventing so many unwanted births. There is no guarantee that all these children would have been (successfully) adopted, while their birth would have caused difficulties and distress to the parents and their families, and potentially led to social problems and crime.

Global consequences of the non-availability of abortion

According to the World Health Organization (WHO), in 2003, out of 193 countries surveyed, there were still four where abortion was not permitted, even to save the pregnant woman's life; 71 where it was not permitted to preserve her physical health; 73 where it was not permitted to preserve her mental health; 110 where it was not allowed on the grounds of rape or incest; and 117 where it was not permitted for foetal impairment. On the other hand, abortion was available on request in only 52 countries. Of the 210 million pregnancies throughout the world, 42 million were terminated voluntarily, but only 22 million within a national legal system. The other 20 million may have been performed by unskilled providers and/or in unhygienic conditions:

> Abortion attempts may involve insertion of a solid object (root, twig or catheter) into the uterus; a dilation and curettage procedure [which scrapes the lining, placenta and embryo/foetus from the womb] performed improperly by an unskilled provider; ingestion of harmful substances; exertion of external force; or misuse of modern pharmaceuticals. In many settings, traditional practitioners vigorously pummel the woman's lower abdomen to disrupt the pregnancy; this can cause the uterus to burst, killing the woman. (WHO, *Unsafe Abortion*, p. 5)

Almost 5 million of the women who have illegal abortions annually suffer temporary or permanent disabilities, while 65,000 to 70,000 die. There is no doubt that these women are human persons, with full moral status. Whether we regard their injuries, pain or deaths as justifiable will depend on whether we regard the human embryo/foetus in the womb as an intrinsically valuable form of human life, which we must try to preserve at all costs, or whether we consider it to have little or no intrinsic value – or at least less than that of the woman in whose womb it is located.

2 Euthanasia, suicide and assisted suicide

Voluntary euthanasia

When someone kills him/herself, by whatever means, it is suicide. If someone helps another person to commit suicide, perhaps by providing the drugs that will make death swift and painless, it is assisted suicide. If someone, because of extreme pain and/or terminal illness, wishes for a 'gentle and easy' death, but is unable to commit suicide, and someone else kills them, for example, by injecting them with a lethal drug, it is voluntary euthanasia. However, assisted suicide and voluntary euthanasia may be difficult to distinguish.

Involuntary and non-voluntary euthanasia

There are two other forms of euthanasia: involuntary and non-voluntary. The former occurs when the life of a suffering person who is capable of giving consent, but who does not, is ended; the latter when the life of a person who is incapable of giving consent, such as someone in a coma, is brought to an end. Another important distinction is between active euthanasia, which involves taking steps, such as injecting drugs, to end someone's life, and passive euthanasia, where a person's life is ended by withholding treatment that would keep them alive. The ethical debate about euthanasia mainly concerns voluntary euthanasia. Almost no one advocates involuntary euthanasia.

Choosing when to die

Unlike abortion, with suicide, assisted suicide and euthanasia, there is no question about whether or not we are dealing with persons who have moral status. Clearly, we are. The issues concern our attitudes towards those who commit, or wish to commit, these acts, and how they are, or should be, treated by the law. Should people be allowed to choose when they die? In Britain, committing suicide is not now a criminal offence, but assisting someone else to die (covering both assisted suicide and voluntary euthanasia) is. But should they be?

Suicide and euthanasia

Clearly, there are parallels between euthanasia and suicide, as both involve ending a life before it ends naturally, so exploring philosophical views about, and religious and other attitudes towards, suicide, should shed some light on the issues surrounding euthanasia. The human instinct is to live, and to go on living. Even if things are difficult, and life is not enjoyable, we still think that it is rational and natural to want to continue to exist, and irrational and unnatural to want to die. However, we recognize that, for some people, in certain circumstances, life is more or less unbearable. And we know that some of these people try to kill themselves. Today, in western society, we do not condemn them, but treat them with compassion. We try to understand their situation; to help them to resolve their problems; and to persuade them that they should not discard their lives.

St Augustine and suicide as a sin

In Britain, those who commit, or attempt, suicide, do not commit a crime. The 1961 Suicide Act revoked the 'rule of law whereby it is a crime for a person to commit suicide' (Section 1). The idea of punishing someone who is so disenchanted with life that s/he tries to end it seems ludicrous, but the pre-1961 law reflected **Christian teaching** that God made human beings in his own image, so human life is sacred (see **pp. 184–5**). As God has given them the gift of life, human beings have a duty to God to respect their own lives, as well as those of others: not to do so is to commit a sin. St Augustine argues the Christian case against suicide powerfully; and his arguments can be applied equally well to euthanasia:

> It is significant that in the sacred canonical books there can nowhere be found any injunction or permission to commit suicide either to ensure immortality or to avoid or escape any evil. In fact we must understand it to be forbidden by the law 'You shall not kill' . . . the text . . . has no addition and it must be taken that there is no exception, not even the one to

whom the command is addressed . . . we take the command . . . as applying to human beings, that is, other persons *and* oneself. For to kill oneself is to kill a human being. (Augustine, *City of God*, pp. 31–2)

Aristotle and suicide as an anti-social act

Suicide was also regarded as an anti-social act, whereby those who attempted it failed in their duty to the state (and their fellow citizens), as their deaths would prevent them serving it in future:

> a man who cuts his throat in a fit of anger is voluntarily doing, contrary to the right principle, what the law does not allow; therefore he is acting unjustly. But towards whom? Surely not himself, but the state . . . It is for this reason that the state imposes a penalty, and a kind of dishonour is attached to a man who has taken his own life, on the ground that he is guilty of an offence against the state, (Aristotle, *Nicomachean Ethics*, pp. 141–2)

In Britain, into the 1950s, unsuccessful suicides might be sentenced to terms of imprisonment, and required to receive counselling from the clergy, possibly preventing further attempts, and/or convincing them that it was wrong to do so. However, it is difficult to apply the 'failure of duty' argument to euthanasia, because those seeking it are probably physically incapable of service to the state or their fellow citizens.

Kant and suicide as failing to treat human beings as ends in themselves

However, Kant puts forward an argument against suicide that is equally effective against euthanasia. Someone sick of life, and contemplating suicide, should ask himself whether the maxim or rule of conduct on which he would act, if he were to do so, would be consistent with his duty to himself as a rational being. Could he will that the maxim of his action should become a universal law of nature, governing the conduct of all rational beings?

> His maxim . . . is: from self-love I make it my principle to shorten my life when its longer duration threatens more troubles than it promises agreeableness . . . It is then seen at once that a nature whose law it would be to destroy life itself by means of the same feeling whose destination is to impel toward the furtherance of life would contradict itself, and would therefore not subsist as nature; thus that maxim could not possibly be a

law of nature and, accordingly, altogether opposes the supreme principle of all duty. (Kant, *Groundwork*, p. 32)

It is contradictory to try to turn the maxim of self-love into a universal ethical law of ending life if it becomes more troublesome than agreeable, when the same maxim impels us to conserve our lives. Committing suicide would also mean using oneself as a means of limiting one's own unhappiness, and not as an intrinsically valuable end-in -itself.

David Hume and the defence of suicide

Hume challenges the view that suicide is an offence against God, other people, or the individual him/herself. Experience (he argues) shows that God does not decide when people's lives should end. He has determined that life and death, like every other event, should be governed by the general laws of the universe, and it does not encroach upon his prerogative if we interfere with these laws, either to shorten life, or to preserve it:

Has not every one, of consequence, the free disposal of his own life? . . . Were the disposal of human life so much reserved as the peculiar province of the almighty that it were an encroachment on his right for men to dispose of their own lives; it would be equally criminal to act for the preservation of life as for its destruction. ('On Suicide', in *Dialogues Concerning Natural Religion*, p. 100)

As for society, a human being who commits suicide does not harm it. He only ceases to be able to contribute to its good; but this does not mean he should prolong his life if it has become intolerable to him: 'Why then should I prolong a miserable existence, because of some frivolous advantage which the public may perhaps receive from me?' (p. 103). Indeed, he may have become a burden to society, perhaps through needing care and attention: in which case, his 'resignation of life' is laudable (p. 103). It may also be the means of fulfilling his duty to himself, and setting an example for others:

age, sickness, or misfortune may render life a burthen . . . I believe that no man ever threw away life, while it was worth keeping. For such is our natural horror of death . . . both prudence and courage should engage us to rid ourselves at once of existence, when it becomes a burthen. 'Tis the only way that we can be useful to society, by setting an example, which, if imitated, would preserve to every one his chance for happiness in life and would effectually free him from all danger or misery. (p. 104)

Hume's defence of suicide is equally applicable to euthanasia: as everything is subject to the operation of general laws, there is no evidence that God determines the length of people's lives, while only the individual can judge when his/her life is not worth living.

The difference between suicide and assisted suicide and euthanasia

The problem is that, unlike suicide, assisted suicide and euthanasia involve the assistance of others, and this is strictly prohibited by the law:

> A person who aids, abets, counsels or procures the suicide of another . . . shall be liable on conviction . . . to imprisonment for a term not exceeding fourteen years. (Suicide Act, 1961, Section 2 (1))

This is why, unlike suicide, Mill's **principle of liberty** does not clearly cover assisted suicide and euthanasia. According to Mill, society is entitled to exercise power over its members to prevent harm to others. When someone commits suicide, s/he harms only him/herself. But, assisting with a suicide, or performing euthanasia, causes harm to others, even if it is at their request.

Euthanasia in the Netherlands

In the Netherlands, the law has permitted voluntary euthanasia, under certain conditions, since 2002. It must be established that a patient faces a future of unbearable and interminable suffering. The request to die must be voluntary and have been fully thought through. Both the patient and his doctor must be certain that there is no other solution, such as the use of pain-killing drugs, that would make life endurable. There must be a second medical opinion, and life must be ended by medically appropriate means. Where there is a risk of incapacitation, the patient must leave written instructions that s/he wishes to die. However, there are allegations that official figures of voluntary euthanasia cases (over 2,000 in 2007) do not include cases where life has been terminated without patients' consent, and that there has been 'an extension of euthanasia to those who are mentally ill or "tired of life" and . . . to those who are unable to consent such as infants and young children' (CofE (c)).

Arguments for euthanasia

For its supporters, voluntary euthanasia is essentially a matter of individual freedom and choice. Only the individual can judge whether life is worth living, or pain unendurable. For the British Humanist Association (BHA), 'reason and respect for others', concern about individual 'quality of life' and 'respect for personal autonomy':

> lead to the view that in many circumstances voluntary euthanasia is the morally right course. People should have the right to choose a painless and dignified end . . . The right circumstances might include: extreme pain and suffering; helplessness and loss of personal dignity; permanent loss of those things which have made life worth living for this individual. (BHA, *A Humanist Discussion of . . . Euthanasia*)

It rejects the view that it is ethically laudable to 'postpone the inevitable', when there is no gain for the suffering person, and advocates voluntary euthanasia, provided there are definite safeguards, such as the involvement of several doctors, counselling and clearly expressed instructions by the patient, to prevent involuntary euthanasia.

A key element in the BHA's case is that voluntary euthanasia is a means of ensuring that people enjoy 'happiness and fulfilment in this life', because 'it is the only one we have'. For those who do not believe in God or a life after physical death, decisions about whether to live or die are matters that affect only human beings. Their perspective is very different from that of religious believers.

Dignity in Dying (DiD) is a British organization that provides information, counselling and support to those who are terminally ill and to their friends and relatives. It also campaigns for a change in the law, to permit medically assisted dying within strict safeguards. DiD highlights the ethical dilemma faced by the relatives and friends of those who are terminally ill. Should they assist them, even though the law forbids it?

> The law makes people juggle their conscience . . . Sometimes relatives help their loved ones to die, at their request, even though this is a serious crime. Relatives can and do face prosecution for murder or assisted suicide even though they believe they acted compassionately. (DiD website)

It is much easier to assert that human life should be preserved at all costs, in the abstract, than when confronted by a loved one who is suffering acutely, who wishes to die, and who needs help to do so.

233

Singer asks whether the advocates of voluntary euthanasia attach too much weight to the individual freedom argument. On justifiable paternalistic grounds, people are prevented from taking heroin. Does the same principle apply to euthanasia? He accepts that Mill may have overrated human rationality, and that it may sometimes be right to stop people acting in ways that are not rational, and that they will regret. However, he does not think that voluntary euthanasia falls into the category of individual choices that paternalism is justified in preventing:

> voluntary euthanasia is an act for which good reasons exist ... occurs only when, to the best of medical knowledge, a person is suffering from an incurable and painful or extremely distressing condition ... The strength of the case for voluntary euthanasia lies in this combination of respect for the preferences, or autonomy, of those who decide for euthanasia; and the clear rational basis of the decision itself. (Singer, *Practical Ethics*, p. 200)

Living wills

DiD recommends that those who are concerned about their treatment, in the event of their becoming terminally ill, should make a living will, stipulating the treatments they would, or would not, wish to receive; and nominating someone who can be consulted about treatment, if a decision is needed. The Mental Capacity Act, 2005 creates statutory rules covering advance decisions to refuse treatment, in the event of mental incapacitation. Such decisions must be written, signed and witnessed, and include an express statement that the decision stands, even if life is at risk.

Arguments against euthanasia

Opponents of euthanasia are not necessarily religious. They include non-religious people who feel that voluntary euthanasia is inconsistent with human dignity and/or capable of being abused. However, the **Christian Churches** strongly oppose it:

> the life of men and women bears the stamp of God ... This is the source of our basic dignity and it is the biblical basis for the sanctity of human life. What God has given, we should not take away. Death is an event marking a transition rather than a terminus. (Methodists (b))

The **Church of England** and **Roman Catholic** bishops (CofE (c)) challenge over-emphasis, by advocates of voluntary euthanasia, on individual autonomy and welfare. They reject the view that a terminally ill patient's perception that their suffering is 'so severe as to be unacceptable', and that their lives have 'no value', justify ending them. If they did, there would be no basis for limiting euthanasia to the terminally ill. Their approach to euthanasia is shaped by their view of human life as God's gift, which should always be 'revered and cherished'. Non-religious **deontological ethicists** would agree that, 'All human beings are to be valued', and that a fundamental objection to voluntary euthanasia is that it involves killing intrinsically valuable human beings, albeit with their agreement.

The bishops warn of the dangers of life-and-death decisions being taken in isolation. Individuals exist 'within complex networks of relationships', and the limits of individual autonomy should be drawn at the point where its exercise could harm others. If the terminally ill are allowed help to die, it could lead to the view that, in general, chronically sick and disabled people are disposable. Thus, Mill's principle of liberty should not be applied to voluntary euthanasia, as it would change 'the cultural air we all breathe', and damage the interests of society's 'vulnerable members'.

The effect on the medical profession

The bishops warn of other undesirable consequences. The obvious people to assist with it are doctors, but they have taken the Hippocratic Oath, which includes such statements (versions vary) as:

> I will use my power to help the sick to the best of my ability and judgement; I will abstain from harming or wronging any man by it . . . I will go to help the sick and never with the intention of doing harm or injury.

Doctors' participation in voluntary euthanasia would lead to an 'undermining of trust' between doctors and patients' (CofE (c)).

Not striving officiously to keep patients alive and the doctrine of double effect

However, the bishops do not maintain that doctors should prolong the lives of the terminally ill by 'all available means'. Where patients are near to death, the 'withholding or withdrawing of medical treatment that is judged futile or burdensome is both moral and legal'. Treatment should be 'proportionate' to the condition of the patient, who may reasonably refuse particular treatments as 'too burdensome'. Again, by the doctrine of double effect:

> Administering doses of pain-relieving drugs that have the foreseen consequence of accelerating death is not intentional killing, if the actual intention is only to relieve pain. (CofE (b))

But, treatment should never be given or refused with the deliberate intention of making the patient die.

The hospice movement and palliative care

The first hospice was opened in London in 1967, and the hospice movement now operates worldwide. In Britain, there are about 200 hospices, with 3,500 beds, offering palliative (concerned with alleviation of suffering) care to the dying. The hospice movement's credo is that death is a natural part of life, and that those who are dying should be cared for in a way that prevents avoidable pain and distress and ensures human dignity. The bishops urge that 'the lessons learned in hospices about pain control, and emotional and spiritual support should be applied throughout the health service to all dying people' (CofE (c)).

Grappling with the issue

The libertarian arguments are cogent, but, however strongly we believe in individual freedom and choice, there are significant problems with permitting voluntary euthanasia. Terminally ill people, possibly in severe pain, are not well placed to make an objective decision about whether to live or die, but advance instructions are not free of problems either. Is it really possible to know, in advance, whether or not we want to end our lives in this or that set of circumstances? Again, if voluntary euthanasia were legalized, it would involve others, who might feel compelled to assist, even if they did not want to. It would also create the possibility of abuse. Terminally ill people might be pressurized into it by relatives or medical authorities, or even have the decision taken for them. The Dutch experience is not altogether reassuring on this point. **Christians** are bound to oppose voluntary euthanasia, as it involves spurning God's gift of life. **Deontologists** will probably object to it, because it involves treating human beings in a way that does not accord with their intrinsic value and dignity. **Kantians**, in particular, would argue that it fails the test of the categorical imperative, by allowing people to treat themselves as a means to the ending of their own suffering.

The **utilitarian** arguments for legalizing voluntary euthanasia are that the preferences of the person seeking euthanasia could be met, and a quantity of pain eliminated. However, this would have to be balanced against the preferences and pain of their family and friends. The **consequentialist** arguments against voluntary euthanasia are that there could be no absolute assurance that nobody would be subjected to euthanasia against their actual preferences; it could reduce the prospects of developing more effective forms of palliative care; it could diminish trust in the medical profession; and it is remotely possible that somebody might miss out on a cure. There are also understandable concerns that legalization might diminish respect for human life, and create a slippery slope into involuntary euthanasia.

References and suggestions for further reading and research

Aristotle, *The Nicomachean Ethics*, trans. J. A. K. Thomson (notes and appendices by H. Tredinnick, Introduction and Further Reading by J. Barnes), rev. edn, London: Penguin, 1976.

Augustine, *City of God*, ed. D. Knowles, Harmondsworth: Penguin, 1972.

British Humanist Association (BHA), at http://www.humanism.org.uk: *A Humanist Discussion of . . . Euthanasia*; *A Humanist Discussion of . . . Suicide*.

Catechism of the Catholic Church, 2nd edn, at http://www.scborromeo. org/ccc.htm (see also http://www.catholic-church.org.uk).

Church of England (CofE), at http://cofe.anglican.org: General Synod's Mission and Public Affairs Division, *Abortion: A Briefing Paper* (2005) (CofE (a)); *Assisted Suicide* (CofE (b)); Church of England House of Bishops and the Roman Catholic Bishops' Conference of England and Wales, *Joint Submission to the House of Lords Select Committee on the Assisted Dying for the Terminally Ill Bill* (2004) (CofE (c)).

Department of Health, *Statistical Bulletin* (Abortion Statistics, England and Wales: 2006) at http://www.dh.gov.uk.

Dignity in Dying (DiD), at http://www.dignityindying.org.uk.

Education for Choice, *More on UK Abortion Law* at http://www.efc.org. uk.

Hospice Information, at http://www.helpthehospices.org.uk.

David Hume, 'On Suicide', in David Hume, *Dialogues Concerning Natural Religion*, 2nd edn, ed. R. H. Popkin, Indianapolis and Cambridge: Hackett, 1998.

Immanuel Kant, *Groundwork of the Metaphysics of Morals*, ed. M. Gregor, Cambridge: Cambridge University Press, 1998.

H. Kuhse, 'Euthanasia', in P. Singer (ed.), *A Companion to Ethics*, Cambridge: Cambridge University Press, 1993.

J. L. Mackie, *Ethics: Inventing Right and Wrong*, Harmondsworth: Penguin, 1977.

The Methodist Church of Great Britain (Methodists) at www.methodist. org.uk: *Abortion and Contraception* (Methodists (a)); *Euthanasia* (Methodists (b)); *Methodist Statement on Abortion*.

John Stuart Mill, *On Liberty*, in John Stuart Mill, *On Liberty and Other Essays*, ed. J. Gray, Oxford and New York: Oxford University Press, 1998.

Office of Public Sector Information, *Statute Law Database*, at http://www. statutelaw.gov.uk. The full text of the statutes referred to can be found here.

H. J. Paton, *The Categorical Imperative*, London: Hutchinson, 1946.

ProLife Alliance, *Submission to the Select Committee on Science and Technology Inquiry into Scientific Developments Relating to the Abortion Act 1967* (2007), at http://www.prolife.org.uk.

P. Singer, *Practical Ethics*, 2nd edn, Cambridge: Cambridge University Press, 1993.

P. Vardy and P. Grosch, *The Puzzle of Ethics*, rev. edn, London: HarperCollins, 1999 (chapters 12 and 13).

M. A. Warren, 'Abortion', in P. Singer (ed.), *A Companion to Ethics*, Cambridge: Cambridge University Press, 1993.

World Health Organization, *Unsafe Abortion*, 5th edn, 2003 at www.who. int/en/.

14 Infertility, Assisted Conception and Embryo Research

1 Infertility and assisted conception

The right to children

Both the Universal Declaration of Human Rights (Article 16) and the European Convention on Human Rights (Article 12), which was incorporated into British law by the 1998 Human Rights Act (see **pp. 280–1**), provide for the right of men and women to marry and/or to have a family. Thus, in Britain, there is a legal right for those who wish to do so to have children. However, in the past, whether or not a couple had children depended on their natural physical capability to reproduce. If this was lacking, they had to remain childless, unless they wished, and were able, to adopt; and there were many childless couples who felt that, in one essential regard, their lives were incomplete. According to the National Health Service (NHS), most couples (85 per cent) do conceive naturally after a year of unprotected sex. However, the remaining 15 per cent do find it difficult to conceive. Those unable to conceive after two years of unprotected sex are diagnosed as infertile.

Infertility and its causes

It used to be assumed that infertility problems were due to the woman, and a stigma attached to her for being barren and failing to give her husband children. In fact, both men and women can be infertile, and there are many possible causes. In women, these range from ovulation problems, such as premature ovarian failure (when the ovaries stop working before the age of forty), to problems with the fallopian tubes (which carry the fertilized egg from the ovary to the womb), with the womb itself (for example, the effects of previous surgery preventing the embryo implanting), or the effects of age: women in their early twenties are twice as likely to conceive as those in their late thirties. Seventy-five per cent of male infertility is caused by abnormal semen, such as a low sperm count, or sperm with low mobility which cannot reach the egg to fertilize it. Other male causes include ejaculatory and testicular problems. Both male and female fertility may be affected by obesity, smoking or stress. These factors are within the individual's control, and those whose infertility is affected by them will need to address aspects of their work or lifestyle. Other causes may require the use of drugs, like clomifene or gonadotropins, which stimulate ovulation, or surgery: for example, to unblock the fallopian tubes, or the epididymis, where sperm is stored in the testicles.

Assisted conception techniques

But, for some couples, none of these procedures work. If they want children, they will either have to adopt them or make use of assisted conception. If the male has a low sperm count, sperm with limited mobility, or is impotent, intrauterine insemination (IUI) can be used. Sperm is taken from the male, and introduced into the woman's womb, via a tube, when the woman is ovulating. However, some infertile couples may need sperm or eggs from a third party donor, in order to conceive. This treatment usually involves in vitro (literally, 'in glass', as opposed to in vivo or 'in body') fertilization (IVF). IVF can also be used when both egg and sperm are supplied by the couple themselves, but they are unable to conceive through normal intercourse, because, for example, of sperm or fallopian tube problems. In these cases, the female is given medication that enables her to produce a larger than normal quantity of eggs. These are then taken from her ovaries, and fertilized with sperm in the laboratory. The resulting embryos are allowed to develop for a few days, and then returned to her body. Although egg and sperm should fertilize normally, albeit in vitro, if there is a sperm penetration problem, the sperm can be injected directly into the egg, using intracytoplasmic sperm injection (ICSI).

'Test-tube' babies

IVF was developed in Britain in the late 1970s, and the first birth of a baby using IVF took place in 1978. It aroused a storm of controversy, with tabloid headlines about 'test-tube' babies, and was followed by the appointment of the Committee of Inquiry into Human Fertilisation and Embryology (the Warnock Committee), which led to legislation (the 1990 Human Fertilisation and Embryology Act), and the establishment of the Human Fertilisation and Embryology Authority (HFEA), to regulate the whole area of fertility treatment.

The novelty factor

But why does controversy attach to a technique that enables otherwise childless couples to have the children they desire? In the early days, as with any scientific innovation, the very idea of fertilization outside the human body seemed extraordinary. However, some 45,000 plus babies have been born through IVF, so there is no longer a novelty factor. Another, related, concern is that children might be distressed, and perhaps psychologically damaged, when or if they discover that they have been conceived by artificial means. But again, the novelty aspect and the initial tabloid references to 'test-tube' babies seem to be the major factors. It is a matter of what is regarded as out of the ordinary. Assisted conception is now relatively commonplace, accounting for about 1.5 per cent of births, so children will not be distressed or embarrassed to find that this was how they were conceived. Thirty years ago, divorce was far less common than it is today. A certain degree of social stigma attached to it, and the children of divorced parents were conscious of this. The situation is very different today.

Creation of surplus embryos

There are religious objections (see below), but one concern, shared by religious and non-religious people, is that IVF involves production of more embryos than are actually required for transfer into the woman's uterus. The surplus embryos are either destroyed, or, with parental consent, used for research purposes. However, for those who regard the embryo as an intrinsically valuable human being from the outset, disposing of the embryos, or carrying out research on them, is to use them in an ethically repugnant way. There is also concern that couples may be pressurized into allowing their surplus embryos to be used for research, even if they do not really wish to do so. The religious and non-religious objections to embryo research are discussed on **pp. 249–50**. An important counter-argument is that 70 per cent of embryos that are fertilized in vivo never implant in the womb, but are washed away during the journey from the uterus.

Health implications of fertility treatments

What about the health implications of infertility treatments? Women may suffer a range of side-effects from such drugs as clomifene and gonadotropins, including nausea, vomiting, abdominal pain and diarrhoea. There is also a greater likelihood of an ectopic pregnancy, where the egg implants in the fallopian tube, not the womb.

Fertility treatment increases the prospects of multiple pregnancy. With IVF, for example, several fertilized eggs are introduced into the woman's uterus, in order to try to ensure success. Multiple pregnancy has health implications, as it is likely to raise the woman's blood pressure, perhaps substantially, making her up to three times more likely to develop diabetes during pregnancy, while half of all twins and almost all triplets have low birth weights. Further, there is the claim that children born as a result of IVF have a higher tendency to birth defects, including the eye disease retinal blastoma. For critics, the birth defects result from the unnatural environment in which an embryo is developed in a laboratory and then inserted into the womb. These are all strong **consequentialist** arguments against assisted conception, as its use involves risks to the mother, the foetus or both.

Emotional stress, success rate and cost

In addition to health risks, there is the stress of undergoing fertility treatment. Those undertaking it see it as their only opportunity to have their own biological children. But their hopes may well be disappointed. Indeed, with IVF, the odds are stacked against success. Although about 80 per cent of the woman's eggs are fertilized successfully in vitro, this is no guarantee of a baby:

> Although the transfer itself [to the woman's body] is a simple procedure, it is after the transfer that things are most likely to go wrong; for reasons that are not fully understood, with even the most successful IVF teams, the probability of a given embryo that has been transferred to the uterus actually implanting there, and leading to a continuing pregnancy, is always less than 20%, and generally no more than 10%. (Singer, *Practical Ethics*, p. 159)

A 2005 HFEA survey of fertility clinics revealed wide variations in their success rate for IVF. The average rate, with women aged 35, was 27.6 per cent, but, while the best clinics achieved 58.5 per cent, the worst managed only 10 per cent.

However, while the outcome is doubtful, the costs are not. The NHS will meet the costs of tests to diagnose infertility, but there is no certainty that they will pay for the treatments, while it is not covered on private medical insurance policies. HFEA estimates that, at a private clinic, each IVF cycle can cost between £4,000 and £8,000. Even if the NHS does foot the bill, unless they are exempt from prescription charges, couples have to pay for fertility drugs (such as the ovulation induction agent, pergonol), themselves, which can cost up to £1,600.

Is it fair to allow people to subject themselves to such an emotionally gruelling process, when the chances of success are so limited, but the costs so high? Perhaps not; but, in a free society, it is accepted that this is a matter for individual decision. Society's responsibility is to provide a satisfactory legislative and regulatory framework, which ensures good practice and prevents profiteering from people's desire to have children. However, given the expense of treatment, and the patchiness of NHS provision, fertility treatment has become something that only the well-off can afford, creating a situation where, in effect, it is possible to purchase the ability to have children.

Fertility treatment on the NHS

According to NICE (National Institute for Health and Clinical Excellence) guidelines, primary care trusts (PCTs), which provide health care at local level, should provide up to three cycles of IVF, funded by the National Health Service. However, a recent survey showed that only one in ten PCTs are doing so, with 17 per cent providing two cycles, and 68 per cent providing just one. There are also long waiting-lists of up to five years for treatment. Thus, whether or not people receive NHS-funded treatment depends on where they live, and such a 'postcode lottery' raises questions of fairness. On the other hand, there is the issue of whether the NHS should be providing fertility treatment at all, in view of the fact that, in some areas, it struggles to provide basic health care and runs hospitals in which low standards of hygiene and cleanliness put patients at risk of contracting 'superbugs', such as MRSA (methicillin-resistant staphylococcus aureus).

Among the NICE guidelines for NHS-funded IVF treatment is the recommendation that it should be limited to women between 29 and 39 years of age. This appears reasonable, as these are the years when women are most likely to conceive, in normal circumstances; are most likely to be able to cope with the physical demands of pregnancy; and during which they and their babies are least likely to experience health problems. It also helps to prevent the problems that may arise from elderly parents trying to bring up young children. However, the counter-argument here is that the guidelines discriminate unfairly against less well-off older women with fertility problems. There is nothing to stop older women, who can conceive naturally, doing so; older women with the financial means can obtain private treatment; while there is also the feminist issue that some men are capable of fathering children well into old age.

Disclosure of donor information

Egg and sperm donation is now complicated by the fact that donors can no longer remain anonymous. Under the Disclosure of Donor Information Regulations (2004), the HFEA must now provide anybody, born as a result of egg, sperm or embryo donation, with full information about the donor, including their name, date of birth, and address, once s/he has reached the age of 18. While it is understandable that people born in this way should want information about their biological parent(s), and it seems right to provide it, this provision may deter prospective donors, and also create emotional distress for all those involved.

Surrogacy

Where a woman is unable to conceive, or to support a pregnancy, one solution is to find a surrogate. With traditional surrogacy, the surrogate woman's own egg is fertilized with the intended father's sperm, which is introduced into her body by artificial insemination. Gestational or host IVF surrogacy is where the would-be parents supply both the egg and sperm, and the surrogate woman 'hosts' an embryo, conceived through IVF.

A friend or relative volunteering to be a surrogate, in order to help an infertile couple, seems noble and self-sacrificing, but a commercial arrangement does not seem ethically acceptable, or consistent with human dignity, as it would involve the surrogate 'renting out her womb' for others' use. In Britain, surrogacy is legal, but payment is not. Under the Surrogacy Arrangements Act, 1985 (as amended by the Human Fertilisation and Embryology Act, 1990), surrogates can only be reimbursed for reasonable expenses. Further, a surrogacy agreement is not enforceable in law, so even in a gestational surrogacy, the would-be parents do not have an enforceable legal right against the surrogate, if she decides to keep the baby.

The religious perspective

There are specific **Christian** objections to assisted conception, reflecting the Christian belief that all life is ultimately God-given and valuable; that this applies to embryos; and that, at every stage of existence, human conduct should reflect what is held to be God's purpose for human beings.

Roman Catholic teaching

The **Roman Catholic Church** has particularly strong objections, based on the belief that such techniques separate the act of procreation from the sexual act; that they give technology the dominant role in bringing a human person into existence; and that they undermine the dignity of parents and children, turning the creation of children into the production of a commodity:

> Techniques that entail the dissociation of husband and wife by the intrusion of a person other than the couple . . . are gravely immoral . . . [and] infringe the child's right to be born of a father and mother . . . bound to each other by marriage . . . The act which brings the child into existence is no longer an act by which two persons give themselves to one another, but one that entrusts the life and identity of the embryo into the power of doctors and biologists . . . contrary to the dignity and equality that must be common to parents and children . . . procreation is deprived of its proper perfection. (*Catechism of the Catholic Church*, paras. 2376–7)

From a secular point of view, this may appear as an over-emphasis on the centrality of the sexual act as the 'natural' way of procreating children. Roman Catholic objections also include the fact that human embryos are destroyed in IVF, and that sperm collection involves masturbation, which is sinful.

The development of Anglican thinking

The **Church of England** used to share the **Roman Catholic Church's** view:

> Artificial insemination with donated semen involves a breach of marriage. It violates the exclusive union set up between husband and wife . . . For the child there is always the risk of disclosure, deliberate or unintended, of the circumstances of his conception. We therefore judge artificial insemination to be wrong in principle and contrary to Christian standards. (CofE (a)).

As well as seeing assisted conception as violating the essence of Christian marriage, within which the procreation of children results from the sexual relationship of two people, united in love, the Church's view (in 1959) was that it would be distressing and psychologically harmful for children to discover that they had been conceived through artificial reproductive methods. But, by the 1980s, the **Church of England** was coming round to the view that the loving relationship between a married couple is not damaged by assisted conception, in the way that it would be if one or other had actual sexual intercourse with another person:

> [it] excludes no more than physical intercourse . . . the semen donated by a third party is no more than a mere fertilizing agent which imports nothing alien into the marriage relationship and does not adulterate it as physical union would. (CofE (a))

However, a 1997 General Synod resolution urged that assisted conception should only be available to women during the years when they would conceive under normal circumstances, and emphasized the central role of marriage as the 'ideal context' for procreating and raising children, and children's need for a father (CofE (a)).

Secular morality

From the point of secular morality, provided that infertility treatments are safe, that they do not lead to a higher incidence of birth defects, and that those who make use of them genuinely want children, and are capable of taking care of them, the **consequentialist/utilitarian** is likely to approve of them, as maximizing happiness. However, if they involve risks to the health of the women using them, or if the children conceived by these means have a greater likelihood of birth defects, **utilitarians** would have reasons for opposing them, on the grounds that they may lead to pain and suffering. For the **deontologist**, a key issue is whether or not s/he regards an embryo as a human person. If s/he does, then those human persons are being used (and, in many cases, discarded) as means to others' ends. Again, are those who resort to assisted conception using themselves as a means to what they perceive as their own happiness, in a way that is inconsistent with human dignity? The **virtue ethicist** might argue that techniques that enable people to have children, when they are physically incapable of doing so, inhibit development of such virtues as fortitude and stoicism, from which the individual and society benefit.

Fairness has already been mentioned. At the moment, assisted conception is not equally available to all. Should it be? If so, we have to decide how much society is prepared to spend on it. Is an upper age limit for women to receive publicly funded fertility treatment a sensible measure, in the interests of the women themselves, of any children that might be born, and of society; or is it discriminatory against older women and, in particular, poor older women? The age question pinpoints another possible problem with fertility treatment: that it may be seen as a kind of 'fall-back position', encouraging the social trend towards people having children later in life, when it suits their career or financial circumstances. However, this may not be to the advantage of children, parents or society. There are also issues, which are discussed on **p. 273**, arising from amendment of Section 13 (5) of the Human Fertilisation and Embryology Act, 1990 (see below), which refers to children's need 'for a father', by the new Human Fertilisation and Embryology Act.

2 Embryo research

Use of embryos for research

Many of the same ethical issues arise in embryo research as in abortion and assisted conception. Does an embryo have the moral status of a human person from the moment of conception, meaning that it should be treated with appropriate respect, and ruling out research? Does it have no intrinsic value, making its use in research unobjectionable, and certainly less so than the use of animals, particularly primates? Or, does it acquire increasing moral status, and entitlement to protection, as it develops?

The genetic blueprint

In natural fertilization, the human embryo is formed when a sperm fertilizes an egg. Together, they form a genome, which is the genetic blueprint of the future human being. After a few days, a blastocyst is formed, comprising cells of two types. An outer layer of cells will become the placenta and other tissue required for the future foetus's development. An inner mass, the stem cells, are the human body's so-called 'master cells'. They are 'pluripotent', which means they have the potential to develop into almost every other type of tissue in the human body. The issue, and potential benefits, of research into these stem cells, and the methods of creating embryos for research, raise further ethical questions.

Implantation and the primitive streak

Fertilization occurs in the upper portion of the fallopian tube. During the first 14 days of its existence, the embryo travels to the womb, where it implants itself; and, at this point the primitive streak, which is the basis of the nervous system, develops.

The primitive streak indicates whether the embryo will develop into one foetus or divide, to form identical twins: until that time, it is impossible to say whether the embryo is one potential human being, or more than one. Another important point is that around 70 per cent of embryos never implant in the womb; they are washed away during their journey from the fallopian tube.

The Warnock Committee, the Human Fertilisation and Embryology Act, 1990 and the Human Fertilisation and Embryology Authority (HFEA)

The Committee of Inquiry into Human Fertilisation and Embryology, chaired by the philosopher Mary Warnock, was appointed in 1982, following the first birth of a child conceived through IVF; and its recommendations were enacted in the Human Fertilisation and Embryology Act, 1990. This dealt with: fertility treatment involving the use of donated eggs or sperm, as in donor insemination and embryos created outside the body (IVF); their storage; and research into human embryos. The HFEA was created to supervise these activities, and to license clinics and research centres. Embryo research can only be conducted on embryos up to 14 days old (the point at which the primitive streak appears), and was initially confined to the purposes of: promoting advances in the treatment of infertility; increasing knowledge about the causes of congenital disease and of miscarriages; and developing more effective contraceptive techniques and techniques for detecting the presence of chromosome abnormalities in embryos before implantation.

Extending the range of embryo research

At that time, the source of embryos was expected to be those created for, but not used in, IVF, which would only be available with the parents' permission. However, embryo research clearly offered opportunities to investigate the causes of serious diseases, and, following a report by the Chief Medical Officer, the Human Fertilisation and Embryology (Research Purposes) Regulations, 2001 were passed, which included in the range of research purposes: increasing knowledge about the development of embryos; increasing knowledge about serious disease; and enabling such knowledge to be utilized in the development of treatments for serious disease.

Ethical issues

Is it ethically legitimate to conduct research on embryos at any stage, under any conditions and from any source? Clearly, those who take the view that the embryo is a human person, with full moral status from the point of fertilization, will condemn it. The **Roman Catholic Church's** view is that a human life starts when the ovum is fertilized: it is 'the life of a new human being with his own growth. It would never be made human if it were not human already' (*Evangelium Vitae*, para. 60). Those **deontologists** who hold that the embryo has moral status as a human person also oppose embryo research, as it means treating the embryo as a means, not an end. On the other hand, one of Peter Singer's arguments in favour of research on embryos of up to 14 days old is that such an embryo cannot (logically) be regarded as a human person (see **p. 225**):

> human beings are individuals, and the early embryo is not even an individual. At any time up to about 14 days after fertilisation . . . longer than human embryos have so far been kept alive outside the body – the embryo can split into two or more genetically identical embryos. This happens naturally and leads to the formation of identical twins . . . prior to this point, we cannot be sure that what we are looking at is the precursor of one or two individuals. (Singer, *Practical Ethics*, pp. 156–7)

One way to settle this issue would be to identify the precise point when a human life begins, and then to give the embryo/foetus the same legal protection as adults or children from that stage. But Mary Warnock holds that there is no such precise point:

> I tried many times to explain that the question '*When does Life begin?*' was the wrong question. What we were really asking was '*When, in the gradual development of the embryo do we begin to think of it as something that merits protection? What, at its various stages, is to be its moral status?*' (M. Warnock, 'Anne McLaren as Teacher', p. 489)

Warnock thus endorses a developmental view of the human embryo. This is the view taken in the Human Fertilisation and Embryology Act, 1990. While no embryo may be used or kept, for research or other purposes, 'after the appearance of the primitive streak' (Section 3 (3) (a)), before that point, which is defined as occurring fourteen days after fertilization (Section 3 (4)), research may be conducted on it.

Religious views

The **Church of England** affirms the sanctity of the human embryo; the need to treat it with respect, from the outset; and the importance of not using embryos for research, unless absolutely necessary. However, it is more sympathetic to the 1990 Act's view that, before the appearance of the primitive streak, embryos do not have the same moral status as they do subsequently. The undifferentiated cells of the fertilized egg, which will form the placenta and umbilical cord, as well as the foetus, do not have clear 'continuity of individual identity' (para. 48) with the foetus in the womb. Not until the appearance of the primitive streak, after which they cannot become twins, is there continuity of identity with the future child and adult; and that is when it is appropriate to refer to an individual human person. Further:

> An absolutist view of the embryo does not accord with actual practice. Funeral services are not held for embryos that fail to implant and are lost. (CofE (b), para. 52)

Stem cell research and cell nuclear replacement

As the stem cells are the human body's 'master cells', with the potential to develop into almost every other type of bodily tissue, research on them could lead to significant advances in medical treatment. Cultivating them, so that they could replace dead or diseased cells in human organs, might make it possible to relieve the suffering of the many thousands of people afflicted by such currently incurable diseases as Alzheimer's and various types of cancer. This was why the 2001 regulations (see above) extended the range of permitted research.

However, surplus embryos, created for IVF, are not the only source of stem cells. As well as being found in foetal tissue and umbilical cord blood, stem cells can also be obtained from embryos that are specially created for research purposes. They are produced by the technique of cell nuclear replacement (CNR), or 'cloning', permitted under the 1990 Act and the 2001 Regulations, in which the nucleus from an adult cell is placed in a human egg that has had its nucleus removed. The embryo is allowed to develop until the blastocyst stage, when the stem cells are isolated, and then differentiated, in vitro, to produce cells that could be implanted in a human patient. This is therapeutic cloning. Cells from embryos that have been created with a cell from a possible patient have the advantage of not being liable to rejection by his/her immune systems after implantation.

The spectre of 'Dolly the Sheep'

The problem is that the CNR technique, used for therapeutic cloning, can also be used for reproductive cloning. It is the first step in the process that created Dolly the Sheep, in 1996. Opponents of therapeutic cloning argue that it sets up a 'slippery slope': if embryos are created for research and therapeutic cloning, it makes it harder to reject reproductive cloning, and then its application to human beings. However, although the initial process of embryo creation for therapeutic and reproductive cloning is the same, the purpose behind the former is different, being designed to produce embryonic stem (ES) cells, exclusively for treatment and therapy. The CNR embryo is allowed to develop only to the blastocyst stage, and it is not implanted in a female uterus in order to produce a baby. Further, the Human Reproductive Cloning Act, 2001 makes the implantation of a CNR embryo in a woman a serious criminal offence, punishable by a fine or up to ten years' imprisonment.

The issue of deliberately creating embryos for research purposes

Fears that allowing production of CNR embryos might lead to reproductive cloning is not the only objection to CNR. For those who regard the human embryo, before the appearance of the primitive streak, as having full, not developmental, moral status, embryo research is wrong, whatever the source of the embryos. Other concerns are that embryos are being deliberately created for research and therapeutic purposes, and that the extended research purposes, under the 2001 Regulations, involve embryos being used for purposes other than research relating to reproductive techniques, which some regard as the only research purposes for which they should be used.

However, CNR embryos are subject to the same tight regulatory framework as other embryos, while the potential benefits of using them for research are enormous. For example, it could aid understanding of the process of cell dedifferentiation: the process by which a differentiated adult cell (one that has developed into a specific type of cell) is 'dedifferentiated' when placed in the recipient egg. A problem, however, has been the limited availability of human embryos for research: a problem that is addressed by the new Human Fertilisation and Embryology Act (see below).

Hybrid embryos

In addition to provisions relating to the welfare of children and same-sex couples (see **p. 273**), the recently enacted Human Fertilisation and Embryology Act, 2008 provides that all human embryos, however produced, are subject to regulation; bans sex selection of offspring for non-medical reasons; and facilitates follow-up research. More controversially, it widens the scope of legitimate embryo research, and (to tackle the problem of the scarcity of human embryos) permits production of 'inter-species' or hybrid embryos, which combine human and animal genetic material. Almost inevitably, this has led to talk of the creation of 'Frankenstein's monsters'.

The hybrid embryos will be produced by CNR, and will involve placing the nuclei of adult human cells in denucleated animal cells, which will then be developed to the blastocyst stage, when the ES cells can be harvested. The embryos will not be allowed to develop beyond this point, and will be subject to the same strict regulatory framework as other embryos. The strong opposition to the proposals seems to derive from fears that such embryos will be used for reproductive cloning, and thus to the creation of hybrid creatures. However, such an outcome is totally prohibited by the Human Reproductive Cloning Act, 2001.

The 'yuk' factor

Medical researchers and charities are delighted with the new Act. For example, Dr Chris Kingswood of the Tuberous Sclerosis Association describes hybrid embryo research as a 'powerful tool for discovering the basic problems in genetic and other diseases and accelerating the chances of finding treatments'. On the other hand, opponents of embryo research, such as the **Roman Catholic Church**, are particularly unhappy about its provisions, with Cardinal Keith O'Brien using his 2008 Easter Day sermon to denounce them as 'grotesque' (*The Times*). In a cautiously supportive response to the consultation that preceded the Act, the **Church of England** observed that the '"yuk" factor', which is the understandable immediate response to the measure,

> is neither a final arbiter of acceptability nor necessarily the artefact of unscientific and uneducated thought. Rather it reminds us to pause and consider carefully where the appropriate boundaries should lie and to seek wisdom to do so. (CofE (c))

While welcoming discovery of the means of 'alleviating presently untreatable diseases', it warns against raising 'unrealistic expectations' among sufferers, and makes the essential point, with which even the Act's most enthusiastic advocates would agree: that laws against bringing any hybrid creatures 'to birth' must be stringently enforced.

References and suggestions for further reading and research

BBC News, at http://news.bbc.co.uk.

Catechism of the Catholic Church, 2nd edn, at http://www.scborromeo. org/ccc.htm (see also http://www.catholic-church.org.uk).

The Christian Institute website at http://www.christian.org.uk contains briefing papers reflecting traditional Christian teaching on a range of issues, e.g. 'Apologetics: The Sanctity of Life'.

Church of England (CofE) at http://cofe.anglican.org: *Science, Medicine, Technology and Environment* (Human Fertilization and Embryology) (CofE (a)); A report from the Mission and Public Affairs Council, *Embryo Research: Some Christian Perspectives* (CofE (b)); *Response to HFEA Consultation on Hybrids and Chimeras* (2007) (CofE (c)); and The Board for Social Responsibility of The Church of England, *Response to the House of Lords Select Committee on Stem Cell Research* (2001).

Department of Health website at http://www.dh.gov.uk provides information about health policy and practice. See *Acts and Bills* section for details of the new Human Fertilisation and Embryology Act, and *Progress on Policy* section for 'Stem Cell Research: Medical Progress with Responsibility'.

T. Drake, 'What's Wrong With In-Vitro Fertilization', at http://www. staycatholic.com (this website contains a range of articles about Roman Catholic approaches to bio-ethical issues).

Evangelium Vitae, encyclical of Pope John Paul II (March 1995), at http:// www.vatican.va.

Human Fertilisation and Embryology Authority website at www.hfea.gov. uk contains information about its work and regulatory activities.

The Human Fertilisation and Embryology Bill, 2007–08 at http://services. parliament.uk/bills/.

The Independent, at http://www.independent.co.uk/life-style/health-and-wellbeing/health-news/.

NHS Direct website at http://www.nhsdirect.nhs.uk contains health information and statistics (see *Common Health Questions*, 'Do I have to pay for IVF treatment?' and an online *encyclopaedia of health issues* (see 'Infertility' and 'In-vitro fertilization'.

National Institute for Health and Clinical Excellence (NICE) website at http://www.nice.org.uk contains their guidelines and information about their work.

The Times, 'Stem-Cell Research – Playing God?' (10 May 2008), at http://business.timesonline.co.uk.

Office of Public Sector Information, *Statute Law Database*, at http://www.statutelaw.gov.uk (the full text of the statutes and regulations referred to can be found here).

Office of Public Sector Information website at www.opsi.gov.uk contains information about the public sector and official publications.

P. Singer, *Practical Ethics*, 2nd edn, Cambridge: Cambridge University Press, 1993.

M. Warnock, 'Anne McLaren as Teacher', *International Journal of Developmental Biology*, vol. 45, pp. 487–90, at www.ijdb.ehu.es.

15 Human and Sexual Relationships

1 Human relationships

The right to form relationships

Article 16 of the Universal Declaration of Human Rights (UDHR) and Article 12 of the European Convention on Human Rights (ECHR) (see **pp. 280, 285–93**) affirm to all men and women of full age, and without any limitation of nationality or religion, the right to marry and to start a family, provided marriage is entered into freely. These articles reflect some of human beings' most powerful instincts: not only to have sexual relations with other human beings, but to form permanent relationships, within which those sexual relations occur, and to procreate and raise a family.

A purely private matter?

Are such relationships purely private matters? Are individuals entitled to form whatever relationships they wish, and to conduct them as they please? Or, is society entitled to interfere? There is no doubt that it has; and UDHR points to the tension that inevitably exists between on the one hand the privacy of individual relationships and on the other hand society's role of regulating its members' relationships and its responsibility to do so, which involves encouraging certain types of relationship and discouraging others. While Article 12 seeks to secure to each individual freedom from 'arbitrary interference with his privacy, family, home', Article 16 declares that the family is the 'natural and fundamental group unit' (in society), which is entitled to societal and state protection.

Marriage and families

Families, involving two married partners, have traditionally been regarded as the best environment within which to raise children as well-balanced individuals, and as an indispensable basis for a stable society. Human relationships are also a matter of religious concern, as all the major world religions, including Christianity, have teachings about the purposes of human beings and human sexuality, and the kind of relationships into which people should and should not enter. Historically, western societies, with Christian-based values, have encouraged marriage, and discouraged other forms of human relationships, either through the sanction of public opinion (moral disapproval), as with cohabitation and procreation outside marriage, or through the sanction of the law (by banning them), as with male homosexuality.

Changing attitudes and individual freedom

In the past 40 years, as religious influence has waned, coinciding with an increase in the use and effectiveness of contraception, attitudes and the law have changed. In its approach to human relationships, society's default position now seems to be that of Mill's **principle of liberty**: that in conduct affecting only himself and his own good, whether physical or moral, the individual is entitled to absolute independence; the only purpose for which society can rightfully exercise power over one of its members, against his will, is to prevent harm to others. Thus, the conduct of adults, when it affects only themselves, and does not harm others, is for them to decide; the law will not interfere. Indeed, although individuals, particularly religious people, and their organizations, have definite ethical views about the rightness or wrongness of what Mill calls **'self-regarding' conduct** (that which affects only the individual) even the sanction of public opinion has become muted.

Society still has a role

However, when relationships involve injury or exploitation of others, or abuse of children, society, through the law, does interfere. There are also situations, such as teenage pregnancy, which has a high incidence in Britain (in 2003, 42.3 conceptions per 1,000 girls under 18, more than five times that in the Netherlands) that society seeks to discourage, in this case both in the interests of the pregnant teenagers themselves, whose educational and career prospects parenthood will blight, and to prevent children being brought up by single parents in circumstances of poverty and deprivation. Again, marriage and now civil partnership are legal, as well as personal, relationships, and society determines the legal framework within which they can be entered into and dissolved.

Utilitarian and deontological approaches

Current social attitudes embody both **utilitarian** and **deontological** approaches. Allowing people to engage in whatever relationships they choose, and to conduct them as they wish, is thought likely to maximize happiness. However, intervention occurs if individuals are being coerced, exploited or abused, in which case they are being treated, not as ends in themselves, but merely as means to the pleasure and gratification of others; and such intervention also has the effect of minimizing the pain experienced by the victims. Of course, some **religious people** and ethicists maintain that certain kinds of sexual activity and relationship, even if entered into freely, are incompatible with God's purpose for human beings or with human dignity.

2 Marriage and cohabitation

The influence of Christianity

In western society, **Christian teaching** has established and reinforced belief in marriage. After God has created man, he decides that: 'It is not good that the man should be alone; I will make a him helper fit for him' (Genesis 2.18). Jesus sums up the nature of Christian marriage, as a loving, permanent and indissoluble union:

> But from the beginning of creation, 'God made them male and female.' 'For this reason a man shall leave his father and mother and be joined to his wife, and the two shall become one flesh'. So they are no longer two but one. (Mark 10.6–8)

St Paul (or a follower – the Epistle's authorship is disputed) draws an analogy between the marriage relationship and that of Jesus to the Christian Church:

> Husbands, love your wives, as Christ loved the church and gave himself up for her . . . This mystery is a profound one . . . however, let each one

of you love his wife as himself, and let the wife see that she respects her husband. (Ephesians 5.25, 32–3)

Elsewhere, Paul represents marriage as a necessary measure for controlling and curbing human lust. In response to the view, expressed by members of the church in Corinth, that Christians should be celibate ('It is well for a man not to touch a woman'), he argues that, 'because of the temptation to immorality, each man should have his own wife and each woman her own husband' (1 Corinthians 7.1–2). However, in the context of the imminent arrival of the kingdom of God ('the form of this world is passing away': 1 Corinthians 7.31), whether or not Christians marry does not really matter: 'Now concerning the unmarried, I have no command of the Lord . . . in view of the present distress it is well for a person to remain as he is. Are you bound to a wife? Do not seek to be free. Are you free from a wife? Do not seek marriage' (1 Corinthians 7.25–7).

The Christian conception of marriage

Any long-term relationship involves commitment by the partners, but the nature of the relationship, and therefore the expectations that partners have of each other, and society of them, differ with religious marriage, civil marriage and cohabitation. The preface to the **Church of England** marriage service (CofE (a)), for example, makes clear the spiritual dimension of religious marriage. It is a 'gift of God in creation', through which the partners may 'know the grace of God'. It has been 'made holy by God'; 'blessed' by Jesus' presence at the wedding at Cana in Galilee (John 2.1–11); and will unite the partners with each other, in 'heart, body and mind', as 'Christ is united with his bride, the Church'. The partners will be able to 'grow together in love and trust' and 'joyful commitment', lasting to the end of their lives. They will enjoy the 'delight and tenderness' of their sexual relationship, and their lifelong union will be the 'foundation of family life', enabling children to be nurtured, and family members to find in each other 'strength, companionship and comfort'. Marriage is also an institution that enriches and strengthens society and the community and that should be upheld and honoured.

The couple make their vows to each other 'in the presence of God and his people':

I, [name], take you, [partner's name],
to be my wife/husband.
to have and to hold

from this day forward;
for better, for worse,
for richer, for poorer,
in sickness and in health,
to love and to cherish,
till death us do part;
according to God's holy law.
In the presence of God I make this vow.

Rightly, the preface emphasizes that marriage is not to be entered into 'lightly or selfishly'.

Civil marriage

In a civil marriage ceremony, in England and Wales, although the couple can exchange vows of their own choosing, the only requirement is a statutory declaration that there is no reason why they should not be married:

I do solemnly declare that I know not of any lawful impediment why, I [name], may not be joined in matrimony to you [partner's name];

and the contracting words:

I call upon these persons here present to witness that I, [name], do take thee [partner's name] to be my lawful wedded husband [or wife].

Vows are not made in the presence of God; the partners are not required to affirm its lifelong nature; and there is no explicit acceptance that the marriage should endure, irrespective of life's hardships and vicissitudes. However, the effect is the same: the partners are legally married, and need to divorce, in order to end their relationship.

The personal and social benefits of marriage

There is evidence that married couples and their children enjoy many advantages over single and cohabiting people and their children; and that society also gains. Studies in the United States, Britain and elsewhere indicate that married people are happier than those who are unmarried; earn and save more; have greater life expectancy; and enjoy better physical and mental health. A study carried out for the Human Services Policy Office (HSP) of the Office of the Assistant Secretary for Planning and Evaluation (ASPE), US Department of Health and Human Services, which focused on research conducted in the United States since 1990, found that:

> there is substantial research evidence suggesting that, for young adults, marriage reduces heavy alcohol consumption . . . and . . . for young men of a reduction in marijuana use . . . Recent work consistently indicates that – for both men and women – marital entry decreases depressive symptoms while marital dissolution increases them. Similarly, those who are stably married report fewer depressive symptoms than do similar adults who are stably unmarried . . . which also suggests that marriage reduces the prevalence of depressive symptoms . . . The studies that are available . . . suggest that growing up with two parents does improve long-term physical health outcomes, particularly for men. (ASPE/HSP, pp. 6–7)

It has been suggested that marriage has these effects, because cohabitants tolerate behaviour, such as smoking and alcohol abuse, that 'husbands and wives would discourage' (Civitas, *The Facts Behind Cohabitation*, p. 2).

The ASPE study recognizes the difficulty of establishing a clear causal connection between marriage and health: 'marriage is likely to be both a cause and a consequence of these health outcomes'; it may be the case that healthier people are 'more likely to marry' (p. 2). However, research outside the United States also indicates a link between marriage, health and happiness. According to Daniel Lees of the New Zealand Maxim Institute, research, such as that by Stack and Eshelman, which measured marital status and happiness 'across 17 nations', shows that married couples are 'more likely to report being happy than those who cohabited' (Lees, *Psychological Benefits of Marriage*).

It also seems that marriage contributes to the stability of society, and the well-being of children, because married partners are far less likely to end their relationships. The family life expert Linda Waite, Professor of Sociology at the University of Chicago and a former President of the Population Association of America, who has made a detailed study of cohabitation in the United States, argues that it is an 'unstable' living arrangement, which can have a negative impact on people's emotional, financial and physical well-being:

> The 'cohabitation deal' . . . will have especially disappointing outcomes for people who expect it to deliver the same benefits the 'marriage bargain' delivers . . . People who cohabit often contend that marriage is just about a piece of paper. We've found . . . that there is quite a big difference

between being married and living together. (*The University of Chicago Chronicle*, March 2000)

In Britain, the average cohabitation lasts less than two years, with fewer than 4 per cent lasting 'for ten years or more' (Civitas, *The Facts Behind Cohabitation*, p. 1). A particularly telling statistic is that, whereas only 8 per cent of married couples have split up within five years of the birth of a child, '52 per cent of cohabiting couples will have' (*Daily Telegraph*, December 2005). Further, there is evidence that the children of married parents have happier and more stable lives, and gain more from education:

> children born to cohabiting couples are more likely to experience a series of disruptions in family life, which can have negative consequences for their emotional and educational development. Children living with cohabiting parents do less well at school and are more likely to suffer from emotional problems than children of married couples. (Civitas, *The Facts Behind Cohabitation*, p. 2)

The ASPE/HSP study confirms the 'intergenerational' benefits of marriage: 'the evidence to date suggests that children from two-parent families live longer and enjoy better adult health than children from single-parent families or whose parents divorced in childhood' (p. 48).

In 2006, almost a quarter of children lived in single-parent families, which tend to be poorer than couple-based families: for example, single-parent families are 'three times more likely to live in rented accommodation', and are also more likely to occupy housing that does not meet 'minimum standards' (The *Independent*, April 2007). Around 20 per cent of children in Britain are 'born to cohabiting couples' (Civitas, *The Facts Behind Cohabitation*, p. 2), who are many times more likely to end their relationships, exposing children to emotional distress, financial hardship and health risks. Given the benefits of marriage, and of family life based on marriage, it is hard to understand why society does not do more to promote and sustain it, for the benefit of its members, especially children, and in the interests of social stability.

Interestingly, John Stuart Mill's **libertarianism** did not include couples being free to have children as they chose:

> laws which . . . forbid marriage unless the parties can show that they have the means of supporting a family . . . are not objectionable as violations of liberty. Such laws are interferences of the State to prohibit a mischievous act – an act injurious to others, which ought to be a subject

of reprobation, and social stigma, even when it is not deemed expedient to superadd legal punishment, (Mill, 'On Liberty', p. 120).

In the light of the evidence, Mill would doubtless have welcomed a strenuous effort by society today, through the use of the sanction of public opinion, to discourage cohabitation and the birth of children to cohabiting or single parents, and to promote marriage, in order to ensure the well-being of children.

How marriage is faring in Britain

Despite its personal and social advantages, marriage is a decreasingly popular option. In 2006, only 236,980 marriages took place in England and Wales, the lowest number since 1895. The number of marriages that were the first for both partners reached its highest point in 1940, at 426,100, which was 91 per cent of all marriages. This contrasts with a figure of 144,120, or 61 per cent, in 2006; 92,870 of the 2006 marriages were remarriages, 39 per cent of the total.

Cohabitation

Cohabitation is a fact of British family life. Of the 17.1 million families of all types in 2006, the number based on cohabiting couples increased from 1.4 to 2.3 million (by 65 per cent), in the ten years since 1996, while the number of families based on married couples fell to 12.1 million. In 2001–03, 21 per cent of women aged 25–9 had cohabited, whereas it was only 1 per cent in 1971–3. As the research into the relative durability of relationships based on marriage and cohabitation indicates, the growing popularity of the latter has important implications for society.

The **Christian Churches**, while recognizing that social changes influence attitudes towards marriage ('There are many challenges to our understanding of marriage – the changes in attitudes towards sexual activity linked with increasing acceptance of contraception, the increased number of couples who delay or choose not to marry but live together' (CofE (b))), remain resolute in their support for it. For example, a resolution of the **Church of England's** General Synod, in February 2004, strongly reaffirmed that: 'marriage is central to the stability and health of human society and warrants a unique place in the law of this country' (CofE (c)).

However, there have been efforts within the Church of England to promote a more tolerant and positive attitude towards cohabitation. A 2003 report, from the Diocese of Southwark, challenged the Church's traditional teaching, that sex before marriage is always wrong, on the grounds that it creates a sense of guilt, and estranges cohabiting couples from the Church, especially as the media take society's view that cohabitation and marriage are the same. Changing the approach need not demean marriage, but could offer a new route into it. The suggestion is that the Church should encourage cohabitees to see the advantages of a permanent relationship, and 'convert' their cohabitation into marriage. However, many cohabitees seem to choose cohabitation, precisely because it is not a permanent, legally binding relationship: they do not wish to make the commitment marriage involves.

Marriage and commitment

The key advantage that marriage seems to have over cohabitation is that it involves commitment: those who marry intend, and declare their intention, to enter a permanent relationship. They are not qualifying their position, or saying that they will 'see how things go':

> When people marry, they commit themselves not only to being emotional and sexual partners, but also to taking care of each other . . . They promise to stick by each other through the ups and downs that occur in everyone's lives. (Civitas, *The Facts Behind Cohabitation*, p. 4)

Some people claim to have objections of principle to marriage, but, while non-religious people will have such objections to religious marriage, it is hard to see what they could be in relation to civil marriage: other than unwillingness to make a commitment. Indeed, a **deontologist** could argue that no one should start a sexual relationship with a member of the opposite sex, particularly if they are not using contraception, unless they are prepared to make a commitment, because to do so is to treat the other person, and any children that might be conceived, as means, not ends in themselves. The **consequentialist/utilitarian** arguments in favour of marriage, as opposed to cohabitation, appear overwhelming, from the viewpoints of both individuals and society.

3 Contraception

The development of contraception

Forms of contraception, to enable couples to enjoy sex without risk of childbirth, have been around for thousands of years, but the vulcanization of rubber, in the mid-nineteenth century, made male barrier contraceptives more effective, by making possible the manufacture of rubber condoms. Female barrier methods, the diaphragm, the vulcanized rubber cap (the Dutch cap) and intrauterine devices, were developed in the late nineteenth and early twentieth centuries. However, increased effectiveness did not make contraception and birth control morally or socially acceptable. Charles Bradlaugh and Annie Besant were prosecuted, and sentenced to six months in jail, for publishing a manual of contraception, in 1876. However, they escaped imprisonment on a technicality. Dr Marie Stopes published a best-selling book, *Married Love*, which advocated contraception, in 1918. Despite strong opposition, particularly from the **Roman Catholic Church**, she opened a family planning clinic in London in 1921, which was followed by others around the country during the 1920s and 1930s. Described by A. J. P. Taylor as 'among the great benefactors of the age' (Taylor, *English History 1914–1945*, p. 165), her work helped to popularize contraception and birth control, leading to the foundation of the National Birth Control Council in 1930, which became the Family Planning Association (FPA) in 1939.

Current attitudes to contraception

By 2004–05, 75 per cent of women in Britain were using at least one method of contraception, the most popular being the oral contraceptive pill (first approved for use in 1961), which is used by 25 per cent of women, followed by the male condom (22 per cent). It is difficult to understand how anyone could oppose contraception, which, by giving women control of their own bodies, affords them autonomy and choice; enables individuals and partners to decide when, and if, to have children; helps to prevent unwanted babies; and, in the form of the condom, limits the spread of sexually transmitted diseases (STIs) and AIDS.

Article 16 of the Convention on the Elimination of All Forms of Discrimination Against Women (CEDAW: see **p. 290**) seeks the same rights for women as men: 'to decide freely and responsibly on the number and spacing of their children and to have access to the information, education and means to enable them to exercise these rights'. However, non-availability, or ignorance about, contraception is one factor contributing to the millions of unwanted pregnancies that occur in the world every year, many of them affecting women in undeveloped countries, where abortion may be illegal or difficult to obtain.

Roman Catholic teaching

The **Roman Catholic Church** prohibits any form of artificial contraception, even between married partners. According to the encyclical (papal letter) *Humanae Vitae* (1968), married love is directed not only to 'loving interchange' between husband and wife, but to the procreation of children (para. 9). Through 'laws written' into their 'actual nature', as men and women, they are 'capable of generating new life' (para. 12). If they perform an act of sexual love that lacks the 'capacity to transmit life' that God, as creator, incorporated into it, they frustrate his 'design which constitutes the norm of marriage', defy his will and deprive sexual love of its 'meaning and purpose' (para. 13).

Artificial contraception, even for 'therapeutic' purposes (concerned with health), is 'absolutely excluded as lawful means of regulating the number of children' (para. 14). If, due to the husband's or wife's health, or other factors, there are good reasons for spacing births, a married couple must use 'the natural cycles immanent in the reproductive system', and have intercourse only during the infertile periods of the wife's menstrual cycle (para. 16). The encyclical warns that artificial methods of contraception could undermine marital fidelity, lower general moral standards and damage the 'reverence' of men for women (para. 17).

The Anglican and Methodist approaches

In the **Church of England**, contraception is not regarded as a sin, and is acceptable to most members, provided both partners agree. Parents are entitled to decide the number and spacing of their children, based on the needs of existing children, maternal and child health, and other factors. Teaching on contraception has evolved over the decades. It was condemned at the 1908 Lambeth Conference (meeting of bishops of the worldwide Anglican Communion), as 'demoralising to character and hostile to national welfare', reflecting anxieties about national birth rates. The 1930 Conference recommended 'complete abstinence' as the best means of limiting family size, but accepted other methods, if used 'in the light of Christian principles'. By the 1958 Conference, it was affirmed to be a matter for individual conscience, while the 1968 Conference rejected the view, in *Humane Vitae*, that artificial methods of contraception are contrary to God's will (CofE (d)). The **Methodist Church** welcomes 'responsible contraception' as a means to marital fulfilment, for example, by spacing children, or preventing pregnancy altogether, for medical reasons (Methodists (a)).

Contraception and promiscuity

The New Testament explicitly and repeatedly condemns fornication or promiscuity (sexual intercourse between unmarried people) and adultery (sexual infidelity by those who are married): for example, 'let the marriage bed be undefiled; for God will judge the immoral and adulterous' (Hebrews 13.4); and, 'Now the works of the flesh are plain: fornication, impurity, licentiousness' (Galatians 5.19). And, although Jesus protected the woman 'caught in the act of adultery', he told her to 'go and do not sin again' (John 8.1–11). Acceptance of contraception does not mean that the **Church of England/Anglican Church** rejects such teachings, or approves sexual promiscuity or extra-marital sex:

> sexual intercourse is an act of total commitment which belongs properly within a permanent married relationship . . . fornication and adultery are sins against this ideal, and are to be met by a call to repentance. (CofE (e))

Its view is that, in addition to 'Scripture, Tradition and Reason', teaching on this issue should be informed by 'human experience'; and the 'experience of Christian married people in relation to contraception' (of the qualitative benefits it brings to marriage) is the reason for the 'change in Anglican thinking between 1930 and 1958' (CofE (d)).

Preventing unwanted pregnancies

In his 1971 Baird lectures, the New Testament scholar and Church of Scotland minister Professor William Barclay, while criticizing the sexual excesses of what was then called the 'permissive society', nonetheless noted that few people would question the use of contraception within marriage, or wish to return to the nineteenth century, 'when Charles Dickens' wife . . . had ten children and five miscarriages in rather less than twenty years' (Barclay, *Ethics in a Permissive Society*, p. 211). He upholds Christian teaching that 'sexual intercourse before and outside marriage is wrong': but what should be done about those who do not accept the 'Christian ethic of sex' (p. 211)? Every effort should be made to persuade them to do so, but, if they refuse, they should use contraception, because: 'anything is better than to bring into the world an unwanted child' (p. 211). Barclay's argument from the point of view of a traditional Christian ethicist is: best, no sex outside marriage; but, failing that, better protected sex than unwanted pregnancies and children.

The causes and consequences of unwanted pregnancies

However, there is still a long way to go in ensuring awareness of, and access to, contraception and birth control. According to the Global Health Council (GHC), lack of information about reproductive health services contributes to 'unwanted pregnancy, unsafe abortion, inadequate antenatal care, and lack of skilled attendance at birth' (GHC, *Women's Health*, p. 1; see also pp. 227–8). Each year, deaths related to maternal causes are estimated at 507,000–585,000 (one woman every minute, every day), with 99 per cent occurring in undeveloped countries (p. 2). Despite the worldwide commitment to providing access to contraception, nearly 30 per cent of the world's 205 million annual pregnancies are unintended, and between 1995 and 2000 almost 700,000 women died from causes related to them (p. 3). Further, women's vulnerability to the HIV virus, particularly in sub-Saharan Africa, is partly attributable to 'deeply entrenched socio-economic inequalities . . . This includes . . . the inability to negotiate condom use' (p. 2). HIV-positive women then risk transmitting the virus to their children, during pregnancy, childbirth or breastfeeding.

4 Divorce

The legal position in Britain

Before the Matrimonial Causes Act, 1857, which allowed judicial divorce, essentially on the grounds of adultery, but with a higher burden of proof for women, it could only be obtained by Act of Parliament. The Matrimonial Causes Act, 1923 removed some of these inequalities, and an Act of 1937 provided for divorce on the additional grounds of cruelty, desertion or incurable insanity. The problem was that, contrary to what was often the case, divorce was granted on the basis of the petitioner's innocence, and the respondent's guilt. This was felt to be unfair, and, partly as a result of initiatives by the then Archbishop of Canterbury, Michael Ramsey, the Divorce Reform Act, 1969 (re-enacted in the 1973 Matrimonial Causes Act) made a marriage's irretrievable breakdown the sole ground for divorce. However, this can only be established if one of five facts apply: adultery, and the petitioner finding it intolerable to live with the respondent; behaviour by the respondent, such that the petitioner cannot be expected to live with him; the respondent's desertion for at least two years; the partners' having lived apart for at least two years prior to the divorce petition, and the respondent agreeing to a divorce; or the partners' having lived apart for five years.

Thus, while the intention of the 1969 and 1973 Acts was 'fault-free' divorce, on the grounds of irretrievable breakdown, this has to be demonstrated against one of five tests, three of which involve fault by one partner, and therefore the temptation for the other to make (exaggerated) allegations of unacceptable conduct. In 1996, the then Conservative government passed the Family Law Act, which, if implemented, would have completely changed divorce law. After attending an information meeting, at which divorce and its consequences were explained, a couple would have had to wait three months before starting proceedings for divorce, the only grounds for which would have been marriage breakdown. If they had children, there would then have been a period for reflection, of up to fifteen months, during which they would have been expected to sort out financial and other matters, and attend a mediation meeting. The divorce would then have been granted, if the applicant still wanted it. The Act might have helped to preserve marriages, by requiring people to think carefully, and to accept mediation, before they ended their marriages. However, the Act's provisions were considered to be unworkable.

Christian teaching about divorce

Although interpretations of Jesus' teaching about marriage and divorce (Mark 10.1–10) differ, he does state that, 'What . . . God has joined together, let not man put asunder', and clearly indicates that marriage reflects God's original purpose for human beings, which he revealed when he created them: that 'each male should be united to one female in an indissoluble union' (Nineham, *Gospel of Saint Mark*, p. 261). According to **Roman Catholic** teaching, marriage is a sacrament (outward and visible sign of inward and visible grace), and the 'marriage bond', 'established by God himself', can 'never be dissolved' (*Catechism of the Catholic Church*, para. 1640). Further, divorce is immoral, because it 'introduces disorder into the family and into society' (para. 2385). However, following enquiry, a marriage can be annulled, for example on the grounds that one party did not freely consent to it (paras. 1628–9).

The **Church of England/Anglican Communion** teaches that marriage is, 'in its nature a union permanent and life-long . . . till death them do part, of one man with one woman' (Canon B30); and, in 1994, the General Synod reaffirmed its belief that it 'should always be undertaken as a life-long commitment' (CofE (f)). The Church recognizes that marriages do fail, and, in certain circumstances, will allow a divorced person to remarry in church. However, under the Matrimonial Causes Act, 1965, no member of the Church of England clergy can be compelled to remarry a person whose marriage has been dissolved, and whose former spouse is still living, or to permit remarriage in their church. And, if they do so, they must establish that a divorced person intends the new marriage to be a lifelong union; and that issues from the previous marriage have been resolved; and find out whether their new relationship was a cause of the previous marriage's breakdown. The **Methodist Church** is generally prepared to marry divorced people whose former spouses are still alive, provided there are no 'major obvious' reasons for not doing so (Methodists (b)).

Non-religious approaches

Christians who believe they have made vows of lifelong fidelity before God are likely to be particularly unwilling to contemplate divorce. However, a **deontologist** could argue that, in civil marriage as well, both partners have made promises to each other that they have a duty to keep, and that divorce is incompatible with this duty. For the **consequentialist/utilitarian**, it would be a matter of trying to determine which course of action would minimize pain for all those involved, including any children and perhaps others who may be affected.

Divorce and its consequences

In 2006, the divorce rate in England and Wales was at its lowest level since 1977. There were 132,562 divorces, compared with 141,750 in 2005. However, 53 per cent of divorcing couples had at least one child under 16, and, of the 125,030 children under 16, who were affected by divorce, 20 per cent were under five and 63 per cent under 11. These statistics indicate the hardship and misery that divorce can cause. Children's lives, as well as those of the couple, are disrupted. They will find themselves living with one or other parent, and ultimately, perhaps, with a step-parent, who may also have children; and their education may be disrupted. There will be distress to grandparents and the family's circle of relatives and friends. Financial arrangements have to be made, and only the wealthy are immune to the financial consequences of divorce. This is not to suggest that divorce should not be permitted. Some marriages may be intolerable for one or other partner, or both, and/or their children, and need to be ended:

> If . . . the emotional and spiritual welfare of the parents and children in a *particular* family could best be served by a divorce, then, wrong and cheap-jack as divorce often is, love justifies a divorce. (Fletcher, *Situation Ethics*, p. 133)

However, the **consequentialist** arguments against divorce are strong, indicating that, especially where children are involved, it should not be (and society, which has to pick up many of the pieces, should not allow it to be) too easily available. Those contemplating marriage should not enter into it 'lightly or selfishly', or have children, unless they are certain of their commitment to each other.

5 Same-sex relationships and civil partnership

Traditional attitudes to same-sex relationships

Are homosexual inclinations and sex acceptable? Are homosexual relationships equivalent to heterosexual ones? Until comparatively recently, the answer, reflecting Christian teaching, was that they are not. As we have seen, Jesus (Mark 10) teaches that God's purpose for human beings is that one man should be united to one woman, in a permanent union. St Paul condemns homosexual sex as defying God's intention, which he has clearly revealed in the natural order. People who engage in it are in the grip of sin:

> For this reason God gave them up to dishonourable passions. Their women exchanged natural relations for unnatural, and the men likewise gave up natural relations with women and were consumed with passion for one another, men committing shameless acts with men. (Romans 1.26, 27)

Those who practise homosexuality have no place in God's kingdom: 'the unrighteous will not inherit the kingdom of God . . . neither the immoral, nor idolaters, nor adulterers, nor sexual perverts' (1 Corinthians 6.9). Thus, **traditional Christian teaching** is that homosexuality runs counter to the God-given natural order, and contravenes natural law (see **p. 125**). For Aquinas, 'unisexual lust' is contrary to heterosexual intercourse, which is the type of sexual relationship that is natural to all animals, including human beings, and which is the form of sexual relationship that God, as creator, intended all animals, including humans, to practise. Therefore, homosexual relationships, by being contrary to nature, and thus to God's will, are 'an unnatural crime' (Aquinas, *Summa Theologica* Ia IIae q. 94 a. 3). Natural law arguments are important elements in both **Roman Catholic** and **Church of England** teaching about homosexuality (see below).

But does this matter? Quite apart from the fact that many people are not

Christians or religious, should the attitudes, even of Christians, about this issue be determined by (one view) of what has traditionally been regarded as 'natural'? Reason and freedom of choice are also part of the natural order, and some Christians invoke them to argue for conduct and actions, such as contraception, that other Christians hold to be contrary to the natural order. Again, arguments from nature could be used to oppose even the treatment of disease. Certainly, they have been used, in the past, to prevent women being given pain relief during childbirth. Indeed, if we were to tie our ethical principles and values to nature, we would collapse 'ought' into 'is', and be unable to use moral language to condemn anything that was deemed 'natural' (see **p. 36**).

For homosexuals, restrictive laws deny them their **'dignity and worth'** as human persons (see **pp. 285–93**), and the opportunity to pursue their own happiness in ways that, as they do not violate Mill's **principle of liberty** (homosexual activities do not harm others), society is not entitled to prevent (see **pp. 9–11**).

Gross indecency and the Wolfenden Committee

In Britain until the 1960s, same-sex relationships were generally considered immoral and unacceptable to society. Male homosexual sex, specifically (lesbian sex has never been illegal in Britain), was against the law, and practising homosexuals, such as Oscar Wilde, were prosecuted and imprisoned (1895) for 'gross indecency', under the Criminal Law Amendment Act, 1885. After the Second World War, homosexuality was seen as a serious social problem, and, in 1954, following a high-profile case involving Lord Montagu of Beaulieu (1954), the then Home Secretary Sir David Maxwell Fyfe set up a departmental committee, chaired by Sir John Wolfenden (Vice-Chancellor of Reading University), to investigate homosexual offences and prostitution.

The Wolfenden Report and the Sexual Offences Act, 1967

The government may have hoped that Wolfenden would produce suggestions about how to deal with, and perhaps 'cure', homosexuality. In fact, their report (1957) concluded that homosexuality could not be regarded as a disease, because, apart from their homosexuality, most homosexuals enjoyed full mental health. Instead, applying Mill's **principle of liberty**, they argued that the law's function is to preserve public order and decency, and to prevent exploitation and corruption, not to enforce particular patterns of behaviour on people; and recommended that private, consensual homosexual activity, between adults, should cease to be a criminal offence. The report

> made a crucial distinction between private actions and public order. Wolfenden proposed that it should not be the function of the law to regulate private behaviour that did not harm anyone else, however distasteful others might find it. Its role was to establish the framework of public order (Weeks, 'Wolfenden and Beyond', p. 1)

The Homosexual Law Reform Society was formed in 1958, to campaign for a change in the law, and in 1967, the Sexual Offences Act was passed, by which homosexual acts, in private, between two consenting adults who had reached the age of 21, ceased to be an offence.

Section 28 and campaigning for equal treatment

However, what Wolfenden and the Sexual Offences Act provided was bare toleration of homosexual acts, under certain defined circumstances. They did not offer 'any endorsement of homosexuality as a valid life choice; it was a problem that needed to be dealt with' (Weeks p. 6). For many gay (a term which came into increasing use during this period) and lesbian activists during the 1970s and 1980s, this was unsatisfactory. Section 28 of the Local Government Act, 1988, which prohibited local authorities from intentionally promoting homosexuality, or permitting it to be taught in maintained schools, as an acceptable alternative family relationship, spurred further campaigning for greater rights and equal treatment for homosexuals. In the late 1980s and 1990s, movements such as Stonewall (founded in 1989)

> positively affirmed the merits of lesbian and gay lives . . . The affirmation of valid identities, built around sexuality but not reducible to it, became the central element of the movement as it developed . . . sustained by a wider sense of belonging. The idea of 'community' became central to this. (Weeks, 'Wolfenden and Beyond', pp. 6–7)

However, efforts to change the law, such as the proposals (1994) to equalize the age of consent for homosexual sex with that of heterosexual sex at 16, were unsuccessful.

Equalizing the age of consent, anti-discrimination legislation and the Civil Partnerships Act, 2004

In the past ten years, there has been a spate of legislation addressing equal rights for gay and lesbian people. The age of consent was reduced to 16 by the Sexual Offences (Amendment) Act, 2000; Section 28 was repealed by the Local Government Act, 2003; while the Employment Equality (Sexual Orientation) Regulations, 2003 ban discrimination in all areas of employment and recruitment, in both private and public sectors. The long-standing ban on lesbians and gays serving in the armed forces was lifted in 2000, and the Adoption and Children Act, 2002 allows same-sex couples (as opposed to individuals) to apply to adopt children. Regulations (2007) under the Equality Act, 2006 makes it unlawful to discriminate, on the grounds of sexual orientation, in such areas as provision of goods and services; education; and the exercise of public functions. The 2008 Human Fertilisation and Embryology Act facilitates infertility treatment for lesbians (and single women: see also **pp. 248–9**) by amending Section 13 (5) of the 1990 Act: fertility clinics will still have to take account of a prospective child's 'welfare' and need for a 'supportive parent', but not specifically for a father.

A particularly significant development is the 2004 Civil Partnerships Act's creation of civil partnerships, which give same-sex couples equal treatment to married couples in a wide range of legal areas, such as tax/inheritance tax, employment and occupational pensions/benefits, and the duty to provide reasonable maintenance and protection from domestic violence. Intending civil partners register their partnership by giving notice of, and then signing, a civil partnership schedule before two witnesses. Registration is a wholly secular process, and the Act rules out a religious service, but couples may arrange for a ceremony, if they wish. Civil partnerships can be dissolved, through a process akin to divorce, on the grounds of irretrievable breakdown. Civil partnership has proved popular: between December 2005 and December 2006, over 18,000 civil partnerships were formed.

Current religious teaching and attitudes

However, the fact that gay and lesbian lifestyles and sex are legal, and generally acceptable, and accepted, within society, does not change religious beliefs that they are wrong. The **Roman Catholic Church** teaches that acts of homosexual sex are 'intrinsically disordered', and contrary to both scripture and 'the natural law' (*Catechism of the Catholic Church*, para. 2357 and see p. 125). However, those subject to homosexual inclinations are to be treated with 'compassion', and given every help with the difficulties 'their condition' imposes on them (para. 2358). They are urged to follow lives of chastity, so that, with the support of friendship, prayer and 'sacramental grace', they will gradually approach 'Christian perfection' (para. 2359). Thus, the Church distinguishes between the homosexual individual, on the one hand, and homosexual practice, on the other. Only the latter is condemned; the individual with homosexual inclinations is to be treated with sympathy, and given support; but s/he must practise self-control and refrain from sexual activity.

A General Synod resolution (1987) affirms the **Church of England's** view that, like fornication and adultery, 'homosexual genital acts' do not meet the Christian ideal; those engaging in them should be treated with compassion, but encouraged to repent (CofE (e)). A House of Bishops' statement (*Issues in Human Sexuality*, 1991) endorses traditional, biblically based Christian teaching, that sexual activity should take place within heterosexual marriage, and that, even in the light of contemporary 'sympathetic and perceptive thinking', the Church cannot regard same-sex orientation and activity as a parallel and equivalent form of human sexuality:

> The convergence of Scripture, Tradition and reasoned reflection on experience . . . makes it impossible for the Church to come . . . to any other conclusion. Heterosexuality and homosexuality are not equally congruous with the observed order of creation or with the insights of revelation. (CofE (e))

Church members are asked to treat lay people, who sincerely believe that they are called to a homosexual way of life, with respect. However, their vocation and consecration disbar members of the clergy from 'sexually active homophile relationships' (CofE (e)).

Specifically in relation to civil partnership, the Church of England reaffirms the 'universal Christian tradition' that sexual activity outside marriage falls short of 'God's purposes for human beings', and its view that heterosexual marriage is essential to social stability and well-being, and the best environment for bringing up children. However, as with divorce, it recognizes the need for legislation to remedy particular injustices, even if it results in developments that conflict with its doctrine and teaching. It welcomes the fact that civil partnerships make possible recognition of individual rights within same-sex relationships, and may help to promote long-term relationships. But, it questions the meaning of the government's declared aim of 'securing culture change through legislation'. While fostering tolerance, and overcoming homophobia, should be encouraged, it cannot endorse the views that civil partnership is equivalent to marriage (thus undermining marriage's 'unique' status), or that it is discriminatory to distinguish between the two (CofE (g)).

The **Methodist Church** does not offer an 'authoritative interpretation' of the 'cluster of resolutions' it has adopted on human sexuality. These condemn promiscuity and sexual exploitation; reaffirm the Church's 'traditional teaching' of chastity outside marriage and fidelity within; welcome participation by 'lesbians and gay men in the church'; and urge members to combat discrimination, and work for justice for all people, whatever their sexuality. It accepts that there will be a 'diversity of interpretations': Methodists must examine their 'aspirations and practice in the light of these resolutions' (Methodists (c)).

Attitudes and the law

The position in Britain is no longer one where homosexual orientation and same-sex relationships are tolerated, as long as they remain in the closet. Homosexuals have extensive legal rights and protection from discrimination. These rights, which reflect changing social attitudes, and contribute to changing them, mean that people can now lead gay and lesbian lifestyles openly. Whereas

> Wolfenden conjured up the individual homosexual making moral decisions about sexuality in private ... The new gay movement .... asserted the importance of public affirmation of gayness as a way of enhancing and legitimising private lives: flaunting it. (Weeks, 'Wolfenden and Beyond', p. 8)

In its response to the civil partnership proposals, the **Church of England** referred to, and questioned, the government's view that culture change can be secured though legislation. Experience shows that legislation does have this effect: that which is made lawful comes to be accepted and, in general, to be morally approved; and it may be the case that this is more likely to happen in societies, like Britain, where most people are no longer part of generally respected, independent sources of moral authority, such as religious groups. But, does the fact that society treats something as lawful mean that all its members must endorse it? As homosexuality and homosexual sex are now lawful, is it no longer morally legitimate to express the view that they are wrong? Should those who question whether gay or lesbian couples should be allowed to adopt (this has posed a particular problem for **Roman Catholic** adoption agencies) or receive infertility treatment keep their views to themselves? Is it no longer acceptable for Christian organizations to declare their beliefs that a homosexual lifestyle is less in accord with God's purpose for human beings than heterosexual marriage?

John Stuart Mill and the libertarian view

A complicating factor is the current view (odd in a country with a long tradition of free speech), that to disagree with people about their views or lifestyle is to show hatred towards them: as if it is impossible to express dissent from a view, without hating, or stirring up hatred against, the person who holds it. Mill's *On Liberty* has long been invoked in support of homosexual freedom and rights. There can be no doubt that they pass the test of Mill's principle of liberty: homosexual inclinations and sex do not cause harm to others, and society is not entitled to prevent them. Mill would also approve of people following gay and lesbian lifestyles, because they generate new ideas and values; contribute to the diversity of patterns of life, which enrich society; and offer a range of alternatives, from which individuals can choose:

> There is no reason that all human existence should be constructed on some one or some small number of patterns . . . Human beings are not like sheep . . . A man cannot get a coat or a pair of boots to fit him, unless they are . . . made to his measure . . . and is it easier to fit him with a life than with a coat . . . ? . . . unless there is . . . diversity in their modes of life, they neither obtain their fair share of happiness, nor grow up to the mental moral . . . stature of which their nature is capable. (Mill, *On Liberty*, pp. 75–6)

But Mill's arguments are not directed at promoting, or defending, a particular view or lifestyle. What Mill argues for so passionately and persuasively, in *On Liberty*, is freedom of expression, diversity of views, and a wide variety of patterns of life, as the means to human progress. And Mill would be as opposed to denying freedom of expression to those who question and oppose homosexuality and a gay lifestyle, as to those who applaud and embrace it:

> If all mankind minus one, were of one opinion, and only one . . . were of the contrary opinion, mankind would be no more justified in silencing that one person, than he . . . would be justified in silencing mankind . . . If the opinion is right, they are deprived of the opportunity of exchanging error for truth; if wrong, they lose . . . the clearer perception . . . of truth, produced by its collision with error. (p. 21)

Recently, the House of Lords forced the government to include protection for free speech in its proposed homophobic hatred law. Thus, although it will (rightly) be a criminal offence to threaten or stir up hatred against gays and lesbians, the Lords' amendment makes it clear that this will not include:

'the discussion or criticism of sexual conduct or practices or the urging of persons to refrain from or modify such conduct or practices' (Christian Institute).

References and suggestions for further reading and research

Aquinas, *Summa Theologica*, at http:/www.op.org/summa/summa.html.

W. Barclay, *Ethics in a Permissive Society*, London: Collins Fontana, 1971.

The Canons of the Church of England, London: SPCK, 1969.

Catechism of the Catholic Church, 2nd edn, at http://www. scborromeo. org/ccc.htm (see also http://www.catholic-church.org.uk).

The Christian Institute website (ch. 14), at http://www.christian.org.uk.

Church of England (CofE) website at http://cofe.anglican .org: *The Marriage Service* (CofE (a)); *Human Relationships* (CofE (b)); *Cohabitation* (CofE (c)); *Science, Medicine, Technology and Environment* ('Contraception') (CofE (d)); *Human Sexuality* (CofE (e)); *Divorce* (CofE (f)); The Archbishops' Council of the Church of England, *Civil Partnership* (2003) (CofE (g)).

Civitas (The Institute for the Study of Civil Society), *The Facts Behind Cohabitation*, at http://www.civitas.org.uk.

Daily Telegraph, 12 December 2005, 'Labour Must Stop Penalising Marriage', at http://www.telegraph.co.uk.

Department for Education and Skills, 'Teenage Pregnancy', at Every Child Matters website, at http://www.everychildmatters.gov.uk, has information about teenage pregnancy and strategies for reducing it.

Directgov website, at http://www. direct.gov.uk/en: *Rights and Responsibilities*, 'Marriage, cohabitation and civil partnerships'.

European Court of Human Rights, *European Convention on Human Rights*, at http://www.echr.coe.int.

ERSC Society Today, *Welfare and Single Parenthood in the UK*, at http:// www.esrcsocietytoday.ac.uk.

Family Planning Association (FPA) website at http://www.fpa.org.uk has information and fact sheets about contraception and family planning.

J. Fletcher, *Situation Ethics*, London: SCM Press, 1966.

General Register Office, *Civil Partnerships* and *Registering a Civil Partnership*, at http://www.gro.gov.uk.

Global Health Council (GHC), *Women's Health*, at http://www.global-health.org.

Humanae Vitae, encyclical of Pope Paul VI (July 1968), at http://www.vatican.va.

D. Lees, *The Psychological Benefits of Marriage*, Maxim Institute Research Note (2007), at http://www.maxim.org.nz/.

N. Lowe, 'Grounds for Divorce and Maintenance Between Former Spouses, England and Wales', at http://www2.law.uu.nl/priv/cefl/Reports/pdf/England02.pdf.

The Methodist Church of Great Britain (Methodists), *Abortion and Contraception* (Methodists (a)); *Weddings* (Methodists (b)); and *Human Sexuality* (Methodists (c)), at www.methodist.org.uk.

John Stuart Mill, *On Liberty*, in J. Gray (ed.), John Stuart Mill, *On Liberty and Other Essays*, Oxford and New York: Oxford University Press, 1998.

Office of Public Sector Information, *Statute Law Database*, at http://www.statutelaw.gov.uk (the full text of the statutes and regulations referred to can be found here).

National Statistics website, at http://www.statistics.gov.uk contains a wealth of national statistical information, including *Marriages* (under 'Society'); News Releases: *Contraception and Sexual Behaviour*; *Divorce Rate Lowest for 22 years*; increase in families mainly in cohabiting couples (under 'focusonfamilies').

The New York Times, 2 October 2008, 'Studies Find Big Benefits in Marriage', at http://query.nytimes.com/.

D. E. Nineham, *The Gospel of Saint Mark*, Harmondsworth: Penguin, 1963.

M. Shoffman, 'Half a Century of Gay Progress', published by Pink News at http://www.pinknews.co.uk.

A. J. P. Taylor, *English History 1914–1945*, Oxford and New York: Oxford University Press, 1965.

United Nations, *Universal Declaration of Human Rights*, at http://www.un.org.

University of Chicago Chronicle 19.11, 2 March 2000, 'Research Looks at Cohabitation's Negative Effects', at http://chronicle.uchicago.edu/.

United States Department of Health and Human Services, Office of the Assistant Secretary for Planning and Evaluation (ASPE), Office of Human Services Policy (HSP), *The Effects of Marriage on Health: A Synthesis of Recent Research Evidence* (Mathematica Policy Research, Inc., June 2007) (ASPE/HSP), at http://aspe.hhs.gov/hsp/07/marriageonhealth/index.htm.

J. Weeks, 'Wolfenden and Beyond: The Remaking of Homosexual History' (2007), *History and Policy*, at http://www.historyandpolicy.org.

16 Equality and Human Rights

1 Defining the terms

Equality

What do we mean by the 'equality' of human beings? That there are no significant differences between them, so everybody should be treated the same? Generally, we do not mean that all humans are identical, but that they have equivalent moral status, and are entitled to equal treatment, in certain fundamental respects (for example, by the law; in terms of the right to vote, in relation to employment opportunities; and so on), because of their common humanity.

Human rights

What are 'human rights'? They do not mean that human beings have a right to do anything they choose. In democratic states, people have a 'right' to have children, in the sense that society must allow them to exercise this choice; but not a right in the sense of an entitlement to have children, even if they cannot produce them by natural or artificially assisted means. Again, if people's 'rights' included exercising their every choice, it would involve harm to others, which society cannot permit, and which, as Mill accepted (see **pp. 9–11** and **pp. 282–4**), it is entitled to prevent. The relationship between human rights and human equality is close. If human beings are fundamentally equal, then, as human beings, they have certain basic rights. Thus, equality and human rights concern the same range of issues.

A deontological, rather than a consequentialist basis

Equality and human rights largely reflect **deontological** ethical principles about the intrinsic value of human beings, who should be regarded and treated as ends in themselves, not merely as means to others' ends. Although it would also be possible to defend them on **consequentialist** grounds, the **utilitarian** might argue that any particular human right should be overridden, either generally, or in particular instances, if doing so would maximize happiness.

Declarations of Human Rights

Equality and human rights are not just theories. They are set out in detail in two great post-Second World War declarations of human rights and freedoms: the Universal Declaration of Human Rights (UDHR), adopted by the General Assembly of the United Nations (UN), in 1948, and the Convention for the Protection of Human Rights and Fundamental Freedoms (the European Convention on Human Rights: ECHR), adopted by the Council of Europe, in 1950, and by some 45 European countries since.

Core human rights treaties

While the UDHR only expresses a consensus among UN member states, as to the intrinsic value of individual human beings, and how they should be treated, it has given rise to six core human rights treaties, which, once adopted by member states ('states parties'), become legally binding on them. They are: the International Covenant on Civil and Political Rights (ICCPR: 1966); the International Covenant on Economic, Social and Cultural Rights (ICESR: 1966); the International Convention on the Elimination of All Forms of Racial Discrimination (ICEFRD: 1966); the Convention on the Elimination of All Forms of Discrimination Against Women (CEDAW: 1979); the Convention Against Torture and Other Cruel, Inhuman or Degrading Treatment or Punishment (CAT: 1984); and the Convention on the Rights of the Child (CRC: 1989).

Human rights in Britain

Britain adopted ECHR in 1953, but until 2000, it was not incorporated into national law. Individual British citizens had to complain of a breach of their rights, under the Convention, by petitioning the European Commission of

Human Rights in Strasbourg, which would investigate the complaint, and then refer it to the European Court of Human Rights, if there was a case to answer. This could only be done when all national legal processes had been exhausted. However, the Human Rights Act (HRA), 1998, incorporates the rights and liberties guaranteed in the ECHR into domestic law. Important aspects of equality and human rights are also covered by such British legislation as the Race Relations Act (RRA), 1976; the Sex Discrimination Acts (SDAs), 1975 and 1986; and the Disability Discrimination Act (DDA), 1995.

2 Thinking about equality

Are human beings equal, even in a 'fundamental' sense? Is it a good thing to believe that they are? Or, does it reduce human beings to the same level, and prevent us appreciating the abilities of the more talented?

Friedrich Nietzsche and Christian teaching (see recommended edition on p. 296)

According to Christian teaching (see **pp. 184–5**), all human beings are made in the image of God, are equally valuable to God, and so merit equal treatment. However, the German philosopher Friedrich Nietzsche (see **pp. 11–14**) did not agree. He thought that talk of equality degraded human beings and diminished society; and he blamed Christianity for preaching socially destructive egalitarianism. In *Beyond Good and Evil*, he points to the destructive effects that religious teachings about human equality have on society. There is a surplus of 'degenerating' and 'suffering individuals'; by making itself a religion for the suffering, and concerning itself with their needs, Christianity has preserved too many of those who should be allowed to perish (p. 56).

For Nietzsche, not injuring, abusing, or exploiting others is appropriate behaviour only towards other, equally powerful, members of the same (ruling) class. Making equality and equal treatment of its members society's *'basic principle'* leads to 'dissolution and decline'; it is contrary to nature, and holds back the able and strong, who have the leadership qualities that society needs (p. 152). They should be encouraged to satisfy their will to power, in order to create a vigorous and successful, if unequal, society. This is not a question of morality or immorality, but of the will to power: exploitation belongs to living things' *'fundamental nature'* (p. 153).

Plato and the Guardians *(see recommended edition on p. 296)*

Plato (*The Republic*: see **pp. 5–9** and **pp. 15–18**) also believed that society needs a ruling elite, whose intelligence and education fit them to govern. However, unlike Nietzsche, he believed that the philosophically trained Guardians, with their knowledge of what is good in itself, so far from oppressing and exploiting other members of society, would sacrifice their own interests, in order to govern well. As a successful and unified society can only exist if its members accept the need for a hierarchy of roles and responsibilities, he argues that society would benefit from having a 'magnificent myth' about its origin (p. 115). While stressing the fact that all members of society belong to the same community, this would teach them to accept their particular (and for some, inferior) roles in it:

> when god fashioned you, he added gold in the composition of those of you who are qualified to be Rulers . . . silver in the Auxiliaries [assistant Guardians], and iron and bronze in the farmers and other workers. Now since you are all of the same stock, though your children will commonly resemble their parents, occasionally a silver child will be born of golden parents . . . Guardians . . . must . . . watch the mixture of metals in the characters of their own children. If one of their children has traces of bronze or iron . . . they must . . . assign it its proper value . . . the State will be ruined when it has Guardians of silver or bronze. (pp. 116–17)

Although Plato emphasizes the Guardians' responsibility to review the abilities of the children in all three classes, and, if necessary, to move them to a different class, his 'magnificent myth' has been widely condemned, both for advocating an official lie and for suggesting that whole classes of people should have permanently inferior positions in society.

John Stuart Mill and democracy *(see recommended edition on p. 296)*

In *On Liberty* (**pp. 9–11**), John Stuart Mill's prime concern is with individual liberty, and ensuring that the increasingly egalitarian and democratic society of mid-nineteenth-century Europe did not prevent the individual from expressing his views freely, and leading his life as he chose. In Mill's view, political change and social progress are only possible if there is individual freedom, so that gifted and innovative individuals can show the rest of society the way forward. He pinpoints the drawbacks of democracy:

It was . . . perceived that such phrases as 'self-government' and 'the power of the people over themselves', do not express the true state of the case. The 'people' who exercise the power are not always the same people with those over whom it is exercised . . . The will of the people . . . practically means the will of the most numerous or the most active *part* . . . The limitation . . . of the power of government . . . loses none of its importance when the holders . . . are . . . accountable to the community . . . the 'tyranny of the majority' is now . . . included among the evils . . . [of] society. (p. 8)

Regrettably (Mill believes), in setting the boundaries between individual liberty and social control, the majority does not think that free development of individuality matters. He maintains that, with democratic governments increasingly pandering to the demands of the masses, whose opinions are shaped by mass-circulation newspapers, the general trend in nineteenth-century society was towards uncritical acceptance of conventional views. Indeed, he is harshly dismissive of democracy and its results: the government of the mediocre is bound to be a 'mediocre government' (p. 74). For new and fruitful ideas, society must look, not to democratic politicians, who take their opinions from the masses that elect them, but to outstanding individuals, who are prepared to defy the 'tyranny of the majority':

all wise or noble things . . . come from individuals . . . when the opinions of masses . . . are everywhere become . . . the dominant power, the counterpoise and corrective to that tendency would be, the more and more pronounced individuality of those who stand on the higher eminences of thought . . . In this age, the mere example of non-conformity, the mere refusal to bend the knee to custom, is itself a service. (p. 74)

Individual freedom underpins the diversity of views and culture that enriches society and fosters progress. In Europe:

Individuals, classes, nations, have been extremely unlike one another . . . have struck out a great variety of paths . . . Europe is . . . wholly indebted to this plurality of paths for its progressive and many-sided development. (p. 80)

Mill makes an eloquent case for the disadvantages of equality and democracy. They can lead to uncritical acceptance of the majority view, which democratic politicians are afraid to challenge, and to the oppression of minorities who do not conform to majority opinion or lifestyle. In its own

interests, a democratic and egalitarian society must ensure individual freedom and freedom of opinion and expression, so that alternative viewpoints
may be heard.

Tom Paine and the Rights of Man *(see recommended edition on p. 296)*

The radical political thinker and campaigner Thomas Paine, whose writings
had a major influence on the American and French Revolutions, champions
political equality and democracy in his *Rights of Man*:

> What is Government more than the management of the affairs of a
> Nation? It is not . . . the property of any particular man or family, but of
> the whole community, at whose expense it is supported . . . Every citizen
> is a member of the Sovereignty, and . . . can acknowledge no personal
> subjection: and his obedience can only be to the laws. (pp. 91–2)

Paine argues that history shows that intellectual abilities are not distributed according to social class. Unless states are governed in a way that reflects this fact of nature, they will be badly ruled, because they do not allow
some of their most able people a part in running their affairs. A representative form of government is calculated to produce the best laws, because it
draws on the wisdom of the whole nation. He calls for general recognition
of natural or basic human rights, which each individual has by right of his
existence, and which were clearly stated in the French National Assembly's
Declaration of the Rights of Man and of Citizens:

> Men are born, and always continue, free and equal in respect of their
> rights . . . The end of all political associations, is, the preservation of the
> natural and imprescriptible rights of man . . . liberty, property, security,
> and resistance of oppression. (p. 65)

These include the individual's right to pursue his own comfort and happiness, provided he does not harm the rights of others. These natural rights
(Paine contends) are the foundation of the civil rights (such as the right to
vote and to have a share in government) that all human beings are morally
entitled to exercise, but which, then and now, societies or states deny many
people.

The Universal Declaration of Human Rights and the inherent worth and dignity of the individual

Paine's insistence on the natural rights, essential equality and inherent dignity of each individual human being is reflected in the Preamble to the UDHR, which affirms that 'freedom, justice and peace' are based on 'fundamental human rights . . . the dignity and worth of the human person and . . . the equal rights of men and women'; and Article 1, which declares that:

> All human beings are born free and equal in dignity and rights. They are endowed with reason and conscience and should act towards one another in a spirit of brotherhood.

3 Being equal and having rights

Right to life and liberty, equality before the law

The right to life, and to not having it ended at another's whim, whether an individual's or the state's, is the most fundamental human right, because without it, no other right matters. In the context of the 'Glorious Revolution' of 1688–9, during which, in defence of liberty and constitutional government, James II was overthrown and replaced by William and Mary, John Locke asserts that no one, including the state, is entitled to end another's life arbitrarily:

> *Despotical power* is an absolute, arbitrary power one man has over another, to take away his life, whenever he pleases. This is a power, which neither nature gives, for it has made no such distinction between one man and another; nor compact can convey: for man not having such an arbitrary power over his own life, cannot give another man such a power over it; but it is the *effect only of forfeiture*. (Locke, *Second Treatise of Government*, p. 89)

UDHR and ECHR seek to secure for all human persons the rights and freedoms that are taken for granted in democratic western society: as well as the right to life (and its protection by law), liberty (which should only be removed after due legal process) and security of the person (UDHR, Art. 3; ECHR, Art. 2). They also prohibit any form of slavery or compulsory labour (UDHR, Art. 4; ECHR, Art. 4).

Equality before the law is when the state, through the law, fulfils its duty to protect the life, liberty, personal security and property of all its citizens equally: not to enable them to do as they please, which could cause harm to others, but to enable them to exercise their freedom, and pursue their chosen activities, without others' arbitrary interference:

> freedom is not . . . a *liberty* for every man to do what he *lists* [wishes] . . . but a *liberty* to dispose, and order as he lists, his person, actions, possessions, and his whole property, within the allowance of those laws [of the state] under which he is, and therein not to be subject to the arbitrary will of another, but freely follow his own. (Locke, *Second Treatise of Government*, p. 32)

In the context of today, this means that the law must treat and protect all human persons equally, without discriminating between them on the basis of their race, sex, or any other factor that is irrelevant to their moral status as human persons: 'All are equal before the law and are entitled without any discrimination to equal protection of the law' (UDHR, Art. 7).

UDHR requires that everybody should receive 'effective remedy' by national courts for any acts that violate their fundamental rights (Art. 8); should not be subject to arbitrary interference with their privacy, family, home or correspondence (Art. 12), or to arbitrary arrest, detention or exile (Art. 9); should have the right to be presumed innocent, until proved guilty in a public trial (Art. 11); and should not be subjected to torture or to cruel, inhuman or degrading treatment or punishment (Art. 5: see below). These requirements are also set out in ECHR (Arts. 3, 5, 6 and 8).

Of course, throughout history, there have been states with laws that, instead of treating their citizens equally and protecting their rights and interests, oppressed (some of) them, and treated them less favourably than others. The laws of South Africa during the apartheid era entrenched the privileged position of the white minority at the expense of the black majority:

> in 1950 the government enacted the Popular Registration Act . . . the basis of *apartheid*, which prescribed registration and classification by race . . . the Native Laws Amendment Act 1957 . . . gave the authorities power to exclude Africans from such places as churches . . . the Separate Amenities Act 1953 . . . declared that separate amenities for blacks and whites need not be equal . . . the General Law Amendment Acts . . . stringently reduced the rights of the individual against the police . . . the Bantu Laws Amendment Act 1963 . . . legalized the eviction of any African from any urban area . . . and turned him into a squatter . . . who was allowed to work but not to settle. (Calvocoressi, *World Politics since 1945*, pp. 401–2).

Political rights and democratic and individual freedoms

UDHR (Art. 21 and ECHR Protocol 1, Art. 3) provides for every human person's right to participate in their country's government, either directly or through freely chosen representatives, and to stand for public office; and that the will of the people, expressed through 'genuine elections', on the basis of 'universal and equal suffrage', and in a secret ballot, should be the basis of government authority. UDHR also provides for the essential democratic and individual rights and freedoms of thought, conscience and religion (Art. 18; ECHR Art. 9); opinion and expression (Art. 19; ECHR Art. 10); peaceful assembly (Art. 20; ECHR Art. 11); marriage and starting a family, with both parties' consent (Art. 16; ECHR Art. 12); movement, choice of residence and asylum (Arts. 13 and 14); and property ownership (Art. 17; ECHR Protocol 1, Art. 1). Individual rights and freedoms are balanced by the individual's duty to the community:

> Everyone has duties to the community . . . In the exercise of his rights and freedoms, everyone shall be subject only to such limitations as are determined by law solely for the purpose of securing due recognition and respect for the rights and freedoms of others. (Art. 29)

In Britain, achieving a universal franchise, the right of all to stand for election to public office, and a secret ballot, took almost a hundred years: from the Great Reform Act of 1832, which eliminated 'rotten boroughs' (where there was no or a tiny electorate), introduced a limited redistribution of parliamentary seats to reflect the distribution of the population, and made a limited increase in the franchise, to the Representation of the People Act, 1928, which finally gave women the same political rights as men. Women did not receive the vote until 1918, when it was given to women aged 30; from 1928, they could vote at 21.

Apart from life itself, personal security and physical health, these rights and freedoms seem to contribute most to making life worthwhile. For the citizens of a democratic society, life without them would be hard to imagine. The same is true of democracy itself. Although Plato dismissed direct democracy, as practised in Athens, as an 'anarchic form of society' (Plato, *The Republic*, p. 294), it is hard to think of any practical alternative to representative democracy:

> By ingrafting representation upon democracy, we arrive at a system of government capable of embracing and confederating all the various interests . . . That which is called government . . . is no more than some

common centre, in which all the parts of society unite . . . This cannot be accomplished by any method so conducive to the various interests of the community, as by the representative system. (Paine, *Rights of Man*, pp. 120–1)

The effectiveness of representative democracy is reinforced by freedom of opinion and expression, and the clash of differing points of view:

a party of order or stability, and a party of progress . . . are . . . necessary elements of a healthy state of political life . . . it is . . . the opposition of the other that keeps each within the limits of reason and sanity. Unless opinions favourable to democracy and to aristocracy, to property and to equality . . . are expressed with equal freedom . . . there is no chance of both elements obtaining their due. (Mill, *On Liberty*, pp. 53–4)

Of course, it could be argued that individual freedom is a luxury of life in a stable democratic society. For Thomas Hobbes, living, as so many people around the world do today, in a country wracked by civil war and religious and ideological conflict (the English Civil War), nothing mattered more than a government capable of enforcing order and ensuring personal security:

during the time men live without a common power to keep them all in awe, they are in that condition which is called war . . . of every man, against every man . . . wherein men live without other security . . . there is no place for industry; because the fruit thereof is uncertain . . . no society, and which is worst of all, continual fear, and danger of violent death; and the life of man, solitary, poor, nasty, brutish, and short. (Hobbes, *Leviathan*, p. 84)

Racial equality

Both UDHR (Art. 2) and ECHR (Art. 14) exclude any form of discrimination, on the grounds of race, colour or nationality, as the basis for political or individual rights. Britain adopted ICEFRD, which condemns and seeks to eliminate racial discrimination, in 1969; and has also signed the 1998 Council of Europe Framework Convention for the Protection of National Minorities (FCPNM), committing it to respecting the ethnic, cultural, linguistic and religious identity of ethnic minorities, and to creating the conditions within which they can maintain their identity.

Legislation against racial discrimination is well-established in Britain. By RRA, 1976 (see p. 281), it is unlawful to discriminate against any person on racial grounds, either directly or indirectly, in employment or the provision of goods, facilities or services. Indirect discrimination occurs when, in job recruitment, for example, a criterion or condition is imposed that, though applied to all applicants, has a disproportionately adverse effect on those from a particular racial group. By Race Relations (Amendment) Act, 2000, as well as local authorities, the whole public sector (such as police and prisons) comes within the scope of race discrimination legislation, and has a positive duty to combat racism and promote equality.

One problem with an initiative like the FCPNM is that it brings together two separate factors: race and culture. Particular racial groups may be associated with particular cultural and/or religious values and beliefs, and it may be difficult to distinguish between unacceptable discrimination and legitimate disagreement with/rejection of certain beliefs and values. The great challenge that multi-racial, multi-cultural and multi-faith societies (and most states in western Europe and North America are all three) face is to create an environment in which different racial and cultural/religious groups respect each other's (different) beliefs and values, within the context of core common values, which in a democratic society must include acceptance of the democratic system, individual freedom and equality.

Gender equality

In the fourth century BC, Plato argued that there are no relevant intellectual or physical differences between men and women that disqualify the latter from a share in government:

> if the only difference apparent between them is that the female bears and the male begets, we shall not admit that this is a difference relevant for our purpose . . . no administrative occupation . . . is peculiar to woman as woman or man as man; natural capacities are similarly distributed in each sex, and it is natural for women to take part in all occupations as well as men. (Plato, *The Republic*, pp. 164–5)

But Plato's arguments generally fell on deaf ears. Despite examples, from Elizabeth I to Jane Austen, of what women could achieve, women's position in Victorian Britain was little better than that in ancient Greece. In 1869, John Stuart Mill described their 'social subordination' as: 'an isolated fact in modern social institutions . . . a single relic of an old world of thought and practice exploded in everything else' (Mill, *Subjection of Women*, p. 491).

He likens the situation of married women, and the unfettered control the law gave their husbands over them, to a form of slavery:

> The law of servitude in marriage is a monstrous contradiction to all the principles of the modern world . . . the sole case . . . in which a human being in the plenitude of every faculty is delivered up to the tender mercies of another human being . . . Marriage is the only actual bondage known to our law. There remain no legal slaves, except the mistress of every house. (pp. 557–8)

In Britain, it was not until 1882 that an extended Married Women's Property Act gave married women the right to separate ownership of property of all kinds; and women were not given full political rights until 1928 (see above).

Although UDHR (Art. 2) and ECHR (Art. 14) declare that the same rights and freedoms should be equally available to men and women, CEDAW (preamble) records what is still the case: that 'extensive discrimination against women continues to exist', violating the 'principles of equality of rights and respect for human dignity'. Discrimination against women is defined (Art. 1) as any sex-based 'distinction, exclusion or restriction', preventing women's full and equal participation in every area of national life. CEDAW signatories agree to pursue 'the full development and advancement of women' in the 'political, social, economic and cultural fields' (Art. 3); to remove any barriers to women taking part in a state's 'political and public life' (Art. 7); to give women full access to educational opportunities, and eliminate any 'stereotyped concept' of the roles of men and women in education systems (Art. 10); and to secure for women the same legal status as men (Art. 15).

Plato thought the only difference between men and women is that the latter bear children. However, this can be a tremendous barrier to female equality. CEDAW (Arts. 11 and 14) requires states parties to ensure that women are not disadvantaged by 'marriage or maternity', and have the same marital rights and responsibilities as men. But if, in the absence of information about, and access to, contraception, they undergo a succession of pregnancies (see pp. 266–7), and have to perform most of the child-rearing responsibilities these entail, they are unlikely to be able to exercise their political rights fully, or to achieve their full career potential. For women, control over their own bodies, and over the 'number and spacing' of children (CEDAW, Art. 16) is an essential element in realization of equality.

In Britain, SDAs make it unlawful to discriminate against a person, directly or indirectly, on grounds of sex and/or marriage, in employment or in the provision of goods, facilities or services. By the Equal Pay Act (EPA),

1970, men and women working for the same employer should receive the same pay and have the same contractual terms if they do similar work or work of equal value. Although EPA has been in place for decades, women still only earn 80 per cent of average full-time male hourly earnings, and there is still talk of a 'glass ceiling' preventing their rising above a certain level in their careers. In 2006, only 6,740 of the directors of companies employing more than 250 people were female, compared with 53,524 men.

Religious equality and freedom

UDHR (Art. 2; ECHR Art. 14) provides that people should not be denied rights and freedoms on religious grounds, and (Art. 18) that there should be religious freedom. This matters, because people's religious beliefs are often those of most importance to them, and which shape their ethical principles (see **pp. 167–70** and **182–200**). In Britain, there has been religious toleration for almost three centuries. Although laws discriminating against **non-Anglicans**, and excluding them from government and municipal office, were not repealed until 1828 (for Nonconformists: Protestants who did not 'conform' to Church of England teaching and practice) and 1829 (for **Roman Catholics**), there was little active discrimination against Nonconformists, or actual persecution of Roman Catholics (the Gordon Riots of 1780 being an exception), during the eighteenth century. Indeed, even during the reign of Elizabeth I (who was personally tolerant), although the Act of Uniformity (1559) required attendance at **Church of England** services, fines were light, and enforcement restrained, until Pope Pius V issued his Bull (edict), *Regnans in Excelsis* (1570), 'depriving Elizabeth . . . of her pretended title to the Kingdom of England, releasing her subjects from their allegiance, and interdicting obedience to her laws' (Neale, *Queen Elizabeth I*, p. 194): after which tougher laws against Roman Catholics were passed and enforced.

While the course of the English Reformation means that England has an 'established' or official church, the **Church of England**, of which the monarch is supreme governor, Britain is a multi-faith, as well as a religiously tolerant, society, with substantial numbers of Muslim, Hindu, Sikh, Jewish and Buddhist citizens. Nobody in Britain is required by law to belong, or not to belong, to any particular religious group, and the Employment Equality (Religion or Belief) Regulations, 2003, covering recruitment, employment and vocational training, and applying to the public and private sectors, ban discrimination on the grounds of religious belief.

In Britain as a whole, religious membership and attendance are in decline. In **Christianity**, Sunday worship attendance, taking account of all denominations, has fallen dramatically over the last few decades. Perhaps unfairly, given Britain's history of religious toleration, John Stuart Mill correlates it with lack of interest in religion:

> so natural to mankind is intolerance . . . that religious freedom has hardly anywhere been practically realized, except where religious indifference . . . has added its weight to the scale. In the minds of almost all religious persons, even in the most tolerant countries, the duty of toleration is admitted with tacit reserves. (Mill, *On Liberty*, p. 12)

What cannot be tolerated in democratic societies are religious beliefs or practices that harm others. Kierkegaard (see **pp. 176–80**) holds up Abraham as an exemplar of faith, but (as Kierkegaard acknowledges) society could not tolerate imitators of Abraham, however sincere. Again, as with Islamic terrorism, perverse or erroneous interpretation of religious teachings can lead members of religious groups to attack democratic societies and democratic freedoms, which those societies cannot tolerate.

Disability equality

The Disability Discrimination Act, 1995, gives important rights to those with a disability, which is defined as a 'physical or mental impairment' that has a substantial and long-term adverse effect on their ability to carry out normal day-to-day activities. Those with disabilities now have the right not to be discriminated against in employment and the provision of goods, services and facilities. Employers must make reasonable adjustments for disabled employees, and service providers must change policies, practices or procedures that make it impossible or unreasonably difficult for people with disabilities to use their services.

Children's rights

By UDHR (Art. 25), motherhood and childhood are entitled to 'special care and assistance', and (Art. 26) everyone has the right to (free elementary) education, although educational opportunities vary enormously around the world. CRC (see **p. 280**) recognizes that children are not able to defend their own rights, and are frequently the victims of conflict, abuse, exploitation or neglect. It spells out the rights of children (those under 18) in detail, and imposes on states parties the obligation to incorporate their rights into domestic law. There are two optional protocols (2000) to CRC, dealing with children's involvement in armed conflicts and the sale of children, child prostitution and child pornography.

Equality of sexual orientation

For discussion of this issue, see **pp. 270–7**.

4 Law and punishment

Should human beings be held responsible for their actions?

UDHR (Arts. 9–11) and ECHR (Arts. 5–6) prohibit arbitrary arrest, and require fair and public trial of those accused of crimes, with the presumption of innocence, but recognize that liberty may be removed from those convicted by a competent court.

But, are we entitled to hold other human beings responsible for their actions, and subject them to punishment? Our view on this will depend on whether or not we think that human beings are (wholly) responsible for their actions (see **pp. 201–17**). If we think that human beings (for whatever reason) cannot act other than as they do, even when they are not subject to external coercion, it is hard to hold them accountable for their actions, or to punish them when they do wrong. On the other hand, if we feel that normal human beings are genuinely free to decide whether or not to perform a particular action, we are entitled to hold them responsible, and punish them.

Making the punishment fit the crime

But, if human beings are responsible for their wrong actions and crimes, what sort of punishments should we impose on them? Our understanding of what is just requires that people should receive the punishment they deserve: that, when a crime has been committed, the punishment should fit it (see **pp. 134–5**). Generally, there is criticism if the sentence a court hands down is perceived to be too lenient (a short sentence for a serious crime of violence), or too harsh (a prison sentence for petty theft).

Cruel, inhuman or degrading treatment or punishment

UDHR (Art. 5; ECHR Art. 3) requires that nobody should be subject to 'torture or to cruel, inhuman or degrading treatment or punishment', reinforced by an Optional Protocol of CAT (see **p. 280**) aiming to prevent torture and other forms of ill-treatment by states parties, through inspections of places of detention, and the promotion of a human-rights-based approach to prison management and reform. However, are there circumstances in which, even in a democratic society, torture would be justified? There is a **utilitarian** argument for torturing a known terrorist, if it would produce information that could enable the police to prevent a terrorist attack, in which innocent lives would be lost. Again, the **utilitarian** could argue that harsh prison conditions are in society's interests, as they will deter both convicted and potential criminals from criminal acts. The counter-argument is that a brutal prison regime brutalizes prisoners, and rules out their rehabilitation, making it more likely that they will re-offend and return to prison. Both the arguments for torture and harsh prison conditions are likely to be rejected by **deontologists**, who would maintain that they involve treating human beings as means (to reducing crime, and protecting society), and ignore the intrinsic value of all human beings, including convicted criminals.

The death penalty

What about the crime of deliberate, premeditated murder? ECHR (Art. 2) originally recognized that human beings could be deprived of life 'in the execution of a sentence of a court'. However, the death penalty is banned in all circumstances by ECHR Protocols No. 6 (dealing with times of peace) and 13 (dealing with times of war). The Presidency of the European Union maintains that the death penalty is a punishment that impairs 'human dignity, increases the level of brutality, and provides no added value in terms of deterrence'. According the Foreign and Commonwealth Office (FCO), 118 countries have abolished the death penalty, while 78 retain it (2004).

Arguments for and against

However, some people argue for the death penalty, on the **consequentialist** grounds that it is a deterrent to murder and crimes of violence, because intending murderers fear being killed themselves (opinions vary as to whether this is he case) and it is less cruel than life imprisonment; and on the democratic grounds that the majority supports it. Opponents argue against it on the **consequentialist** grounds that it is not actually a deterrent; that life imprisonment is a harsher punishment; or that it encourages violence, because it involves the state behaving violently towards its own citizens; and/or, on the **deontological** grounds that it should not be permitted, even if it is a deterrent, because it breaches respect for intrinsically valuable human beings.

Mill and Kant

Both Mill and Kant defended the death penalty. Mill maintains that, if someone commits murder, 'the greatest crime known to the law', and shows no remorse or sign that he will ever again be fit to 'live among mankind', depriving him of 'the life of which he has proved himself to be unworthy' is the most appropriate way that society can attach to the crime 'the penal consequences' essential for preserving the lives of its citizens: he thinks it is also the 'least cruel mode in which it is possible adequately to deter from the crime', and he warns against leaving society without effective deterrents against crime (Mill, House of Commons, April 1868, in *Utilitarianism*, pp. 65 and 71).

Mill's argument is mainly **consequentialist**: the death penalty deters murder; but he also indicates that deprivation of life is the fitting punishment for one who, by taking away another's, has shown himself unworthy of his own. Kant bluntly makes this point about **respect for the intrinsic value** of the murdered human person being expressed in his murderer's execution:

Even if a civil society were to dissolve itself . . . the last murderer remaining in prison must first be executed, so that everyone will duly receive what his actions are worth and so that the blood-guilt thereof will not be fixed on the people because they failed to insist on carrying out the punishment. (Kant, *Metaphysical Elements of Justice*, p. 102)

But, given human fallibility, could we always be sure we were executing the right person? 'The forfeiture of life is too absolute, too irreversible, for one human being to inflict it on another, even when backed by legal process' (Kofi Annan, quoted by FCO).

References and suggested further reading

P. Calvocoressi, *World Politics Since 1945*, 4th edn, Harlow: Longman, 1982.

Church Society website at http://www.churchsociety.org has information about Church of England church attendance.

European Court of Human Rights, *European Convention on Human Rights*, at http://www.echr.coe.int.

Foreign and Commonwealth Office (FCO) website, at http://www.fco.gov.uk, contains information about human rights issues.

Thomas Hobbes, *Leviathan*, ed. J. C. A. Gaskin, Oxford: Oxford University Press, 1998.

Immanuel Kant, *The Metaphysical Elements of Justice*, trans. J. Ladd, Indianapolis: Bobbs-Merrill, 1965.

John Locke, *Second Treatise of Government*, ed. C. B. Macpherson, Indianapolis/Cambridge: Hackett, 1980.

John Stuart Mill, *On Liberty*, in John Stuart Mill, *On Liberty and Other Essays*, ed. J. Gray, Oxford and New York: Oxford University Press, 1998.

John Stuart Mill, *The Subjection of Women*, in *On Liberty and Other Essays*, ed. J. Gray, Oxford and New York: Oxford University Press, 1998.

John Stuart Mill, House of Commons, April 1868, in John Stuart Mill, *Utilitarianism*, ed. G. Sher, 2nd edn, Indianapolis/Cambridge: Hackett, 2001.

Office of Public Sector Information, *Statute Law Database*, at http://www.statutelaw.gov.uk (the full text of the statutes and regulations referred to can be found here).

J. E. Neale, *Queen Elizabeth I*, Harmondsworth: Pelican, 1971.

Friedrich Nietzsche, *Beyond Good and Evil*, trans. M. Faber, Oxford and New York: Oxford University Press, 1998.

Office of the High Commissioner for Human Rights (OHCHR), *Convention on the Elimination of All Forms of Discrimination against Women*, at http:www.unhchr.ch.

Thomas Paine, *Rights of Man*, Mineola, NY: Dover, 1999.

Plato, *The Republic*, trans. H. D. P. Lee, 2nd edn (revised and reissued with new Further Reading), London: Penguin, 2003.

The International Committee of the Red Cross (ICRC) website, at http://www.icrc.org, contains information about International Humanitarian Law.

C. L. Ten, 'Crime and Punishment', in P. Singer (ed.), *A Companion to Ethics*, Cambridge: Cambridge University Press, 1993.

United Nations, *Universal Declaration of Human Rights*, at http://www.un.org.

P. Vardy and P. Grosch, *The Puzzle of Ethics*, rev. edn, London: HarperCollins, 1999.

17 Issues of War and Peace

1 What is war?

Throughout history, war has been generally condemned, but constantly resorted to, as a means of settling disputes between states or groups of states. Wars can be on various scales, from localized conflicts to world wars, involving millions of people. Unlike personal disputes, or clashes between street gangs, wars are normally fought between states or alliances of states, and involve distinct, rival political communities. These may exist within one state, in which case it is a civil war. Wars originate from a variety of causes. Many, from the Persian invasions of Ancient Greece, to Hitler's invasions of Poland and Russia, have started because of one state's desire to conquer another and acquire its territory, making them wars of aggression by one side, and of self-defence by the other. There are wars of liberation, as in the War of American Independence, when a people seeks to free itself from colonial rule, or, as in the First Gulf War, states act to free one state (Kuwait) from oppression by another (Iraq). Wars, from the Crusades to the Vietnam War, have been fought for religious or ideological reasons: to champion the cause of religion, or to propagate, or prevent the spread of, a particular political ideology.

Do the same ethical principles apply to states as to individuals?

Wars inevitably involve violence, death and injury. Yet, when individuals act as states do in war, and kill or assault others, they are condemned morally, prosecuted by the law, and executed or imprisoned. However, wars are often said to be right, and those in the armed services who fight them are applauded. So, do the ethical principles that guide individuals within civilized societies not apply even to civilized, democratic states in their relations with other states? One important consideration is why a state goes to war: an aggressor state will be censured, perhaps even by its own citizens, while a state that fights to defend itself against attack will be praised.

Yet, intuitively, we may feel individuals and states are not governed by the same standards. While people regard the conduct of an individual who pursues only his own interests and ignores those of others as ethically unacceptable (or criminal), they generally expect a government to put their state's interests above those of others. But then a state is not an individual. It is a community of people, on whose behalf its government acts, and whose collective interests it is responsible for safeguarding. The analogy between an individual acting selfishly, and a state doing so, is imperfect. A state that pursues its interests to the point of war seems acceptable in a way that an individual following such a course of action would not be – unless, of course, it is a totalitarian state, where government policy aims to satisfy the interests and preferences of a ruling elite, not those of the majority. In general, while the people of a democratic state may support their government's decision to go to war, they will only do so if they see the war as necessary, in order to preserve the state's essential interests, such as when it is the victim of aggression. Citizens of a democratic state do not expect their government to pursue national interests without regard for those of other countries, in a way that provokes war; and they expect it to try to resolve disputes by peaceful means.

Making war less terrible

War is always terrible, but it can be made less so, if the states abide by certain established rules, and do not engage in it at all, unless they are justified in doing so. As war is such a common occurrence, philosophers and others have devoted a lot of thought to the reasons that justify war, and the rules that should govern its conduct. So-called '**just-war theory**' goes back to ancient times, and has been developed by such Christian thinkers as Augustine and Aquinas.

2 The realist approach

Carl von Clausewitz and war as the continuation of policy by other means

Some philosophers and statesmen have argued that war is a necessary and legitimate means of pursuing political objectives. This '**realist**' viewpoint holds that there are times in history when states cannot achieve their political objectives by ordinary political or diplomatic means. They must either give them up, or go to war. In *On War*, the Prussian soldier and philosopher of war Carl von Clausewitz famously describes war as 'a mere continuation of policy by other means' (p. 22). It is always

> called forth by a political motive. It is therefore a political act . . . if we reflect that war has its root in a political object, then naturally this original motive which called it into existence should also continue the first and highest consideration in its conduct. (p. 21)

Even if it could be avoided, war may be the most rapid or effective means for a state to achieve its ends, in which case its government may go to war, provided its military resources are adequate:

> war is . . . a real political instrument . . . a carrying out of the same by other means. All beyond this which is strictly peculiar to war relates merely to the peculiar nature of the means which it uses . . . the political view is the object, war the means, and the means must always include the object in our conception. (p. 22)

Count Cavour and the practice of realism

In nineteenth-century Europe, war was used for political ends, in the unification of Italy and Germany, and the following episode from the former illustrates the 'realist' approach. In July 1858, Count Camillo Benso di Cavour, prime minister of the northern Italian kingdom of Piedmont-Sardinia, who wished to unify the various Italian states into one country, made a secret agreement with the Emperor Louis Napoleon of France. In exchange for Savoy and Nice, which belonged to Piedmont-Sardinia, and on condition that Piedmont-Sardinia could provide a pretext to justify conflict to the rest of Europe, France agreed to support it in a war to drive Austria out of Italy. Piedmont-Sardinia could then seize Lombardy and Venetia, which were under Austrian rule, and create a kingdom of northern Italy under its king, Victor Emmanuel II.

Means and ends

Through the war that followed, Piedmont-Sardinia gained Lombardy. Therefore, Cavour was partly successful in his immediate objective, and

wholly successful in his ultimate objective: the unification of the whole of
Italy was completed in 1870. But can Cavour's cynical realism be justified? Both he and Louis Napoleon used the thousands of French, Austrian
and Piedmontese soldiers, who died in the bloody battles of Magenta and
Solferino, as mere means to their ends. There was further loss of life before Italy was unified, causing pain and distress to those killed or injured
and their families and friends, while Cavour had frequent recourse to lies,
manipulation and deception. Indeed, he acknowledged that, 'If we did for
ourselves what we do for our country, what rascals we should be!' True,
many Italians, then and subsequently, wanted unification, so its achieve-
ment made them happy, but it caused unhappiness to those who opposed
it. In the longer term, a united Italy may have been more prosperous and
strong than a collection of disunited statelets, but its later history involved a
repressive fascist dictatorship under Benito Mussolini; the unprovoked and
brutal invasion of Abyssinia (Ethiopia) in 1935; and alliance with Hitler's
Germany, during the Second World War. It could be argued not only that
the end did not justify the means, but that it would have been better if the
end had not been achieved.

3 The just war

Ius ad bellum: going to war for the right reasons

So, what makes a war just?

Aristotle

Aristotle (see also **pp. 104–14**) accepts that wars are inevitable, but insists
that 'leisure and peace' are preferable (Aristotle, *Politics*, p. 289). He deplores states such as Sparta that make waging war their main activity:

> a city [is not] to be deemed happy or a legislator to be praised because he
> trains his citizens to conquer and obtain dominion over their neighbours
> . . . Neither should men study war with a view to the enslavement of those
> who do not deserve to be enslaved. (p. 290)

States have a right to defend themselves and to fight to prevent the enslave-
ment of their citizens; but the aim of war is not conflict for its own sake, or
conquest, but to secure peace:

the legislator should direct all his military and other measures to the provision of leisure and the establishment of peace . . . Since the end of individuals and of states is the same, the end of the best man and of the best
state must also be the same . . . there ought to exist in both of them the
virtues of leisure; for peace . . . is the end of war. (pp. 290–1)

Aquinas

Thomas Aquinas (see also **pp. 121–9**) developed 'just-war theory', holding
that three conditions must be fulfilled for a war to be just. First, war must be
declared by a state's ruler, who has the proper authority to do so:

it is not the business of a private individual . . . the care of the common
weal is committed to those . . . in authority, it is their business to watch
over . . . the city, kingdom or province. (Aquinas, *Summa Theologica* IIa
IIae q. 40 a. 1)

The cause must be just:

those who are attacked, should be attacked because they deserve it on
account of some fault . . . A just war . . . avenges wrongs, when a nation
or state has to be punished. (IIa IIae q. 40 a. 1)

The belligerents must have a right intention:

so that they intend the advancement of good, or the avoidance of evil.
Hence Augustine says . . . 'True religion looks upon as peaceful those
wars that are waged not for motives of aggrandizement, or cruelty, but
with the object of securing peace, of punishing evil-doers, and of uplifting
the good'. (IIa IIae q. 40 a. 1)

Augustine

Augustine (354–430) bemoans the fact that even just wars create misery for
all involved, including those fighting in a just cause who are compelled to do
so by others' injustice:

the misery of these evils is not yet ended . . . the wise man, they say will
wage just wars . . . if he remembers that he is a human being, he will
rather lament . . . the necessity of waging just wars; for if they were not
just, he would not have to engage in them . . . it is the injustice of the

opposing side that lays on the wise man the duty of waging wars. (Augustine, *City of God*, pp. 861–2)

Authority to declare war

Aquinas's first condition of a just war is that it be declared by the state's proper authority, which is responsible for governing it, not by a private individual or a faction within the state. In medieval times, that would have been a king or emperor. Today, we might say that a state is justified in going to war provided it is itself a legitimate state: one with a government that its own citizens regard as legitimate, which respects their rights, and which is not itself committing aggression against other states; and that only a democratic state can satisfy these criteria.

A just cause

The obvious example of a just cause would be a state going to war to defend itself, or another state or states, against aggression. But, if a state goes to war to seize territory, or to prevent a neighbouring state becoming a successful economic rival, or to consolidate its government's position by deflecting internal discontent towards an outside foe, it would not have a just cause. Where one state commits an act of aggression against another, for example by invading its territory, it tramples on the rights of that state and its citizens and, if successful, destroys them; it deprives the victim state of its sovereignty and territorial integrity, and its citizens of their liberty. By doing so, the aggressor state gives up its right not to have war waged against it, to put right the wrong that it has done.

In both 1914 and 1939, Britain had just cause for declaring war on Germany, because the latter was an aggressor state that had invaded the territories of other states: Belgium (whose neutrality it was committed by treaty to respecting) in 1914 and Poland in 1939. In both cases, Britain went to war reluctantly, and only after it had made every effort to avoid war. Indeed, nobody could have tried harder to avoid conflict, in the 1930s, than the British prime minister, Neville Chamberlain. In 1991, Britain, as part of a multi-member coalition, went to war with Iraq, to put right the wrong of Iraq's invasion of Kuwait, and to restore Kuwait's sovereignty and territorial integrity. One of the main reasons for debate about whether or not the United States and Britain had just cause to invade Iraq in 2003 is doubt about whether they had exhausted all peaceful means of resolving the issues surrounding Iraq's alleged possession of weapons of mass destruction.

Humanitarian (compassionate) grounds, such as protecting innocent people from death or injury, provide just cause for sending troops into the territory of a sovereign state(s), as in the case of former Yugoslavia, during the 1990s. Military intervention to stop terrorist aggression such as that by al-Qaeda against the United States and its citizens in September 2001 (9/11), which involved invading Afghanistan in order to remove the Taliban government that was sponsoring international terrorism, is also justified. US and British forces are still there, in order to prevent the Taliban overthrowing the new, legitimate government of Afghanistan.

Right intention

Aquinas points out that right intention must accompany a just cause. Just cause must not be a mere pretext to disguise such aims as territorial expansion. Further, a state must declare war publicly, thus informing its own citizens that they are going to war, and letting the enemy state know that a state of war exists between the two countries.

Other aspects of ius ad bellum

War should be a state's last resort. It must not be undertaken quickly or lightly, but only after every other avenue of resolving differences has been explored. A state should not go to war unless it has a reasonable prospect of success, as this would only result in violence and death with no possible benefit. It should apply the principle of proportionality, weighing up the benefits and evils that are likely to arise from war. However, these **consequentialist** approaches may be unacceptable in some situations, as well as difficult to apply in practice. They would generally stop a small state resisting aggression by a more powerful one, as Poland did against Germany, and Finland against the USSR, in 1939. But, although their resistance was unsuccessful, were these two small countries wrong to fight? A **deontologist** might argue that their governments had a duty to their citizens, and their citizens to each other, to resist aggression and to fight for freedom. In ancient times, careful weighing of the possible consequences would have prevented the Greek city-states from resisting Persian invasions of Greece, as the odds were so heavily stacked against them. This application of just war theory would have ruled out the overwhelming Greek victories at Marathon, Salamis and Plataea, as well as the Spartans' noble self-sacrifice at Thermopylae – and strangled western civilization in its cradle.

Crimes against peace

Augustine deplored the fact that human beings were compelled to fight just wars, due to others' injustice. The Second World War demonstrated just how unjust a state, ruled by ideologically driven fanatics, contemptuous of human life, could be. After it was over, several Nazi leaders, including Hermann Goering, Joachim von Ribbentrop and Rudolf Hess, were tried for war crimes at Nuremberg, and sentenced either to imprisonment or death. In 1950, certain Principles of International Law, which had been recognized in the Charter of the Nuremberg Tribunal and the Tribunal's Judgement, were adopted by the United Nations (UN). Principle III stipulates that a person is not relieved from responsibility for acts constituting crimes under international law, on the grounds that he committed them as head of state. Principle VI (a) recognizes crimes against peace: planning, preparing, initiating or waging a war of aggression, or a war that violates international treaties, agreements or assurances; or taking part in a common plan or conspiracy to accomplish any of these acts.

Ius in bello: fighting war by the rules

All is not fair in war

Is all fair in war, as in love? This is not the view humanity has taken. As it has evolved, just-war theory requires not only a just cause and right intention, but that wars be fought with force that is proportional to achieving military objectives; that military force be applied to military personnel and targets, not civilians and non-combatants; that any international treaties relating to banned weapons, such as weapons of indiscriminate effect or mass destruction, be obeyed; and that prisoners of war be properly treated. These requirements are expressed in a range of international agreements that are part of international humanitarian law. They aim to regulate the conduct of wars, and make them less brutal than they would be otherwise.

War crimes and crimes against humanity

Nazi Germany waged an unjust war, and waged it unjustly; and it was a war that, due to more sophisticated and destructive weapons, had a greater impact on civilians than previous ones. Principle VI of the Nuremburg Tribunal Principles deals with war crimes and crimes against humanity. The first group covers such breaches of acceptable customs of war as ill-treatment, or deportation for slave labour, of an occupied territory's civilian population; murdering or ill-treating prisoners of war; killing hostages; plundering public or private property; and wanton destruction of cities and towns, without military justification. The second group includes murder, extermination, inhuman acts against civilian populations, and persecutions on political, racial or religious grounds.

Many of these were directed at German atrocities, such as savage treatment of civilian populations in occupied territories; the murder of millions of Jews in death camps; and the wholesale plunder of art treasures from conquered countries. However, Allied hands were not completely clean. In an effort to cripple Germany's productive capacity, Britain and the United States 'saturation-bombed' German cities, hitting civilian populations and their homes, rather than German industry: 'Indiscriminate bombing could aim only at the centres of towns, and most factories were in the suburbs. Many houses were destroyed, and few factories' (Taylor, p. 571).

The crime of genocide

In response to Nazi atrocities, particularly against the Jews, the newly formed UN adopted the Convention on the Prevention and Punishment of the Crime of Genocide, in 1948. This (Article 2) defined genocide as killing, deliberately imposing conditions likely to bring about the physical destruction of, or attempting to prevent births among, any national, ethnic, racial or religious group, in whole or part. In 1968, due to fear that surviving Nazi war criminals might go unpunished, the UN affirmed that, because of their terrible nature, which time cannot efface, statutory limitations would not apply to war crimes and crimes against humanity.

The International Criminal Court (ICJ)

This came into operation in 2003. Cases of alleged genocide, crimes against humanity and war crimes can be referred to it. Anybody, from heads of state to ordinary soldiers, can be brought before the court, and sentences range from life imprisonment to fines and forfeiture of the proceeds of crimes. Alleged war criminals can be indicted by states, by the court's own prosecutor, or by the UN Security Council. A hundred states have ratified the treaty that establishes the Court, but not the United States, China, Russia, India or Pakistan.

The Geneva Convention and the Red Cross

In June 1859, Henri Dunant, a Swiss citizen, witnessed the aftermath of the battle of Solferino (see above). This bloody battle, which played an important part in the ultimate unification of Italy, was fought mainly between France and Austria, and resulted in 40,000 dead and thousands of wounded. Dunant was appalled by the primitive medical arrangements and pressed for establishment of voluntary relief organizations, which could care for the wounded, and an international agreement that would protect them from attack. His initiative was the origin of the Red Cross, and, in 1864, several countries signed the Geneva Convention, agreeing to look after soldiers wounded in battle, irrespective of nationality. The Convention also accepted that Red Cross personnel, hospitals and equipment, which would be identified by the Red Cross emblem, would be neutral and immune from attack.

The four Geneva Conventions of 1949

In 1949, following the Second World War, four Geneva Conventions were signed. Convention I (the original Convention) deals with sick and wounded soldiers, and Convention II extends this protection to sailors. Convention III relates to humane treatment of prisoners of war, and Convention IV deals with civilian populations under the control of the enemy or an occupying power. By the first two Conventions, sick or wounded soldiers or sailors are to be regarded as non-combatants, in need of protection. Warring states must treat sick or wounded enemy military personnel with the same care as their own; collect and identify the dead, as quickly as possible; and not attack medical establishments. By Convention III, prisoners must be treated humanely; allowed to inform their families that they have been taken prisoner and to correspond with them; adequately housed, clothed and fed, and given access to medical treatment; not forced to give any information, other than name, age, rank and service number; and not compelled to do dangerous, degrading or unhealthy work. Convention IV provides that civilian populations must be humanely treated; not discriminated against on the grounds of race, religion or political opinion, or forced to give information; allowed to practise their religion, and have their religious beliefs and practices respected; and not be used to shield military operations.

The 1977 Protocols

These two Protocols to the Geneva Conventions ruled (Protocol I) that armed conflicts in which people are fighting against colonial domination, alien occupation or racist regimes are to be regarded as international conflicts, to which the Geneva Conventions apply; and sought (Protocol II), as 80 per cent of the casualties of armed conflicts were victims of non-international conflicts, to extend the essential rules of law to internal wars.

The Hague Conventions

As well as the original Geneva Convention, the Geneva Conventions built on the Hague Conventions. In 1899, an international peace conference took place at The Hague, with the aim of maintaining 'universal peace', by reducing excessive armaments. This objective was not achieved, but the First Hague Convention extended the Geneva Convention to sailors (see above); banned certain kinds of weapons, including so-called 'dum-dum' bullets, which expanded on impact and made injuries worse; and established a Court of Arbitration, at The Hague, to which states could refer disputes. A second conference (1907) failed to achieve its major objective of reducing armaments, during the period of mounting international tension preceding the outbreak of war in 1914. It did reiterate the previous Convention's ban on 'asphyxiating or deleterious gases' (weapons with indiscriminate effects, whose use would be contrary to the just conduct of war), but this was generally ignored during the First World War.

The Geneva Protocol to the Hague Convention, 1925

During the First World War, poison gas was used extensively, causing terrible suffering and some 90,000 deaths. The Treaty of Versailles (with Germany: 1919), and the treaties with the other defeated enemy states, banned them from manufacturing or importing poisonous gases; and, in 1925, the League of Nations convened a conference designed to secure general international acceptance of the ban. The Geneva Protocol to the Hague Convention, prohibiting the use in war of asphyxiating, poisonous or other gases, and of bacteriological methods of warfare, was signed in that year. These weapons were not used during the Second World War.

Biological and chemical weapons and anti-personnel mines

The 1925 Convention only prohibited use of chemical and bacteriological weapons. In 1971, the UN General Assembly adopted a Convention (Biological Weapons, 1972), banning development, production and stockpiling of biological and toxin weapons. It was accepted that there was no purpose in their development, as there would be no military advantages in using them. There are also no possible circumstances in which their use would be ethically justifiable: the most thoroughgoing **consequentialist** would have to concede that it would be impossible, even in theory, to establish that it would benefit the user, because their long-term effects, including ones detrimental to the user, could never be calculated.

Agreement on chemical weapons was achieved in 1992 (Chemical Weapons Convention, 1993), which banned development, production and stockpiling of chemical weapons, and required existing weapons to be destroyed. In 1997, eighty-nine states adopted a Convention prohibiting the use, production and stockpiling of anti-personnel mines, another weapon which has indiscriminate effects, and which has caused terrible injury and suffering, to both combatants and civilian populations.

Nuclear weapons

Nuclear weapons are weapons of mass destruction, the effects of which cannot be confined to military personnel, equipment or bases. Although, unlike biological and chemical weapons, their use is not definitely banned, the ICJ has indicated that it would breach the principles and rules of international humanitarian law.

Their use against Japan

However, shortly after their development by the United States, during the Second World War, they were used against Japan. On 6 and 9 August 1945, atomic (A) bombs were dropped on the Japanese cities of Hiroshima and Nagasaki. The consequences were appalling. Within, and close to, the fireball created by such a nuclear explosion:

> everything will evaporate or melt . . . Second degree burns to unprotected skin may occur 3 km from the explosion, and at 2 km third degree burns will be frequent . . . At less than 2 km, thermal radiation can be expected to kill most people directly exposed to it. (*Nuclear Weapons*, p. 57)

In 1976, the Mayors of Hiroshima and Nagasaki calculated that, in Hiroshima, up to 150,000 had died by December 1945, and 200,000 by 1950; in Nagasaki, up to 80,000 and 100,000, by the same dates (p. 63).

Then and since, it has been argued that use of nuclear bombs was justified, on the grounds that it minimized Allied casualties; that total casualties

(Allied and Japanese) were lower than if the Allies had had to invade the Japanese mainland; and that the war ended sooner than it would have otherwise. This was Churchill's view:

> To avert a vast, indefinite butchery, to bring the war to an end, to give peace to the world . . . by a manifestation of overwhelming power . . . seemed, after all our toils and perils, a miracle of deliverance . . . The final decision . . . lay . . . with President Truman . . . but I never doubted what it would be, nor have I ever doubted since that he was right. (Quoted in Liddell Hart, *History of the Second World War*, p. 692)

Joseph Fletcher (see **pp. 147, 152**) holds that these considerations justify Truman's action. It was the **most loving** in that situation: 'On a vast scale of "agapeic calculus" President Truman made his decision about the A-bombs on Hiroshima and Nagasaki' (Fletcher, *Situation Ethics*, p. 98). Certainly, there was no need to invade Japan; Emperor Hirohito announced its surrender on 14 August 1945.

These **utilitarian** and **situationist** arguments for the use of nuclear weapons, in 1945, could be applied to comparable situations. And, even if it could be proved that, in fact, the overall effect of not using them would have been to minimize pain (that the combined Allied and Japanese casualties, caused by an invasion, would have been fewer than the actual Japanese casualties that resulted from dropping the bombs), the Allied action could still be justified, on the grounds that a belligerent state's duty, to preserve the lives of its own soldiers, sailors and aviators, takes precedence over that of reducing enemy casualties.

However, successful defence of the Allied action is predicated on the thesis that, unlike Germany, a few months earlier, the Japanese government was not prepared to accept unconditional surrender, and was determined to go on fighting. There is evidence that the Japanese government was seeking peace, but that their approaches, mainly through the Russian leader, Josef Stalin, were overlooked or ignored. US Fleet Admiral Leahy, Chief of Staff to President Truman, had no doubt that the bombing of Hiroshima and Nagasaki was unnecessary: 'The Japanese were already defeated and ready to surrender because of the effective sea blockade and the successful bombing with conventional weapons' (Liddell Hart, *History of the Second World War*, p. 697).

Nuclear deterrence

For decades after the end of the Second World War, conflict between the two superpowers, the United States and the Soviet Union (and their allies) was ruled out by both sides' (NATO and the Warsaw Pact) possession of nuclear weapons, thus deterring attack by the other side. Nuclear deterrence has been condemned as immoral, on the grounds that, if the two sides were serious about using the weapons in actual conflict, they were prepared to perpetrate indiscriminate slaughter across the globe, possibly rendering large parts of it uninhabitable, through radiation; but that, if they were not, they dishonestly subjected the world to a protracted period of fear (the Cold War), as nobody could be sure that they would not. This fear was particularly acute during the Cuban Missile Crisis (1962), when the United States, under President John F. Kennedy, successfully faced down Russian attempts to site nuclear missiles on the territory of its ally, Cuba. On the other hand, nuclear bombs or missiles have not been used since 1945, while the threat of so-called mutually assured destruction (MAD) seems to have helped to ensure peace between the two superpowers.

Nuclear Non-Proliferation Treaty

The problem is that, once created, nuclear know-how could not be 'disinvented', only controlled. An important element in attempting to prevent another use of nuclear weapons is the 1968 Nuclear Non-Proliferation Treaty (NPT), which has been signed by 189 countries. This recognizes five states, the United States, Britain, Russia (formerly the Soviet Union), China and France as nuclear weapons states (NWSs). They undertake not to use nuclear weapons against non-nuclear weapons states (NNWSs), and not to help them to manufacture or acquire nuclear weapons. NNWSs can develop nuclear technology for peaceful purposes, and NPT is monitored by the International Atomic Energy Agency (IAEA). However, India, Pakistan and Israel, known to have nuclear warheads, are not signatories to NPT, while North Korea, which was, withdrew from it (2003), and is thought to be developing nuclear weapons technology. Iran, another NPT signatory, is accused of trying, or planning, to do so. On the other hand, South Africa, which developed a nuclear capability under its apartheid regime, has disarmed itself under NPT.

For decades, there has been talk of disarmament, and reducing the number of nuclear weapons in the world. However, countries that possess them are unlikely to follow South Africa's example and renounce them, while potential enemies still have them. Particular causes of concern are the tensions between the nuclear-armed states of India, Pakistan and China; the fact that, given the unstable situation in the Middle East, Israel has them; and the prospect of 'rogue' states, like North Korea and Iran, possessing them.

Comprehensive Nuclear Test-Ban Treaty

The UN General Assembly adopted a Comprehensive Nuclear Test-Ban Treaty (CTBT) in 1996. The Treaty totally bans any nuclear weapon test explosion, preventing qualitative improvement of weapons, and will establish a global verification regime, to monitor compliance. Over 100 countries have ratified CTBT, which will come into operation when signed and ratified by all 44 of the states that took part in the Conference on Disarmament that led to it, and which have nuclear power or research reactors.

4 Making peace, keeping the peace and pacifism

Making peace

Another factor that can contribute significantly to maintaining peace is what happens when a war ends. How will the victor treat the vanquished? Will there be reprisals and expropriations, or will moderation and the desire not to sow the seeds of future discord prevail? At the end of the dynastic and territorial struggles between France and Britain, during the late seventeenth and eighteenth centuries, the victor's overriding aim was to secure as many of its objectives as possible, without much concern for future peace. Thus, the radical politician and journalist John Wilkes likened the Peace of Paris, which ended the Seven Years' War (1763), to 'the peace of God, for it passeth all understanding': notwithstanding her enormous gains under the treaty, Britain, on this occasion, had not extracted as much as she might have from her overwhelming victories during the war.

Although Napoleon and France had ravaged Europe with war for over 20 years, the First Treaty of Paris (1814) treated France generously, with a view to preventing future conflict. She was not disarmed; there was no war indemnity; and she kept the works of art she had seized from defeated enemies during the Revolutionary and Napoleonic Wars, and some of her territorial gains. Even after Napoleon had terrified the Allies by returning from exile in Elba, and had inflicted further warfare and loss of life on Europe, culminating in the Battle of Waterloo, the terms of the Second Treaty of Paris, though tougher, were still far from harsh. As a result: 'There was no great war in Europe for a century and no major war until 1853; the territorial settlement remained the political basis of Europe for thirty years' (Grant and Temperley, *Europe*, p. 133).

It is often said that the harshness of the Treaty of Versailles (1919) with Germany, at the end of the First World War, caused German resentment, and led to the Second World War. Certainly, Germany was forced to give up large areas of territory; significantly reduce her armed forces and armaments; accept responsibility for starting the war (the War Guilt Clause); and agree to pay unspecified reparations for damages done to the Allies. However, given the terrible loss of life and suffering, the Allies' terms do not seem unreasonable. Germany itself was not invaded or occupied; and, in 1939, it was able to start another world war. Indeed, it could be argued that the Treaty was not harsh enough. At the end of the Second World War, Germany had to agree to unconditional surrender, was divided up into zones of occupation by the Allies, and, for more than four decades, was two states: West and East Germany. However, first West Germany, then the whole of Germany, following its reunification (1990), has become a peaceful, democratic state.

Keeping the peace

Major wars usually produce a desire for peace, and, in the nineteenth and twentieth centuries, have led to the establishment of mechanisms or organizations for maintaining it.

The Concert of Europe

There was an attempt to create such a system after the Revolutionary and Napoleonic Wars, through congresses or conferences of the major European powers (Britain, Austria, Prussia, Russia) that had defeated Napoleon, and which were later joined by France. However, the so-called 'Concert of Europe' broke down, because Britain did not share the other members' desire to meddle in other countries' internal affairs, and to suppress internal revolutions against repressive regimes. But, the congress system 'left as a tradition . . . the practice of international conferences, inherited by the twentieth century', in the forms of the League of Nations and the UN (Grant and Temperley, *Europe*, p. 133).

The League of Nations

After the First World War, the League was established (its Covenant was written into the Treaty of Versailles), to 'promote international co-operation and to achieve international peace', and thus to prevent a repetition of the horrors of the First World War. President Wilson of the United Sates, in particular, had high hopes of its contribution to future peace: 'As racial hatreds die down, the power of the League will assert itself, wrongs will be healed and remedies applied' (quoted in Grant and Temperley, *Europe*, p. 429). And certainly the League looked impressive on paper. Members undertook to 'respect and preserve as against external aggression the territorial integrity and existing political independence of all Members' (Covenant, Art. 10). 'Any threat of war' was to be a 'matter of concern to the whole League', which would 'safeguard the peace of nations' (Art. 11). Disputes were to be submitted to arbitration or 'enquiry by the Council' (Art. 12); and, if a League member went to war, in breach of Covenant undertakings, it would be deemed to have made war 'against all other Members' and subjected to trade and/or financial sanctions, while the League Council would consider whether to use force against it (Art. 16). It was also hoped that the League would help to secure general disarmament (see above). In reality, the League foundered on the United States Senate's refusal to ratify the Treaty of Versailles and to participate; and on the ambitions of such countries as Japan, Germany and Italy, which pursued their own interests, in defiance of the League. After Hitler became Chancellor of Germany, in 1933, he proceeded to tear up the Treaty of Versailles, and the League did nothing to stop him: nor did it take effective action over Japan's invasion of Manchuria (1931); or Mussolini's invasion of Abyssinia (1935); or oppose Italian and German intervention in the Spanish Civil War in support of Franco (1936–9).

The United Nations

Following the Second World War, the United Nations was created (1945), to 'save succeeding generations from the scourge of war, which twice in our lifetime has brought untold sorrow to mankind'; enable people to 'live together in peace with one another as good neighbours'; and to maintain 'international peace and security' (UN Charter, Preamble). The Charter also refers to the aims of preventing and removing 'threats to the peace', suppressing 'acts of aggression', and settling international disputes peacefully (Art. 1.1); developing friendly international relations, based on respect for the principles of 'equal rights and self-determination', and strengthening 'universal peace' (Art. 1.2); achieving international co-operation, to solve 'economic, social, cultural, or humanitarian' problems; and promoting respect for 'human rights' and 'fundamental freedoms', without distinction of 'race, sex, language, or religion' (Art. 1.3). These are noble aims, but, more than 60 years after the UN came into being, they are a long way from being accomplished: there have been numerous wars and conflicts since 1945. Peace, international co-operation and respect for human rights and freedoms require more than the existence of an organization committed to achieving them: at the very least, they require national governments to stop putting what they perceive as their own interests first. There are also issues, as in the Middle East, where both Israel and the Palestinian Arabs lay claim to the same territory, that seem incapable of any solution.

Pacifism

One response to the inevitable miseries of war is not to add to them. The individual can refuse to join the armed services, or to commit acts of violence. Such a position is certainly consistent with Jesus' teaching about love in the Sermon on the Mount (see **pp. 191–2**), where (Matthew 5.9) he describes the 'peacemakers' (those who create peace on earth) as 'sons of God'. This is the view of the Religious Society of Friends, or Quakers, founded in the seventeenth century by George Fox, who 'deny all outward wars and strife . . . for any end, or . . . pretense whatever; this is our testimony to the whole world . . . the Spirit of Christ, which leads us into all truth, will never move us to fight' (Quaker Declaration of Pacifism). During the First World War, opponents of the conflict founded such organizations as the Fellowship of Reconciliation, which held that all human beings are one in Christ, and that evil can only be overcome by love; and the No Conscription Fellowship, which specifically opposed the Military Service Acts (1916) that replaced voluntary recruitment with compulsory military service. Those who had a conscientious objection to it could apply to a local tribunal for exemption. However, they were often treated unsympathetically, and many sincerely held claims were rejected. Some conscientious objectors agreed to do non-combatant service, such as ambulance work, but those who refused any kind of compulsory service were: 'drafted into military units, and sentenced to imprisonment . . . when they refused to obey the order of an officer' (Taylor, *English History*, p. 54).

Conscience requires courage

Indeed, being a conscientious objector, or speaking out against the First World War or its conduct, required courage. The philosopher Bertrand Russell (1872–1970) 'could see no principle at stake . . . which would justify the suffering and loss of life. He was appalled by the enthusiasm with which our entry into the war was generally greeted' (Ayer, *Russell*, p. 20). He campaigned vigorously against it and in support of the No Conscription Fellowship. As a result, he was twice sentenced to imprisonment; spent six months in prison; and was dismissed from his lectureship at Trinity College, Cambridge. When he was then offered a post at Harvard, the government refused him a passport. During the Second World War, although there was almost universal support for fighting Hitler, there was none of the enthusiasm for war itself that had been present in 1914. Nobody could be ignorant of the horrors of modern warfare, and conscientious objectors were treated more sympathetically. Of the 58,000 people who applied for registration, 40,000 were 'given conditional, and 2,900 unconditional exemption' (Taylor, *English History*, p. 457).

Pacifism and peace

But is pacifism right? Is it always right? Russell, who acknowledged that 'love of England' was one of his most powerful emotions, conceded that it may sometimes be necessary to fight: 'in the Second World War he thought that the evils of Nazism warranted armed resistance' (Ayer, *Russell*, p. 20). But, this raises the further question of whether the individual, who is also a citizen of his country, from which he receives the benefits of its protection, is entitled to pick and choose the causes for which he will fight. Nazi Germany was undoubtedly a more evil state than the Germany of Kaiser Wilhelm II, but both sought to destroy Britain's independence and freedom.

Aristotle held that wars should be fought, not for their own sake, but to secure the end of peace (see above). This raises the question of whether pacifism and non-violence are the best means of achieving peace. In some situations, is war the only means of doing so? Mohandas (Mahatma: Great-souled) Gandhi developed, and practised, non-violent resistance, based on the Hindu doctrine of *ahimsa* (non-violence, respect for life), which included peaceful protests, non-cooperation and public fasts, to achieve India's independence from Britain. But during the Second World War, when Britain was in the forefront of the battle against the evils of German Nazism and aggressive Japanese militarism, Gandhi adopted a neutral stance. Though condemning fascism, he was unwilling to support Britain, demanding an

315

'immediate reconstruction of the Indian government, so as to make the Viceroy no more than a figurehead' (Pelling, *Winston Churchill*, p. 490). But which was the greater threat to peace and freedom (including India's) in the world: Britain or the enemies against whom she was waging a just war? Perhaps those like Churchill who accept that in some situations war is a necessary evil, in order to achieve peace, do more to secure peace in the long term than those like Gandhi who pursue peace only through peaceful means.

References and suggestions for further reading

Aquinas, *Summa Theologica* IIa IIae q. 40 a. 1–4, at http://www.op.org/summa.

Aristotle, *Politics*, trans. B. Jowett, Oxford: Clarendon Press, 1908.

Augustine, *City of God*, ed. D. Knowles, Harmondsworth: Penguin, 1972.

A. J. Ayer, *Russell*, London: Fontana, 1971.

J. B. Bury, *A History of Greece*, London: Macmillan, 1963.

P. Calvocoressi, *World Politics since 1945*, 4th edn, London and New York: Longman, 1982.

Carl von Clausewitz, *On War*, trans. J. J. Graham, Ware: Wordsworth, 1997.

R. C. K. Ensor, *England 1870–1914*, Oxford: Oxford University Press, 1936.

J. C. Fenton, *Saint Matthew*, Harmondsworth: Penguin, 1963.

L. Fischer, *The Life of Mahatma Ghandi*, London: HarperCollins, 1997.

J. Fletcher, *Situation Ethics*, London: SCM Press, 1966.

A. J. Grant and H. Temperley, *Europe in the Nineteenth and Twentieth Centuries*, 6th edn, London: Longman, 1952.

Laws of War and International Humanitarian Law. The Avalon Project website at Yale Law School (http://www.yale.edu/lawweb/avalon) and the Red Cross website (http://www.icrc.org) contain databases of these, including the texts of all the documents referred to. The British Red Cross website (http://www.redcross.org.uk) also contains a wide range of information, including about its history; weapons of war; modern warfare; nuclear weapons; and the International Criminal Court.

B. H. Liddell Hart, *History of the Second World War*, London: Cassell, 1970.

J. McMahan, 'War and Peace', in P. Singer (ed.), *A Companion to Ethics*, Cambridge: Cambridge University Press, 1993.

The Military Service Acts, 1916 (c.104 and c.15). See the Long, Long Trail website at http://www.1914–1918.net.

Nuclear Weapons: Report of the Secretary-General of the United Nations, Brookline, MA: Autumn Press, 1980.

B. Orend, 'War' (rev. 2005), in E. N. Zalta (ed.), *The Stanford Encyclopaedia of Philosophy*, at http://plato.stanford.edu.

H. Pelling, *Winston Churchill*, Ware: Wordsworth, 1999.

Quakers of Britain website at www.quaker.org.uk.

A. J. P. Taylor, *English History 1914–1945*, Oxford and New York: Oxford University Press, 1965.

S. Watson, *The Reign of George III*, Oxford: Oxford University Press, 1960.

L. Woodward, *The Age of Reform 1815–1870*, 2nd edn, Oxford: Oxford University Press, 1961.

P. Vardy and P. Grosch, *The Puzzle of Ethics*, rev. edn, London: HarperCollins, 1999.

18 Animals and the Environment

1 Anthropocentric ethics

Ethics is mainly concerned with human beings and their well-being, so it is **anthropocentric**: it is almost exclusively concerned with human beings and their well-being. Irrespective of the differences between ethical and metaethical theories, the aim of ethics and the reason why it exists is to define and regulate our responsibilities to other human beings and also to ourselves. But is this how it should be?

Animals

Human beings do not exist in a vacuum. We share our world with other beings, animals. Although they are not rational and self-conscious, they are sentient or conscious and clearly capable of experiencing suffering and pain. Ethics has not ignored them completely. In developed western countries, at least, there is a consensus that animals should not be cruelly treated or allowed to suffer unnecessarily. However, they are not given the same moral status as human beings. Their value is seen as instrumental, not intrinsic: they are spared cruel treatment, only to the extent that it is consistent with human needs. Many are kept in unnatural and uncomfortable conditions in factory farms, and then slaughtered, in order to provide us with cheap food. They are subjected to painful experiments, to ensure the safety of medicines for human beings. But is this **ethical 'speciesism'** (limiting moral status to human beings) justified? We obviously possess moral status, but do animals, too?

The environment

Then there is the environment itself, the planet earth and all its non-sentient organisms? Do we have ethical responsibilities to it and its contents, beyond the merely prudent one of promoting, or at least limiting anthropogenic (harmful human) behaviour towards those aspects of the planet that serve human needs, whether as means of survival, sources of nourishment, or opportunities for relaxation and enjoyment? Do we need to rethink our **anthropocentrism**, whereby the ultimate justification, even of conservation, is what is good for us?

2 Animals and animal rights

A nation of animal lovers?

In Britain, we like to portray ourselves as a nation of animal lovers, but there is evidence that contradicts such a claim. Between 2003 and 2006, the number of animal cruelty complaints investigated by the RSPCA increased from 105,932 to 122,454, while the number of convictions fell only slightly from 1,829 to 1,647. For the sake of the producers' convenience, factory farming often involves the declawing and debeaking of hens and the dehorning of cattle, sheep and goats. In 2003, apart from almost 500,000 rats, more than 5,000 dogs, 500 cats, 400 horses and 3,000 primates were used in animal experiments. But does this matter? A Kantian might argue that, as rational beings are the only ends-in-themselves, whom we have a duty not to treat as means, animals, as merely conscious and so non-rational beings, lack moral status, and so we can treat and exploit them as we please for food, sport, entertainment and so on.

Albert Schweitzer and reverence for life

Albert Schweitzer argues that, as human beings, we have a 'will-to-live', and that we act naturally when we affirm it, and treat our own lives with reverence, rather than as something insignificant that we could easily throw away (Schweitzer, *My Life and Thought*, pp. 142–3). However, as rational, thinking beings, we should universalize this respect for our own lives, and extend to 'every will-to-live the same reverence for life' as we accord our own (pp. 142–3). For Schweitzer, we only become truly ethical beings when we move beyond anthropocentrism and realize that 'life, as such, is sacred', which includes not only animals but plants as well (p. 143):

Only the universal ethic of the feeling of responsibility in an ever-widening sphere for all that lives – only that ethic can be founded in thought. The ethic of the relation of man to man is not something apart by itself: it is only a particular relation which results from the universal one. (p. 143)

Jeremy Bentham and the moral status of animals

For **utilitarians**, animals, as sentient beings, are capable of experiencing pain. Therefore, they could argue that we should always seek to minimize their pain, even if we do use them to serve our own interests. Jeremy Bentham points out that, although animals are capable of happiness, as a result of human neglect of their interests, they have been 'degraded into the class of *things*' (Bentham, *Introduction*, p. 310). For Bentham, it is not wrong to slaughter animals for food, or kill those that threaten us:

> we are the better for it, and they are never the worse. They have none of those long-protracted anticipations of future misery which we have. The death they suffer in our hands commonly is . . . a speedier, and by that means a less painful one, than . . . would await them in the inevitable course of nature. (p. 311)

But, we are not entitled to make them suffer. He draws a parallel between the way slaves had been treated, due to their being regarded as an inferior sort of human being, and contemporary treatment of animals; and looks forward to a time when 'the number of legs, the villosity [hairiness] of the skin' are not seen as adequate reasons for denying animals moral status. So, where is the line to be drawn? Moral status should not, Bentham argues, be restricted to rational beings:

> Is it the faculty of reason, or . . . discourse? . . . the question is not, Can they *reason*? Nor, Can they *talk*? But, Can they *suffer*? (p. 311)

Bentham holds that, in fact, 'a full-grown horse or dog is beyond comparison a more rational . . . animal, than an infant of a day, or a week, or even a month' (p. 311). But it is their capacity to suffer that entitles animals to moral status. However, though conscious, they are not self-conscious, and so do not have equivalent moral status with human beings. We can slaughter them for food, because they will not be aware, as the prospective victims of cannibals would, of their fate: they do not undergo miseries of anticipation. However, they must be killed humanely, to minimize their suffering.

Peter Singer and regarding animals as persons

But should we go further, and regard animals as persons? The **preference utilitarian** Peter Singer (see also **pp. 98–102**) maintains that the apparent oddness of calling an animal a person may just reflect the sharp distinction we draw between the human species and others. But are any non-human animals 'rational and self-conscious beings, aware of themselves as distinct entities with a past and a future' (Singer, *Practical Ethics*, pp. 110–11). Singer believes that research indicates that apes, chimpanzees and gorillas can be taught to communicate with human beings, through sign language, and that apes 'use signs to refer to past or future events, thus showing a sense of time' (p. 112). He also believes that these animals may not be exceptional: just that being taught a language has enabled them to demonstrate an ability that other animals may possess.

For Singer, there should be no sharp dividing-line on the scale of moral status, separating the human species from all the others, because some non-human animals are persons. He maintains that the only 'defensible version of the doctrine of the sanctity of human life' is that human beings have a 'personal life'; if human life has special value, it is because 'most human beings are persons' (p. 117). However, if some non-human animals are autonomous persons, with preferences or interests to be satisfied:

> we should reject the doctrine that places the lives of members of our species above the lives of members of other species. Some members of other species are persons; some members of our own species are not. No objective assessment can support the view that it is always worse to kill members of our species who are not persons than members of other species who are. (p. 117)

Tom Regan and animals as 'subjects-of-a-life'

The **deontologist** Tom Regan maintains that certain animals have intrinsic or inherent value, and so we have a duty to treat them with respect, and not as means to our ends. The view that only rational moral agents, as 'ends in themselves', have moral value fails to recognize that some human beings, such as infants and those with mental disabilities and disorders, are 'human moral patients', not agents; nonetheless, we still have 'direct duties' to them (Regan, *Animal Rights*, p. 239). As we cannot consistently maintain that moral patients 'can never be harmed in relevantly similar ways' to moral agents, we cannot 'nonarbitrarily' regard the former as 'lacking inherent value' (pp. 239–40). However, we cannot exclude 'normal mammalian animals, aged one or more' from the category of moral patients (p. 239).

Both human moral patients and animals are 'subjects-of-a-life'. This involves more than just being alive and conscious. Subject-of-a-life individuals have:

> beliefs and desires; perception, memory, and a sense of the future, including their own future; an emotional life . . . the ability to initiate action in pursuit of their desires and goals; a psychophysical identity over time. (p. 243)

Mammalian animals satisfy the 'subject-of-a-life criterion', because their 'experiential life fares well or ill for them', irrespective of its effect on others, including human beings (p. 243). They conduct their lives

> logically independently of their utility for others and logically independently of their being the object of anyone else's interest . . . [they] have a distinctive kind of value – inherent value. (p. 243)

For Regan, mammalian animals' moral status has important implications for our ethical responsibilities towards them. Animal husbandry as a whole, not just factory farming, is unjust, because 'it fails to treat farm animals with the respect they are due, treating them instead as renewable resources having value only relative to human interests' (p. 394). We must stop supporting it by not purchasing meat. We should also give up hunting and trapping animals, as the pleasures that derive from these pursuits can be enjoyed without harming animals. We should not kill animals for scientific research, as the deaths, not just the suffering of beings with inherent value, is morally wrong; and, as we do not know where to 'draw the line between those animals that are, and those that are not, subjects-of-a-life', we should 'err on the side of caution' (p. 396). Even medical research should be condemned, because it reduces the value of mammalian animals to their 'possible utility relative to the interests of others' (p. 397).

Genesis, Aristotle and Aquinas

Christian teaching originates from the Old Testament, where not even higher animals are regarded as having moral status and a 'right' to compassionate treatment. According to Genesis (see pp. 184–5), God created only human beings in his own image, and then instructed them to subdue the earth, and to exercise dominion over every other living thing. Not only every plant, but every beast of the earth and bird of the air has been given to human beings, suggesting that God has given human beings a free hand to treat animals as they like, unless doing so contravenes a specific religious rule, such as those found in Leviticus: 'This is the law pertaining to beast and bird and every living creature that moves through the waters and . . . swarms upon the earth, to make a distinction between the unclean and the clean . . . between the living creature that may be eaten and . . . that may not be' (Leviticus 11.46–7).

Aristotle says much the same thing about the relationship between human beings and animals, basing his conclusion on what the natural order tells us:

> we may infer that, after the birth of animals, plants exist for their sake, and that the other animals exist for the sake of man . . . for food, and for the provision of clothing . . . nature makes nothing incomplete . . . the inference must be that she has made all animals and plants for the sake of man. (Aristotle, *Politics*, p. 40)

Aquinas takes over Aristotle's argument and fuses it with Genesis. There is no sin in using things for their purpose, so it is not wrong to 'use plants for the good of animals, and animals for the good of man'; and the latter cannot be used as food, unless they are 'deprived of life' (Aquinas, *Summa Theologica* IIa IIae q. 64 a. 1). According to Genesis, God has given the 'beasts of the earth' to human beings for their use, so, by 'Divine ordinance', animal (and plant) life is 'preserved not for themselves but for man' (IIa IIae q. 64 a. 1). Further, their lack of reason is a sign that animals are 'naturally enslaved and accommodated' to human use; thus, if someone kills an animal belonging to another, his sin is not killing, but damage to property (IIa IIae q. 64 a. 1). According to **Roman Catholic** teaching, it is

> legitimate to use animals for food and clothing . . . Medical and scientific experimentation on animals is a morally acceptable practice if it remains within reasonable limits and contributes to . . . saving human lives. (*Catechism of the Catholic Church*, para. 2417)

Another view of Christian teaching

However, the phrase 'within reasonable limits' indicates a different perspective within the **Christian tradition**. Although animals are not made in God's image, he entrusted them to human beings. They are part of God's natural created order, and a higher part than the non-sentient world. Although God made animals to serve human needs, human beings must respect them, together with the rest of creation, not primarily because of their duty to the animals, but because of their duty to God: 'Animals are entrusted to man's stewardship; he must show them kindness' (*Catechism of the Catholic Church*, para. 2457). Human dominion over the natural order is not that of a cruel tyrant, empowered to treat other creatures as he pleases, but that of the responsible steward, who cares for the rest of creation, especially animals, and avoids inflicting unnecessary pain on them, even when he is using them, as in food production, for his own purposes: 'It is contrary to human dignity to cause animals to suffer or die needlessly' (para. 2418). A resolution of the **Church of England** General Synod recognizes: 'the welfare of animals and their just treatment as an essential part of our responsibility towards creation' (CofE (a)). The **Methodist** view is that: 'Unnecessary and unjustifiable experiments and trials . . . should not take place. Intensive factory farming methods which ignore the welfare of animals are to be condemned' (Methodists (a)).

Andrew Linzey and 'theos-rights'

Andrew Linzey has developed Christian thinking about animals. He rejects an instrumentalist view of animals as 'speciesist'; it privileges one species, human beings, giving them a unique moral status. For Linzey, animals are part of God's creation, and have God-given or 'theos-rights', and thus moral status:

> God the Father gives life . . . By positing the rights of the creature we do no more . . . than claim God's right in his creation and the integrity of his redeeming work . . . The value of the theos-rights perspective is that it enables us to question the all-too-easy assumption that human personality . . . is the only kind of value to God . . . The theos-rights perspective . . . does not deny that human beings have especial value to God . . . it simply resists the view that humans alone have special value and that theos-rights can be denied to animals . . . in the end the basis of judgement should not be what *we* value but what *God* values. (Linzey, *Christianity and the Rights of Animals*, pp. 71–7)

If we treat animals badly, we are bad stewards and we wrong God. Our duty to him is to treat animals well, which may require giving up animal experiments and factory farming.

There are affinities between Linzey and other animal liberationist philosophers. However, the ultimate justification for treating animals well is duty to God, not **utilitarian** concern with the interests/preferences of animals (Singer) or **deontological** recognition of their rights as persons (Regan):

From a theological perspective, what is the function of a steward but to safeguard what God has given and to value what God values? (p. 87)

Growth of concern for animals

In Britain, attitudes to animal welfare, as they developed during the nineteenth century, reflected a mixture of the sense of the responsibility to animals that Christian stewardship involves, and **utilitarian** concern to minimize their suffering. The Cruelty to Animals Act, 1876 prohibited animal experiments that were calculated to cause pain, unless they were essential for advancing scientific knowledge, or of use for saving or prolonging human life or alleviating human suffering; and it specified the use of anaesthetics, to minimize pain. Similarly, the Protection of Animals Act, 1911 made it an offence for the owner of an animal to cause it unnecessary suffering, through acts of commission (actively mistreating it) or omission (allowing it to suffer through neglect).

Current animal welfare issues

The Animal Welfare Act, 2006 imposes harsher penalties (fines up to £20,000 and imprisonment for up to 51 weeks) for pet owners if they neglect or cruelly treat animals. They now have an explicit 'duty of care' to look after their pets, which includes catering for their needs and ensuring they receive necessary veterinary treatment. Certain practices, such as docking tails for cosmetic reasons, are also banned. As the statistics for RSPCA investigations and prosecutions testify (see above), cruelty to pets is still widespread. However, what give rise to greater concern and controversy, in Britain and elsewhere, are the issues of animal experiments and intensive methods of rearing animals for food production.

Animal experiments

In Britain, animal experiments are covered by the Animals (Scientific Procedures) Act, 1986. This provides a regulatory framework for laboratories where research on animals is conducted, which includes frequent Home Office inspection. Animals must have appropriate accommodation; veterinary expertise must be available; research must be conducted by trained and experienced researchers. The legislation also requires that: the potential benefits justify use of animals; they will only be used if non-animal methods will not suffice; that as few animals as possible are used;

and that dogs, cats and primates are used only if other species, such as rats, are unsuitable.

The regulatory regime seems rigorous, and the advocates of animal research, such as the Research Defence Society (RDS) and the Coalition for Medical Progress (CMP), argue that it is essential. First, the legislation, such as the Medicines Act, 1968 and European Directives, require new drugs to be tested on animals: 'all new medicines must be studied in animals before they are tested in people: this is vitally important to protect human volunteers and patients taking part in clinical trials' (RDS). It is also scientifically necessary:

> The animal tests aim to show the potential of the medicine . . . to cause various toxic effects in the body. These can affect specific organs, such as the liver or the heart or . . . foetal development . . . By using two different species . . . about 7 in 10 toxic reactions in humans can be predicted. (RDS).

There are also compelling historical reasons for doing research on animals. The Medicines Act was passed as a result of the thalidomide tragedy in the 1950s, when babies were born with serious deformities, because: 'No pre-testing of Thalidomide [a pregnancy drug] in pregnant animals meant its horrific side-effects were not detected until after it started to be prescribed' (CMP).

However, this still means that non-human animals are subjected to possibly painful testing for the benefit of human beings. Is this justified? The pro-testing arguments seem more persuasive when the focus is on testing medicines. But, as opponents such as the British Union for the Abolition of Vivisection (BUAV) point out, animal experiments are carried out for a range of purposes, which include agricultural and space research and tests for the safety of household products. For example, the Draize eye test (to test for the skin irritancy of such products) involves:

> a substance being dripped into one eye of a rabbit. The eye is then examined for signs of bleeding, ulceration, redness, swelling and discharge . . . The albino rabbit is traditionally used . . . it is cheap, docile . . . and has large eyes. (BUAV)

Even if animal suffering is justified for experiments to test (life-saving) drugs, is it justified for tests of this kind? Some argue that it is not justified, even if it is the only means of ensuring that the drugs used by humans are safe; and even if there is no realistic alternative. As human beings are the intended beneficiaries, why not conduct the experiments on them? At least they would be volunteers. The fact that we do not 'can only be explained in terms of simple prejudice' (BUAV). BUAV also questions the reliability of animal experiments, which 'tell us about animals, not people'.

Factory farming

Since the rise of supermarkets, where 90 per cent of people in Britain now buy their food, there has been an expectation that food will be cheap and (at least until recent sharp price rises, reflecting world commodity shortages) get even cheaper. Most human beings consume meat and/or animal products, and keeping down the cost of animal-based food seems to be achievable only by treating animals as commodities to be processed. For example, most egg-laying hens are not kept in natural, free range conditions, but in cramped cages:

> five hens are packed into a cage of only 45 × 50 cm . . . The average wing span of a hen is 76 cm – so movement and natural behaviour is severely restricted. Thousands of cages are stacked into windowless sheds . . . Up to 90,000 birds are packed in these sheds . . . The combination of a lack of fresh air and daylight, selective breeding and caging in overcrowded conditions has led to the spread of diseases and to distress and suffering. Prolapses . . . cancers, infectious bronchitis . . . (VIVA)

Not only are factory farming methods cruel, they harm human health and the environment. Excessive use of antibiotics runs the risk of creating 'resistant strains of bacteria' in animals, which can be passed on to humans; small farms and farmers, who use more animal- and environment-friendly methods are unable to compete, and are forced out of production; wildlife and the landscape are damaged, and bio-diversity diminished (AFF). And how efficient are these supposedly cost-effective methods? Indeed, is it sensible to rear and kill animals for food at all? Would we not make more efficient use of our resources if the land devoted to producing foodstuffs for livestock were given over to growing food we could consume directly:

> Nor is animal production in industrialised societies an efficient way of producing food . . . most of the animals . . . have been fattened on grains and other foods that we could have eaten directly. When we feed these grains to animals, only about 10 per cent of the nutritional value remains as meat for human consumption . . . Their flesh is a luxury, consumed because people like its taste. (Singer, *Practical Ethics*, pp. 62–3)

Fox-hunting

Another major controversy has been over fox-hunting. The Hunting Act, 2004 bans hunting with dogs in England and Wales. The main argument against fox-hunting is the cruelty to the fox, which can be condemned on **utilitarian** grounds (the fox experiences fear as it is pursued, and pain when it is killed) and/or **deontological** ones (a fox is a 'subject-of-a-life', and should be treated with respect). It is also unnecessary, because foxes can be controlled in other, less cruel ways, which are still permitted. There is the further point that fox-hunting involves taking pleasure in inflicting pain on animals and may have undesirable effects on those who take part. On the other hand, apart from the claims that it is necessary as a means of controlling the fox population, banning fox-hunting infringes Mill's **principle of liberty**. Those who want to hunt are only harming foxes, which can be killed anyway, and society is not entitled to prevent them doing so, if they wish.

Thus, those who support fox-hunting could combine an **anthropocentric libertarian** argument with an **anthropocentric utilitarian** argument: that the pleasure that the human fox-hunters derive from being free to pursue their sport should always outweigh any pain the fox may suffer from being pursued. However, its opponents could combine **utilitarian** and **deontological** arguments, in relation to the fox, with the quantity of pain or diminished pleasure they experience themselves, when they see or hear about foxes being killed in this way. A further **anthropocentric** argument, which was and is invoked by supporters of fox-hunting, relates to the economic and social benefits of fox-hunting for the rural economy. However, a **Church of England** briefing paper pointed out that, if fox-hunting is incompatible with the consideration human beings 'owe to animals', these factors would not by themselves 'justify it' (CofE (b)); and this argument can be applied to other areas where inflicting pain on animals is defended on such grounds.

Utilitarian and deontological approaches

A **utilitarian** approach does not necessarily rule out any kind of exploitation of animals. Even if it is accepted that non-human animals are persons, whose pleasures, preferences or interests should be taken into consideration, the **utilitarian** could always argue that those of human beings, who are at the top of the hierarchy of persons, should outweigh those of animals, who are lower down the scale; and that the lower down the scale they are, the less their preferences or interests need to be considered. The **utilitarian** need have no problem with killing animals for food or other purposes, provided fear or suffering is eliminated, or minimized. However, the **deontologist**, who recognizes (some) animals as intrinsically valuable persons, will either have to abstain from actions and practices, including killing them for food and carrying out research on them, that infringe their rights as moral subjects, or determine the extent to which, and in what circumstances, the rights of self-conscious human persons should take precedence over those of merely conscious animal persons.

The human–animal community

The environmental philosopher J. Baird Callicott (following Mary Midgley) provides an interesting insight into where things have gone wrong in the relationship between human beings and animals. He does not agree with some of the animal liberationists, that animals have equivalent moral status to human beings: 'Even to those deeply sympathetic to the plight of animals there is something deeply amiss in the concept of *equal* moral consideration or *equal* moral rights for animals' (Callicott, *In Defense of the Land Ethic*, p. 55). However, with industrialization and urbanization, many human beings are no longer, as they were in a predominantly agricultural society, part of a 'mixed human–animal community', which generates mutual 'sociability – sympathy, compassion, trust, love', between species, and prevents erection of a 'species-barrier' (p. 52). Now, however, we have 'depersonalized and mechanized' animals, and the disgust we feel towards factory farming and animal experimentation reflects our guilt at having 'broken trust with erstwhile fellow members of our traditionally mixed communities' (p. 55).

As a society, we can of course repudiate our schizophrenic attitude towards animals, which regards them, anthropomorphically, as characters in a Beatrix Potter story and, at the same time, treats them merely as animated chunks of meat or bottles of milk, and restore a sense of the mixed human–animal community in which animals are treated with respect and allowed to enjoy their lives but, at the same time, used with the minimum of pain and suffering to serve human needs.

3 The environment and human stewardship

The challenges we face

What about environmental issues in general, which include global warming and climate change, ozone depletion and the threat to biodiversity? They all affect human and non-human animals, as they relate to the quality of our environment and its present and future viability.

Global warming and climate change

The more highly industrialized the world is, and the more voracious our appetites as consumers, the bigger our impact on the environment. We burn ever-growing quantities of fossil fuels, such as oil, coal and gas, which increases the levels of carbon dioxide (7 billion tonnes a year from this source) and other so-called 'greenhouse' gases (methane and nitrous oxide) in the atmosphere. These enwrap the world, hold in the heat and cause it to get warmer. Other human activities also contribute to global warming. For example, we cut down forests, removing trees that reduce carbon dioxide levels in the atmosphere; we insist on breeding animals for food, which is wasteful of resources (see above) and generates methane; we do little or nothing to restrain population growth (see **pp. 263–7, 338**); and so on.

Inevitably, these activities have an effect. Since the late 1990s, we have had some of the warmest years since records started. The Arctic ice sheet is diminishing by almost 10 per cent each decade, while glaciers around the world are also getting smaller, releasing methane into the atmosphere. On the other hand, deserts are getting larger, leading to water shortages, particularly in Africa. However, global warming is also associated with extremes of weather, resulting in rising sea levels, storms and floods, which leave thousands of people homeless and impoverished. Even in Britain, 'the cost of storm and flood damage doubled over the five years to 2004' (Climate Concern UK). According to Greenpeace, 'within 50 years, one-third of all land-based species could face extinction. If we carry on the way we are now, by 2100 the planet will be hotter than it's been at any point in the past two million years.' We seem to be like homeowners who not only neglect to repair and maintain their house, but kick down the doors, smash the windows and pull slates off the roof.

Ozone depletion

The ozone layer denotes the ozone within the stratosphere, the second major layer of the earth's atmosphere. Although ozone itself is an irritating and corrosive gas, the ozone layer is vitally important, because it absorbs up to 99 per cent of the sun's ultraviolet light, which can harm living cells and, as far as human beings are concerned, can cause skin burns and cancers and eye damage. In 1985, analysis of the British Antarctic Survey data showed the ozone levels for Antarctica were down by 10 per cent. This confirmed the findings of previous studies that linked ozone depletion to the effects of chlorofluorocarbons (CFCs: carbon with chlorines and fluorides), which had been used as refrigerants since the 1920s.

Biodiversity

This refers to the variety of the earth's life forms; variations within animal and plant species; and the different ecosystems of which the species are part. In all sorts of ways, human activities endanger or diminish biodiversity. Growing populations, and rising lifestyle expectations, mean that the countryside and its wildlife are concreted over for houses, roads and airports. In agriculture, the demand for cheap food (see above) has led to intensive farming, which has involved chopping down trees and grubbing up hedgerows, and so removing wildlife habitats and destroying plant species, which are also killed by widespread use of fertilizers and herbicides. According to Defra, 'In the UK we have lost over 100 species during the last century, with many more species and habitats in danger of disappearing.'

The attitudes of rich and poor

We cannot afford to ignore these issues, and there are initiatives at international, national and local levels to address them. For example, the Kyoto agreement (1997) committed developing countries to reducing greenhouse gas emissions by at least 5.2 per cent between 2008 and 2012; the Montreal Protocol (1987) lays down a schedule for phasing out CFCs; while, in Britain, the 2000 Countryside and Rights of Way Act gives stronger protection to the most important wildlife habitats (Sites of Special Scientific Interest: SSSIs), helping to preserve biodiversity. But, quite apart from anxieties in developed countries about the impact of such initiatives on prosperity and the standard of living, are environmental concerns a luxury only affluent western societies can afford?

From the lofty heights of our prosperity, we can renounce a degree of material consumption without too much discomfort. However, this is not the case with poor or developing countries, which are far from reaching our standards of prosperity. They are unlikely to restrain industrial development and consumption, even when confronted with compelling arguments about their environmental impact. And the developed world seems both culpable and hypocritical here. While preaching self-denial to developing countries, which do not think they have much to deny themselves, industries in developed countries have transferred production to these countries, where costs, but also environmental controls, are lower, risking greater pollution and environmental damage.

The basis for environmental concern and action

We are confronted with a range of environmental issues. But why should we address them? Some people do not seem to worry: they think we should carry on as we are, enjoy our lifestyles and hope for the best. Most people's reasons for concern and action are **anthropocentric** and/or sentient-creature-centric: we need to act to preserve the planet for ourselves, for other animals, and for future generations. But satisfying the preferences/interests of, or fulfilling our duties to, other (and future) human beings and animals are not the only reasons for grappling with the issues. What about the planet as a whole and/or the non-sentient entities within it? Do we have obligations to them? For example, with bio-diversity, is our only concern to preserve species, because they are of direct use to human beings, or to make the planet more habitable or beautiful? Or is there an obligation to preserve landscapes and plant species because they are valuable in themselves? And what about the religious dimension? For religious people, concern for the environment is part of their duty to God.

Christian teaching about creation and the environment

According to **Christian teaching** (see **pp. 184–5**), God created the universe and all it contains from nothing. Therefore, human beings, as rational creatures, made in God's image, have a duty to God's natural order. They must:

> respect ... the integrity of creation ... Use of the mineral, vegetable, and animal resources of the universe cannot be divorced from respect for moral imperatives. Man's dominion over inanimate and other living beings granted by the Creator is not absolute; it is limited by concern for the quality of life of his neighbour, including generations to come; it requires a religious respect for the integrity of creation. (*Catechism of the Catholic Church*, para. 2415)

Thus, the **Roman Catholic tradition** provides a succinct statement of the Christian basis of environmentalism: recognition that the created natural order belongs to God, not us, and is good ('Because creation comes forth from God's goodness, it shares in that goodness': para. 299); that we are its stewards, accountable to God, not its outright owners ('God willed creation as ... an inheritance destined for and entrusted to him [mankind]': para. 299); and that we must conserve it, not exploit and damage it, for selfish, short-term profit ('The order and harmony of the created world results from the diversity of beings and from the relationships which exist among them': para. 341).

Creator and sustainer

God is not only the creator, but also the sustainer of the natural order ('With creation, God does not abandon his creatures to themselves . . . but . . . upholds and sustains them in being': para. 301), which is not yet 'complete', and which he is guiding towards its 'ultimate perfection' (para. 302). As rational beings, we can also learn about God through the natural order: 'Our human understanding, which shares in the light of the divine intellect, can understand what God tells us by means of his creation' (para. 299).

A call to change our lifestyles

The **Church of England** points out that all faith traditions, by acknowledging God as the 'source of all things', accept that human beings do not have 'mastery and dominance of the created order', but are 'stewards of that which is not their own to exploit' (CofE (c), p. 2). They have a particular duty to 'hand on unharmed their legacy of an exquisitely beautiful, vastly intelligent, single sourced yet wholly diverse creation' (p. 2). However, during the twentieth century, creation has been increasingly harmed by 'human action and lifestyle choices' (p. 3). As well as urging and supporting government and international environmental initiatives, Christians must recognize that concern for God's creation calls them to change their own way of life. For, Christians are among those whose 'resource-hungry lifestyles' (as in western Europe and especially the United States) would, if replicated across the globe, require 'five planets' worth of resources' to satisfy (p. 4).

Acting at local level

One strand of the **Church of England's** response is to develop local environmentalism, based on the Church's 'centuries old parish system', which encompasses 'every person and the creation itself within that geographical boundary' (p. 5). The concept of the 'eco-congregation' encourages parishes to conduct an audit of energy uses, to determine the size of its carbon footprint, and then to devise means of reducing it (p. 5). As well as urging the government to 'introduce robust policies to reduce carbon emissions', and regretting the 'disproportionate responsibility of developed nations for climate change' and its impact on 'poorer communities throughout the world', the **Methodist Church** urges its congregations to recognize the need for a 'radical new lifestyle', and to 'monitor and reduce their carbon emissions' (Methodists (b)).

Operation Noah

Churches in Britain support Operation Noah, a joint project between the Christian Ecology Link and the Environmental Issues Network of Churches Together in Britain and Ireland, established in 2001, in response to 'the threat posed to the whole of God's creation by human-induced global warming'. It seeks to transform thinking about environmental issues in Britain, so that people understand that natural resources are not unlimited; that the earth cannot cope with ever-increasing levels of pollution; and that economic growth cannot continue indefinitely. They will then be willing to give up irresponsible lifestyles, tied to 'boundless consumption of goods and services'. Its 'core goal' is national legislation to reduce individual annual carbon emissions from the current 9.5 tonnes to 1 tonne by 2030.

The Gaia hypothesis

Named after the Greek mother goddess, this theory, put forward by the research scientist James Lovelock, suggests regarding the whole biosphere as a massive self-regulating organism, capable of initiating and sustaining life, whatever happens. Like Christian belief that God created and sustains the world (see above), the data, natural phenomena, are the same, but interpretation of their origin and value differs from the ordinary secular one. Thus, instead of taking the view that life on earth developed when conditions existed to support it, this hypothesis suggests that 'Gaia', or the earth's life-initiating and sustaining capacity, created life-supporting conditions; and some natural phenomena lend themselves to this interpretation: the 'salinity of the sea, and the oxygen content of the atmosphere . . . have been constant for billions of years, and this very constancy requires explanation' (Brennan, *Thinking About Nature*, p. 129). Believing the Gaia hypothesis could lead to a quasi-religious attitude to the earth, and reinforce the will to conserve it. However, the compatibility of a hypothesis with certain data, or possible beneficial effects of believing it, do not make it true. Accepting the Gaia hypothesis would be as much an act of faith (and persuasive for some of the same reasons) as the belief that God created and sustains the world: 'We have to be wary of thinking from the design-stance about the various ways in which the earth seems anomalous when compared with other planets' (p. 130).

Shallow ecology and deep ecology

Within secular environmental ethics, a convenient division is between 'shallow' ecologists, whose environmental concern focuses on human and animal well-being, and 'deep' ecologists, who argue that all natural entities, not only self-conscious or conscious ones, have intrinsic value, rather than the merely instrumental one of serving the latter's needs. Whereas shallow ecologists hold that the environment should be protected and preserved, because it is in the interests of humans and animals, deep ecologists call for some form of biospheric egalitarianism: equal moral status for all natural entities.

Although a **utilitarian** case can be made for deep ecology, along the lines that all natural entities, rational, sentient and non-sentient (such as rivers and mountains), have 'interests', which need to be weighed against each other, the **utilitarian** deep ecologist would have the problem of explaining what 'interests' mean, in relation to non-sentient entities: unlike rational and sentient beings, plants, rivers and mountains cannot experience pleasure or the satisfaction of interests and preferences in the way that rational and sentient beings do.

Peter Singer and the sentient creature boundary

Peter Singer's position (and see above) is that 'the boundary of moral consideration' should be extended to include all sentient creatures, but not beyond. He asks if, for example, 'aspects of the flooding' of a valley can be shown 'to have intrinsic value . . . independently of their effects on human beings or non-human animals' (Singer, *Practical Ethics*, p. 277). He stresses the difficulty of plausibly extending an ethic beyond sentient beings with 'wants and desires' (p. 277). It may look possible, if the moral boundary is confined to living things:

> We know what is good or bad for the plants in our garden: water, sunlight, and compost are good; extremes of heat or cold are bad. The same applies to plants in any forest . . . so why not regard their flourishing as good in itself, independently of its usefulness to sentient creatures? (p. 277)

But the problem (Singer maintains) is the absence of 'conscious interests' to guide decisions as to the 'relative weights to be given to the flourishing' of different types of living things (p. 277). Is 'a two-thousand-year-old Huon pine more worthy of preservation than a tussock of grass' (p. 277)? It seems obvious that it is: but this reflects our preferences and interests, not those of the Huon pine or the grass. Philosophers like Paul Taylor have argued that every individual living thing is a 'teleological centre of life', which is seeking to preserve itself and realize its good (Taylor, *Respect for Nature*, p. 121); and that, once we appreciate this, we will see all living things as we see ourselves, and be willing to value their lives as we do our own. And talk of plants 'seeking' water or light, so that they can survive, does indeed suggest that they possess a will to live and are ends-in-themselves. But reflection shows that, as plants are not conscious and cannot engage in intentional behaviour, such language is metaphorical and misleading:

> one might just as well say that a river is pursuing its own good and striving to reach the sea . . . in the absence of consciousness, there is no good reason why we should have greater respect for the physical processes that govern the growth and decay of living things than we have for those that govern non-living things. This being so, it is at least not obvious why we should have greater reverence for a tree than for a stalactite, or for a single-celled organism than for a mountain. (pp. 279–80)

Thus, for Singer, the ethical basis of environmentalism and conservation is what satisfies the ascertainable preferences and interests of rational and sentient beings, who have moral status, not the (in Singer's view, unascertainable) 'interests' of all individual living entities. And the latter would not qualify for moral status and rights against Regan's 'subject-of-a-life' **deontological** criterion either (see **pp. 321–2**).

John Baird Callicott and Aldo Leopold's land ethic

Despite their differences, the approaches of Singer, Regan and Taylor are all individualistic: their concern is with the interests or rights of individual natural entities, although they draw the boundaries of moral status at different points in the hierarchy of being. But, what about the environment as a whole? John Baird Callicott, a disciple of the influential American environmentalist Aldo Leopold's 'land ethic', maintains that the biotic community as a whole has intrinsic value: 'ethical considerability' is extended from people to 'nonhuman natural entities' (Callicott, *In Defense of the Land Ethic*, p. 15). Valuing the whole environment has major implications for the ethical significance of animals, and even human beings. While animal liberationists seek to eliminate animal suffering, Leopold was indifferent to it, and enjoyed hunting: he was concerned about 'the disappearance of species of plants as well as animals and for soil erosion and stream pollution', indicating, not different ethical perspectives, but a 'profoundly different' cosmic vision (pp. 17–18).

Rejecting the ethical focus on sentience

Callicott points to differences between, and incoherencies within, the arguments of the animal rights philosophers: Singer wants 'equal consideration of the divers interests of all *sentient* animals'; but what would be the effects, on the natural environment as a whole, of setting domestic animals free (p. 39)? Again, animal liberationism fails to recognize that domestic animals, like chickens, are actually 'creations of man', so it is 'incoherent' to contend that factory farms 'cruelly' frustrate the 'natural behaviour' of what are 'living artifacts': it would make 'almost as much sense to speak of the natural behaviour of tables and chairs' (p. 30). Callicott disputes Regan's claim that showing proper respect for the rights of the individual animals who constitute the biotic community would preserve the community itself. For example, if we respect the rights of 'individual whitetail deer to live unmolested', and do not cull herds, so far from being preserved, the 'plant members of some communities would be seriously damaged, some beyond recovery' (p. 43).

The coherence of the land ethic

Callicott confronts the objection that a moral theory that argues for inclusion of plants, soil and water in the same ethical class as animals and people, and yet allows some to be slaughtered and eaten, or hunted, perhaps cruelly, is itself incoherent. This objection fails to grasp Leopold's categorical imperative:

> 'A thing is right when it tends to preserve the integrity, stability, and beauty of the biotic community. It is wrong when it tends otherwise'. What is . . . noteworthy . . . in this proposition, is the idea that the good of the biotic *community* is the ultimate measure of . . . the rightness or wrongness, of actions. (p. 21)

The land ethic can demand moral consideration for plants, as well as animals, but allow the latter to be killed, or trees to be felled, because nothing, in itself, has 'the right to life' (p. 57). The emergence of ecology reinforces the land ethic and makes it more persuasive. The landscape no longer appears as 'a plurality of separate individuals', but as a 'unified system of integrally related parts' (pp. 22–3). The land ethic takes, as its standard for assessing the relative value of its constituent parts, the good of the biotic community as a whole.

A special status for human beings?

The land ethic does not exempt human beings from moral evaluation in the context of the whole biotic community. On the contrary, human beings constitute the major part of the threat to its well-being:

> A global population of more than four billion persons ... presents an alarming prospect ... a global disaster ... The extent of misanthropy in modern environmentalism thus may be taken as a measure of the degree to which it is biocentric. (p. 27)

As well as emphasizing the practicability of the land ethic, as offering a single standard for deciding the 'competing individual claims' of the biotic community's 'myriad components', Callicott draws attention to the idea of the 'mixed community' of humans and animals (see p. 329) as a source of guidance as to how we should determine human obligations to animals, and as to how the rights and responsibilities of rational and sentient creatures relate to those of the biotic community (p. 37).

The land ethic is a useful corrective to **anthropocentrism** and sentience-centrism, and it also offers a valuable criterion against which to test environmental decisions and priorities: the right ones are those that are in the interests of the biotic community as a whole. But it does not provide a 'single standard' for such decisions, because inevitably, as the human beings who make and set such decisions and priorities, we do not regard ourselves as just so many more 'components' of the biotic community; and we will insist that environmental decisions respect our special status.

Andrew Brennan and respect for natural entities

Andrew Brennan argues that we should respect all natural entities, including 'mountains, cliffs, rivers', because, like human beings, they are 'independent, particular, highly individual' things, which also derive some of their significance from interactions with other entities, including ourselves: 'We can leave our marks on mountains and a chalk cliff ... But such things ... leave their marks on us: as challenges to climbers ... objects of beauty and awe to observers' (Brennan, *Thinking About Nature*, p. 196). Natural communities, systems, objects, and 'even the land forms around me deserve my respect ... simply by being what they are ... and interacting with other items in the way they do' (p. 197).

Issues and reasons

We face a range of environmental challenges. There are those who dismiss or minimize them, but most people seem to agree that they demand urgent action at local, national and international level. However, concern for the welfare of rational and sentient creatures, present and future, is not the only reason why we ought to act. Environmental initiatives can also be justified on grounds that are not (mainly) **anthropocentric** or sentient-creature-centric. But, would there be reasons for acting, even if we knew that all rational and conscious beings were going to cease to exist, and would ultimately derive no benefit from environmental initiatives? G. E. Moore asks us to contemplate two worlds, one 'exceedingly beautiful' and the other 'simply one heap of filth', neither of which human beings will ever contemplate, and asks whether it is 'irrational to hold that it is better that the beautiful world should exist' (Moore, *Principia Ethica*, p. 135).

References and suggestions for further reading and research

Animal Freedom Foundation website at http://www.animalfreedom.org.

Aquinas, *Summa Theologica* IIa IIae q. 64 a. 1, at http://:www.op.org/summa.

Aristotle, *Politics*, trans. B. Jowett, Oxford: Oxford University Press, 1908.

J. Bentham, *An Introduction to Principles of Morals and Legislation*, Mineola, NY: Dover, 2007.

A. Brennan, *Thinking About Nature*, Athens, GA: University of Georgia Press, 1988.

A. Brennan and Y.-S. Lo, 'Environmental Ethics' (rev. January 2008), in E. N. Zalta (ed.), *Stanford Encyclopaedia of Philosophy*, at http://plato.stanford.edu.html.

British Union for the Abolition of Vivisection (BUAV) website at www.buav.org.

J. Baird Callicott, *In Defense of the Land Ethic*, Albany, NY: State University of New York Press, 1989.

Catechism of the Catholic Church, at www.scborromeo.org/ccc.htm (see also http://www.catholic-church.org.uk).

Church of England (CofE) website at http://cofe.anglican.org: *Science, Medicine, Technology and Environment* (Animal Welfare and Environment) (CofE (a)); *Hunting with Hounds* (A briefing paper by Professor Michael Banner for the Board of Social Responsibility, 2000) (CofE (b)); *The Environment Debate: A Briefing from the Mission and Public Affairs Council* (CofE (c)).

Climate Concern UK website at http://www.climate-concern.com.

Coalition for Medical Progress (CMP) website at http://www.medical-progress.org.

Department for Environment, Food and Rural Affairs (Defra) website at http://www.defra.gov.uk.

R. Elliot, 'Environmental Ethics', in P. Singer (ed.), *A Companion to Ethics*, Cambridge: Cambridge University Press, 1993.

Friends of the Earth website at http://www.foe.co.uk.

Greenpeace website at http://www.greenpeace.org.uk.

L. Gruen, 'Animals', in P. Singer (ed.), *A Companion to Ethics*, Cambridge: Cambridge University Press, 1993.

L. Gruen, 'The Moral Status of Animals' (rev. July 2003), in E. N. Zalta (ed.), *Stanford Encyclopaedia of Philosophy*, at http://plato.stanford.edu. html.

A. Linzey, *Christianity and the Rights of Animals*, London: SPCK, 1987.

Methodist Church of Great Britain (Methodists) website at http://www.methodist.org.uk: *Animal Welfare: The Methodist Church's View on Animal Welfare* (Methodists (a)); *Caring for Creation in the Face of Climate Change* (Methodists (b)).

Office of Public Sector Information, *Statute Law Database*, at http://www.statutelaw.gov.uk (the full text of the statutes referred to can be found here).

G. E. Moore, *Principia Ethica*, ed. T. Baldwin, rev. edn, Cambridge: Cambridge University Press, 1993.

National Aeronautics and Space Administration (NASA) website at http://www.nas.nasa.gov.

Operation Noah website at http://www.operationnoah.org.

T. Regan, *Animal Rights*, Berkeley/Los Angeles: University of California Press, 1983.

Research Defence Society (RDS) website at http:// www.rds-online.org.uk.

Royal Society for the Prevention of Cruelty to Animals (RSPCA) website at http:www.rspca.org.uk.

A. Schweitzer, *My Life and Thought*, London: Guild Books, 1955.

P. Singer, *Practical Ethics*, 2nd edn, Cambridge: Cambridge University Press, 1993.

P. Taylor, *Respect for Nature*, Princeton NJ: Princeton University Press, 1986.

P. Vardy and P. Grosch, *The Puzzle of Ethics*, rev. edn, London: HarperCollins, 1999 (chapters 17 and 18).

Vegetarians International Voice for Animals (VIVA) website at http://www.factoryfarming.org.uk.

Verdict Research website at http://www.verdict.co.uk.

R. Wade, 'Animal Welfare and Ethical Concerns', *Australian EJournal of Theology* at http://dlibrary.acu.edu.au.

In Conclusion

This book is designed to support the teaching and learning of the AS and A2 Religious Studies Ethics/Religious Ethics units and those aspects of AS/A2 Philosophy concerned with moral philosophy.

All the examination boards publish sample questions, as well as the specifications, and a lot of material is available on their websites. It is also possible to obtain past papers from them. These often remain relevant, even following specification changes.

The **website addresses** for the four examination boards covering England and Wales are:

AQA: www.aqa.org.uk
Edexcel: www.edexcel.org.uk
OCR: www.ocr.org.uk
WJEC/CBAC: www.wjec.co.uk

Below is a selection of AS/A2 level-type issues and questions, with page references to where relevant information to help understand and answer them is to be found in this book. The questions about religion refer explicitly to Christianity, as this is the religion covered in this book.

1   (a) Outline Plato's theory of the forms and explain the importance of the form of the good. (**pp. 15–18**)
    (b) Evaluate the view that there is no such thing as a moral truth. (**pp. 15–27**)

2   (a) Explain the difference between ethical prescriptivism and ethical descriptivism. (**pp. 20–1, 49–50, 53–64**)
    (b) Critically assess the claim that morality is logically grounded in human needs. (**pp. 14–5, 49–64**)

3 (a) Explain what Moore means by the naturalistic fallacy and the open question argument. (**pp. 27–31, 36–39, 41, 89, 95**)
(b) 'Mill did not commit a naturalistic fallacy, even if Bentham did'. Discuss. (**pp. 27–31, 36–39, 41, 89, 95**)

4 (a) Outline one of Kant's formulations of the categorical imperative, and explain its importance as a test of moral maxims. (**pp. 71–8**)
(b) Assess the value of the categorical imperative in making decisions about abortion. (**pp. 71–8, 221–8**)

5 (a) Outline Mill's version of utilitarianism, and explain the principal ways in which it differs from Bentham's. (**pp. 86–103**)
(b) 'Utilitarians are bound to support the legalization of euthanasia.' Discuss. (**pp. 86–103, 228–37**)

6 (a) Explain what Aristotle meant by eudaimonia and why he believed that intellectual development is the key to happiness. (**pp. 104–14**)
(b) 'One society's moral virtues may be regarded as vices in another.' Discuss. (**pp. 104–19**)

7 (a) Outline the Natural Law theory of ethics, and explain its appeal to those who believe in God. (**pp. 120–9**)
(b) Evaluate the view that the Natural Law approach to ethics rules out certain forms of sexual relationship and conduct. (**pp. 120–9, 255–77**)

8 (a) Outline the situational approach to ethics, and explain Fletcher's objections to prefabricated ethical rules and regulations. (**pp. 138–53**)
(b) Evaluate the view that no situation that demands an ethical response is ever exactly like another. (**pp. 138–53**)

9 (a) Outline the theories of hard and soft determinism, and explain the differences between them. (**pp. 201, 204–14**)
(b) 'If determinism is true, nobody can be held responsible for what s/he does.' Discuss. (**pp. 201–18, 293–5**)

10 (a) Outline Christian teaching about the nature of human beings, and explain why human life is precious to God. (**pp. 182–97**)
(b) Evaluate the view that Christians have a duty to oppose embryo research. (**pp. 182–97, 247–53**)

11 (a) Outline the theory of the just war, and explain why it is more likely

to be practised by democratic than non-democratic states. (**pp. 300–8**)
(b) Evaluate the view that no sincere Christian would be prepared to fight in a war. (**pp. 145–6, 186–99, 314–6**)

12 (a) Outline Christian teaching about animals, and explain why there are differing attitudes among Christians towards them. (**pp. 184–5, 322–5, 328**)
(b) 'Human beings will only take care of the environment if their survival depends on it'. Discuss. (**pp. 329–39**)

Index

INDEX